The Peace Business

The Peace Business

Money and Power in the Palestine-Israel Conflict

MARKUS E. BOUILLON

I.B. TAURIS
LONDON · NEW YORK

Published in 2004 by I.B. Tauris & Co Ltd
6 Salem Road, London W2 4BU
175 Fifth Avenue, New York NY 10010
www.ibtauris.com

In the United States of America and in Canada distributed by Palgrave Macmillan,
a division of St Martins Press, 175 Fifth Avenue, New York NY 10010

Copyright © Markus E. Bouillon, 2004

The rights of Markus E. Bouillon to be identified as the author of this work have been
asserted by the author in accordance with the Copyright, Designs and Patent Act 1988.

All rights reserved. Except for brief quotations in a review, this book, or any part
thereof, may not be reproduced, stored in or introduced into a retrieval system,
or transmitted, in any form or by any means, electronic, mechanical, photocopying,
recording or otherwise, without the prior written permission of the publisher.

Library of Modern Middle East Studies 37

ISBN 1 85043 443 3
EAN 978 1 85043 443 6

A full CIP record for this book is available from the British Library
A full CIP record for this book is available from the Library of Congress

Library of Congress catalog card: available

Printed and bound in Great Britain by MPG Books Ltd, Bodmin from
camera-ready copy supplied by the author

Contents

List of Tables and Figures	vi
Exchange Rates, Abbreviations and Acronyms	vii
Note on Transliteration	x
Chronology of the Middle East Peace Process	xi
Acknowledgements and Foreword	xv
Introduction	1
Social Forces, Politics and International Relations	9
The Economy, Business and Politics	23
Business Interests in Peace and Co-operation	51
Business Ties between Israel, Jordan and the PA	75
Business Leaders and Political Elites	105
Peace, Social Equality and Democracy	128
The Regional Failure of the Peace Business	149
Conclusion	166
Notes	173
List of Interviews	205
Bibliography	209
Index	233

List of Tables and Figures

Table 1: Israel's Economy at a Glance	24-25
Table 2: Jordan's Economy at a Glance	34-35
Table 3: JIC Holdings, 1994	37-38
Table 4: The Palestinian Economy at a Glance	42
Table 5: Blacklisted Jordanian Companies, 2000	63-64
Table 6: Portfolio of the Century Investment Group, 2000	78-79
Table 7: Truck Traffic between Israel and Jordan	83
Table 8: Jordanian and Israeli Exports, 1997	84
Table 9: Projected Employment in Palestinian Industrial Parks	89
Table 10: Palestinian Trade with Israel and Jordan, 1990-1998	93
Table 11: Jordanian-Palestinian Trade, 1995-1998	99
Table 12: Truck Traffic between Jordan and the PA, 1997	102
Table 13: Costs of Palestinian Imports from Jordan	103
Table 14: PCSC Holdings, 1999	123
Figure 1: The Palestine Development and Investment Company	47

Exchange Rates

(June 2002)

$1 = NIS 4.95   NIS 1 = $0.20
$1 = JD 0.71   JD 1 = $1.42

Acronyms and Abbreviations

ABA	Arab Businessmen Association
ACC	Arab Co-operation Council
ACC	Amman Chamber of Commerce
ACI	Amman Chamber of Industry
AIC	Arab Industrial Company
APC	Arab Potash Company
APIC	Arab Palestinian Investment Company
Aqaria	Palestine Real Estate Investment Company
ATS	Arab Technology Systems
BOT	Build, Operate, Transfer
CBEO	Co-ordinating Bureau of Economic Organisations
CBJ	Central Bank of Jordan
CCC	Consolidated Contractors Company
CCS	Computer Communications Systems
CEO	Chief Executive Officer
CFO	Chief Financial Officer
CPRS	Center for Palestine Research and Studies
DIC	Discount Investment Corporation
ECC	Economic Consultative Council
ECF	Economic Cooperation Foundation
ESC	Economic Security Council
ESCWA	Economic and Social Commission for Western Asia
EU	European Union
FDI	Foreign Direct Investment
FEZ	Free Economic Zone
FICC	Federation of Israeli Chambers of Commerce
FJCC	Federation of Jordanian Chambers of Commerce
FTA	Free Trade Agreement
GCC	Gulf Co-operation Council
GDP	Gross Domestic Product
GIE	Gaza Industrial Estate
GNI	Gross National Income

GNP	Gross National Product
GSS	General Security Service
GTZ	Gesellschaft für Technische Zusammenarbeit (German Agency for Technical Assistance)
HCH	Housing and Construction Holding Company
HCIF	Higher Commission for Investment and Finance
IBRD	International Bank for Reconstruction and Development (The World Bank)
ICBS	Israeli Central Bureau of Statistics
IDBH	Israel Discount Bank Holding
IDF	Israel Defence Forces
IEC	Israel Electric Corporation
IFC	International Finance Corporation
IEI	Israel Export Institute
IMA	Israel Manufacturers Association
IMF	International Monetary Fund
INTAJ	Information Technology Association of Jordan
IPCRI	Israel-Palestine Centre for Research and Information
JABA	Jordanian-American Business Association
JBA	Jordan Businessmen Association
JCC	Jerusalem Cigarette Company
JCFC	Jordan Cement Factories Company
JCIC	Jordan Ceramic Industries Company
JCIEC	Jordan Commercial and Industrial Estates Corporation
JD	Jordanian Dinar
JEA	Jordan Engineers Association
JEC	Joint Economic Committee
JEDCO	Jordan Export Development and Commercial Centres Corporation
JEDICO	Jerusalem Development and Investment Company
JEIC	Jordan Engineering Industries Company
JFIC	Jordan Fertiliser Industries Company
JGIC	Jordan Glass Industries Company
JIC	Jordan Investment Corporation
JMCC	Jerusalem Media Communications Centre
JPMC	Jordan Phosphate Mines Company
JPRC	Jordan Petroleum Refinery Company
JTA	Jordan Trade Association
JTC	Jordan Telecommunications Company
JTI	Jerusalem Tourism Investment Company
MAS	Palestine Economic Policy Research Institute
MEBRD	Middle East Bank for Reconstruction and Development
MEED	Middle East Economic Digest
MEMRI	Middle East Media Research Institute
MENA	Middle East and North Africa
MK	Member of Knesset

NAPCO	National Aluminium Profile Company
NEEC	Near East Energy Company
NGO	Non-Governmental Organisation
NIE	Nablus Industrial Estate
NIIC	Northern International and Industrial Company
NIS	New Israeli Shekel
OPIC	Overseas Private Investment Corporation
OT	Occupied Territories
PA	Palestinian Authority
PADICO	Palestine Development and Investment Company
Paltel	Palestine Telecommunications Company
Paltrade	Palestinian Trade Centre
PBA	Palestinian Businessmen Association
PCBS	Palestinian Central Bureau of Statistics
PCSC	Palestinian Commercial Services Company
PECDAR	Palestinian Economic Council for Development and Reconstruction
PIEDCO	Palestine Industrial Estates Development Company
PIEFZA	Palestinian Industrial Estates and Free Zones Authority
PIPA	Palestinian Investment Promotion Authority
PITA	Palestinian Information Technology Association
PLC	Palestinian Legislative Council
PLO	Palestine Liberation Organisation
PNC	Palestinian National Council
PSE	Palestine Securities Exchange
PSEC	Private Sector Executive Committee
PTIC	Palestine Tourism Investment Company
PTPC	Palestinian Trade Promotion Corporation
QIZ	Qualifying Industrial Zone
REDWG	Regional Economic Development Working Group
RSS	Royal Scientific Society
SDC	Siemens Data Communications
SEA	Single European Act
SEZ	Special Economic Zone
SME	Small and Medium-Sized Enterprises
SOLAM	Schools Online at Middle East
SSC	Social Security Corporation
UNCTAD	United Nations Conference on Trade and Development
UNDP	United Nations Development Programme
UNRWA	United Nations Relief and Works Agency
UNSCO	UN Office of the Special Coordinator in the Occupied Territories
USA	United States of America
VAT	Value Added Tax
WTO	World Trade Organisation
YEA	Young Entrepreneurs Association

Note on Transliteration

Arabic and Hebrew are, as T. E. Lawrence, or Lawrence of Arabia, once remarked, almost impossible to transcribe in English. In this study, most individual names are transliterated in the way individuals choose to transcribe their own names, or in the form most commonly used in newspapers and reports. Thus, the name of Jordan's former ruler appears as King Hussein, not Husayn.

Where original titles of source documents are given, however, both Arabic and Hebrew are transcribed in the most common manner, following the system in use in the International Journal of Middle East Studies (IJMES). The Arabic *qaf* is represented by *q*; *kha* is transliterated as *kh*; and *ghayn* is shown as *gh*. *'Ayn* and *Hamza* are both represented by a simple apostrophe. The Hebrew *samekh* and *sin* are both transcribed as *s*; the Hebrew *het* or *khet* is rendered *h*, in order to distinguish it from *khaf* (*kh*). Finally, the Arabic definite article *al-* is not assimilated. This simplified system of transliteration, I hope, will make this study as accessible and comprehensible as possible.

Chronology of the Middle East Peace Process

30 October-1 November 1991: Madrid Peace Conference. Palestinians, in a joint delegation with Jordan, at-tend the Madrid talks between Jordan, Syria, Israel and Lebanon. Direct bilateral talks begin among Israel and Syria, Lebanon, Jordan and participants from the Occupied Territories. Multilateral negotiations begin on arms control, security, water, refugees, the environment and economic development.

28-29 January 1992: Moscow Multilateral Talks. The organisational meeting for multilateral talks on regional issues such as arms control, refugees and the environment is held in Moscow. Rounds one, two and three convene in 1992 in Lisbon and London.

9 September 1993: Mutual Recognition. Israel and the PLO agree to recognise each other after 45 years of conflict, building on a pact already initiated on Palestinian self-rule in the Israeli-occupied Gaza Strip and in Jericho. PLO leader Yasser Arafat signs a letter recognizing Israel and renouncing violence.

13 September 1993: Declaration of Principles Signed. Israeli Prime Minister Yitzhak Rabin and PLO Chairman Yasser Arafat meet and watch Israeli Foreign Minister Shimon Peres and PLO Executive Council Member Abu Abbas sign the Oslo agreement.

14 September 1993: Israel-Jordan Common Agenda. The Israel-Jordan Common Agenda is agreed in Washington, D.C., marking the end of the state of war between the two nations and paving the way for talks leading to a formal peace treaty.

29 April 1994: Paris Protocol. The Israel-PLO economic agreement signed in Paris (later incorporated into the Interim Agreement) sets the parameters for Israeli-Palestinian economic relations in Gaza and Jericho. The protocol covers trade and labour relations as well as money, banking, and taxation issues.

4 May 1994: Gaza-Jericho Agreement Signed. At a ceremony in Cairo, Prime Minister Rabin and Chairman Arafat sign the Agreement on the Gaza Strip and the Jericho Area. The new agreement sets out terms for the implementation of the Declaration of Principles and includes annexes on withdrawal of Israeli military forces and security arrangements, civil affairs, legal matters, and economic ties.

25 July 1994: Washington Declaration. The Washington Declaration, embracing the underlying principles of the Israel-Jordan Common Agenda, is signed.

29 August 1994: Transfer of Power to PA. The Agreement on the Preparatory Transfer of Powers and Responsibilities is signed at Erez, a checkpoint between Israel and the Gaza Strip. The expansion of Palestinian self-rule in the West Bank over education, taxation, social welfare, tourism, and health is completed by December 1994.

26 October 1994: Israel-Jordan Peace Treaty. The Treaty of Peace between the State of Israel and the Hashemite Kingdom of Jordan, which had been initiated on 17 October by Israeli Prime Minister Rabin and Jordanian Prime Minister Majali, is signed at the White House.

30 October-1 November 1994: First MENA Conference. Representatives from 61 countries and 1,114 business leaders gather in Casablanca. GCC countries partially lift the secondary and tertiary boycotts of Israel. The final declaration stipulates that 'the creation of a private sector regional chamber of commerce and business council be encouraged to facilitate intra-regional trade.'

7-8 February 1995: Taba Declaration. Egyptian, Palestinian, Jordanian, Israeli, and American trade leaders convene at Taba to discuss regional economic co-operation. They call for the implementation of signed agreements, increased private sector contact and participation in regional projects.

28 September 1995: Oslo II-Agreement. The Israeli-Palestinian Interim Agreement on the West Bank and the Gaza Strip is signed in Washington, D.C. The agreement contains 31 articles and seven annexes (redeployment and security, elections, civil affairs, legal matters, economic relations, co-operation programmes, and prisoner release).

29 September 1995: First Trilateral Committee Meeting. Secretary of State Warren Christopher, Israeli Foreign Minister Shimon Peres, and Chairman Yasser Arafat convene the first meeting of the US-Israel-Palestinian Trilateral Committee.

29-31 October 1995: Second MENA Conference. Representatives from 70 countries and more than 1,000 business leaders establish contacts and sign a number of business deals in Amman, most prominent among them planned joint ventures between the Jordanian APC and the Israeli Dead Sea Works as well as an Enron project to deliver Qatari natural gas via Jordan to Israel. The Regional Economic Development Working Group (REDWG) monitoring committee secretariat is established as a permanent body in Amman.

4 November 1995: Rabin Assassinated. An Israeli university student, Yigal Amir, assassinates Israeli Prime Minister Yitzhak Rabin following a peace rally in Tel Aviv.

13 March 1996: Sharm El-Sheikh Summit. Egyptian President Hosni Mubarak hosts a 'Summit of the Peace-makers' in Sharm El-Sheikh to call for a halt to extremism and violence in the midst of suicide bombing against Israelis and Israeli retaliatory strikes in South Lebanon, which hit refugee camps.

31 May 1996: Binyamin Netanyahu Israeli Prime Minister. Likud Party leader Binyamin Netanyahu becomes Prime Minister of Israel, having defeated Labour's Shimon Peres in early elections called after the assassination of Yitzhak Rabin.

September 1996: Riots in Occupied Territories. In the midst of a hardened mood following operation 'Grapes of Wrath' in South Lebanon and an ongoing debate around the planned settlement Har Homa, Netanyahu authorises the opening of a tunnel under the Temple Mount, which houses the Al-Aqsa Mosque. Four weeks of bloody and violent riots follow.

12-14 November 1996: Third MENA Conference. After Rabin's assassination, Netanyahu's electoral victory, and the September riots, the Palestinian private sector boycotts the conference, protesting against Israeli closures and other obstacles impeding development. The conference is overshadowed by the stalemate in the peace process and does not yield any major successes.

17 January 1997: Hebron Redeployment. Following extensive mediation by Jordan's King Hussein, the Protocol Concerning the Redeployment in Hebron is signed between Israel and the PLO.

16-18 November 1997: Fourth MENA Conference. After the Arab League decides to freeze the process of normalisation with Israel, to reinforce the primary boycott against Israel and to suspend all negotiations on the multilateral track in March 1997, the conference in Doha is boycotted by 9 Arab states, among them the PA. It brings together 850 business leaders and officials from over 60 countries. Brokered by the United States, Israel and Jordan sign the agreement on the Qualifying Industrial Zones (QIZ), allowing jointly manufactured goods free access to the US market.

31 January-1 February 1998: Annulment of PLO Charter Articles. US Secretary of State Madeleine Albright tours to the Middle East and puts forth a proposal for simultaneous steps by the Palestinians on security and by Israel on further redeployment. In what she calls a step forward, Chairman Arafat gives her a letter detailing which parts of the PLO Charter can be considered annulled.

15-23 October 1998: Wye River Memorandum. President Clinton, Secretary of State Albright and other US officials broker intensive negotiations between Israel and the Palestinian Authority, leading to the Wye River Memorandum, which is signed at the White House on 23 October.

30 November 1998: Middle East Donors Conference. President Clinton hosts a Middle East Donors Conference in Washington at which some 40 nations pledge over $3 billion in economic assistance to the Palestinian National Authority.

12-15 December 1998: Clinton Addresses Palestinian Legislative Council. President Clinton visits the Palestinian Authority and Israel. Clinton witnesses a vote by the Palestinian Legislative Council (PLC) in Gaza 'fully and forever' rejecting conflict with Israel.

7 February 1999: King Hussein Dies. King Hussein of Jordan dies of cancer in Amman. His son, King Abdullah II, succeeds him. World leaders conjoin at the late king's funeral in Amman on 8 February and praise the king's vision and role in the peace process.

17 May 1999: Ehud Barak Israeli Prime Minister. Ehud Barak is elected Prime Minister of Israel, defeating Binyamin Netanyahu 56 per cent to 44 per cent in direct voting. He pledges to pull Israeli troops out of Lebanon within one year and to make peace his top priority.

1-5 September 1999: Sharm El-Sheikh Accord. Secretary Albright travels to Morocco, Egypt, Israel, the West Bank and Gaza, Damascus and Beirut to consult with regional leaders on developments in the peace process, and attends the signing of the Sharm El-Sheikh accord on 4 September.

21 March 2000: New Bilateral Talks. Palestinian-Israeli talks commence at Bolling Air Force Base near Washington, D.C. and last one week, but don not yield an agreement.

2-4 May 2000: Israeli Withdrawal from Lebanon. Israel announces the completion of its withdrawal from southern Lebanon; the UN Security Council votes on 18 June to confirm the withdrawal.

11-25 July 2000: Camp David Talks. Abortive talks between Israeli and Palestinian leaders at Camp David to address the most difficult of final status issues, including Jerusalem and the return of Palestinian refugees.

28 September 2000: Al-Aqsa Intifada. A controversial visit by Ariel Sharon to holy sites in Jerusalem triggers an eruption of violence, turning into the Al-Aqsa Intifada. Sharon becomes Prime Minister in 2001, following Barak's resignation.

Source: Adapted from US Department of State, International Information Programmes, Middle East Peace Process Chronology; usinfo.state.gov/regional/nea/summit/chron.htm

Acknowledgements and Foreword

This book is based on a thesis that was made possible to a large degree through the help and funding of many individuals and institutions. The specific sources I have used and relied on necessitate, I feel, a word on the impartiality, objectivity, and confidentiality of this study.

A scholarship from the Israeli government, one of the parties subject to my research, has enabled me to carry out fieldwork in the region during the academic year 2000-2001. I am most grateful for the support that was extended to me. But a study such as this will inevitably be subjected to scrutiny, if not outright rejection, given that one of the major sources of my funding is also one of the objects of study and certainly has interest in a specific interpretation of the subject matter of this book. I therefore wish to clarify – and also extend my gratitude in this respect – that the Israeli Ministry of Foreign Affairs has not in any way attempted to infringe on my academic freedom as a young researcher, nor have individuals associated with the Israeli government attempted to influence my judgement. As a researcher, one is often severely restricted by financial limitations, and my fieldwork would not have been possible without the Government of Israel-scholarship. In this sense, despite the potentially partisan, and to some people probably suspect, financial background to this book, all conclusions, both right and wrong, in this study are 'impartial', and entirely my own. Naturally, some readers may be tempted to dismiss this work as inevitably flawed, and I will not convince them with my writing here. My wish is to be judged entirely on the basis of my own research and my own conclusions. I am confident that the arguments put forward in this book demonstrate my 'impartiality,' if such a thing exists, or at least, for my independent judgement on the evidence I have gathered during nine months of fieldwork in Israel, Jordan, and the Occupied Palestinian Territories of the West Bank and Gaza Strip.

Having said so, I feel that a second word is needed in order to clarify what I mean by 'impartiality' and 'objectivity.' My years of academic dealing with the Middle East, and more specifically, the conflict revolving around the land of Palestine, have taught me that there is not only a great deal of distrust towards the 'other' in conflict and peace-making, but also towards any 'outsider.' Moreover, I have learnt that much of the battle is increasingly being fought by means of research and academic literature.

While I believe that my being an 'outsider', meaning that I am not personally involved in the conflict, makes me a somewhat 'impartial' and 'objective' observer, I have learned that often, the judgement of the 'outsider' is rejected by both sides precisely because she or he is but an 'outsider.' In many discussions, I had to stand my ground for an unpopular opinion. In Israel, where I was attempting to explain the Palestinian psyche and perception of 'self' and 'other' in the conflict, I was often told that I as a German should know better, and certainly be more sensitive to the needs and fears of Israelis. Or, I was simply told I did not know what I was talking about, since I did not live in the region. Both assessments are, in my view, as wrong as the charges I often encountered on the Palestinian and Jordanian sides. Here, I was often either told that as a German, I was a friend of the Jewish anyway, and my having Israeli friends only served to prove the accusation correct, or I was an imperialist or neo-colonialist European.

As for the extension of the battle into academia, to me it proves that the social scientist simply cannot achieve the much-espoused ideal of 'objectivity.' I personally do not believe in the possibility of remaining 'objective,' for the social scientist is part of, and interactive with, the world that she or he is trying to describe and explain. Our own convictions are always reflected in our work, however hard we may try to disguise them. The present book is no exception. Given the importance and influence that academic writing has assumed in the struggle over Palestine, as reflected in the work of Edward Said, or in the debate around Joan Peters' 'From Time Immemorial,' or the ferocious debates underlying the work of the New Historians (one of whom, Avi Shlaim, happened to be my supervisor), I consider it important to make clear to the reader my own standpoint. This may also serve as a reference to the many people on all three sides with whom I have discussed the conflict and whom I have tried to convince so many times – often in vain – that I can make a contribution to the resolution of a conflict that is not my own, strictly speaking, and whose resolution or continuation will not really affect my everyday life as much as theirs.

As a young German, I set out studying my own country's history, including its darkest moments. My attempt to come to terms with a guilt complex on the one hand, and the outright rejection of historic responsibility on the other, led me to delve into the study of the Holocaust, an interest that further led me to study the history of the Jewish Diaspora, Jewish thought, and the history of the Jewish people up to and throughout the creation of the State of Israel. When I began my national service in a vocational training village for mentally disabled in the North of Israel in 1994, I was firmly established on the Israeli side. The Jewish state was the only solution to make up – however inadequately – for the persecution and rejection the Jews of Europe had endured throughout centuries, before most of them were slaughtered and killed purely for being what they were: Jews. Against this background, and the terror I experienced at first hand with the series of bomb attacks during 1994 and 1995, I came to understand Israelis and the worldview that guides many of them until the present day.

When I returned to Europe, I took up the study of political science, history, and Middle Eastern studies, or Islamic studies, as it is usually called in Germany. I began learning Arabic, after I had become fluent in Hebrew whilst in Israel, and started reading up on the other side of the conflict, the Palestinians. I began to see the glorious War of Independence in a different light. I learned the meaning of Al-Nakba, the catastrophe of 1948, began to understand the notion of Deir Yassin, the attachment that people dwelling in poverty in refugee camps in Lebanon, Syria, and Jordan retained to their homeland, when they were not granted political rights and deprived economically. In 1998, I came to Jordan for a research internship of six months. During this time, I learned to understand the fears of expulsion, dispossession, deprivation, and I also learned to understand the delicate balance between Transjordanians and Palestinians in Jordan, and the inherent danger of a notion such as 'Jordan is Palestine.' And I learned that Israel is the stronger side in this conflict.

In line with my leaning towards critical theory and post-positivist reasoning, my personal ethic leans towards sympathy with the weak, the poor, the deprived, and towards finding a way for a change towards a more just, a more sustainable, and a more participatory system. Precisely because I grew up in Germany, and because I was trapped so often in accusations that I should be more patriotic, or when I dared to be, less nationalist, I wished Israelis would understand and be more accommodating. And precisely because I could understand the Palestinian and Jordanian experiences, I could understand their fear of domination and hegemony. And, as I have repeatedly tried to convince my Israeli friends, it is in the interest of Israelis that the Palestinian aspiration for a viable, enduring national home is satisfied. There is no other way of achieving Israel's deep desire for personal and national security.

To my Palestinian and Jordanian friends, and to those still suspecting my standing on the Israeli side of the conflict, I can only say that the State of Israel is a reality they have to come to terms with. Built on expropriation, expulsion, and inherently discriminatory it may be, but ultimately Israel will persist, and the people of the region will have to live together. Precisely for that reason, I believe that Israel will have to come to terms with itself and its history, and it will have to become a true part of the Middle East and accommodate another people firmly established in the region – the Palestinians.

In what follows, I take issue with all three sides, represented by a certain social group, businesspeople. My overall position is critical towards the developments in the economic area of the peace process that began in Madrid in October 1991. My critical analysis, I hope, will enable the academic community, readers interested in the region, policy-makers and the people of the region to understand the failures of the past, not in order to consolidate what has been 'achieved' in an even more sophisticated way, but to overcome the entrenchment of injustice and inequality both domestically and regionally, within all three societies and between the three entities. Ultimately, it will be the people of the region who will have to live in peaceful co-existence. As an 'outsider' and as a passive observer, I can only and solely want to point to the failures of the recent past and the inherent problems and obstacles. To bring about change is the task of the people in the region, not mine. But I do hope that this book contributes to the identification of the problems, and to overcoming them. This is the sole partiality I wholeheartedly espouse.

Aside from the Israeli government, two one-year scholarships from the German Academic Exchange Service (DAAD) enabled me to pursue my studies abroad. In 1998-99, I was funded during the completion of a Masters programme at the School of Oriental and African Studies in London. In the final year of my doctorate, the academic year 2001-2002, a scholarship for doctoral students enabled me to concentrate fully on the writing up of the thesis in Oxford. The Oxford Project for Peace Studies Fund, under the supervision of the Social Studies Faculty Board, supplemented my scholarship whilst in the region with two grants, which made fieldtrips to Jordan possible and covered my airfare to the Middle East. I am very grateful for this support.

But my studies that took me to Israel first, then to Freiburg, Amman, London, Oxford, and Jerusalem, with many other travels and visits in between, would not have been possible without the support of my parents. They have seen very little of me ever since I left school and, only a week later, Germany, and they have never complained but on the contrary, supported me. For this, I am more grateful than I could ever say.

Many other people have shaped my thinking and have helped me a great deal along the path that has finally yielded this book. The Haverim of Kfar Tikvah, volunteers, workers, and 'members;' Roswitha Badry who taught me Arabic, Persian, and most of what I know about Islamic civilisation; Wolfgang Welz who taught me what political science is; and Clemens Juergenmeyer, who taught me that it was worth studying a 'different' part of the world and encouraged my adventures within the rigid German system of higher education. Eberhard Kienle was my teacher at SOAS and has since been a friend, who tirelessly provided me with references. Olaf Köndgen gave me the chance to learn about Jordan and to publish, for the first time and for the second. Martha Sara, Mona Awajat, and Alia Z. Toukan from the Konrad Adenauer Foundation in Amman have provided me with information, contacts, newspaper clippings, endless cups of coffee and much more, whenever I came to Amman, and the Sara family has grown to be my Jordanian family. Efraim Kleiman of the Hebrew University encouraged and supported my application for the Government of Israel-scholarship and gave me long lists of references and contacts. Miki Yungreis, then at the Israel-Jordan Chamber of Commerce, not only clarified issues for me that I would have never grasped myself, but also helped me in identifying the right people to talk to. St. Antony's College was the most stimulating environment, with its international student body and the wide range of intellectual activities. Avi Shlaim was a supervisor who found the right strategy of encouraging me without influencing my thinking according to his own. The friends I found in Freiburg, London, Oxford, Jerusalem, Ramallah and Amman have supported me in many ways, often through the lifeline of cyberspace. Yoav Alon became a friend in Oxford and helped me survive in the turmoil of the Al-Aqsa Intifada, tirelessly supporting me and providing food, accommodation, entertainment, as did Efrat Lev and Yaron Deckel, himself one of the foremost experts on Israeli political affairs. I am also particularly grateful for Yoav's detailed review and his comments on the first draft of this study. Much further thanks is due to Myriam Ababsa, Hayden Bellenoit, Hilary Driscoll, Nicole Evans, Sam Halabi, Ala Hamarneh, Jens Hanssen, Florian Harms, Jalal Husseini, Peter Kramper, Anne Le More, Hartmut Mayer, Claas Morlang, Emma Murphy, Dinah Neuwirth, Shany Payes, Christopher Parker, Prof. James Piscatori, Gordon Peake, Jochen Prantl, Nandini Ramnath, Silke Rauschenbach, Angela Steinegger, Ralph Stobwasser, Thomas Welschof, Christoph Wilcke, Ken Wilson, Matthias Wulff, and Gökhan Yucel. Most important in the preparation of the final manuscript for the present book, though, has been my wife, Asima, to who I wish to dedicate this book, with both love and admiration.

To all the people named above, and many more, I am deeply indebted and will always be grateful. Many of those who helped me while I was in the Middle East cannot be named here for reasons of personal and institutional security. I promised to protect them as my sources and to guarantee their business interests that often crucially depend on going unidentified, and although I may not always agree with their approach, my research would not have been possible without their help. I therefore wish to extend my deepest gratitude to them; without them, this book would never have come into existence. All interpretations, conclusions, omissions, faults and errors, however, are entirely my own.

Markus E. Bouillon

The two parties view the economic domain as one of the cornerstones in their mutual relations with a view to enhance their interests in the achievement of a just, lasting, and comprehensive peace. Both parties shall co-operate in this field in order to establish a sound economic base for these relations, which will be governed in various economic spheres by the principles of mutual respect for each other's economic interests, reciprocity, equity and fairness.

Preamble, Paris Protocol on Economic Relations between the Government of Israel and the PLO Representing the Palestinian People, 29 April 1994.

Viewing economic development and prosperity as pillars of peace, security and harmonious relations between states, peoples and individual human beings, the parties, taking note of understandings reached between them, affirm their mutual desire to promote economic co-operation between them as well as within the framework of wider regional economic co-operation.

Art. 7, Treaty of Peace between the State of Israel and the Hashemite Kingdom of Jordan, 26 October 1994.

Introduction

In the immediate aftermath of the signing of the Israeli-Palestinian Oslo accords in 1993 and the peace treaty between Israel and Jordan in 1994, general optimism characterized the literature on the economic aspects of peace in the Middle East. Taking up the work of scholars who had advocated a warm peace between Egypt and Israel by indicating potential areas of mutually beneficial economic co-operation,[1] much of this literature argued in a functionalist manner that economic co-operation among the participants of the peace process could strengthen and consolidate peace through 'spill-over effects'. Economic interests would strengthen co-operation and create political ramifications to perpetuate the peace process. Peace, the argument ran, would not only offer a vast array of opportunities and effect overall economic development in the region, but would also lead to increasing regional co-operation, which would in turn strengthen the peace process under a 'virtuous-circle scenario'.[2]

The most fervent proponents of this line of thought argued, 'economic relations might make formal peace more stable, or might precede formal peace treaties and help the peace process along.'[3] This highly optimistic perspective, advocated by many Israeli scholars,[4] was met by a rather sceptical view put forward mainly by Arab economists. These expressed their conviction that although agreements on economic co-operation could 'lubricate the hard-core political negotiations,' it would be agreement on political terms that would dominate the potential success on the economic front.[5] Other Arab writers complemented this claim, however, in that they promoted a pragmatic view and accepted the premise of 'benefits for all,' albeit under the condition of reciprocity and a fair distribution of peace dividends.[6] In response, a majority of writers based their arguments on the assumption of a 'just, comprehensive and lasting peace' and of domestic economic reform and measures of liberalization, but were also cautiously optimistic.[7]

Among the most ardent supporters of this approach was Shimon Peres, Israeli Foreign Minister in Yitzhak Rabin's Labour government, who outlined his far-reaching vision of a 'new Middle East' in a book he published in 1993. Recognizing that the political process of peace-making was inextricably linked to other issues such as economic development and democratization, Peres advocated his vision of a future Middle East based on four fundamental pillars. These pillars, which were to mutually reinforce one another, were democratization, political stability, regional security, and regional economics, eventually effecting regional integration, as had been the case in post-World War II Europe.[8]

The multidimensional and functionalist approach to peace-making in the Middle East advocated by Peres and the Israeli scholars was reflected in the structure of the peace process itself, which involved two parallel tracks. Bilateral talks between Israel and the respective Arab parties were to deal with the political issues. A multilateral track that also involved the international community was to deal with the future of the Middle East as a region, with cross-national affairs ranging from environmental issues to regional economic development. The conception of the multilateral track, revolving around a regional core that consisted of Israel, Jordan, the Palestinian Territories, and Egypt, was explicitly functionalist in nature, as Joel Peters pointed out:

> The idea of the multilateral track is grounded in a functionalist view of international co-operation and peace according to which the enmeshing of the states in the region in an ever-widening web of economic, technical and welfare interdependencies would force them to set aside their political and/or ideological rivalries [...] From progress in the multilaterals would emerge a vision of what real peace might entail and the benefits that would accrue to all parties, thereby facilitating progress in the bilateral talks. Functional co-operation would eventually spill over into regional peace.[9]

The multilateral track was not only considered to create a web of apolitical interactions, which would strengthen the peace process, but was also seen as a supplementary instrument to enhance confidence and trust between the negotiating parties. Working groups under the auspices of the international community dealt with water, environmental issues, refugees, arms control and regional security, as well as regional economic development. However, the multilateral track yielded few results beyond rhetoric.

The functionalist conception of peace-making was supported by a growing body of literature on behalf of the international community, which strove to demonstrate the potential areas of co-operation. The World Bank prepared various reports on Gaza and the West Bank as well as on Jordan in 1993 and 1994, which outlined the necessary steps to realize the huge benefits peace seemed to promise.[10] German tutelage for one of the areas within the multilateral framework, trade, resulted in two detailed studies, which analysed existing trade patterns and potential benefits to the parties and recommended practical steps to increase the scope of trade among Middle Eastern states.[11] Moreover, the intention to realize the vision of a new Middle East was manifested in the annual Middle East and North Africa economic summits, which were held under the auspices of the United States, the European Union, and the World Economic Forum until 1997. The MENA conferences – held in Casablanca in 1994, in Amman in 1995, in Cairo in 1996, and in Doha in 1997 – were the most publicized and perhaps the most successful attempt to bring together the states of the region and the international community in order to promote economic co-operation and induce overall development for the region. The belief in the consolidating effects of economic co-operation also led the European Union to pledge financial support for many of the envisaged projects of inter-state co-operation and was an important factor in the so-called Barcelona process, the Euro-Mediterranean partnership initiative of the EU.[12]

From Functionalism to Disillusionment with the 'new Middle East'

In recent years, however, the climate of optimism has receded and been transformed into one of pessimism and disillusionment. Although support for the functionalist approach was reiterated as late as 1998, especially in the context of the Israeli-Palestinian-Jordanian triangle, economic co-operation remained limited and overall economic development was not generated.[13] In September 2000, the picture changed further. The second Intifada followed the inconclusive talks at Camp David between Israelis and Palestinians and brought the Oslo peace process to its end. Until then, Israel had unilaterally benefited from the peace process and particularly the end of the Arab secondary boycott, which boosted foreign direct and portfolio investment in the Israeli economy and induced overall growth. At the same time, however, gains from co-operation were allegedly marginal.[14] Within the multilateral framework, the MENA conferences were suspended in the aftermath of the last summit in Doha in 1997, when, after Egypt and Saudi Arabia had already officially boycotted the proceedings, no participant volunteered to act as the next host.[15]

Both Jordan and the autonomous Palestinian Territories experienced considerable setbacks even prior to the Intifada. Although the Jordanian-Palestinian-Israeli triad had been expected to perform a role similar to the one the Benelux countries performed for Europe, actual results in terms of successful co-operation were rare.[16] In July 1998, Jordan's Foreign Minister Jawad Anani described Jordanian-Israeli relations as 'almost at a standstill and at a minimum level of co-ordination,' after many projects of intergovernmental co-operation had not got off the ground or had been cancelled altogether.[17] The Palestinian economy deteriorated rather than improved, and the process of 'de-development' of the Occupied Territories by the Israelis continued unabated, as Sara Roy showed.[18]

While some observers, especially in the media, blamed the obstructionist policies of Binyamin Netanyahu's Likud government between 1996 and 1999, other critics traced the failure of regional economic co-operation to take off to the basic structure of the peace process. The argument here was that the peace process was fundamentally flawed in favour of Israel, but it did not exceed beyond pessimistically stating that 'the existing framework for negotiations could not secure a lasting peace' and that the future of peace was up to the politicians.[19] The resulting perspective on economic co-operation asserted that the proposed schemes of regional economic integration merely served to disguise Israel's bid for regional hegemony.[20] Moreover, instead of creating a network of interdependence, regional economic co-operation between Israel and its neighbours would resemble the core-periphery relations between the rich industrial states of the North and the underdeveloped world in the South and result in dependence.[21] As a consequence, in the Arab countries, both the alleged hegemonic aspirations of Israel and the supposed evolution of a pattern of dependence would result in domestic instability and the undermining of the very regimes that had opted for peace. Arab governments would almost certainly repress opposition against a peace seen as creating a dependency relationship. The internal climate of conflict and violence, in turn, would have a negative impact on economic development.[22]

Indeed, despite a great deal of rhetoric by the governments, the average Palestinian and Jordanian were highly disappointed by the failure of the anticipated 'peace dividend' to materialize. The eruption of the Al-Aqsa Intifada in this sense was not only the result of the political stalemate, but also a consequence of the economic underpinnings of the peace process. What potential there existed for socio-economic benefits from peace had been debated controversially. The Jordanian and Palestinian leaderships, however, strongly fostered expectations among their populations, in order to 'sell' the peace agreements. The deeply felt grassroots disillusionment in the context of ongoing economic crisis greatly strengthened the base of Islamist groups such as Hamas and Islamic Jihad among Palestinians as well as the Muslim Brotherhood in Jordan, which opposed peace and 'normalization' with Israel. Popular sentiment against the peace process and the resulting political instability or reversal of liberalizing measures, as happened in Jordan, illustrated that Peres' four pillars of the 'new Middle East' – democratization, political stability, regional security, and regional economics – were indeed interrelated, albeit in a very different way from that predicted by Peres. This also suggests that the domestic dynamics underlying and accompanying the process of peace-making play a crucial role for the future of the peace process. This argument has long been recognized by political scientists concerned with the peace process.[23] Students of political economy and the economic dimension of peace, however, only recently took up this line of thought.

Most studies dealing with the economic dimension of the peace process subscribed to the basic vision of economic co-operation as a vehicle for peace and took issue with the macroeconomic obstacles and problems of economic policy, instead of the underlying political economy.[24] Yet, it may be crucial to identify the unbalanced distribution of even potential benefits in order to understand the failure of the economic aspect of peace, if not the peace process altogether. Laura Drake, for example, pointed out that

> unless the economic, cultural, and interpersonal aspects of a future peace are supported at the level of civil society, particularly among the educated and well-informed, any Arab-Israeli peace that might be reached will remain a peace of kings and presidents, and it will be vulnerable to the same societal and political shocks as are the rulers holding it in place.[25]

In recent years, consequently, a new approach to the study of regional economic co-operation and the economic dimension of peace emerged. Where the early proponents of functional co-operation among the participants in the Middle East peace process were concerned with inter-state co-operation and favoured large infrastructure projects that would then benefit the societies at large, more emphasis has recently been placed on private sector co-operation, industrial joint ventures, and cross-border trade. Transnational ties have been assumed to be of crucial importance for generating economic development in the Middle East.[26] Ali Çarkoğlu, Mine Eder, and Kemal Kirişci have argued that only if regional domestic forces were taken into account and 'co-operative incentives on the international scene are balanced with the expectations and open demands of the domestic forces that shape the region,' then regional economic co-operation would not be bound to experience failure. They have suggested that the mobilization of domestic actors, collaboration and interaction among domestic constituencies across countries, and the creation of business ties and functional co-operation among the societies are 'keys for creating peace in the region.'[27]

Against the positive role that Çarkoğlu, Eder and Kirişci assigned private entrepreneurs in the peace process, J. W. Wright argued that businessmen 'have ceded their moral integrity to financial incentives which are based on conflict continuation' and would therefore not support the peace process. While a majority of people in the Middle East would support a peace process leading to economic and political stability, it would be the political-economic elites who in fact favoured the creation of at best unequal ties. The emergence of radical opposition movements and the cycle of violence produced by them, Wright argued, would effectively be in the interest of entrepreneurs, who would benefit from a persistence of the conflict.[28] While both sides in this debate have recognized the 'close and dynamic relationship between economic liberalization, democratization and peace in the Middle East'[29] and the linkage between political economy, domestic politics, economic co-operation and the peace process, the conclusions they reached were diametrically opposed to one another. Çarkoğlu, Eder, and Kirişci themselves therefore suggested that further research be carried out to analyse in-depth 'different kinds of domestic coalitions and their power within the government' in order to determine 'the role of domestic actors and their links to the foreign-policy process.'[30] This is the task of the present study: What role did private entrepreneurs and business communities in Israel, Jordan, and the Palestinian Territories play in the peace process until its disruption through the Al-Aqsa Intifada?

The Role of the Business Sector in the Peace Process

The debate among students of the political economy of Middle East peace, and specifically, between Çarkoğlu, Eder, and Kirişci on one side, and Wright on the other, is the conceptual departure point for this book. There seems to be a consensus in the literature that Israel, Jordan, and the Palestinian Territories form the core of an emerging Middle Eastern region.[31] A plethora of literature has dealt with potentials for co-operation in different areas, and a large number of scholars have engaged in identifying feasible pathways of fostering co-operation and of removing obstacles in the way of prosperity for Middle Eastern states and societies. Another approach has so far focused on the political processes of peace-making and has pointed out the crucial importance of domestic politics in the peace process. Rarely, however, have students of the Middle Eastern peace process attempted to link these two perspectives and to investigate the interrelations between domestic political economy, regional economic co-operation, and the inter-state peace process. The present study seeks to address this gap. With the outbreak of the Al-Aqsa Intifada in September 2000, this theme has gained even greater significance. The question is no longer purely hypothetical – whether businesspeople in the three countries can assume a crucial role in peacemaking – but can be extended to ask why business failed to promote peace.

This study, therefore, enquires into the role that the business sectors in Israel, Jordan, and the Palestinian Territories played throughout the peace process. Has the proposition put forward by Çarkoğlu, Eder, and Kirişci been adequate: Did businessmen play a crucial role in cementing the peace process through the creation of business ties across borders? Or were businessmen, as Wright has suggested, engaged in an essentially mercantilist project of obstructing the peace process in order to maintain their privileged domestic position? What were the interests of the business sectors in the peace process, what were their attitudes towards peace, normalization, and co-operation? How did entrepreneurs attempt to influence policy-making and therefore, the direction of the peace process? Was their role a positive one in that they supported the process and cemented peace, or did they seek to obstruct it? The overarching question – what role did the business sector in the three countries play in the peace process? – is thus broken down into different lines of inquiry. The purely economic sphere – did businessmen co-operate, who, how, and why? – is second in importance to the political-economic dimension here, although it is a preliminary field of enquiry on which the latter is based. Founded on the conception of peace-making as a multidimensional process, the emphasis of this study lies on the interests of the business sectors within the three core parties of the Middle Eastern peace process and how they sought to exert influence on the formulation and implementation of foreign (economic) policy. At the same time, this study represents the first detailed empirical survey of business co-operation amongst Israelis, Jordanians, and Palestinians.

Chapter 1 of the present book spells out the general theoretical framework of the study. Issue is taken not only with the long-standing level-of-analysis debate and the question, how important domestic politics are in the realm of foreign policy and international relations. The argument also assesses the significance of domestic economic interests and the domestic political economy for international politics. Chapter 2 introduces the reader to the economies of Israel, Jordan, and the Palestinian Territories, and outlines the structure, role, and organization of the business sectors within the respective economies.

In Chapters 3 and 4, the interests of businessmen in peace and 'normalization' as well as their engagement in co-operation are explored. These chapters are based on a broad range of primary sources, involving publications by professional associations and organizations, as well as interviews with a variety of entrepreneurs. In Chapters 5 and 6, the influence of entrepreneurs on policy-making, particularly in terms of the foreign policies relating to co-operation and peace, but also domestically, is assessed. In Chapter 5, business sector-government relations, the nature and methods of lobbying and influencing, and the role of entrepreneurs as emissaries and negotiators are traced. Chapter 6 summarizes the role of businesspeople in the peace process and their engagement in advancing or obstructing peace within each of the three entities.

While all these chapters deal with the role of the business sectors in the peace process separately within each of the three countries, Chapter 7 analyses their influence from a comparative perspective. This helps us to understand the dynamics of the peace process at large. It also gives us a sense of how peace and cooperation on one side, and domestic politics, economic liberalization, and political liberalization and democracy on the other, have been linked in the Middle Eastern peace process. Moreover, this chapter leads back to the abstract theoretical question of how important domestic political-economic structures and social forces are in the realm of the peace process in the Middle East and in international relations at large.

Given that the subject matter of this study are recent developments in the Middle East and that inevitably, a strong emphasis is placed on non-archival materials and interviews, one might well doubt the value of the conclusions reached. Yet, the wealth of information available today from a broad range of different sources makes it possible to embark on a project of such contemporary nature. Laurie Brand argues in her study on Jordan's 'political economy of alliance-making' that her conclusions are based on 'informed analysis of a preponderance of the *available* evidence' (her emphasis):

> Those who study the third world are not in a position simply to wait until a 25-year-rule expires for the declassification of release of documents. One works under the assumption that such documents will probably never be released, or may never have existed in the first place [...] For some, these obstacles would suggest that a study such as this should not have been attempted, or that its conclusions are suspect. As for the former contention, the idea that we should avoid the study of major areas of the world because we have less than perfect evidence is cowardly and exaggerates the accuracy of the data available on Western states. As for the latter, research on this level of politics in the developing world is often like working on a jigsaw puzzle with many missing pieces. The trick is to combine all the existing pieces in such a way as to make the most coherent picture, in the process not excluding pieces that may complicate the picture simply for the sake of parsimony.[32]

Despite significant differences in terms of the analytical and theoretical framework, this study shares Brand's premises and is designed in a somewhat similar methodological fashion. Brand's independent variable, so to speak, is Jordan's domestic political-economic structure, which is used to explain the kingdom's foreign policy, studied with reference to different cases but with respect to one country only. The independent variable in the present study, in contrast, is domestic political-economic agency, the influence of which on foreign policy is determined. Unlike Brand's work, besides, the present study of one case over a relatively short period of time – i.e. the Middle East peace process from 1993 to the outbreak of the second Intifada in 2000 – is not carried out purely inductively. Rather, it is informed by a critical-theoretical approach to international relations, which highlights the significance of social force in international politics.

Maybe a last word is in order to clarify what this book is *not* about. This study deals with the role of businesspeople from Israel, Jordan, and the Palestinian Territories in the peace process, or, on a more theoretical level, with the impact of domestic political economy on regional relations. In this sense, the present study does not engage in the identification of potentials for co-operation, as many macroeconomic studies have done in the past. Rather, it investigates the views of businesspeople, government officials and others, as well as the consequences of actual co-operation. Furthermore, this book concentrates on the two broadly defined areas of trade and industry when considering co-operation, in the form of subcontracting, joint ventures, joint manufacturing or the like, and deliberately shuns other sectors, which deserve more specialized attention. Among these are infrastructure, cultural and educational, environmental and health co-operation, which are mostly inter-governmentally dealt with. Two other important areas, in which the private sectors are heavily involved but which have their own dynamics, are tourism and agriculture. The overall consequences of collaboration in these sectors, however, do not seem to lead to any different conclusions than this study presents.

1

Social Forces, Politics and International Relations

Most conventional theoretical accounts of international relations, foreign policy, and co-operation either single out the structure of the international system, or focus on either the state or society as the determining variables for foreign policy outcomes and co-operation. However, a theoretical framework that transcends the 'level-of-analysis' debate provides a more comprehensive lens through which to view and understand international politics. This can be achieved by incorporating society, the state, and international relations and basing the account on the domestic material foundations of social relations and the specific configuration of the state-society complex. Foreign policy and the specific engagement in, and the nature of, co-operation are crucially shaped by the domestic struggle for hegemony between social forces and socio-economic interests, which mould discourse, ideas, state institutions, and social power, and strongly influence foreign policy behaviour.

Functionalism and Its Critics

Functionalism, Neo-Functionalism and the Realist Challenge
Much of the writing on regional economic co-operation in the early era of peace in the Middle East was dominated by economists and based on classical-liberal beliefs, informed by an explicitly functionalist approach. David Mitrany had first developed Functionalism in the 1930s and 1940s. This approach stressed the importance of technical co-operation among experts as a pathway to peace and universal welfare, as functional co-operation would bring together mankind in technical, social, and economic co-operation and thus prevent warfare in international politics: 'Peace requires that we should extend and strengthen the fields of positive international agreement and co-operation.'[1] Transnational interaction on the basis of functional differentiation would replace inter-state competition and would gradually shift the regulatory focus of international affairs onto a supranational level. This would help to overcome animosities and cement peace in the international system.

In the 1950s, Ernst B. Haas reformulated Mitrany's essentially prescriptive and idealistic conception of how peace could be achieved and advanced through functional co-operation into an explanatory theory of regional integration in Europe. Transnational interaction and integration, in Haas' view, was not an intended method of achieving peace, but the accidental outcome of co-operation, which gradually evolved and expanded.[2] This argument formed the core of Haas' explanation of the emergence of European regional co-operation and integration, which was the result of technical co-operation gradually weaving a web of increasing economic, social, and political interdependence and eventually leading to political integration. Beginning with the European Coal and Steel Community, sectoral co-operation and integration had 'spilled over' into the realm of high politics. It set in motion a process of further regional integration, which Haas ultimately expected to yield a unified political community.[3]

Haas' theory of Neo-Functionalism and his optimistic prognosis, however, were weakened by the lack of political integration in European regionalism throughout the late 1960s and 1970s and the emphasis on a *'Europe des patries,'* as advocated by French President Charles de Gaulle. A surge towards European integration suddenly occurred during the mid-1980s and early 1990s, with the Single European Act (SEA), the introduction of the Common Market, and the transformation of the European Community into the European Union. Only then did Neo-Functionalism and Functionalism enjoy a revived interest amongst both practitioners and international relations scholars. This was also fuelled by a parallel worldwide resurgence of regional schemes of co-operation.[4]

In this context, it was no coincidence that although there were few explicit references to Mitrany or Haas, it was their perspectives that essentially shaped both the design of the peace process and much of the early optimistic writings on economic co-operation in the Middle East. Apolitical co-operation in fields such as infrastructure, telecommunications, industry and trade, it was hoped, would help overcome and resolve the vast political differences between the parties and thus 'spill over' into the realm of high politics, where it would eventually effect political co-operation and integration. Yet, it had always been one of the most important criticisms levelled against both approaches that they underestimated the significance of power politics and sought to 'de-politicize' international affairs. Indeed, empirical research on regional integration in Europe demonstrated that European regional co-operation had not been set in motion by functional collaboration, but had been a means to reassert national sovereignty and 'rescue' the nation-state.[5] Likewise, the breakdown of the peace process with the eruption of the Al-Aqsa Intifada in September 2000 illustrated the failure of (Neo-) Functionalism to predict and achieve peace in the Middle East, conceptually as well as practically.

These arguments and developments appeared to fit into the theoretical framework of Realism, the dominant theory of international relations.[6] The Realist tradition had also shaped those arguments sceptical of schemes of regional co-operation in the Middle East, which viewed the peace process as biased in favour of Israel and considered economic co-operation to be a manifestation of Israel's power and dominance in the region. According to Realists, relations between states resembled a Hobbesian state of nature under the condition of anarchy, i.e. in the absence of an overarching regulatory authority, in the international system. As a result, states sought to maximize power in order to guarantee their survival and security. Hence, war was a recurrent pattern and co-operation a difficult and dangerous affair.[7] Joseph Grieco summed up the three basic assumptions of Realism:

> First, states are the major actors in world affairs. Second, the international environment severely penalizes states if they fail to protect their interests or if they pursue objectives beyond their means; hence they are 'sensitive to costs' and behave as unitary-rational agents. Third, international anarchy is the principal force conditioning the external preferences and actions of states.[8]

Early Realist writers such as Hans Morgenthau or E. H. Carr had based their interpretations of the perennial pursuit of power in international relations on an essentially pessimistic view of human nature.[9] In contrast, later Realists such as Kenneth Waltz sought to demonstrate that state behaviour and the characteristics of international politics were logically deductible from the anarchical structure of the international system:

> The national system is not one of self-help. The international system is [...] In a self-help system each of the units spends a portion of its effort, not to forwarding its own good, but in providing the means of protecting itself against others [...] In anarchy, security is the highest end [...] The goal the system encourages them to seek is security.[10]

Thus, the condition of anarchy made co-operation other than in the form of military alliances unlikely, if not impossible. States were concerned with their gains and losses relative to those of other states; international politics was a zero-sum game, in which one state's loss was automatically another state's gain. Only the so-called balance of power, an equilibrium in the military power of different states or alliances, which would make a resort to war too costly an affair, preserved peace and stability in the international system. Neo-Realism also introduced a clear distinction between the realms of domestic politics and international affairs. Foreign policy was conditioned by the structure of the international system, and domestic societal factors were therefore irrelevant.[11] As Waltz argued, 'by depicting an international political system as a whole, with structural and unit levels at once distinct and connected, Neo-Realism establishes the autonomy of international politics and thus makes a theory about it possible.'[12] This theory revolved around the impact of systemic anarchy on the foreign policy behaviour of states. All other accounts of international relations and foreign policy were 'reductionist' in Waltz's view.[13]

The Neo-Neo Debate, Constructivism and a Marxist Alternative

These systemic-structuralist premises found full acceptance in the work of Neo-Liberal Institutionalists such as Robert Keohane when they revived the Functionalist approach in the late 1970s and 1980s.[14] The Neo-Liberal perspective was strengthened by the growth of global and regional interdependence, exemplified in the emergence of international institutions and regimes as well as an increase in economic interconnectedness, which Realism could not explain adequately. Keohane and his followers subscribed to Waltz's view that anarchy in the international system dictated the pursuit of self-interest. However, according to Neo-Liberals, states were not so much concerned with their gains relative to those of others, but with their absolute gains. Employing rational choice and game theory, Neo-Liberals demonstrated that states were able to overcome mutual suspicion and realize their common interests in mutually beneficial co-operation.[15]

These arguments triggered the prolonged 'Neo-Neo' debate, which shaped the academic study of international relations during the 1980s and well into the 1990s. It revolved around the prospects for co-operation and stability through interdependence, which Neo-Realists viewed pessimistically and tended to dismiss, while Neo-Liberal Institutionalists maintained that international affairs were manageable through international regimes.[16] Closely related was the Neo-Liberal argument that the increasing institutionalization of world politics and growing interconnectedness would further enhance transparency and co-operation among states and thus, cement stability and peace in international relations.[17] However, this claim and the anticipation of a linear evolution of increasing co-operation, which followed the writings of Mitrany and Haas, made Neo-Liberal Institutionalism vulnerable to a Realist counter-challenge.

In the face of the undeniable reality of economic interdependence, Neo-Realists refined their arguments and developed the so-called 'hegemonic stability theory:' Co-operation and the pattern of increasing economic interconnectedness in the global economy since the 1970s were contingent upon the existence and consent of a hegemon, who, as the most powerful actor, dictated the rules of co-operation in line with its own preferences.[18] In contrast, Keohane had argued that co-operation was possible without the existence and consent of a hegemon (from which argument he derived the title of his book, 'After Hegemony'), because self-interested states would pursue their absolute gains and realize them in mutually beneficial co-operation.[19]

While the debate between Neo-Realists and Neo-Liberal Institutionalism concentrated on the prospects for co-operation and the role of hegemony, both approaches shared many basic assumptions, which attracted growing criticism during the 1990s. Both remained focused on the structure of the international system and its effects on states. Both assumed states to be rational-unitary actors, with pre-defined interests; strategic power and security – or relative gains – in the Realist view; welfare and economic power – absolute gains – in the Neo-Liberal interpretation. Neither approach questioned how states' interests were actually constituted and defined. As one critic of Waltz's Neo-Realism wrote, it said 'very little about the impact of domestic factors. It talks a great deal about states as self-interested actors competing in an anarchical world but leaves the identity of the "self" and the nature of the interests unexplained, or simply assumed.'[20] This criticism equally applied to Neo-Liberal Institutionalism, as Christian Reus-Smit pointed out: 'Like

Neo-Realists, Neo-Liberals treat state interests as exogenous to inter-state interaction, and see no need for a theory of interest formation.'[21] Keohane himself admitted: 'No system-level theory could be complete. Without a theory of interests, which requires analysis of domestic politics, no theory of international relations can be fully adequate.'[22]

Kenneth Waltz had claimed explicitly that his theory of international politics was not a theory of foreign policy. However, the overriding importance attached to the structure of the international system in his work as the determinant of states' behaviour left little place for other factors contributing to or accounting for co-operation and foreign policy outcomes.[23] This was not the sole inherent inconsistency in Waltz's theory, as Richard Ashley pointed out. Neo-Realism, and Neo-Liberal Institutionalism with it, served to legitimize an artificial and obscuring distinction between the international and the domestic political spheres and to narrow the space for enquiry into the nature of international politics.[24] Unfortunately, radical post-structuralist and post-modern critiques and meta-theoretical explorations such as Richard Ashley's or Rob Walker's had little impact due to the failure of such writers to present a viable empirical research agenda and their refusal or inability to offer a theoretical alternative.[25]

However, Ashley's criticism of Waltz's work in particular and the Realist tradition more generally also questioned the lack of a 'concept of social power behind or constitutive of states and their interests.'[26] John Gerard Ruggie's critical review of Waltz's structuralist perspective similarly illustrated how the principle of sovereignty was a means of establishing a mode of social relations between states. Both Ruggie and Ashley, thus, highlighted the importance of the social foundations of international relations.[27] These criticisms were taken further in the work of the so-called 'Constructivists,' who raised questions about how states' interests were constituted. As Alexander Wendt argued, both 'Neo-Realism and Neo-Liberalism are "under-socialized" in the sense that they pay insufficient attention to the ways in which the actors in world politics are socially constructed.'[28] Wendt went on to single out interactive processes of socialization and learning as the determinants of state behaviour. Anarchy as such did not condition self-help and the quest for power and security, but was 'what states made of it.'[29] Self-help and the pursuit of power under anarchy were 'learned' and emerged from social interaction: 'States are *socialized* to want certain things by the international society in which they and the people in them live.'[30]

With their focus on socialization among states in international affairs, Constructivists followed the work of the so-called English School, which had much earlier argued that states formed an international society.[31] However, most Constructivists remained focused on the structure of the international system and its consequences, instead of leaving systemic theories behind altogether. Thus, Wendt argued that his 'social theory of international politics' was not a theory of foreign policy. It was, like Waltz's approach, both systemic and structural.[32] As a result, Constructivists failed to fulfil their own theoretical premises. While they accounted for the formation of state interests, they resolved the so-called 'agent-structure problem' with resort to the structure alone.[33] Constructivism hence did not live up to its own argument that agents and structures were mutually constitutive. In addition, Constructivists neglected the material foundations of social relations in economic interests and the socio-economic circumstances of individuals and states.

An alternative approach, which was traditionally concerned with an account of interest formation, yet also incorporated the material basis of social relations, was the Marxist perspective. The Marxist tradition had also shaped those arguments put forward against the Functionalist perspective on peace and co-operation in the Middle East, which had pointed out that the vast inequalities between Israel and its Arab neighbours were bound to lead to economic dependence, rather than interdependence.

Since the publication of Lenin's theory of imperialism, which 'in effect converted Marxism from essentially a theory of domestic economy to a theory of international political relations among capitalist states,' Marxist thought had primarily been concerned with inequality and uneven development in the capitalist world economy.[34] On the basis of Lenin's theory, the Neo-Marxist account of Dependency argued during the 1960s that economic growth in the developed countries of the West had occurred only due to outward expansion and the exploitation of peripheral states, which provided raw materials for the economically advanced core regions of the world economy. Elites in the periphery were part of the system and helped to sustain it by taking part in the preservation of the periphery's dependent status within a global system of exchange relations between rich and poor; North and South. Consequentially, peripheral states were to achieve growth only by severing the bonds, which tied them to the capitalist world economy. The realization of nationalist aspirations replaced the international proletarian revolution as the solution advocated by this form of Neo-Marxism.[35]

However, Dependency theory painted a highly static picture and essentially failed to account for the fact that development in the periphery in fact depended on inclusion in the world economy.[36] Immanuel Wallerstein's World-Systems approach transcended beyond the analysis of Dependency theory yet was similarly based on the interpretation that the world system comprised a series of commodity chains. The world economy was divided into a core and periphery, with a hybrid form of semi-peripheral societies, which stabilized the system and achieved a degree of development.[37] Thus, for Wallerstein, like for Dependency theorists, capitalism could not be related to a particular mode of production or economic organization within the state, but was necessarily an international phenomenon, based on exchange relations.[38]

Conceptually, this interpretation meant that these Neo-Marxist accounts left the bounds of domestic political economy behind.[39] Effectively, the Marxist perspective offered a systemic-structuralist theory of international politics. Its normative concern with emancipation or revolution notwithstanding, it became, as Keohane wrote, 'nearly indistinguishable from the doctrine of political realism.'[40] As in Neo-Realism, states struggled for wealth and power, and the differential growth of power was the key to international conflict and political change.[41] Marxist theories of international relations had drawn attention to issues of development and inequality, and had combined the economic and political dimensions of international relations. Yet, the development towards the Dependency and World-Systems perspectives meant that Marxism could not really trace its account of international relations to societal roots anymore, but only to a global logic of capitalism, in which modes of exchange relations between states determined international relations. The Marxist perspective thus became vulnerable to the crucial criticism levelled against all systemic-structuralist theories of international relations: 'States do not operate at the mercy of the structures of the international system,' whether it was simply anarchic, socially constructed or subjected to the logic of global capitalism.[42] Instead, the social foundations of international relations, often located in domestic politics and society, had to be taken into account in order to understand and explain co-operation, conflict, and foreign policy.

Social Forces, Material Interests, Foreign Policy and Co-operation

Domestic Origins of Co-operation and Foreign Policy

The idea that domestic politics had an impact on foreign policy and international relations ran counter to the static systemic-structuralist approaches of Realists, Neo-Liberals, Constructivists, and structural Marxists. It had long been the source of criticism levelled against these perspectives. The debate on whether the determining factors of international politics were to be found on the systems level or on the state or individual levels became known as the 'level-of-analysis' problem in international relations. Critics of systemic structuralism pointed out that these perspectives had eschewed 'any empirical concern with the domestic and internal variations within the separate nations' and produced 'a sort of "black box" or "billiard ball" concept of the national actors,' which in itself had proven insufficient to explain the actual behaviour of states.[43]

Graham Allison's work on the Cuban missile crisis, for example, demonstrated forcefully that the systemic-structuralist approach of Realism in particular bracketed crucial factors in explaining the course of the crisis. Allison applied two alternative models to explaining the foreign policy behaviour of the United States during the crisis, the 'organizational behaviour model' and the 'governmental politics model,' which needed to supplement, if not supplant the 'black box model.' Since government was a 'vast conglomerate of loosely allied organizations, each with a substantial life on its own,' one could understand governmental behaviour 'less as deliberate choices and more as *outputs* of large organizations functioning according to regular patterns of behaviour.'[44] Alternatively, one could conceptualize foreign policy as the result of bargaining games played 'among players positioned hierarchically within the government', who perceived situations differently or might try to further their own political positions.[45]

A very similar perspective was Robert Putnam's conceptual metaphor of 'two-level games.' On the one hand, statesmen participated in international bargaining processes and sought to realize their aims. On the other hand, they had to see through the ratification process domestically, which considerably limited their manoeuvrability in the international negotiations and affected the policy outcome, according to Putnam.[46] The two-level games approach ascribed to society a certain influence on the policy outcome but remained simplistic, as it only dealt with the domestic process of ratification and failed to problematize the process of initial preference formation. The perspective thus also provided a bridge to those Realist models of foreign policy decision-making that recognized 'the need to examine the policy-making process within a country when dealing with questions involving foreign policy,' yet insisted on the power of the state and the independence of decision-makers from societal influences. Stephen Krasner, for example, had maintained that although 'central decision-makers may be frustrated in their efforts to further the national interest by opposition not only from external actors but from domestic ones as well,' ultimately, foreign policy was formulated autonomously by government officials.[47]

Accounts like Krasner's were strongly influenced by a more general attempt to 'bring the state back' into political science and sociology during the 1980s.[48] Stephen Hopgood's work on American environmental foreign policy accepted the premise of state autonomy, yet sought to illustrate that government officials made decisions and implemented policies in policy contexts defined by societal and international elements and restrained by an 'envelope' of shared values among the officials.[49] Although Hopgood thus sought to incorporate societal influences into his theoretical framework of foreign policy-making, he maintained himself that his approach was state-centred. Like the models and approaches put forward by Allison, Putnam, and Krasner, Hopgood's work focused on the state and in particular, the Western model of a democratic state, in which government officials and state institutions played a crucial role in the formation of state interests and the implementation of foreign policy.

However, as critics of such statist approaches argued, any perspective 'which focuses on the state in abstraction from civil society is simply inadequate. It is inadequate because it fails to perceive the dialectical relationship between state and society.'[50] In contrast to the state-centred perspectives, Peter Katzenstein, for example, had pointed out in his work on the political and material bases of foreign policy:

> The governing coalitions of social forces in each of the advanced industrial states find their institutional expression in distinct policy networks which link the public and private sectors in the implementation of foreign economic policy.[51]

Katzenstein's approach pointed towards the significant role of social forces and drew attention to the configuration of state-society relations. In particular, it focused on the interrelations between political and economic elites, which accounted for the formation of state interests and provided the foundation for engagement in co-operation.

Katzenstein was a representative of the so-called Pluralist tradition, which conceptualized the state as subjected to societal influences. It had understood foreign policy, and indeed, policy in general, as an outcome of the 'ongoing struggle for influence among domestic social forces or political groups.' In contrast to the state-centred approaches put forward by Allison, Krasner, Putnam, and Hopgood, according to this perspective, 'state officials or institutions play neither an autonomous nor significant intervening role in shaping or constraining policy.'[52] Pluralism took the state to be a passive arena, in which societal interests competed for influence and shaped foreign policy, or as Stephen Krasner charged, a 'cash register that totals up and then averages the preferences and political power of societal actors.'[53]

The Pluralist approach had the advantage of tracing the social foundations of government policy, in that it stipulated the proposition: 'Societal ideas, interests, and institutions influence state behaviour by shaping state preferences.'[54] Yet, at the same time, the perspective inherently assumed the concept of a liberal democratic state and of democratic interest politics, where, as Krasner pointed out:

> If the state has any active role to play […] it is to maintain the basic rules of the game: to make sure that all groups have equal opportunity to compete. Government activity must be characterized by fairness. It must create an order within which individuals can express their own needs and wants.[55]

Pluralists also put forward an extended argument, which claimed that because of the significance of interest politics and societal interests, it was particularly difficult for democracies to go to war with one another.[56] Interestingly, this literature on the 'democratic peace theory' or the 'liberal zone of peace' provided the very ground on which Çarkoğlu, Eder, and Kirişci had based their argument that domestic political forces would be crucial players in the Middle East peace process:

> An important factor here would be the emergence of domestic players with a stake in economic liberalization capable of influencing governmental policy. This is more likely to happen in a more democratic and open domestic political environment. Such an environment would also facilitate transnational relations and coalition formation among national interest groups that would perceive a benefit from regional co-operation.[57]

Essentially, hence, the Pluralist perspective, and the approach to peace-making in the Middle East advocated by Çarkoğlu, Eder, and Kirişci, were both grounded in the conception of a liberal democratic decision-making process in which all groups had equal access, at least ideally, and competed on an equal footing. This, however, was neither the reality within Western liberal democracies, nor even less so in states which adhered less to the ideal-typical model of a liberal democracy. The Pluralist perspective failed to provide an adequate theoretical account for the consequences of domestic inequality and different configurations of domestic power and influence, which were not tied so rigidly to the concept of the Western liberal democratic state. The democratic peace theory, in particular, could not simply be transferred to the Middle East, where the development of democracy had been limited. In addition, Pluralism assumed a permanently changing base of interests, instead of investigating the historical evolution of existing interests, which were grounded in socio-economic realities and which could remain coherent over time.

In contrast to the Pluralist perspective, Laurie Brand's work on the political economy of Jordan's engagement in shifting alliances, for example, demonstrated forcefully that economic interests could play a determining role in shaping foreign policy behaviour and co-operation. Her argument was that Jordan's foreign policy followed from the state's role as a distributor of resources, which it obtained from outside.[58] Behind the concern with economic security stood the regime's interest to secure its survival domestically through the continued allocation of resources.[59] This argument fitted well into a broader literature on the foreign policies of new states in the developing world, which pointed out:

> The sphere of foreign policy is often used to solve problems in internal politics. This necessarily implies that the realm of foreign policy is seen as secondary to the sphere of domestic politics, and the international consequences of the actions that a government takes are seen as of less importance to itself than those consequences that most nearly touch its citizens.[60]

Yet, Brand's work focused on the role of the state and failed to trace the roots of foreign policy further to the specific domestic political-economic configuration of state-society relations, which shaped Jordanian foreign policy during the 1970s and 1980s. In fact, only an encompassing account of the domestic political-economic underpinnings of state and society could account for an adequate theory of interest formation. This approach would investigate the material foundations of social relations and explain the engagement in specific foreign policies, and forms of co-operation, while simultaneously problematizing the consequences of domestic and international, political and economic inequalities.

The State-Society Complex and Domestic Political Economy in International Relations

The work of Robert Cox on the domestic underpinnings and social basis of foreign policy, co-operation, and international relations pointed in this direction and offered an alternative perspective. It included a suitable theory of interest formation and an encompassing account of the material and historical foundations of international politics. Cox pointed out that the respective configuration of state-society relations in any given state had to be understood as a crucial variable in shaping foreign policy, co-operation, and international relations. As he argued,

> There has been little attempt within the bounds of international relations theory to consider the state-society complex as the basic entity of international relations. As a consequence, the prospect that there exists a plurality of forms of state, expressing different configurations of state-society complexes, remains very largely unexplored.[61]

In opposition to the systemic structuralism of Neo-Realism, Neo-Liberalism, Neo-Marxism, and Constructivism, Cox demonstrated that the conventional distinction between state and civil society, which made the separation of the realms of international and domestic politics possible, was inadequate:

> Traditional international relations theory maintains the distinctness of the two spheres, with foreign policy appearing as the pure expression of state interests. Today, however, state and civil society are so interpenetrated that the concepts have become almost purely analytical (referring to difficult-to-define aspects of a complex reality) and are only vaguely and imprecisely indicative of distinct spheres of activity.[62]

At the same time, against those perspectives, which focused exclusively on either the state or societal influences, Cox argued: 'Beware of underrating state power, but in addition give proper attention to social forces and processes and see how they relate to the development of states and world orders.'[63]

Cox's argument was grounded in a definition of the notions of state and civil society and the nature of state-society relations based on the writings of the early Twentieth-century Italian Marxist theorist, Antonio Gramsci. The state and civil society, Gramsci had argued, were not distinct entities, but were bound in a dialectical relationship, determined by the social relations of production. The nature of the state was shaped by the class structure, on which the state rested. The capitalist bourgeoisie exercised hegemony over society not only through its control over the means of production. It also gained the acquiescence of the working class and the petty bourgeoisie in the hegemonic social order by making concessions, to such a degree that its hegemony became the dominant common consciousness.

As a result of this analysis, Gramsci had enlarged his definition of the state to involve not only the elements of government, but also the 'underpinnings of the political structure in civil society.' These included 'all the institutions which helped to create in people certain modes of behaviour and expectations consistent with the hegemonic social order.'[64] In other words, 'where the hegemonic class is the dominant class in a country or social formation, the state (in Gramsci's enlarged concept) maintains cohesion and identity [...] through the propagation of a common culture.'[65] Thus, hegemony was a form of social contract, which emphasized the consent of the ruled, rather than the coercion of the ruler, as a basis for authority, and was hence embedded in the institutions of the state:

> There is a close connection between institutionalization and what Gramsci called hegemony. Institutions provide ways of dealing with conflicts so as to minimize the use of force. There is an enforcement potential in the material power relations underlying any structure, in that the strong can clobber the weak if they think it necessary. But force will not have to be used in order to ensure the dominance of the strong to the extent that the weak accept the prevailing power relations as legitimate. This the weak may do if the strong see their mission as hegemonic and not merely dominant or dictatorial, that is, if they are willing to make concessions that will secure the weak's acquiescence in their leadership and if they can express this leadership in terms of

universal or general interests, rather than just as serving their own particular interests. Institutions may become the anchor for such a hegemonic strategy since they lend themselves both to the representation of diverse interests and to the universalisation of policy.[66]

On the basis of this theoretical framework, Cox went on to demonstrate how the social relations of production shaped the contemporary world order. The dominant capitalist classes of the industrialized world had established their hegemony first domestically, then also internationally.[67] Cox transcended the conventional level-of-analysis debate by integrating the different spheres into one theoretical framework. In doing so, he heeded Anthony Brewer's earlier claim that

> The question of the appropriate level of analysis – world-system, nation state, unit of production or whatever [...] is a non-problem. There can be no question of choosing to analyse at one of these levels, and ignoring the others; any adequate account of the world system must incorporate all of them, and their interrelations.[68]

Cox's analysis was, as Andrew Linklater pointed out, 'not an exercise in economic reductionism.'[69] This was due to the significance Gramsci had attached to the realm of ideas and discourse. Cox followed his reasoning and used the concept of

> 'hegemony' to mean a structure of values and understandings about the nature of order that permeates a whole system of states and non-state entities [...] Hegemony derives from the ways of doing and thinking of the dominant social strata of the dominant state or states insofar as these ways of doing and thinking have acquired the acquiescence of the dominant strata of other states. These social practices and the ideologies that explain and legitimize them constitute the foundation of hegemonic order.[70]

The contemporary world order, according to Cox, was a manifestation of the existence of a transnational hegemony of the capitalist class, or the bourgeoisie:[71]

> Social forces are not to be thought of as existing exclusively within states. Particular social forces may overflow state boundaries, and world structures can be described in terms of social forces just as they can be described as configurations of state power. The world can be represented as a pattern of interacting social forces in which states play an intermediate though autonomous role between the global structure of social forces and local configurations of social forces within particular countries.[72]

With his interpretation of a transnational hegemonic social order, or of a global hegemony, established and maintained by the capitalist classes of the industrialized countries, Cox translated and transposed Gramsci's original analysis onto the international level. However, in doing so, Cox largely neglected the internal processes within states. His concern with world order led Cox to understand differing configurations of state-society complexes only as expressions of different modes of social relations of production on a global level, i.e. as expressions of different world orders.

Yet, in contrast to this interpretation, one could conceive of differing state-society complexes, moulded by the social relations of production and the state of, or struggle for, domestic hegemony, within the contemporary world order. Foreign policy behaviour would then be shaped by the domestic political-economic underpinnings of the state-society complex. Gramsci himself had reasoned that the sphere of international politics logically followed the realm of social relations in domestic politics.[73] Following Gramsci, Cox had pointed out – in particular in opposition to the notion of hegemony prevalent among Realists and structural Marxists – that hegemony had analytical applicability not only at the international level, but also in the domestic arena: 'When the concept of hegemony is introduced, it becomes necessary to ask, what is the form of power that underlies the state?'[74] This form of power is determined not only by the universal force of capitalism, but also by state-specific factors, based on the specific historical evolution of each society or state and their political-economic underpinnings, in addition to a variety of other systemic and domestic variables.

Thus, the foreign policy behaviour of states could be conceptualized as being determined largely, though certainly not entirely, by the state of hegemony within society. Where a hegemonic order was in place, Cox had argued, 'state actions are constrained by knowledge on the part of the state's agents of what the class structure makes possible and what is precludes. This has nothing to do with specific manipulation of state policies or the actions of particular "actors" but with the general understandings about the tasks and limits of the state.'[75] However, while the struggle for hegemony could be understood as a universal process, the actual establishment and maintenance of hegemony is not necessarily a universal reality, but is contingent upon the specific historical evolution of each state and society.

Hence, it could be argued that relations between states and societies largely follow from the respective state of hegemony in any given state. In other words, the foreign policy of states is shaped and conditioned primarily by the domestic struggle for hegemony. Hegemony, thus, is not simply a matter of existence. It intrinsically entails a historical process, which in itself involves a wide range of factors. Dominant social forces attempt to establish their hegemony, domestically and then, on the basis of that, also internationally, but they might also fail in their attempt and provoke opposition. Thus, it is the struggle for hegemony, not the existence of hegemony – which is only one possible outcome and thus one potential manifestation of the struggle for hegemony – that crucially shapes the foreign policy behaviour of states, although other factors also play a role in determining the eventual foreign policy course taken.

This understanding provides the theoretical framework of the present study. It enquires into the role Israeli, Jordanian, and Palestinian businesspeople played in the peace process until its disruption with the outbreak of the Al-Aqsa Intifada. It investigates the domestic and transnational political and economic interests of these social forces and outlines their role in the peace process. Having placed the business communities in the context of their respective domestic political and political-economic environment, the respective state-society complexes in Gramscian terminology, the preferences of these communities and their impact on the preference formation of the state are investigated. In a next step, this study investigates and outlines those processes leading to a transnationalization of the domestic struggle for hegemony, and the dialectical relationship between the domestic and regional struggles in the political and economic arenas. It demonstrates that indeed, the specific configuration of state-society relations plays a crucial role in shaping foreign policy behaviour and the nature of co-operation, in accordance with the prevailing domestic hegemonic social order, or as a resultant of the domestic struggle for hegemony.

At the same time, as this study further illustrates, the realms of domestic and foreign policy and political economy are dialectically linked and impact upon each other. Cox had argued that the principle of hegemony or of the hegemonic struggle domestically, not 'only serve the most powerful economic and political interests in the dominant states but provoke, in turn, the principal forms of opposition and conflict.'[76] As this study outlines, the processes set in motion as the foreign policy outcome of a particular configuration of state-society relations in the three entities under investigation had consequences, which in the end significantly impacted on and altered both the domestic and the regional state of and struggle for hegemony. Foreign policy, thus, is primarily conditioned and shaped by the domestic hegemonic struggle, yet the policy outcomes of the domestic political-economic configuration of the state-society complex in turn have repercussions on the struggle for hegemony.

This dialectical relationship manifests the inherent historicity of foreign policy and international relations. It also clearly transcends the divide between the realms of domestic and international politics and draws attention to the political-economic configuration of the state-society complex as the basic entity for the analysis of international relations. While doing so, however, the inherently historical approach taken in this study recognizes the interplay of a variety of factors at any given time. Singling out the domestic struggle for hegemony as the crucial factor, this study also involves other, concurrent elements and events on the systemic and domestic levels, and hence seeks to provide a comprehensive account of the evolution and effects of regional business co-operation among Israelis, Jordanians, and Palestinians.

2

The Economy, Business and Politics

This chapter provides an overview of the Israeli, Jordanian, and Palestinian economies, their business sectors, and the role the governments have played in them. The economic, political, and social structures of Israel, Jordan, and the Palestinian Territories have had their own particular histories and manifested themselves in distinct ways. However, there have been striking similarities in terms of the underlying power structures in all three entities. All three economies are dualistic in nature, characterized by a divide between an economically dominant alliance of the government and large business enterprises on the one hand, and a majority of much less influential small and medium-sized enterprises on the other. Despite processes of reform and liberalization, in particular in Israel and Jordan, economic as well as political power has remained or become even further centralized in the hands of a small circle of political and economic elites in all three entities in recent years.

Israel

From Etatisme to Export-Oriented High-Tech Liberalism

Once a traditional economy based mainly on agriculture, light industry and labour-intensive production, Israel used to be described as the 'most socialist economy of any nation outside of the Eastern bloc' until the mid-1980s.[1] Nevertheless, from 1922 to 1973, Israel's high rates of growth had been second only to Japan.[2] Development had been achieved through a highly centralized, state-driven economic policy, making Israel a world record-holder in high taxes and foreign debt, fuelled also by high defence expenditure and the costs associated with the absorption of large numbers of immigrants.[3] In July 2000, Israel's total population was estimated to surpass 6 million, of which roughly 1.25 million were Arabs, compared to a total population of 750,000, of which about 150,000 were Arabs, in May 1948. Defence expenditure had peaked at more than 30 per cent of GNP during the 1970s and still equalled 15.2 per cent of GDP in 1989, but had already started decreasing following the 1979 peace agreement with Egypt.[4]

Table 1: Israel's Economy at a Glance

Poverty and Social		Israel		High-Income Countries
2000				
Population (millions)		6.2		903
GNI per capita ($)				27,510
GNI ($ billions)				24,829
Annual Average Growth, 1994-2000				
Population (per cent)		2.4		0.7
Labour force (per cent)		3.3		0.9
Most recent estimate				
Poverty (per cent of population)				
Urban population (per cent of total)		91		77
Life expectancy at birth (years)		78		78
Infant mortality (per 1,000 life births)		6		6
Illiteracy (per cent of population age 15+)		4		<5
Key Economic Ratios and Long-Term Trends	**1980**	**1990**	**1999**	**2000**
GDP ($ billions)	21.8	52.5	100.8	110.3
Gross domestic investment/GDP	22.4	25.1	21.0	19.3
Exports of goods and services/GDP	43.8	34.7	35.7	40.0
Gross domestic savings/GDP	6.8	14.4	11.4	12.4
Current account balance/GDP	-4.0	0.3	-1.9	
Interest payments/GDP				
Total debt/GDP				
Average annual growth	**1980-1990**	**1990-2000**	**1999**	**2000**
GDP	3.5	5.1	2.2	5.7
GDP per capita	1.7	2.2	-0.2	3.5
Exports of goods and services	5.5	9.2	8.7	
Structure of the Economy	**1980**	**1990**	**1999**	**2000**
Per cent of GDP				
Agriculture				
Industry				
Services				
Private consumption	53.1	55.6	59.6	59.1
Imports of goods and services	59.3	45.4	45.3	47.0

Table 1: Israel's Economy at a Glance, continued:

Average annual growth	1980-1990	1990-2000	1999	2000
Agriculture				
Industry				
Services				
Private consumption	6.2	6.9	4.6	
Imports of goods and services	4.3	8.7	14.5	
Prices and government finance	**1980**	**1990**	**1999**	**2000**
Domestic prices (per cent change)				
Consumer prices	131.0	17.2	5.2	1.1
Implicit GDP deflator	134.7	15.9	6.7	2.0
Government finance (per cent change)				
Current revenue				
Current budget balance				
Overall surplus/deficit	-16.2	-5.3	-2.1	
Trade	**1980**	**1990**	**1999**	**2000**
$ Millions				
Total exports (fob)	5,538	12,080	25,794	31,338
Total imports (fob)	9,784	16,793	33,160	38,130
Export price index *(1995=100)*	76	95		
Import price index *(1995=100)*	87	98		
Terms of trade *(1995=100)*	87	97		
Balance of Payments	**1980**	**1990**	**1999**	**2000**
$ Millions				
Exports of goods and services	8,668	17,312	35,891	
Imports of goods and services	11,511	20,228	40,816	
Resource balance	-2,843	-2,916	-4,925	
Net income	-757	-1,975	-3,281	
Net current transfers	2,729	5,060	6,324	
Current account balance	-871	170	-1,881	
External Debt	**1980**	**1990**	**1999**	**2000**
$ Millions				
Total debt outstanding				
Total debt service				
Official grants				
Foreign direct investment	51	151	2,363	

Source: Adapted from the World Bank, Israel at a Glance, www.worldbank.org/data/

German reparations, then increasing American financial aid had enabled the government to assume a leading role in developing the country.[5] In a market economy divided into three sectors, the public sector and collectivist institutions such as the General Federation of Labour, the Histadrut, had dominated over the private sector. The Histadrut, formed in 1920, had not only represented workers, but had also incorporated Kibbutzim and Moshavim; had provided an extensive range of services to its members, 1.8 million in 1994 or 42 per cent of all salaried workers in the economy; and had been a major employer in its own right. Through its holding company, the Hevrat Ovdim, the Histadrut's economic enterprises had included the leading corporations in industry (Koor), building (Solel Boneh), insurance (Hasneh), and banking (Bank Ha'Poalim), employing 25 per cent of Israel's workforce. Its firms had generated as much as 27 per cent of the country's industrial product in 1986.[6] Because of its close ties to the government, which for decades meant the ideologically related Labour alignment, the Histadrut had been a 'key economic and political force of power,'[7] 'second only to the government itself in economic policy-making.'[8] But due to its very nature as an institution of and for workers, the Histadrut had not aspired to create profits, nor did its firms have to be profitable, since the Federation had access to capital unrelated to its business activities, in the form of membership fees.[9]

Until the 1990s, the government had been the single most important actor in the economy. It had not only been the country's biggest employer and its biggest customer; it had also controlled important resources such as land, money, raw materials, and water. No firm had been allowed to issue bonds or shares without the approval of the Minister of Finance. Foreign exchange had been controlled, and the government had regulated and directed most of the flow of capital.[10] It had allocated and distributed funds and subsidies, and set wages and prices.[11] Effectively, the government had decided what to produce through licence requirements for the production of certain goods, subsidies and import bans.[12] Under these circumstances, much production had been carried out under monopolistic or oligopolistic conditions. The granting of monopolies and the high subsidies paid by the government as part of a strategy of import substitution had been met by a promise of investment, employment, and exports on behalf of the firm. As a result, it was virtually impossible to be successful in business without a favourable government attitude.

All funds accumulated by insurance companies and pension funds had to be invested in special bonds issued by the Ministry of Finance or in Hevrat Ovdim plants. Thus, the Histadrut, whose holding company the Hevrat Ovdim was, had enjoyed a distinct advantage without having to run its enterprises in an efficient manner. When this arrangement was discontinued in 1980, several Histadrut enterprises, among them Solel Boneh and Koor, at the time owning 11 per cent of the Israeli manufacturing industry, found themselves near bankruptcy and had to be bailed out by the government.[13] These developments coincided with balance-of-payments problems for the government due to the fast rate of growth and the high levels of governmental expenditure, mainly for defence purposes, since the 1970s. In 1984, the economic crisis peaked, with inflation running as high as 445 per cent. Only in July 1985 did a national unity government manage to approve an Emergency Stabilization Plan, cutting the budget deficit by $1.5 billion (7.5 per cent of GDP), devaluating the Shekel by 20 per cent, and reducing export subsidies. The programme was a success: Inflation was reduced to 16.4 per cent in 1988; the ratio of external debt to GNP dropped from around 90 per cent to 25 per cent.[14]

On the basis of this programme, Israel underwent drastic reforms during the 1990s. The influx of 600,000 Russian immigrants between 1990 and 1994 heralded a new phase of economic expansion. The economy grew faster than any other industrial economy between 1991 and 1996, averaging over 5.2 per cent per year, and despite the sudden increase of its total population, unemployment amounted to only 6.3 per cent in 1995.[15] The business sector of the GDP grew even faster, at more than 7 per cent annually, signifying a trend towards a more liberal, business-friendly economy, although there was 'still a high degree of concentration of economic might at the centres of power.'[16] The trend was fuelled not only by manpower, but also by an influx of foreign direct investment and trade deregulation, in addition to renewed efforts at privatization and capital market reform.[17] On the basis of its military industry, Israel, which had the highest proportion of engineers in the population worldwide, became a major high-tech producer. By the late 1990s, about 85 per cent of Israel's industrial exports were technology-oriented.[18]

The total value of Israeli exports had risen from only $18 million in 1950 to $780 million in 1971, and reached almost $21 billion by 2000. From 1991 on, Israel gradually dismantled its protectionist trade regime and began exposing the domestic market to foreign imports. Administrative limitations on imports from third countries were cancelled and higher rates of customs tariffs imposed instead, which were then also reduced, according to their degree of influence on local production, while allowing Israeli industry time to adjust to competition. The final stage of this process came to an end in September 2000, when tariff rates reached a maximum range of 8-12 per cent. Israel was the sole country in the world to have both a European Union and a US free trade agreement (FTA), the latter fully effective from 1995 on. Among its most important markets were the Occupied Territories, to which Israel was connected through a one-sided customs union.[19]

The Tripartite Division of the Israeli Economy

Until the mid-1990s, the distortion in free market competition due to the Histadrut's role in the economy had strongly affected the privately-owned part of the business sector, and thus, 'it may be inaccurate to use the term "private sector" for any of Israel's companies,' as Ira Sharkansky remarked:

> Managers learned to profit not by offering products that could compete in the international market, but by offering proposals that would earn subsidies from government offices. Alliances between powerful bureaucracies and the firms that received government aid were counted among the elements that protected the status quo and retarded growth.[20]

In consequence, not only the Histadrut and the state were closely connected, but the private sector and the government as well, as were private sector firms and those enterprises controlled by the Labour Federation. While the private sector accounted for much of Israel's national income and employment and owned a large majority of industrial plants, it was composed of mainly small or medium-sized firms, usually controlled and managed by one or more family owners. The nature of the Israeli economy was essentially dualistic, i.e. split into a competitive periphery and a dominant core of big conglomerates, in which the traditional sectoral cleavage between government, Histadrut, and private capital had largely been transcended.[21]

The economic crisis of the 1970s and 1980s, however, led to a dramatic circumscription of the Histadrut's economic and political power.[22] It lost most of its enterprises and was deprived of a third of its members when new pension schemes and health insurance policies were introduced, abolishing many of the exclusive benefits that had hitherto been associated with membership in the Federation. A new leadership changed the organization's name to New Histadrut in 1994 and decided to henceforth focus on the trade union aspect, while the state and the 'private' sector assumed a more central role in the economy than before.[23] The Histadrut's industrial flagship, Koor, underwent drastic transformations, illustrating the demise of the Labour Federation and the new alliance between government and private sector. Indeed, 'the history of Koor is the history of the Israeli economy in microcosm.'[24]

In the early 1950s, eager to diversify and inspired by Ben-Gurion's determination to develop a local arms industry, Koor had set up the telecom specialist, Telrad, and the artillery supplier, Soltam, which politically made a major contribution to the technological edge and helped Israel win wars. Financially, these companies figured prominently in an export-oriented defence industry, which by the 1980s became Israel's major source of foreign currency.[25] But Koor's expansion into virtually all sectors of the economy, in combination with its political role, meant that it began losing money. In 1988, 126 out of Koor's 130 subsidiaries were unprofitable. Under its new CEO, Benny Gaon, Koor shed as much as 40 per cent of its workers, or 4 per cent of the entire Israeli labour force, and by 1995, the American Shamrock Group had completely taken over the conglomerate, ending its association with the Histadrut.[26] Within a few years Koor established itself once again as Israel's most profitable industrial company, with 20,000 employees in some 30 subsidiaries and a net income of $156 million in 1995, and accounted for over 7 per cent of Israel's entire annual industrial output and exports.[27] Koor became the first Israeli multinational and integrated itself into the global business community. Further changes occurred when, in July 1998, the American Claridge Group took over control from Shamrock and the new leadership under Jonathan Kolber stipulated a new business strategy aimed at making Koor the largest technology holding company in Israel.[28] Koor's transformation illustrated the changes in the Israeli economy, from the state-dominated, quasi-socialist business sector with its focus first on agriculture, later on military industry, to a globalized, liberal economy.

Like Koor, most big business firms underwent major transformations, but their power and influence persisted. Big business had traditionally comprised five core conglomerates, Bank Ha'Poalim, Bank Leumi, Israel Discount Bank Holding (IDBH), Koor, and Clal, which for decades used to be involved in all key sectors of the economy. Clal, for example, had shareholdings in the electronics, metals, food, clothing, textiles, and cement industries. Although it was founded privately, 41 per cent of its shares were owned by Bank Ha'Poalim, which itself was held by the Histadrut and later, by the government. The private IDBH owned the Discount Bank, which in turn controlled 34 per cent of Clal, as well as, through the IDB Development Corporation, the Discount Investment Corporation (DIC), another major holding company.[29] By 2000, Clal was fully merged into the DIC; the IDB Development Corporation also held Azorim Investment and Clal Insurance. During 2001, the group underwent further restructuring, simplifying the holding structure and solidifying the control over the group by the Recanati family.[30]

Both Bank Leumi and Bank Ha'Poalim had originally become involved in non-banking activities during the crisis of the 1980s, when the large conglomerates had failed to repay loans, and the banks acquired equity. During the 1990s, the government had restricted such non-banking activities. Bank Ha'Poalim had to sell its shares in Clal, Delek, Ampal, and Koor. But by 2000, the banks re-emerged; Bank Leumi purchased 20 per cent of the Israel Corporation, previously owned by the government and now held by the private Eizenberg Group, a new big business conglomerate. The Discount Bank was separated from the DIC, but started investing independently into telecommunications and infrastructure. Bank Ha'Poalim purchased 20 per cent of Clal Insurance.[31]

The Eizenberg Group held 41 per cent of the Israel Corporation or Israel Chemicals and together with the DIC and Bank Ha'Poalim owned Shikun v'Pituah.[32] The Israel Corporation held the industrial heavyweights, Dead Sea Works, Rotem Amfert, and Dead Sea Bromine as well as the largest transportation firm, Mifalei Tovala. Another big business firm was the Dankner Group, a private family business spread out across a number of sectors. The family was one of the richest in Israel, owned Dankner Investments, and controlled Bank Ha'Poalim through the shares held by its subsidiary, Salt Industries, together with Arison Investments. Arison also held a 35 per cent stake in the Housing and Construction Holding (HCH), another erstwhile Histadrut enterprise and parent company to Solel Boneh.

Despite the transformations and the complex holding structures of the core conglomerates, the underlying power structure, centralizing economic influence in a few core businesses, has not changed. Indeed, as Michael Shalev argued,

> The recent liberalization process need not be overestimated. Even though local and foreign private investors have acquired controlling interests in segments of big business, the existing groups were also strengthened in the 1990s by opportunities for expansion furnished by some major privatizations and by boom conditions in construction and infrastructure. The top

executives who formerly ran firms in the public and Histadrut sectors continue to be major players in big business.[33]

The 'small-economy' firms, in contrast, have always functioned independently from one another, with only loose business and professional associations. Into this category also fell the private enterprises of 'Israeli Arabs,' i.e. Palestinians with Israeli citizenship, who generally occupied a 'most peripheral status in all branches of the economy.' In consequence, entrepreneurial activity has been rare, significantly disadvantaged in comparison to Jewish-Israeli business, and figured at the lower end of the small economy.[34] Overall, the Israeli political economy has not been receptive towards small entrepreneurs, but has favoured a 'special breed of entrepreneurs,' which emerged in the era of state-regulated capitalism.[35]

Political Business and Interest Politics

The conventional categorization into a public and a private sector never really applied to the Israeli economy, and this used to have important political consequences. As much as the Histadrut represented 'big business' and 'big labour' simultaneously, the government, too, incorporated political as well as business interests.[36] Consequently, representatives of state and Histadrut-owned firms were openly active alongside major private industrialists in the Israel Manufacturers Association (IMA), and as a group with similar interests, big business wielded considerable political influence. In 1976, Yair Aharoni showed that the big companies and groups had a 'great deal of influence on economic policy and on the manner in which the resources of the state are allocated.'[37]

This created a highly politically charged interdependence. While both Histadrut and private sector were dependent on the government for the allocation of capital, the government was bound in its decision-making by the influence of big business, and politicians and civil servants acted under the constraints of big business interests.[38] Domestic capital formation became a circular affair, but the arrangement in effect expressed and ensured the identity of the political and economic elites in Israel.[39] One symptom of the dependency relationship between government and business was the electoral 'business cycle,' where business leaders resorted to generous funding of the ruling party in return for favourable economic policies.[40] The interdependence between big business and the government was also a factor leading to the prolonged economic crisis and hyperinflation at the beginning of the 1980s, due to the business sector's reliance on the government for financial assistance, which was granted in accordance with the former's interests. Business thus wielded a great deal of power.

The large conglomerates, mainly engaged in defence-related production, benefited considerably from the crisis, increasing their shares in net profits of the business sector from less than 3 per cent in the early 1970s to an average of 15 per cent during the early 1980s.[41] With the growing concentration of capital in the core conglomerates and the subsequent concentration of power, the representatives of big business were increasingly in a position to extract resources from the government in return for their support. The electoral business cycle was transformed in favour of big business, and this was one reason why the government could not resolve the crisis until 1985.[42] Since then, however, the big conglomerates have managed to adapt to the new circumstances and have remained at the core of the Israeli political economy. Bichler and Nitzan suggested that big business reflected the 'power/class structure of Israeli society.' Since the 1950s,

> This structure has been consolidated through a growing web of reciprocal business ties; as well as through personal, kinship, and cultural bonds among the Israeli business, political, and military elites – ties which eventually led to the emergence of an Israeli ruling class.[43]

It was in this sense that the Israeli political elite included 'not only the government but also the managers of the large firms [...] – having a sort of old-boy network.'[44] As early as 1973, Yuval Elizur and Eliahu Salpeter pointed out that there existed intimate links within a core elite group of 'several hundred or a several thousand at most,' and that there was a high degree of mobility within this political and economic elite stratum.[45] The fluid interchange of management personnel between government and public industry also included the private sector, and thus the interests of one elite stratum were buttressed in all three sectors. This made it later possible to advocate liberalization, which in fact served the interests of the elites.[46]

Daniel Maman showed that the Israeli business groups were tied together not only through business relations, but also via social ties. Managers sat on boards of other groups and firms, and joint ventures served as institutional linkages among different enterprises. Similarly, policy forums, which were 'institutional settings for encounters between state and non-state organizations,' linked the managers of different businesses with each other and with political decision-makers.[47] With the decline of the Histadrut, which was closely connected to a political party, the Labour alignment, and recent trends on the Israeli political scene, exemplified in the direct election of the prime minister in 1996 and 1999, interest politics have become more flexible and more important.[48] Partly through personal acquaintances and partly on the basis of their contributions to political candidates and parties, businesspeople established close relations with senior politicians.[49] Despite the recent changes, economic and political elites have remained tightly connected.[50] In addition, professional associations and interest groups also utilized private contacts.[51] The business sector was organized under the roof of the Co-ordinating Bureau of Economic Organizations (CBEO), which represented the sector as a whole.[52] Within this umbrella organization, the Israel Manufacturers Association (IMA) was of particular importance. Founded in 1921, it represented 1700 industrial enterprises, or about 90 per cent of the industrial sector, and pursued its interests mainly through direct and high-level contacts to relevant ministers.[53] The Federation of Israeli Chambers of Commerce (FICC), the roof organization of six regional chambers, represented Israeli merchants. The FICC, also a member of the CBEO, operated very much in the same way as the IMA, but had less influence.[54]

Thus, the Israeli economy was characterized by a dualism between government-owned and other big business firms on the one hand, and the majority of small and medium-sized companies on the other, and dominated by the government and big business elites. These were connected in a variety of institutions, socially, and through joint business ventures to such an extent that a coherent political-economic elite stratum emerged, which made economic policy and pursued interest politics in a highly personalized manner. Smaller enterprises, in contrast, had little political influence and were marginalized in politics as in the economy.

Jordan

The Rentier Economy

Jordan's total population approached 5 million in 2000; up from 2.1 million in 1979. An estimated 60-75 per cent of the population are of Palestinian origin.[55] For decades, Jordan relied on remittances from skilled workers in the Gulf, which amounted to as much as 20 per cent of GDP or almost double the value of exports until the early 1980s.[56] Its second major source of income had been foreign aid, first from Britain, then the United States, and later the oil-rich Gulf states.[57] As a result, Jordan had been indirectly dependent on oil during the 1970s and 1980s, since both remittances and foreign aid were linked to the oil price.[58] Another consequence of the importance of capital transfers from workers and foreign governments was the 'bloated state-sector' and the centrality of the government in the economy.[59] Jordan thus became a 'rentier economy', or an 'exoteric state', which was 'predominantly based on revenue accruing directly from abroad,' and in which the state was the 'inevitable intermediary in the collection and redistribution of foreign revenue of public origin.'[60] Other characteristics of the rentier economy included:

> Limited development of indigenous productive forces; a standard of living far higher than the level of indigenous productive forces would have suggested or allowed for; state services and infrastructure far more extensive than the GDP would have permitted; and a very high percentage (nearly 50 per cent) of the work force on the state payroll.[61]

Jordan's external trade was characterized by a large structural deficit, due to the small domestic manufacturing base and the necessity to import food and manufactured goods. Imports covered only about 40 per cent of exports, and although the trade deficit decreased recently, it still amounted to more than $2 billion annually. Most imports came from the EU and the United States, while Jordan's Arab neighbours were its most important export markets, accounting for as much as 43 per cent of exports in 1996.[62] The kingdom's single most important trade partner was Iraq, which also provided most of Jordan's oil needs and foreign aid during the 1980s.[63]

Jordan had witnessed rapid economic growth until 1967, when it lost the West Bank, which had accounted for as much as 38 per cent of the kingdom's GDP.[64] The economy slowly recovered and then enjoyed unprecedented growth until the mid-1980s.[65] With the decay of oil prices, however, the Jordanian economy gradually slid into a deep crisis in the mid-1980s. Workers returned from the Gulf and remittances decreased. Jordan's foreign debts amounted to more than $6 billion, and the kingdom could not meet its obligations anymore. The Jordanian Dinar had to be devaluated by almost 50 per cent in 1988.[66] In 1989, Jordan and the International Monetary Fund (IMF) agreed on a structural adjustment programme, inciting violent riots in April, when subsidies on basic commodities were removed almost overnight. This crisis led to the introduction of cautious measures of political and economic liberalization, with relatively free elections, attempts at privatization, and an increasing rhetoric about the need to attract investment, although success remained limited.[67] Iraq's invasion of Kuwait and the ensuing war in 1991 then brought Jordan's economy almost to a standstill. The adjustment programme with the IMF had to be suspended. According to the Central Bank of Jordan, the economy suffered losses of more than $1.5 billion, or 35 per cent of Jordan's GDP of 1989, in 1990 alone.[68] In contradiction to all expectations, however, the influx of 300,000 returning workers from the Gulf actually triggered a short-lived economic boom in the early 1990s.[69]

The peace process, and with it the relief of a significant share of Jordanian foreign debt, was hoped to usher in a new era of prosperity.[70] However, the continued embargo against Jordan's most important export destination, Iraq, posed major problems. The economy exhibited sluggish growth from 1996 onwards, coupled with a high population growth rate, and Jordanians experienced a decline in real per capita income. Unemployment was high; unofficial estimates put the figure at 25 per cent or more. Jordan's debt, rescheduled in 1999, still stood at $7 billion, or 92 per cent of GDP, in April 2000.[71] Nevertheless, the Jordanian government accelerated the path of privatization and economic reform during the second half of the 1990s, in particular after King Abdullah's succession to the throne in 1999. A new investment law was passed in 1995 and complemented by another law passed in 2000. In 2000, Jordan also became a member of the WTO and concluded a free trade agreement (FTA) with the United States.[72]

The Role of the Government in Business and the 'Big 7'

Jordan had traditionally been considered a free-market economy.[73] Most of the country's productive assets were privately owned, and accordingly, direct state-ownership was relatively small. Public enterprises, not including government services, only accounted for about 14 per cent of GDP in 1992.[74] Nevertheless, as Laurie Brand pointed out, it would be inaccurate to infer that the government played only a minor role, since the boundaries between the public and private sectors were blurred.[75] The government was the kingdom's largest employer and the largest purchaser of goods and services.[76]

As in Israel, the business sector was not divided into a public and a private sector, but rather into a 'big' economy, dominated by political-economic elites and state officials, and the privately owned small and medium-sized enterprises. Decisions on imports were made through centralized units. Prices for both imported and exported goods, as well as many domestically sold commodities, were set by the

Table 2: Jordan's Economy at a Glance

Poverty and Social		Jordan	Middle East and North Africa	Lower-Middle Income Countries
2000				
Population (millions)		4.9	296	2,046
GNI per capita ($)		1,710	2,040	1,140
GNI ($ billions)		8.4	602	2,327
Annual Average Growth, 1994-2000				
Population (per cent)		3.1	2.0	1.0
Labour force (per cent)		4.1	2.8	1.3
Most recent estimate				
Poverty (per cent of population)		12		
Urban population (per cent of total)		74	59	42
Life expectancy at birth (years)		71	68	69
Infant mortality (per 1,000 life births)		26	44	32
Illiteracy (per cent of population age 15+)		10	35	15
Key Economic Ratios and Long-Term Trends	**1980**	**1990**	**1999**	**2000**
GDP ($ billions)	4.0	4.0	8.1	8.3
Gross domestic investment/GDP	36.7	31.9	20.8	22.5
Exports of goods and services/GDP	39.9	61.9	43.6	44.4
Gross domestic savings/GDP	-7.6	1.0	2.6	3.8
Current account balance/GDP	7.1	-10.2	5.0	0.7
Interest payments/GDP	2.0	7.6	4.5	4.3
Total debt/GDP	49.8	203.4	110.8	100.7
Average annual growth	**1980-1990**	**1990-2000**	**1999**	**2000**
GDP	2.5	5.0	3.1	3.9
GDP per capita	-1.2	1.0	0.0	0.8
Exports of goods and services	4.8	2.6	0.5	7.1
Structure of the Economy	**1980**	**1990**	**1999**	**2000**
Per cent of GDP				
Agriculture	7.9	8.1	2.4	2.2
Industry	28.0	28.1	25.6	24.8
Services	64.1	63.8	72.0	73.0
Private consumption	78.8	74.1	72.8	72.4
Imports of goods and services	84.2	92.7	61.8	63.1

Table 2: Jordan's Economy at a Glance, continued:

Average annual growth	1980-1990	1990-2000	1999	2000
Agriculture	6.8	-2.0	-20.4	7.1
Industry	1.7	4.7	4.9	3.8
Services	2.3	5.0	3.2	4.9
Private consumption	1.9	4.5	2.8	1.9
Imports of goods and services	1.2	1.2	0.5	4.3
Prices and government finance	**1980**	**1990**	**1999**	**2000**
Domestic prices (per cent change)				
Consumer prices	11.0	16.1	0.6	0.7
Implicit GDP deflator	1.1	11.4	-1.6	-0.6
Government finance (per cent change)				
Current revenue	54.6	40.2	31.0	30.2
Current budget balance		8.7	2.5	1.1
Overall surplus/deficit		2.6	-3.4	-4.7
Trade	**1980**	**1990**	**1999**	**2000**
$ Millions				
Total exports (fob)	431	1,064	1,769	1,817
Total imports (fob)	1,799	2,600	3,717	4,597
Export price index *(1995=100)*	85	80	94	90
Import price index *(1995=100)*	113	100	102	105
Terms of trade *(1995=100)*	75	80	92	86
Balance of Payments	**1980**	**1990**	**1999**	**2000**
$ Millions				
Exports of goods and services	1,181	2,511	3,534	3,536
Imports of goods and services	2,417	3,754	4,990	5,796
Resource balance	-1,236	-1,242	-1,456	-2,260
Net income	36	-215	-155	-27
Net current transfers	1,481	1,046	2,016	2,345
Current account balance	280	-411	405	59
External Debt	**1980**	**1990**	**1999**	**2000**
$ Millions				
Total debt outstanding	1,971	8,177	8,942	8,397
Total debt service	210	625	647	781
Official grants	1,127	672	390	404
Foreign direct investment	34	38	154	751

Source: Adapted from the World Bank, Jordan at a Glance, www.worldbank.org/data/

state. Consequently, the government decided who and what was to be supplied and consumed in the market. Due to the restriction of free market competition, entrepreneurs sought to satisfy the government so as to win privileges through its policies, rather than meet customer demands of quality, price, and sustainable supply.[77]

The government was also involved in much of the production process via its indirect ownership of many companies. Until the mid-1990s, the government wholly owned and directly administered several entities, the boards of which were generally appointed by the cabinet.[78] In addition, the government had almost virtual control over a number of other enterprises, in which it shared equity with the private sector, and through the government-owned Jordan Investment Corporation (JIC) and the Social Security Corporation (SSC) held significant shares in a number of formally private sector companies.[79]

In 1994, the JIC held shares in 46 firms; the SSC had a portfolio of 54 public shareholding companies and 24 unlisted shareholding companies.[80] In mining, the government owned 38.4 per cent of the Jordan Phosphate Mines Company (JPMC) and 53 per cent of the Arab Potash Company (APC), which accounted for a third of total exports. In manufacturing, the government's shares amounted to 23.2 per cent of the whole capital in manufacturing shareholding companies. 87 per cent of the governmental share was held in the four largest companies, the Jordan Cement Factories Corporation (JCFC), the Jordan Petroleum Refinery Corporation (JPRC), the Jordan Glass Industries Company (JGIC), and in the Jordan Engineering Industries Company (JEIC).[81] These four companies, the JPMC and the APC, and the Jordan Fertilizer Industries Company (JFIC), formed the 'Big 7' of the Jordanian economy, acting as a 'catalyst for economic development' and providing 'training for the future engineers and managers of Jordan.'[82]

The Big 7 recently underwent some changes, beginning with the JGIC, which began incurring losses in the mid-1980s and was liquidated in 1997.[83] But despite privatization efforts, the government retained much control, since most measures saw the sale of minority stakes to foreign partners, which have relied on managements drawn from the Jordanian elite. A 1995 law allowing for foreign ownership of Jordanian companies restricted the foreign share in most cases to 50 per cent until 2000, when new legislation finally permitted full foreign ownership.[84] Thus, privatization proceeded slowly and has been opposed by many elements among the elite. A 20 per cent stake in the JCFC was offered in 1996, then increased to 33 per cent and sold to French interests. Similarly, the Telecommunications Corporation, wholly owned by the government until then, was transformed into the Jordan Telecommunications Company (JTC) in 1997 and sold a 40 per cent stake to France Telecom in December 1999. The chairmen of both companies had vehemently protested against privatization.[85]

As a result of the government's central role in the economy, the absolute private sector, i.e. that which was not controlled by the government, was largely refined to agriculture and quarrying.[86] In the 1980s, industry contributed about 18 per cent of GDP. Of this share, the potash, phosphates, and petroleum refinery industries generated almost 60 per cent, or almost 10 per cent of total GDP. Small

Table 3: JIC Holdings, 1994

Company name	JIC Share (per cent)	Capitalization (million JD)	Employees
Majority Holdings:			
Arab Potash Company (APC)	55.3	765.1	2,134
Jordan Cement Factories Co. (JCFC)	49.5	174.7	2,753
Jordan Phosphate Mines Co. (JPMC)	42.4	128.1	5,516
Minority Shares:			
Cairo Amman Bank	10.0	50.0	1,301
Jordan Worsted Mills	14.1	30.8	192
Jordan National Shipping Lines	18.7	21.8	96
Jordan Press Foundation	15.0	25.1	378
Housing Bank	5.1	68.4	2,206
Jordan Paper & Cardboard Factories	27.4	12.6	238
Jordan Petroleum Refinery Co. (JPRC)	5.5	59.8	3,989
Public Mining Company	51.0	3.0	57
Jordan Tanning	15.0	7.2	261
Jordan Tobacco & Cigarettes	13.3	6.2	946
Jordan Ceramic Industries Co (JCIC)	4.0	15.8	529
Industrial, Commercial, Agricultural	2.5	22.8	528
Arab Pharmaceutical Manufacturing	1.2	46.8	1,002
Jordan Dairy	12.8	4.3	180
Business Bank	2.0	21.8	276
National Textile & Plastic Industries	10.0	3.1	112
Jerusalem Insurance	4.7	4.5	101
Jordan Himeh Minerals	30.0	0.3	19
National Multi-Industries	0.6	14.0	130
Jordan New Cable	0.4	15.0	103
National Chlorine Industries	0.4	11.6	109
Arab Food & Medical Appliances	0.3	3.9	22
El-Zay Ready Wear Manufacturing	0.1	14.4	2,179
Arab Jordan Investment Bank	0.1	37.0	303
Arab Engineering Industries	15.0	-	19
Shares in Loss-Making Companies:			
Agriculture Marketing & Processing	59.4	-	19
Jordan Spinning & Weaving	18.0	13.5	509
Jordan Tourism & Spa Complex	30.8	3.1	158
Machinery Equipment & Maintenance	26.5	0.9	42
Intermediate Petrochemical Industries	1.3	11.3	119
Jordan Sulpho Chemicals	1.2	7.8	122
Jordan Industrial and Match Company	2.9	2.2	81
International Tobacco & Cigarettes Co.	0.2	17.5	233
Arab Investment & International Trade	0.1	5.1	142

Table 3: *JIC Holdings, 1994, continued:*

Company name	JIC share (per cent)	Capitalization (million JD)	Employees
Shares in Non-Listed Companies:			
Agriculture Marketing & Processing	89.9		
National Food (Shafa) Processing Co.	84.1		
Jordan TV & Radio	75.7		67
Industrial Estate Corp.	67.5		
Jordan Poultry Processing & Marketing	40.7		164
Dar al-Sha'b Press	32.1		
Jordan Lime	11.5		
Jordan Dead Sea Industries	10.0		

Source: The World Bank, Jordan Privatization Note, Privatization Technical Assistance Mission, December 9-15, 1995, Annex 6: Major Shareholdings of JIC in 1994 (excludes sold companies)

and medium-sized enterprises in the industrial sector, on the other hand, contributed only 7.2 per cent to GDP, although about 85 per cent of the industrial labour force was involved in it, compared to 12 per cent in the mining and manufacturing industries.[87] In 1994, small industries in Jordan with less than five workers constituted about 90 per cent of all industrial establishments and about 45 per cent of total industrial employment. Adding the medium-sized industries, i.e. those with 5-24 workers, the total percentage of SMEs represented 98 per cent of all industrial establishments. SMEs contributed 26.9 per cent to GDP in 1994, according to the Department of Statistics, as compared to 31.9 per cent of GDP for large enterprises. Trade, and in particular exports, were dominated by the public sector and the large enterprises, while SMEs were marginalized.[88]

The divide between big and small business was exacerbated by the fact that the – however blurred – distinction between public and private sector roughly followed the communal divide, as Laurie Brand showed. Jordanians of Palestinian origin 'overwhelmingly constituted the private sector, while Transjordanians have been disproportionately represented in the state bureaucracy.'[89] This communal division contributed to the discrimination against private business, although several Palestinian merchant families emerged and formed part of the elite, mainly in the quasi-private sector. This elite, termed the 'king's Palestinians' or the 'Palestinian G7', included, *inter alia*, the Masri, Nuqul and Salfiti families and the owners of the Arab Bank, the Shouman family. It was closely tied to King Hussein, and gained business success through its loyalty to the palace.[90]

The Overlap of Political and Economic Elites

Until 1990, the so-called Economic Security Committee (ESC) decided on economic policies, rather than the king, the palace and the cabinet, which only infrequently dealt with economic issues, on the one hand, or the private sector on the other. Comprising only a handful of ex officio cabinet members who were chosen by the prime minister in consultation with the king, 'the ESC appears to have been the institutionalized form of an inner circle for economic policy.'[91] Almost equally important, albeit less in the process of decision-making, but even more so in the context of implementation or obstruction of certain policies, was the large bureaucracy, which accounted for about 50 per cent of the country's employment.[92] The private sector was 'not consulted by the government in formulating economic policies,' although private sector organizations always existed.[93]

The Federation of Jordanian Chambers of Commerce (FJCC), a federation of local chambers, of which the Amman Chamber of Commerce (ACC) was the most important one, comprised of about 70,000 members belonging to branches in all major towns by the late 1980s. Until the early 1960s, the ACC had brought together the most important merchants, which were closely connected to the palace. Sabri Tabba'a, the second president, had served in the Senate during the 1950s; his younger son, Hamdi, a Minister of Industry and Trade in 1986, was JCFC chairman during the late 1990s and president of both the Jordanian Businessmen Association (JBA) and the Arab Businessmen Association (ABA). Muhammad Ali Bdeir served in the Lower House from 1951 to 1954 and in the Senate from 1989 to 1993. He was ACC president several times during the late 1940s, the 1960s, and 1970s.[94] The Bdeir and Tabba'a families dominated the ACC as well as the Amman Chamber of Industry (ACI), founded in 1964, in which membership was compulsory. In 1987, the number of members in the ACI exceeded 4,000, although only 20 per cent of these members were entitled to vote, since a minimum level of capital and employment was needed to qualify for voting rights.[95] As a result, the ACI was strongly dominated by those companies, which were in effect public sector firms.

Although both merchants and industrialists frequently claimed that they played a significant role prior to the onset of reforms in 1989, their influence was in fact severely limited and private sector institutions served at best as tools of co-option. In addition to often conflicting or contradictory interests, the private sector was '"parasitic", heavily dependent upon implementing government-commissioned projects,' and did not oppose government policy.[96] This pattern did not change significantly, when from 1985 onwards, various governments espoused privatization and economic liberalization. In fact, as Laurie Brand pointed out, private sector entrepreneurs complained that the measures first introduced by Prime Minister Zayid al-Rifa'i widened the gap between big business and the small and medium-sized enterprises and served the interests of large private capital, which was closely connected to the palace.[97]

This pattern fitted into the larger picture of Jordan as a rentier state, which was characterized by the alliance of political-economic elites that sustained Hashemite rule. Elite circulation to preserve the power base of the regime took place not only at the ministerial level, but also reached into the large enterprises. A list of board members of the kingdom's Big 7 read like a who's who of Jordan's largest and most influential families, such as the Asfour, Tabba'a, Bilbeisi, Talhouni, Kurdi, Touqan, Bdeir, Abu Hassan, Masri, and Kawar families, who also dominated the ACC, the ACI and the JBA:

> The individuals recruited are part of the country's commercial, financial, and state bourgeoisie, and together comprise the country's national bourgeoisie. Many members of the country's commercial and financial bourgeoisie are from the merchant families, who were the pillars of Jordan's economy from the 1940s to the 1960s. A circulation of elites takes place so these individuals remain in some high government or financial position with ties to the state.[98]

Moreover, since public sector employment represented about 50 per cent of total employment, the implementation of privatization could be seen as a retreat of the state from its historical responsibility and a breach by it of a social contract between the leaders and the people; it therefore proceeded very slowly.[99] Employment in the bureaucracy and the large, state-controlled enterprises has been an important form of distribution and co-option in Jordan. Due to the reliance on external rents, the state evolved as primarily an allocator, rather than an extractor, of resources. In consequence, the longer this relationship between state and citizen continued, 'the more set people's expectations of the state's distributive role were and the more difficult breaking such a pattern or attempting to encourage new patterns became.'[100] As Abu Shair pointed out:

> Large numbers of people became totally dependent on the state for their income. Such people, in particular the East Jordanians, are politically significant for the country's stability because of their loyalty and support, which is based on their economic dependence on the state. In other words, there is a contract of shared benefits.[101]

East Jordanians, in particular, were the bedrock of the regime and were therefore mainly employed in the bureaucracy, whereas Palestinians were mainly active in private sector business. The ethnic divide in the labour market and the politics underpinning it, therefore, made it even more difficult for the private sector to participate in the process of economic policy-making, since Transjordanian bureaucrats rarely reacted with sympathy or assistance to the requests of Palestinian businessmen.[102] Beyond the bureaucracy, public sector enterprises, or those in the private sector, which were under the control of the state, were an important means for the state to provide people with income as well as to favour and reward individuals, whose continued support was important for the regime.[103] Only those enterprises, whose Palestinian owners were loyal to the king, were rewarded and achieved success, thus being co-opted into the elite. One example was the Consolidated Contractors Company (CCC), run by Hassib Sabagh and Sa'id Khoury, who besides the Shouman and Masri families, formed part of the Palestinian G7.[104]

Jordan is still largely organized along tribal and family lines and has been characterized by a personalized style of business and politics, where 'the small group of decision-makers is bound by a network of family, school, regional, or business ties.'[105] This pattern has not changed despite the recent measures of privatization and liberalization. In spite of meetings and consultations with the private sector, 'the government usually does things its way, and only a few of the private sector's suggestions and requirements are incorporated.'[106] Although King Abdullah reintroduced the Economic Consultative Council (ECC) in December 1999, aimed at recommending economic, legislative, and administrative reforms, the council soon came under fire from both the old elite, which felt sidelined, and the small economy, which could still not make itself heard. The council brought together 20 public and private sector representatives, some of whom came from well-known and long-established business families and the remaining of whom represented the new business elite that emerged during the 1990s and became the new bedrock of the regime.[107] Thus, the Jordanian economy has been characterized by the dominance of political-economic elites, which have sustained the Hashemite monarchy. The government, itself under the control and ultimate authority of the monarchy, controlled all sectors of the economy, and the business sector was largely co-opted into the patrimonial rentier-state system, which characterized Jordan. Despite recent changes, the majority of small and medium-sized businesses remain marginalized and excluded from the circles of power, which are formed by the political-economic elites in Jordan.

The Palestinian Territories

'De-Development' and Macroeconomic Decline after the Oslo Accords
The Palestinian economy in this study is defined as the areas of the West Bank and Gaza Strip. Although the Palestinian Authority (PA) had only partial control over those areas, economic activity in areas A (fully under PA control), B (joint control), and C (fully Israeli-controlled) exhibited similar characteristics.[108] In 1997, a total population of 2.9 million lived in the West Bank and Gaza, 1.9 million of which in the West Bank and 1 million in Gaza.[109] Prior to the occupation in 1967, both territories were largely underdeveloped and depended on agriculture and unilateral capital transfers, in the West Bank workers' remittances, in Gaza mainly contributions from the United Nations Relief and Works Agency (UNRWA).[110]

Under the Israeli occupation of the West Bank and the Gaza Strip, the single most important factor determining the course of economic development was the 'imposed, incomplete, economic integration between Israel and the Palestinian economy' until 1993.[111] The customs union with Israel increased effective tax levels approximately fourfold, which, in combination with a host of non-tariff barriers and the Arab boycott against Palestinian products containing Israeli inputs, caused an increasing concentration on the Israeli market, together with a complete dependence on Israeli goods.[112] About 90 per cent of imports to the West Bank came from Israel. Israel and Jordan, via the so-called policy of the open bridges, ab-

Table 4: The Palestinian Economy at a Glance

Poverty and Social	1996	1999	2000
Population (millions)	2.5	2.8	2.9
GNI per capita ($)	1,570	1,800	1,610
GNI (billion $)	4.0	5.1	4.7
Population growth (per cent)	3.9	3.7	3.7
Labour force (per cent)			
Poverty (per cent of population)			
Urban population (per cent of total)			
Life expectancy at birth (years)			
Infant mortality (per 1,000 life births)		22.8	
Illiteracy (per cent of population aged 15+)			
Key Economic Ratios and Long-Term Trends			
GDP ($ billions)	3.6	4.2	4.2
Gross capital formation (per cent GDP)	34.4	39.9	
Exports of goods and services/GDP	19.3	17.1	
Current account balance/GDP			
Interest payments/GDP			
Total debt/GDP			
Average annual growth			
GDP	1.2	7.4	-6.2
Structure of the Economy			
Per cent of GDP			
Agriculture	15.8	8.9	
Industry	24.7	28.9	
Services	59.9	62.2	
Imports of goods and services	68.2	74.8	
Prices and government finance			
Domestic prices (per cent change)			
Inflation, GDP deflator	8.5	5.1	3.2
Balance of Payments			
$			
Aid per capita	217.0	180.3	

Source: Adapted from the World Bank, World Development Indicators Database, April 2001, devdata.worldbank.org/

sorbed about 50 per cent of exports each until the late 1980s.[113] In the Gaza Strip, Israeli provided virtually all imports and absorbed as much as 82 per cent of all exports in 1982.[114]

Private sector growth and industrial development were obstructed by Israeli policies. The export of Palestinian labour, mainly to Israel, became the sole engine of growth.[115] Industry contributed only a small percentage of GDP and remained limited to small firms engaged in subcontracting for Israeli firms in the textiles industry. In consequence, the Occupied Territories became fully 'integrated "provinces" of the Israeli economy,' however with the combined GDP of the Territories equalling only 5 per cent of Israel's, thus indicating the massive inequalities implied in the relationship.[116] As Sara Roy argued, the Israeli government pursued a policy of 'de-development,' which was 'predicated on the structural containment of the Palestinian domestic economy and the deliberate and consistent dismemberment of that economy over time.'[117]

The outbreak of the Intifada in 1987 even worsened the economic situation:[118] GNP decreased by 30-35 per cent between December 1987 and January 1991; per capita GNP fell by 41 per cent.[119] Domestic investment also declined.[120] Israel's own difficulties during the 1980s and the general regional slowdown in economic growth also contributed to the economic crisis, which the Territories experienced.[121] The Gulf War of 1991 effectively stopped remittances, direct aid, and income from wages in Israel, with frequent closures and curfews imposed on the Territories, which were maintained in 1992 and 1993 and increased unemployment and poverty.[122]

In this context, the Israeli-Palestinian Declaration of Principles was signed in September 1993. Its economic provisions, together with the 'Paris Protocol on Economic Relations' of April 1994, provided the foundations for the economic relationship between the Palestinian Territories and Israel and effectively stipulated an 'attenuated one-sided customs union.'[123] Israel retained control over critical resources. Although the protocol gave Palestinian goods free access to the Israeli market and vice versa, it kept imports from third parties under Israeli control, with import taxes collected by Israeli customs authorities and then transferred to the PA. Import taxes became one of the most important sources of revenue for the PA. Yet, the Israeli treasury still accrued most taxes, since most imports to the Territories were declared as Israeli exports to the West Bank and Gaza, equalling as much as 60 per cent of Israel's exports to the Territories.[124] For products on three lists (A1, A2, and B), the PA was free to set its own tariffs. However, the potential to establish a less discriminatory trade regime with those lists was limited since Israeli tariffs on those goods were already either zero or very low.[125]

Yet, the most serious problem the failure to implement the Paris Protocol created was the de facto separation of the two economies:[126] Instead of assuring the continuity of Palestinian employment in Israel, as the agreement stipulated, Israel substituted foreign workers for Palestinian labour.[127] The main reasons were the closures Israel maintained after the Gulf War and during the Interim Period due to frequent terrorist attacks. They led to a drop in employment of Palestinians in Israel from about 30 per cent to 7 per cent in 1996 and a steep decline in income.

Following the closure of the Territories in March-April 1996 after a wave of suicide bombings, 66 per cent of the Palestinian labour force was either unemployed or severely underemployed.[128] Closure also meant a decrease in trade, with imports being cut by around 25 per cent and exports by almost 50 per cent between 1992 and 1995.[129] The closures, overall, had a devastating effect on Palestinian economic activity.[130] GDP fell by about 14 per cent during 1992-96, while private investment declined by about 60 per cent.[131] The developments in trade also meant that the Territories grew even more dependent on Israel as the most important destination for exports. Israel absorbed 95 per cent of all exports in 1998.[132]

Due to the reduction in employment opportunities in Israel and the political necessity to provide jobs, the newly established Palestinian Authority (PA) soon became the single largest employer of Palestinians, creating at least 65,000 jobs between 1993 and 1997. By mid-1998, the PA employed almost 50,000 civilians and 40,000 police for a total of almost 90,000 public servants, or 20 per cent of the total labour force.[133] In this sense, the PA became the main distributor of economic resources and jobs.[134] It increasingly resembled a rentier state, which controlled the influx of donor aid, created economic dependence and thus, political loyalty to the proto-state institutions.[135] The Al-Aqsa Intifada, which broke out in September 2000, not only destroyed the little infrastructure in place, but also led to soaring rates of unemployment and poverty and effectively undermined the PA's rule, after the Palestinian economy had finally shown signs of recovery during the first half of 2000.[136]

Small Business and the New 'Big Business' under the PA

Under occupation, the Palestinian business sector was small and underdeveloped. In 1965, more than three quarters out of a total number of 3,829 industrial units in the West Bank employed less than five persons. Only four, increasing to five by 1967, employed more than 100 persons. In Gaza, there were 769 industrial units in 1960, which on average employed 2.3 workers.[137] Only two enterprises employed more than 100 workers in 1967.[138] Under occupation, industrial activity stagnated and remained the smallest sector in the Territories, confined to labour-intensive, low-productivity manufacturing.[139] Local trade was concentrated in the hands of a few large-scale wholesalers.

Subcontracting arrangements with Israeli firms, most visibly in the textiles industry, became one of the most important entrepreneurial activities in the Territories, based on cheap unskilled or semi-skilled Palestinian labour.[140] Since Palestinian businesses were dependent on raw materials imported from or via Israel and the domestic market was small, subcontracting was an almost inevitable development. By the late 1980s, 70 per cent of textiles and footwear were manufactured for Israeli firms and re-sold under Israeli labels.[141] While this opened up employment opportunities, subcontracting did not provide a stimulus for further development of the existing industries in the territories. As Sara Roy argued for Gaza, subcontracting was 'Israel's major source of industrial investment in the Gaza strip economy,' and it effectively 'transformed Gaza's industrial base into a de facto free zone operating for the benefit of Israeli producers.'[142]

By 1994, 20 per cent of Gaza's industrial establishments were small sewing shops, employing an average of five people per shop, with a small investment of about $2,000 per employee.[143] Altogether, 10,433, or 90 per cent, of all firms in the Territories employed less than ten workers in 1994; 73 per cent employed less than five.[144] Discriminatory policies and practices were enforced against Palestinian businesses and entrepreneurs:[145] Palestinian manufacturers paid 35-40 per cent more taxes than their Israeli counterparts, which made their production costs higher and undermined competitiveness.[146] Complicated certification and licensing procedures, restrictions on types and quantities of imports, and complex labelling requirements in addition to constraints on Palestinian exports via Israel to the Arab countries due to the Arab boycott against Israel further limited Palestinian production and export capacities.[147]

Exports were low, not exceeding 18 per cent of total sales in 1994, and largely restricted to goods produced under subcontracting arrangements, since foreign markets remained largely closed to Palestinian producers.[148] Palestinian entrepreneurs had to obtain licences to carry out investment plans, which were only rarely granted when 'the military government believed that they did not conflict with the interests of Israeli producers.'[149] Most of these restrictions also limited the scope for trade and commerce within the Territories. Wholesale and retail trade had been the most important sector in the Territories before 1967 but declined under the Israeli occupation, since trade was largely one-way, from Israel into the Territories, which became Israel's second most important market after the United States, and contributed to the growing deficit that reached $854 million in 1992.[150]

With the outbreak of the Intifada in 1987, the conditions for business grew even worse. A new military order conditioned the issuing of permits and licences in 23 different categories on payment of all taxes as well as approvals from as many as seven authorities. Many small-scale businessmen went without these licences, which made their businesses illegal activity and led to the demolition of factories when discovered. Industrial output consequently declined by 22 per cent in 1988; by February 1989, industrial production in Gaza had fallen by 50 per cent.[151] Even more damaging to the Palestinian business sector were the closures that began with the Gulf War in 1991 and continued through much of the early years of the peace process. Imports to the West Bank and Gaza fell by almost 30 per cent between 1992 and 1996. Importers, subcontractors, and manufacturers alike were all hit hard. Due to the limitation on the number of trucks allowed into and out of Gaza, business opportunities were severely restricted.[152]

Due to new Israeli licensing policies issued in 1992 and the high expectations for growth, the number of registered establishments increased significantly after 1994, exceeding the total number of registrations during the 1980s by mid-1995. However, the Palestinian economy experienced a concentration of capital in a few core conglomerates.[153] These were run directly by the PA or PA officials, wealthy Diaspora Palestinians with close ties to the PA, and a few of the local businesspeople who had run successful businesses during occupation and established a good relationship with the PA.[154] The largest of those companies was the Palestine Development and Investment Company (PADICO), set up in 1993 by the Palestinian G7 from Jordan.[155] With a working capital of $1.5 billion, it engaged in industrial projects, tourism, and developed telecommunications through its subsidiary, the Palestine Telecommunications Co. (Paltel), as well as industrial parks in the Palestinian Territories through another daughter, the Palestine Industrial Estates Development Co. (PIEDCO).[156] PADICO also owned the Palestine Securities Exchange (PSE). A second conglomerate was the Arab Palestinian Investment Company (APIC), which created 700 jobs locally in several industrial and trade enterprises. Its investors included members of the Saudi royal family, most of the Palestinian G7, and the PA-owned Palestine Commercial Services Co. (PCSC).[157] Among the local big business companies was the Nassar Investment Company, a stone and marble manufacturer, which employed Samir Huleileh, a former Assistant Deputy Minister of Trade, negotiator at the multilateral talks, and consultant for the PLO's Welfare Association, as its Marketing Director.

The economy also came to be characterized by the emergence of state-controlled monopolies as well as quasi-monopolies and state-controlled conglomerates, such as the PA-controlled Sharikat al-Bahr (Sea Co.) and the Palestinian Commercial Services Company (PCSC) in the West Bank, which held shares in 29 companies. Monopolistic conditions could be found in petroleum, cigarettes, and cement, which were estimated to accrue as much as $300 million in revenues to the PA that only had a total budget of $1.7 billion in 1997. The concentration of capital in those companies illustrated the increasing evolution of a dualistic economy, split into a politicized core of large conglomerates and privately owned small and medium-sized enterprises, since the establishment of the PA.

The Decay of Traditional Elites, the G7 and the Tunisian Profiteers

Traditionally, large land-owning families had wielded both economic and political power in the agriculturally dominated West Bank and Gaza.[158] Under occupation, the old landed families retained their power in Gaza due to their economic strength, while in the West Bank the traditional landed elite had to contend for power with a new class of urban merchants and traders. As a result, Gaza was held under tight control by the military authorities, while a more subtle strategy of co-option, in particular of merchants with economic interests in maintaining the status quo, was pursued in the West Bank.[159] In both territories, however, with the confiscation of land by the Israeli authorities and the growing dependence of the Palestinian economy on employment in Israel, land, labour, and patronage networks lost their significance, and the power of the traditional families declined, while a new private business elite emerged alongside a new middle class.

The Palestinian political elite originated in refugee camps or in small villages, while economic power came to rest with the new stratum of entrepreneurs, which could be found among importers and subcontractors who benefited from the structural integration of the Territories into the Israeli economy.[160] In the West Bank, a subcontracted Palestinian business class evolved, which 'dominated and even replaced the weak nationalist bourgeoisie that had been privileged under Jordanian rule.'[161] At the same time, however, these businessmen were subjected to restrictive Israeli policies. The political economy of Palestine under occupation was

Figure 1: The Palestine Development and Investment Company (PADICO)
(registered in Liberia in 1993; total investment: US$ 350 Million by April 2000)

Chairman: Munib Masri; **Vice-Chairman:** Nabil Sarraf;

Board members: 1. Sabih Masri; 2. Shukry Bishara; (Arab Finance Holding/Arab Bank); 3. Yazid Mufti (Cairo Amman Bank); 4. Abdel Qader Dweik (Housing Bank); 5. Munir Khoury (Said Co.); 6. Khaled Masri (Al-Masira Investments); 7. Kamil Sadeddin (O. S. Investments); 8. Hussein Sharqawi; 9. Khalil Talhouni (until death in May 1999); 10. Ramzi Dalloul; 11. Riad Sadik; 12. Zahi Khouri; 13. Azmi Abdulhadi; 14. Farouk Toukan; 15. Mahdi Saifi; 16. Nidal Sukhtian; 17. Hatem Halawani.

Palestine Real Estate Investment Co. (Aqaria)
Capital: $21 Mio.
Chairman: N. Sarraf
PADICO share: 52%

→

- Hay An-Nada (500-apartment neighbourhood in Gaza, for Ministry of Housing
- Masayef Steps (Elegant private housing complex in Al-Bireh)
- Bethlehem Tourist Bus Terminal (BOT for municipality; 15 years)
- Al-Bireh Central Bus Station (BOT for municipality; 22 years)

Palestine Electrical & Electronics
Capital: $5 Mio.
Samsung TV sets
PADICO share: 14%

Palestine Plastics Industries
Capital: $7 Mio.
PADICO share: 23%

Palestine Poultry
Capital: $14 Mio.
4 farms, producing 30% of market demand
PADICO share: 63%

Palestine Industrial Investment Company (PIIC)
Capital: $21 Mio.
Chairman: N. Sukhtian
PADICO share: 78%

Palestine Securities Exchange (PSE)
Capital: $2.8 Mio.
Chairman: S. Masri
PADICO share:

→ *24 companies listed in the manufacturing, banking, insurance, and services sectors.*
Market capitalization: $849 Mio. (1999).
First fully automated stock exchange

Palestine Telecommunications Co. (PALTEL)
Capital: $95 Mio.
Chairman: S. Masri;
PADICO share: 23%

Working Lines 1997: 83,331
Working Lines 1999: 222,198
Cellular Phones 1999: 22,000
Payphones 1999: 2,031

Palestine Industrial Estate Development & Management Co. (PIEDCO)
Capital: $10 Mio.
Chairman: F. Toukan
PADICO share: 83%

→ Gaza Industrial Estate (GIE) operational since 1999; phase II was to begin in mid-2000; Other zones planned in Jenin, Tulkarem, Hebron, Qalqiliya, Rafah and Nablus; Total development cost: $180 Mio.

Palestine Tourism Investment Company (PTIC)
Capital: $28 Mio.
Chairman: M. Saifi
PADICO share: 35%

→ *Jacir Palace Inter-continental Bethlehem Hotel (Five stars)*

Jerusalem Tourism Investment Co. (JTI)
Capital: $25 Mio.
Chairman: M. Saifi
PADICO share: 95%

Sources: PADICO annual report; PADICO website www.padico.com

subordinated to the political-economic regime of Israel: Palestinian entrepreneurs formed the 'small economy,' and Israeli businessmen represented 'big' business, irrespective of the actual size of their enterprises, in the integrated Israeli-Palestinian economy. As one observer put it:

> A whole generation of Israeli manufacturers tried to crush the very possibility of capitalist industrial development in the Territories. The Israeli occupation authorities operated as an arm of the Israeli bourgeoisie, making it impossible for a Palestinian capitalist to obtain the thousand and one approvals required for establishing a large business without producing a document stating that he would not be competing with an Israeli company.[162]

Policies were decided on and imposed by the Israeli authorities, which implemented protectionist measures in favour of the Israeli business sector. Palestinian entrepreneurs inside the Territories had little influence on policy-making, since business associations and chambers of commerce were largely dysfunctional. Chambers of Commerce had been established prior to the Israeli occupation but elections were suspended between 1972 and 1992; members who left or died were not replaced.[163] Trade unions, which could have assumed an important political role in view of the significance of Palestinian labour in the integrated Israeli-Palestinian economy, were banned altogether until 1979. Even thereafter, little unionist activity occurred until the outbreak of the Intifada.[164]

Palestinians outside the Territories, therefore, dominated Palestinian politics and business. The PLO was first based in Egypt, then in Jordan; and after its expulsion from Jordan in 1970-71 and the Israeli invasion of Lebanon in 1982 established itself in Tunis. The Palestinian Diaspora community came 'to be recognized for its entrepreneurial spirit and strong work ethic' and began to form a wealthy elite on the basis of businesses established in Europe and the United States as well as their role in the oil economies of the Gulf. This elite, alongside with a younger generation of academics, engineers, doctors, and business managers throughout Europe and the Middle East channelled funds into the Territories and supported the PLO financially. Most important among them were the Palestinian G7 from Jordan and the Shouman-run Arab Bank. Hassib Sabagh from CCC was called the 'financial link' for his role of intermediary between Arafat and foreign politicians.[165] The biggest conduit for private aid was the Geneva-based Welfare Association, sponsored by more than 100 of the richest Diaspora Palestinian businessmen.[166] Yet, this Diaspora community remained politically inactive apart from funding the PLO and after 1993, exhibited a wait and see attitude and preferred to maintain their businesses in the Diaspora.[167]

Two political-economic forces began to take shape from the late 1980s onwards, which came into competition and open conflict or engaged in co-operation and co-option after the establishment of the PA. One was the political elite of the PLO that formed the PA, the other were the forces that emerged prior to and during the first Intifada. Under worsening economic conditions in the West Bank and Gaza, social charities, religious groups, professionals, entrepreneurs, and workers co-operated in the resistance movement. These groups became institutionalized, established close links to the PLO and formed the backbone of the Intifada.[168] However, the Intifada was highly damaging to the Palestinian economy, and it did not alter the overall political-economic balance, either inside the West Bank and Gaza, or between the Territories and Israel.[169]

The arrival of the PA fundamentally changed the picture, when a new economic regulatory authority established itself, with both access to resources, in the form of donor assistance and tax collection, and policy-making power. Through the Palestinian Economic Council for Reconstruction and Development (PECDAR), donor aid was disbursed to establish the quasi-state institutions of the PA, dominated by the old PLO elite, the so-called 'Tunisians,' who only arrived in the Territories in 1994 after decades in the Diaspora. In the context of a worsening economic situation, civil society was weakened, and through its access to funds, the PA managed to extend its influence over much of the Palestinian society.[170] With declining employment opportunities in Israel and the general weakness of the economy, job creation was the PA's first economic priority. The drop of employment in Israel was paralleled by the rapid expansion of the newly established public sector, which transformed the PA into the largest employer of Palestinian labour. The resulting increase in government expenditures, however, led to a decline in the budget share for social services and contributed to a weakening of the small private sector.[171] In addition, with the establishment of 'at least 13 monopolies under the control of no more than five individuals, who are members of the PA's inner circle,' the PA became a de facto competitor to local business. Despite its repeated commitment to private sector-led growth and a market economy, the PA effectively weakened the private sector and centralized economic power in a few conglomerates, with a tacit understanding that those businesses not directly run by the PA would support its rule, in return for business opportunities.[172] Small enterprises had to compete with one another in a struggle for business opportunities and sources of income under the impact of closures.

Increasingly, the Palestinian political economy became transformed into a dualistic economy, with the already existing private sector, driven by a primary interest in maintaining previous levels of trade and income, on the one hand, and an emerging economic core that was closely connected to the PA on the other. While small enterprises were tied up in the competition between themselves, new political and economic elites emanated, largely within and around the institutions of the emerging proto-state. Hajo Rabe argued:

> While the private business elite has certainly not disappeared from the scene, its significance has been weakened, and it has been superseded by new, powerful actors, which have been in various capacities connected to the institutions of the proto-state [...] This new elite that has emerged can be roughly divided into two categories; first there is a small and relatively cohesive and closed circle around President Yasser Arafat, with the clear mission of generating revenues for the Authority [...] Secondly, evidence suggests that there is a larger and much more loosely connected stratum of officials in

the proto-state institutions, who have entered commercial activities and partnerships with members of the private sector and, some argue, the security services [...] This further points to the close co-operation between the new political and economic elites, and to the emergence of a new complex within the political and economic spheres.[173]

While this political-economic core elite stratum increasingly consolidated its power, the small and medium-sized enterprises outside the network grew weaker. The PA increasingly transformed itself into a rentier quasi-state. The political-economic elites used 'the resources of the state to allow for the primitive accumulation of capital' and distributed 'these "privileges" tactically in ways that allow the regime to hold its power.'[174] PADICO, the conglomerate set up by the Palestinian G7 from Jordan, and APIC, the group dominated by Palestinians from Saudi Arabia, both formed a tacit understanding with the PA, helping it to assert its control over Palestinian society in return for profits. Interest politics functioned in a highly personalized manner and depended on access to the PA core elite.

As in Israel and Jordan, therefore, power in the Palestinian economy came to be centralized in the core elites, which pursued highly personalized interest politics and marginalized most ordinary Palestinians. The three economies of Israel, Jordan, and the Palestinian Territories, thus, were all characterized by the dominance of large conglomerates and political-economic elites, while the majority of small and medium-sized enterprises were marginalized and excluded from the circles of power and political decision-making. In all three entities, the division between the public and private sectors was overshadowed by this differentiation into an advanced core of political-economic elites and their enterprises and peripheral capital. In all three entities, in addition, the distinction between these two sectors grew more pronounced during the 1990s and the years of the peace process. The structure of the political economies of Israel, Jordan, and the Palestinian Territories provided the foundations from which the economic dimension of peace developed. Other factors clearly affected the impact of the peace process, such as, at the domestic level, the rise of an Islamist opposition and, at the systemic level, the extent of support from outside powers. But there is no doubt there was an economic consequence: Peace exacerbated the pre-existing divisions in the three economies. Co-operation was driven largely by the elites, who pursued their own interests, while smaller and medium-sized companies exhibited a diverging attitude, as the following chapter will show.

3

Business Interests in Peace and Co-operation

Israeli businesspeople eager to end the Arab boycott and to expand their activities paved the way for the peace process and drove it. However, Israelis were largely pursuing their self-interest, promoting regional economic co-operation in order to gain access to new markets, most of which were to be found overseas, while seeking to maintain their economic hegemony especially over the Palestinians. The formula for co-operation was found with the discovery of Jordan as a cheap and convenient manufacturing base. In Jordan, businesspeople remained reluctant at first and were often fierce in their public rejection of ties with Israelis, while claiming access to the Palestinian market; at the same time, they entertained a considerable interest in dealing with Israel behind the façade of public rejection. The same applied to many Palestinians, who were dependent on Israel in any case and sought to maintain business relations while realizing their nationalist ambitions.

The Israeli Business Sector

Peace, Privatization and Profits

The transformation of the Israeli economy during the 1990s was intrinsically linked to the peace process, a connection best captured in the equation of 'peace and privatization.'[1] Big business needed to expand, and thus, 'after the beginning of the Intifada in 1987, the large corporations in Israel started to publicly promote the benefits of regional reconciliation.'[2] As Kadri and MacMillen argued, 'the calls for peaceful co-existence inside Israel were, in part, based on that segment of a growing capital, which could flourish if it expanded into the surrounding region.'[3] In 1989, the 'Business Week' reported that for the first time,

> The pragmatic Israeli business community is putting behind-the-scene pressure on the Shamir government to negotiate with the Palestinians […] Israeli businessmen know that without peace with the Arabs, there is little chance of the country building a stable civilian economy.[4]

In 1992, Dov Lautman, Chairman of the textiles concern Delta Galil and IMA President, and FICC President Danny Gillerman both started calling on Prime Minister Rabin to view the abolition of the Arab boycott as a top priority. In January 1993, Lautman asked Foreign Minister Shimon Peres to 'discuss the role of the business community in the political process and in the negotiation of bilateral and multilateral trade accords with the leadership of the Manufacturers Association.'[5] Gillerman, in a news conference in February 1993, argued: 'The economy at the end of the day will be the key to any successful peace agreement [...] As businessmen, we can create facts, if possible, even before an official agreement is signed.'[6] In consequence, the IMA sought to commence talks with Palestinian businessmen in order to facilitate economic co-operation and through it, advance the political talks.[7]

Koor CEO Gaon best exemplified the new attitude of Israeli big business. At the Jerusalem Business Conference in November 1994, he argued that it was the 'responsibility of companies such as Koor [...] to develop a regional economy of peace,' and called on the leading industrial concerns 'to take the lead, to take the risk, and invite foreign capital for joint investment projects in Israel as well as in the region.'[8] A year earlier, Gaon had already announced Koor's involvement in a first, $60 million joint venture involving two Palestinians brokers to invest in industrial projects in the Palestinian Territories and the Arab world, which however soon ground to a halt.[9] In 1994, Gaon also declared that two Koor subsidiaries, Telrad and Tadiran, were considering investing in communication companies in neighbouring Arab states.[10] But while he saw himself as a leader of the peace process, even Gaon had to admit to the actual interest of big business, which saw the real peace dividend not in the benefits of deals with Jordanians or Palestinians, but in the opening of doors to third countries, such as India, Japan, China, or the emerging South East Asian markets.[11] Gaon maintained his public commitment to peace after his departure from Koor in 1998, as Chairman of the Israel-Jordan Chamber of Commerce and as Chairman of a special commission to develop economic links with Arab nations at the IMA.[12] In February 1998, he said that the Middle East no longer interested the world and that 'the peace process must be privatized and taken out of the politicians' hands,' calling for the establishment of a joint lobby by supporters of peace in Israel, Jordan, Egypt and the PA, in order to pressure governments into advancing the peace process.[13] His new company, Gaon Holdings, however, took full advantage of the new opportunities abroad. It set up a venture capital fund in partnership with the Austria Bank and the British Jupiter International Group to target information technology and life sciences, while his promise to also invest in Middle Eastern IT companies remained a lip service.[14]

By that time, big business' real objective, setting the peace process in motion in order to open up new markets, had been achieved. The large conglomerates turned their attention elsewhere, continuing to pay lip service to the peace process, but without actual engagement. As Allan Retzky argued, 'the real economic benefits of peace were reaped overseas. From the economic point of view, Israel's peace dividend lay in the increasing internationalization of its economy,' due to the dissolution of the Arab boycott against Israel.[15] Koor once again illustrated this underlying motivation. With Gaon's departure from Koor, the new CEO, Jonathan Kolber, introduced a new business strategy and did not even maintain his predecessor's public promotion of the peace process. Koor's only successful peace project, PDI Peace Development, an agricultural joint venture with the Jordanian government-owned Social Securities Corporation, represented only a 'very minor investment' among Koor's new business activities, which continued quietly in the background but was not actively pushed by the new Koor leadership.[16] According to the initiator of the project, a former close aide to Rabin, the project had in fact effectively been stalled since 1998.[17]

Big business had pushed for peace, but its underlying objective had been to gain access to hitherto closed markets. Gabby Bar, Head of the Middle East and North Africa desk at the Israeli Ministry of Trade and Industry, said the peace process had provided Israel not only with recognition from the Arab parties, but also meant an end to the secondary and tertiary boycotts and a boost to relations with third countries, which had hitherto maintained only low-profile relations, such as Japan. Arab markets were not as important to Israel as other, international markets, which had hitherto been off-limits for Israelis.[18] Abraham Atar, Marketing Director of Tadiran, said, 'Asia, and especially China and India, are clearly the Big Story of Israeli global penetration,' after diplomatic ties had been established with both in 1991.[19] Amit Segev, Deputy CEO of another former Histadrut flagship, the Housing and Construction Holding Co. (HCH), expressed a similar view, saying that much more important than relations with Israel's Arab neighbours was the opening of new markets and a general strengthening of the economy. HCH was engaged in BOT projects in Central Europe, Central America, and Africa, but did not have any major business with Arab partners.[20] Likewise, Badia Tannus, Chairman of B. S. T., a Nazareth-based construction company, said his company had attempted to enter the Palestinian and Jordanian markets, but had then turned towards more promising projects in Poland and Hungary.[21] The Global Wires Group, a cables manufacturer, initiated contacts in Amman in 1995 and became involved in a deal in Jordan, but cancelled the engagement in 1999, and instead expanded into the Indian market.[22] Several textiles companies re-located operations to South East Asia, which offered cheap and reliable production.[23]

The awareness that the actual peace dividend would be reaped outside the region was also expressed in the attitude of Israeli businesspeople at the MENA conferences. On their way to the first meeting in Casablanca in 1994, businessmen cautioned that the meeting would not result in large numbers of closed deals, but was a basis for future agreements.[24] Danny Gillerman, the FICC President, prepared his co-attendants for the second conference in Amman in 1995, advising them 'to go to Amman with minimum expectations [...] I feel nothing important will happen in Amman.' Even the official publications prepared for the conferences were not to be taken too literally. Yossi Vardi, one of the authors, said the idea was only to make non-Israelis feel 'more optimistic.' How much significance was attached to countries outside the region was illustrated when Gillerman urged his fellow business leaders to prepare themselves and to follow up contacts:

> We are great at giving our business cards and promising to follow up, and then we disappear [...] They return to Korea and Singapore and the business opportunity dissipates.[25]

While both Gillerman and Dan Propper, IMA President and Chairman of the Osem food concern, emphasized the need for reciprocal business relations with Israel's Arab neighbours, Gillerman also reminded his audience that the goal was not the Arab world, but the Far East, Europe, and the United States.[26] Since the first two economic conferences drew the largest attendance from third countries, it was unsurprising that many Israeli businesspeople did not attend the Cairo conference in 1996 nor the 1997 Doha meeting anymore, which were also overshadowed by the stalemate in the peace process.[27]

At the same time, however, a new potential for business relations was discovered, namely the transferring of labour-intensive industries from Israel, where they could not remain competitive due to legislative reforms ending the protectionist regime on the domestic market and because of high labour costs, to Arab countries. The textiles industry, for example, had grown considerably between 1990 and 1994, but now faced competition from cheap imports due to a drop in tariffs from more than 70 per cent to 12 per cent for clothing and 8 per cent for textiles until 2000 and an end to quotas on textile imports within a decade.[28] Some companies, such as Zikit, moved out of the textiles industry altogether. The core of the Israeli textile industry – by 1995, Delta Galil, Dov Lautman's company, alone accounted for 14 per cent of total textile exports, and nine firms, among them Delta, the Clal subsidiaries Polgat, Gibor, and Kitan, as well as Nilit, Macpell, Gottex, Lodzia and Caesarea Wardinon, accounted for half the industry's exports – adapted by moving to foreign locations, among them Jordan and Egypt.[29] Amir Hayek, Director-General of the Israel Export Institute (IEI), reflecting the interest of the crisis-shaken textiles industry, advocated the production of high-quality textiles in Israeli-Arab co-operation, with the labour-intensive manufacturing process carried out in Arab countries, while Israel would provide know-how, quality control, and marketing.[30] Likewise, the three companies at the core of Israel's edible oils industry were reported to be holding talks in 1999 to shift operations abroad, to Egypt, Jordan, Turkey, or Romania, since they had lost their competitive edge due to the reduction of tariffs and the subsequent exposure to cheap imports.[31]

Jordan as a Manufacturing Base for Israeli Industry

The business community was particularly interested in Jordan. In addition to a pre-history of peaceful relations and economic interaction before the signing of the peace treaty, King Hussein was hugely popular in Israel, and Israelis felt safer and more comfortable in Amman than in Ramallah or Gaza.[32] As soon as the peace treaty was signed, FICC President Gillerman urged the government to 'move rapidly towards signing an Israel-Jordan trade agreement,' which he believed 'could serve as a model for other nations in the Arab world.'[33] According to a study conducted by the Jordan Export Development and Commercial Centres Corporation (JEDCO) during 1995, 146 Israeli companies were interested in co-operating with Jordanian companies in various areas such as subcontracting, joint ventures, technology transfer, and licensing. Most ventures, however, never made it beyond the planning stages.[34] The Israeli euphoria was often not accompanied by a realistic business sense, and many projects were cancelled even before the trade and transportation agreements came into effect.[35] In addition, many Israelis gradually came to realize that Jordan offered only a very limited market, which could not absorb most Israeli products because of their sophistication and price.[36]

The main interest of Israeli companies lay in moving manufacturing operations to Jordan, where labour costs were lower than in Israel and ranged between less than half to two-thirds of the wages paid to Palestinians.[37] In addition, falling profits and increasing competition in the domestic market, as well as a reduced comparative advantage internationally due to rising production costs, made joint ventures with Jordanian companies a 'logical' move.[38] An internal report of the Israeli Ministry of Trade and Industry expecting the lay-off of up to 14,000 Israeli workers in traditional industries, recommended the re-location of labour-intensive units to neighbouring countries, in particular Jordan, in 1998.[39] Moshe Nahum, Head of the IMA's Foreign Trade and International Relations Department, pointed out that Israeli textile companies were not competitive anymore on world markets and that Jordan was a convenient option for them to re-locate, since it was so close. However, he also stressed, the movement out of Israel had less to do with the achievement of peace, rather than the opening up of Israel's economy to global markets and competition.[40] In September 1997, Kitan's Deputy General Manager, Gidi Laks, concluded, 'it is only a matter of time before all sewing workshops in Israel are closed and transferred to Jordan.'[41] This interest did not alter with the changes at the top in Jordan: When King Hussein's dismissed Crown Prince Hassan, one of the most ardent supporters of regional economic integration, Dov Lautman said in an interview, 'we're not in Jordan just due to the pro-Israeli regime. It's a matter of common economic interest, and therefore we have no cause for concern.'[42]

The advantage Jordan offered as a manufacturing base to the ailing traditional Israeli industries, and the pressure that drove them to Jordan, were therefore reflected in strong protests whenever Israelis felt the status quo was threatened. Thus, Nahum pointed out that the Jordan-United States free trade agreement (FTA), concluded in 2000, could harm the growth of economic co-operation between Israel and Jordan, and that this treaty, as well as Jordan's association agreement with the EU, would encourage Jordanian imports from the USA and the EU at the expense of Israeli imports.[43] Likewise, when the Jordanian government requested a modification of the trilateral agreement on the Qualifying Industrial Zones (QIZ), allowing jointly manufactured goods free access to the US market, in order to reduce the required Israeli contribution, the IMA asked the Ministry of Trade and Industry not to surrender to the Jordanian demands.[44] Despite the protest, the modification was ratified, and in general, Israeli businesspeople were very eager to maintain good relations with Jordan, where many Israeli companies invested in manufacturing plants.

Due to this interest, Israeli businesspeople established a bilateral Chamber of Commerce in Tel Aviv in 1995, with Benny Gaon as its chairman, which by 2000 had 130 members, half of whom were actually engaged in Jordan.[45] Even Binyamin Netanyahu, who was not very popular with the business community, included three leading businesspeople, Benny Gaon, Dov Lautman, and Shaul Eizenberg from the Eizenberg Group, in his delegation when he met King Hussein in Amman in 1996.[46] In 1999, IMA President Oded Tira, FICC President Gillerman, and Lautman met with King Abdullah in Amman, inviting him to set up a co-ordinating committee with Israel's private sector.[47] Politically, Jordan was considered a role model for a 'warm' peace. Economically, Jordan was discovered as a cheap manufacturing base. Jordan was thus important both to politicians and entrepreneurs, but any change in the status quo was rejected once Israelis had established themselves there.

Integration, Separation and the Status Quo
Towards the Palestinians, Israelis were equally enthusiastic at the beginning, when in September 1993, 'everyone was dreaming of the great potential for future ties.' But within one year, 'many were questioning what, if anything, their Palestinian neighbours could offer them to cement the peace economically or to earn future profits.'[48] However, 'despite their stated position to co-operate,' there was 'no sign by the bulk of Israeli industrialists to a more equitable division of the pie [...] no effort on the part of the Israeli importers to share with potential Palestinian importers their sole foreign agencies or representations.'[49] The Israeli reluctance to engage in co-operation with Palestinian entrepreneurs was a result of revenues already lost or under threat, due to the changing political context. Most Israelis did not favour any alteration to the status quo of economic relations.

A survey carried out by the IMA at the end of 1993 among 372 Israeli companies, representing over one-quarter of Israeli industry, found that although 85 per cent of those companies were interested in co-operating with Palestinian firms in the West Bank and the Gaza Strip and 96 per cent expected the Oslo Accords to have a positive impact on economic growth, 36 per cent expected the interim period of the Oslo process to affect them negatively; 74 per cent expected that Palestinians would establish competing industries. The value of lost revenue, which was expected as a result of the interim period, totalled $1.4 billion in sales. Firms predicted a decrease in exports to the West Bank and Gaza Strip, particularly in building material, wood and textiles. 9,000 workers were expected to lose their jobs in the industrial sector. Israelis feared that the PA would lower VAT, which would enable Palestinian producers to undercut Israeli prices. The hope that the new arrangement would lead to overall economic growth, thus, was not based on co-operation with Palestinians, but on an end to the Arab boycott, which all surveyed companies were hoping for and expecting to lead to strong export growth.[50] In particular smaller businesses and business associations feared Palestinian competition. The Poultry Farmers' Association, for example, warned in 1993 that cheaper egg prices in the Territories might put Israel's 7,800 chicken farmers out of business, if an open border policy allowed Palestinians to sell their eggs in Israel. In consequence, the association called on the government to take a stand to protect Israeli poultry farmers.[51]

While the small economy in Israel in particular feared any disruption of the status quo, big business realized the strategic importance of the Palestinian issue. The core conglomerates' underlying motivation was the need to expand, which necessitated an end of the Arab boycott, which in turn required a peaceful settlement with the Palestinians. Yet there was also a second factor at work, the interest to maintain and make use of cheaper Palestinian labour. Thus, Israeli entrepreneurs opposed the closures of the Palestinian Territories, which the Israeli government began imposing in the context of a deteriorating security situation, because the absence of Palestinian workers severely disrupted sectors such as construction and agriculture.[52] Throughout 1996, Benny Gaon kept trying to organize a meeting between Yasser Arafat and a delegation of Israeli top executives, including himself, Dov Lautman, and the CEOs of Clal, the Dankner Group, Telrad, Strauss Dairies, Bank Ha'Poalim, Bank Leumi, and the First International Bank.[53] In December, Gaon announced that the group had offered Arafat to help the PA to build up light industry in the Territories – the sector in which Israel was losing its competitive edge due to high labour costs.[54] Amiram Shor, Chairman of the Israel Software Houses Association and the MLL Group, said in 1993 that Israeli software companies would be among the first in the business sector to benefit from the peace accord with the Palestinians.[55] This interest was further enhanced when by the late 1990s Israel faced a shortage of programmers and high-tech personnel. This fuelled the project of the Khaddourie high-tech industrial park, which the PA planned near Tulkarem, close to the Israeli high-tech centres of Herzliya and Netanya.[56] Despite the initial reluctance to co-operate with Palestinians, a number of Israeli companies were said to consider investing in the park. The Peres Centre for Peace supported the establishment of the park through its Peace Technology Fund, in which Koor and Clal had invested $20 million each, and to which the DIC, Teva, and others had also contributed.[57]

The Khaddourie Park was one of nine joint Israeli-Palestinian industrial parks originally planned. The concept had first emerged in 1994, and after lengthy debates revolving around the legal framework and possible sites – the Israeli side had favoured joint parks located on the border, under Israeli legislation and with Israeli tax incentives for investors, but the Palestinians had rejected this, and the parks were thus planned and developed unilaterally – the Gaza Industrial Estate (GIE) at Karni, developed by the PADICO-subsidiary PIEDCO, was chosen to be a pilot project.[58] Ten Israelis were negotiating to establish factories in Karni during a first phase of operations, according to PADICO's Director-General. On touring the site, IMA President Dan Propper stressed the importance of Palestinian labour and said, 'most factories that are leaving Israel would otherwise go out of business, and at least this way the profits and management can stay in Israel.'[59] Other large Israeli companies were also hoping to set up factories in the park in order to expand by entering the Palestinian market, such as Strauss, one of Israel's largest dairy concerns, or Coca-Cola Israel, which invested in the National Bottling Co. in the GIE.[60]

The main interest on the Israeli side, however, was to turn the joint parks into showcases of a peaceful Middle East, with production based on cheap Palestinian labour and Israeli marketing know-how, which would enhance exports and open up new markets. Stef Wertheimer, Chairman of the ISCAR Group and a former Member of the Knesset (MK), for example, had long advocated his vision of a peaceful Israel based on export-oriented capitalism.[61] Wertheimer had built several industrial parks in developmental regions inside Israel, and he began planning to establish a similar park located in the Israeli-Egyptian-Palestinian triangle, near the Gaza Strip, in 1998.[62] According to Avraham Asheri, Wertheimer's close aide, a former Director-General at the Ministry of Industry and Trade and CEO of the Israel Discount Bank, however, the Egyptian response was not very positive. The project was then planned as the Israeli sister park to PIEDCO's second industrial park in the Gaza Strip at Rafah. Agreement was reached in August 2000 between the ISCAR Group, the Dankner Group, and PADICO, to buy mutual 20 per cent shares in the respective parks, before the outbreak of the Intifada 2000 delayed plans.[63]

As a result of the many conflicting interests with regard to economic relations with the Palestinians – fear of competition, dependence on Palestinian labour, desire to enter Arab markets, aspirations to co-operate in order to expand overseas – the Israeli business community debated ferociously, which economic arrangement between Israel and the PA would be best. The main divide ran between industrialists and merchants, but also between big business and the small economy. Big business, and in particular industry, favoured economic integration, which would boost exports, while traders and the small economy advocated at least clear regulations, if not economic separation. The best solution, most agreed, was to maintain the status quo, protecting Israeli manufacturers and preserving Israeli dominance. This attitude was basically the outcome of a report on the 'Economic Implications of the Establishment of Autonomy in the Territories and Ways for its Integration with the Israeli Economy,' presented by a committee of the CBEO, chaired by Danny Gillerman, in 1993, which was largely incorporated into the Israeli position at the Paris economic talks in 1994.[64] A survey the IMA conducted among its members in 1999 showed that 38 per cent of Israeli industrial enterprises preferred to retain the economic status quo with the PA. 36 per cent wished full economic integration and a customs union, and only 11 per cent wanted a physical boundary separating the two entities.[65]

This view stood in contrast to a position paper put out in 1999 by the FICC, which favoured economic separation between the two economies, with a clear physical border, albeit under a free trade agreement (FTA).[66] The motivation underlying this position was the desire to prevent the uncontrolled movement of goods between the two areas, which harmed the interests of Israeli traders.[67] In particular, the so-called border markets that sprang up near the Green Line, where many Israelis shopped on Saturdays, enjoying the low prices Palestinian wholesalers could offer, posed a problem for Israeli merchants.[68] In addition, cheap Palestinian products, often imitations and forged brand products, led to losses amounting to 'hundreds of millions of dollars,' which the FICC complained about in an urgent memorandum to the Ministers of Industry and Trade, Public Security, and Finance in 1999.[69] The IMA supported the claim and the idea to establish a free trade area between Israel and the PA, with harmonized taxes and full borders.[70] At an IMA meeting in November 1999, industrialists discussed the competition they were facing, prompting one observer to write: 'There arose a fleeting impression of little Israel confronted by some industrial power threatening momentarily to swamp the home market.' Overall, the IMA assessed that industrial sectors employing 63,000 workers (16 per cent of the industrial labour force), with a share of 17 per cent in domestic market sales, were confronted by unfair competition due to lower production costs in the PA and demanded resolution of this problem in a permanent status agreement.[71] Only the biggest businesses, which were not threatened by potential Palestinian competition, diverted from this position. Dov Lautman, for example, said that the economic accord should aim for building the Palestinian economy, which in turn would increase demand for Israeli goods and services: 'Any increase in their standard of living will increase our exports.'[72] The Chairman of the Bank Ha'Poalim subsidiary Peilim Portfolio Management, Yoram Gabbai, who had also participated in the economic negotiations with the Palestinians in Paris in 1994, argued that, 'integration was the only viable option.'[73]

The outcome of the internal debates among Israeli industrialists and between the IMA and the FICC was a compromise, based on the common interest of ensuring Israeli dominance over potential Palestinian competition with regard to importing foreign goods and to Israeli manufacturing, while maintaining trade relations between the two entities. Thus, the IMA presented a memorandum to Minister of Trade and Industry Ran Cohen in December 1999, which was only partially based on the results of its survey from the preceding month. In the memorandum, the IMA advocated the gradual establishment of a customs union, with physical borders and customs controls, thus meeting the demands and fears of smaller businesses and traders. Its recommendation included

> The creation of a single, symmetrical customs union ('external cover'), within which trade relations are free (but) controlled, which will ensure fair competition on the internal market and an optimal realization of mutual benefits in the unity of the two economies. This recommendation necessitates a transition period, which would be determined to gradually bring the two markets into harmonization and to enable the construction of (the basis for) a market economy in the PA.[74]

Oded Tira, IMA President since 1999, made clear that industrialists insisted on affording specific sectors temporary protection for an adaptation period, and that a bureaucratic barrier be set up between the two economies. Under this arrangement, the PA should receive tax refunds on products sold by Israeli importers in the PA, which would avoid the encouragement of direct imports, pushing Israeli importers off the market.[75] Ultimately, thus, the position of the Israeli business community towards economic relations with the Palestinians reflected both the desire of big business for economic integration, while safeguarding the interests of both smaller industries and of Israeli merchants.

Jordanian Businessmen, Merchants and Entrepreneurs

Public Reluctance and the Dependence on Iraq

Jordanian businessmen were initially cautious in dealing with their Israeli counterparts. Before the conclusion of the peace treaty in October 1994, a Jordanian industrialist said, 'Jordanians have this image of Jews as being master businessmen, and in the end they worry that they will just dominate.'[76] Public opinion was sceptical about the economic benefits of the peace process. In 1993, only 26 per cent of Jordanians had been found in favour of 'normalization' with Israel, while 65 per cent opposed it. By early 1996, a majority of 57 per cent favoured normalization, with 36 per cent against it, yet only 8 per cent thought that easing the Arab boycott was a 'very good idea.'[77] By 1998, with the stalemate of the peace process and deteriorating bilateral relations, almost 80 per cent of Jordanians believed that Israel was their enemy.[78] Businesspeople, in particular those who stood to lose in the context of a worsening economic situation, mirrored those views in their public statements.[79]

Mamduh Abu Hassan, Chairman of the Jordan Ceramic Industries Co. (JCIC), founder and first President of the Jordan Businessmen Association (JBA), a former board member of the Central Bank of Jordan (CBJ) and the JPMC, a long-standing ACC board member and former member of the Senate, said 'you cannot overcome 50 years of continuous enmity by pushing a button.' Abu Hassan explained he did not want to deal with Israelis, and, he added, this attitude was probably shared by most Jordanian businesspeople. It was 'becoming natural' not to do business with Israel.[80] Similarly, Thabet Taher, a former JPMC General Manager, Minister of Energy in 1989, JPRC Chairman between 1997 and 1999, and now Chairman of a JPRC spin-off, Petra Drilling, as well as JBA Vice-Chairman, said Jordan's natural markets were the Palestinian and Iraqi ones, and signing the peace treaty meant effectively losing markets; the PA market because of Israel's domination, which resulted in only a very small market share for Jordan, the Iraqi market because of the threat of a boycott against Jordanians dealing with Israel and because of the UN embargo against Iraq. According to Taher, there was a common feeling, at least among JBA members, that 'unless there is goodwill […] there is no point in co-operating with Israelis.'[81]

As a result of this attitude, the JBA, the ACI, and the FJCC decided not to support the establishment of a regional business council with Egyptians, Palestinians, and Israelis in October 1996. According to JBA Chairman Hamdi Tabba'a, the creation of such a council was premature, and there would be no need for a regional business council 'should Israel prove to be committed towards the implementation of agreements with the Arabs.'[82] These statements came at the time of the third MENA conference in Cairo 1996, when a clear shift was noticeable in the focus of the meeting from business involving Israel to inter-Arab as well as Arab-African and Arab-Asian economic co-operation and only a few Jordanians attended.[83] Already for the 1995 Amman summit, the government, which had been eager to present Jordan as a centre of the emerging 'new Middle East,' had had to appoint a ten-member 'Private Sector Executive Committee' (PSEC), because the business associations refused to co-operate in the preparations for the conference.[84] Before the fourth MENA conference in Doha in November 1997, Muhammad Halaiqa, the Secretary-General of the Ministry of Industry and Trade and later Minister himself, admitted, 'the private sector is reluctant to participate because of the attendance of Israel.'[85] In the end, the Jordanian delegation included only three private sector representatives, ACI President Khaldoun Abu Hassan, FJCC President Haidar Murad, and Wa'el Touqan, President of the Contractors Association. ACI Vice-President Wasef Azar called on Arab and Jordanian businessmen to 'do their utmost to make Israel feel their strong protest against its anti-peace practices.'[86] When the agreement on the Qualifying Industrial Zones (QIZ) between Israel, Jordan, and the United States was signed at the conference, a large number of businesspeople opposed the agreement, which had been initiated by the Americans in order to reward Jordan for its pro-peace stance. One entrepreneur said: 'The Israelis will make use of Jordan's manpower at Jordanian rates, which means fantastic savings to them. We will simply be tools in the Israeli economic wheel.'[87]

The attitude of Jordanian businessmen towards normalization, however, was also shaped by their dependence on the Iraqi market. Since the Gulf Crisis, many Jordanian companies had developed food and pharmaceutical products for the Iraqi market, and for most of these, Iraq was their sole client. ACI Vice-President Azar pointed out, 'about a quarter of a million people are involved in one aspect or another of doing business with Iraq, in addition to the transit of Iraqi goods through Jordan.' Thus, when King Hussein increasingly began criticizing Saddam Hussein and moving towards Israel in 1995, 'almost everyone, from a small grocer to large supermarket owners,' was worried over the possible consequences on Jordanian business of a suspension of ties with Iraq.[88] Top business delegations repeatedly visited Iraq, attempting to boost relations and to urge Iraqi officials to continue relying on Jordanian imports of food and medicine under the food for oil-programme, while the Jordanian government was clearly reluctant to bolster ties.[89] The Iraqi hostility towards Israel forced Jordanians to choose between established ties with Iraq and the new relations with Israel: During the visit of a Jordanian commercial delegation to Baghdad in September 2000, the Iraqi government threatened that it would not trade with Jordanian firms that maintained ties with Israel and the PA, claiming that it held a list with the names of 85 Jordanian enterprises doing business with Israel.[90]

The Hidden Interest in Co-operation

Behind the façade, however, most Jordanian entrepreneurs had either been enthusiastic about prospects for co-operation with Israel, or cautious but willing to follow their king, who had hoped for a huge peace dividend. Only when this peace dividend failed to materialize and the peace process itself became stalled, many turned in their disappointment to the side of those who rejected the peace treaty and normalization. This was fuelled by the impression that Israeli businesspeople only came to sell their products and make a profit, but not to really interact with their Jordanian neighbours. Alleged or factual problems included the selling of old machines, half-hearted commitments, or the case of an Israeli businessman who sold chemicals in Jordan which turned out to be hazardous waste.[91]

Nevertheless, Jordanians were interested in co-operating with Israelis. As early as November 1994, less than one month after the peace treaty was signed, two members from the Talhouni family, which held Zara Investments and owned several hotels in Jordan, were reported to have met with officials from the Haifa municipality to discuss investment prospects in the Israeli town.[92] Israel's first ambassador to Jordan, Shimon Shamir, said he was flooded with calls from businessmen who were looking for Israeli partners in 1995.[93] In July 1994, Yahya Kadamani, a partner in the JETT bus company, said he was certain Jordan would profit from the peace process and that JETT wanted to restore the pre-1967 Jerusalem-Amman coach service.[94] As soon as the transportation agreement between Israel and Jordan was then signed in 1995, hundreds of private Jordanian operators applied for licences to operate direct coach routes between Jordan and Israel, leading to a compromise that all operators formed one public share-holding company with a capital of JD 10 million.[95]

One Jordanian businessman in particular stood out. Omar Salah, educated in Britain and the United States, returned to Jordan soon after the Oslo Accords in 1993 and founded the Century Investment Group. He began forging contacts with Israeli industrialists to establish joint ventures between Israeli companies and various Jordanian industries. As he said, 'I realized that this transitional period in the Middle East, from conflict to peace, had fantastic business potential.'[96] By 1997, Century operated 12 joint ventures with Israeli companies, all officially with international investors. Salah was a crucial player in bringing about the QIZ agreement, and was named 'Global Leader for Tomorrow' by the World Economic Forum in Davos in 1998.[97] Although even Salah kept a rather low profile in public, he became a role model for the pragmatic young business generation in Jordan.

This new generation was largely Western-educated, many of them the sons of government officials and influential families, and wanted to make profits, not politics.[98] A small, intimate circle of this pragmatic new generation in Jordan was interested in reaping the benefits from co-operating with Israeli companies and became involved mainly in business under the QIZ agreement. Emad al-Shamma', for example, first General Manager of Sari International, the third company in Jordan to take advantage of the QIZ agreement, and then a consultant to foreign companies operating under the agreement, said, 'only businesspeople are the forbearers of peace, politicians can only lay the framework.' Exposure to an international environment and pragmatism were traits common to all those young businesspeople dealing with Israelis. The peace process, according to Shamma', helped Jordan to begin realizing its potential, and in this sense, the QIZ agreement was only one engine of growth and development for Jordan, together with the free trade agreement (FTA) with the United States or Jordan's WTO accession.[99]

Two brothers from the Fakhoury family were also part of this circle. Kamil, the younger one, worked for Specialized Industrial Compounds, which ran the first privately-owned QIZ near Amman.[100] The elder brother, Emad, had been Jordan's first commercial attaché in Tel Aviv from 1995 to 1999, before spending a year as

Century CEO until he was appointed Royal Commissioner for Investment and Economic Development for the Aqaba Special Economic Zone (SEZ) in late 2000. As he said, many of the young business leaders had strong anti-Israeli sentiments, but were also pragmatic enough to realize the potential the QIZ agreement offered and make use of it.[101] Another good example of the new pragmatism was a young Transjordanian lawyer who studied Hebrew in Israel for six months in 1995 and made contacts with Israeli and foreign businesspeople. Upon his return, he began representing foreign companies, mainly from South Asia, but also Israelis under the cover of foreign passports, and helped to finalize ten deals in the textiles industry, with QIZ operations located in the governmental Al-Hassan Industrial Estate near Irbid.[102]

Table 5: Blacklisted Jordanian Companies, 2000

Companies Active in the al-Hassan Industrial Estate (QIZ) near Irbid		
Company	Individual Name	'Crime'
Century Investment Group (with all its enterprises)		
Crystal Readymade Garment Co.	Muhammad Ali Majid Manager: Altaf Majid	
International Luggage Manufacturing Co. [Boscan International]	Charlie Chang	
Millennium Readymade Garments	Nidal Abu Haj Manager: Dee Pak	
Best Knit Co.	Manager: Ahmad Bataineh	
Sari International for Clothes [Howard Brykes]	Ahmad Abu Bakr, Manager: Emad al-Shamma'	Subsidiary of the Israeli branch
Al-Mutaqdamah For Readymade Clothes	Joseph Hadad	
South Asian Garment Co. [Sunny]		
Century Standard Textile Co.	Hazem Abdellatif	
El-Zay Readymade Co.	Muhammad al-Tork	Has special regulations; is located outside the al-Hassan Industrial Estate
Arab-Italian Co. for Furniture	Khalil Jilani	Uses raw materials from Israel
Hilmi Armush Co. for Transportation		Agent for Zim, the Israeli shipping company, and franchise holder for all McDonald's branches

Table 5: Blacklisted Jordanian Companies, 2000, continued:

List of Companies Dealing with the 'Zionist Enemy'		
Company	Individual name	'Crime'
Century Investment Group (al-Hassan Industrial Estate)	Ziyad Salah; Omar Salah	Founding company of the QIZ, in which Jews have invested, according to one of the shareholders; containing the following plants: -Century Gold Industries, George Alama' -Century Standard Textile Co., Hazem Abdelatif -Century Electronics Co., Agil Baidun -Centurywear Co., Nadeem al-As'ad -Century Tailoring Co., Ali Sharif
RMC (Ready Mix Concrete)	Abdel Razaq Dajani; Assaf Jabasheh	Signed joint venture with the Israeli Ras Mal company
Five (5) Continents for Travel Services	General Manager: Mahmoud Salah Al-Din Nabiyeh	Representatives for the Israeli airline, El Al
El-Zay Readymade Co.	General Manager: Muhammad al-Tork	Uses industrial raw materials from Zionists
International Luggage Manufacturing Co. [Boscan International]	General Manager: Charlie Chang	Chinese [Hong Kong] company based in al-Hassan Industrial Estate; uses industrial raw materials from the Zionists
Ja'far al-Kurdi & Co.		Uses bromide-methyl gas from the Zionists
Tamar for Gardens and Agriculture Co.	Muluh al-Issa and sons	Uses cement imported from the Zionists
Abdelhay al-Majali Co.	Abdelhay al-Majali	Subsidiary of Israeli company dealing in agriculture, bananas, and water management
Middle East Co. for Agriculture & Trade	Jacques-Georges Khiyat	Uses seeds and fodder from the Zionists and imports through the port of Haifa
Petra Engineering Industries Co.	Osama Hussein	Exports Petra air-conditioners to the Zionists
Hotel Imperial Ambassador	Ahmad Abdelhady Abu Matar	Hosted the Israeli embassy's reception for the year 2000
National Exhibitions Co.	Fakhry Nasser	Organized Israeli trade fair
Al-Aswaq al-Urdunniya Press and Publications	Mustafa Abu Labdeh	Invested into the pro-peace newspaper Sawt al-Salam and attended the Israeli embassy's reception

Source: 'Muqawama' (Resistance), Newsletter of the Professional Associations' Anti-Normalization Committee, 21 January 2001[103]

The young lawyer, however, as most other Jordanian businesspeople involved in co-operation, tried to keep his engagement secret. Jordanian entrepreneurs said the persisting stigma of trading with the Jewish state forced them to adopt a low profile in order to avoid being labelled 'collaborators'. Rami Qutub, Managing Director of International Freight Services and Trading Co. and the Jordanian agent for Arkia, for example, complained: 'Too many Jordanians who are doing business with the Israelis are trying to hide the fact from the public for fear of retribution.'[104] But the danger to businessmen dealing with Israelis was considerable. The acting head of the Jordan Engineers Association (JEA), Husni Abu Gheida, for example, said in 1996 that those dealing with Israelis 'ought to be ostracized by their colleagues because they are putting their personal interest above those of the Arab nation.'[105] While membership in the JEA was compulsory for all engineers in order to obtain a business licence, the JEA stood at the helm of an 'anti-normalization movement' in Jordan.

The pressure from public opinion and the anti-normalization movement, including Islamist groups, leftists, and the influential professional associations, on Jordanian businesspeople to refrain from co-operating, was perhaps most visibly exerted when an Israeli trade fair was planned to take place in Amman in November 1996 and repeatedly delayed.[106] When the fair finally opened in the second week of January 1997, it was almost left without visitors, while a broad coalition of political activists, opposition movements, trade unions, and professional associations, organized in a 'Committee for the Cancellation of the Israeli Trade Fair,' demonstrated against the fair outside. The government, in a move widely interpreted as almost supporting the protesters, had stated that it would neither deter opposition, since 'all citizens had the right to demonstrate,' nor would it interfere and cancel the event, since it was committed to the peace treaty.[107]

The pressure of the anti-normalization movement on Jordanian entrepreneurs steadily increased and was the reason why most businesspeople involved in co-operation kept a low profile. In 1998, Mtri Twal, General Manager of Five Continents Travel Services, which represented the Israeli air carrier El Al, said, 'working with El Al is fulfilling my dream of peaceful coexistence.'[108] After the Al-Aqsa Intifada erupted, however, in November 2000, his company announced in an advertisement in the English-language Jordan Times under the bold-lettered heading 'important notice' that it had terminated its contract with the Israeli airline. Under the pressure of public opinion and the threat of losing customers, the company had given in.[109] This step came as a reaction to the first publication of a 'blacklist' by the 'Committee Against Normalization,' a coalition body involving most professional associations in Jordan, in its newsletter Muqawama (Resistance).[110] A second list of companies and individuals accused of normalization was published in February 2001, but prompted the government to crack down on the movement.

Shortly before the publication of the first list, JBA Chairman Tabba'a had called Israel 'an enemy,' which had 'proven that it does not deserve peace.'[111] A newspaper dedicated to support normalization, Sawt al-Salam ('The Voice of Peace'), which appeared for the first time in September 2000, also attracted a great deal of criticism, and in fact, had to be printed in Ramallah, because no Jordanian publishing house was willing to take on the job.[112] Given the strong pressure exerted by public opinion and in particular, the anti-normalization movement, it was only natural that Jordanian businessmen sought to keep a low profile and maintain their Israeli contacts secretly. Not even the new Intifada, however, disrupted business, and co-operation continued smoothly.

Great Interest in the Palestinian Market

Given the large population of Palestinian origin, and that according to polls more than 90 per cent of Jordanians believed their ties with the Palestinians to be stronger than relations with any other Arab country, Jordanians were highly interested in trade with the Palestinians.[113] Kamal Kakish, Chairman of the Jordan Trade Association (JTA), pointed out that if Jordan could gain a 10 per cent share in the more than $2 billion worth of goods that Palestinians in the West Bank and Gaza imported annually, almost exclusively from Israel, this would give a major boost to the Jordanian economy: 'For us, the Palestinian market is very important [...] It should be our No. 2 market, after Iraq.'[114] JBA Deputy-Chairman Fakhri Bilbeisi stated: 'One of the biggest economic gains of peace will be the opening of the Palestinian market, which is a natural market to Jordanian products.'[115]

Ties between government institutions and private sector organizations alike were close. The first Jordanian trade exhibition, organized by JEDCO, took place in Ramallah in November 1996.[116] In September 1998, JEDCO opened a permanent office in Ramallah to facilitate commercial transactions and expand the range of services provided for Jordanian and Palestinian businessmen.[117] The JBA was the first organization to start building relations when it organized the 'First Jordanian-Palestinian Conference' in Amman in June 1995. The JBA and the Palestinian Businessmen Association (PBA) then signed a protocol on a joint business council in July, which however remained largely ineffective.[118]

With Israel's continued involvement in Jordanian-Palestinian relations, due to its control over borders, and obstacles such as the back-to-back transportation agreement, lengthy security checks, and Israeli customs, standards and certification specifications, Jordanian businessmen grew increasingly frustrated. Muhammad Noureddin al-Hamouri, for example, was one of a number of Jordanian and Palestinian investors who had intended to set up a $50 million investment project in Jenin, expecting to create more than 3,000 jobs, but who decided to freeze it after the election of Binyamin Netanyahu as Prime Minister in May 1996.[119] A private business consultant pointed out:

> Many businessmen were hoping to invest in the West Bank; they had problems with the old Israeli government, and now with the right-wing coming to power, many investors are very discouraged from carrying out their plans or even from going through with existing ones before the situation becomes clearer.[120]

JCIC Chairman Mamduh Abu Hassan, who had not had any business with the West Bank before, obtained a standards licence for his products even before the peace treaty was signed. But, he claimed, since the Israeli authorities could not reject his tiles on grounds of insufficient standards, his products were then overvalued when customs were calculated, with the result that JCIC became uncompetitive. JCIC then tried Palestinian importers, as well as an official agent in the PA, but it did not work, and like most other Jordanians, Abu Hassan abandoned his efforts to enter the Palestinian market.[121]

In fact, it was not only the Israeli attempt at retaining dominance over the Palestinian market, but also the problem that Palestinians and Jordanians were actually competitors, which undermined the Jordanian interest in co-operation. As early as 1993, Jordanian businesspeople had expressed their worries over losing investments by wealthy Palestinians living in Jordan, who would choose to invest in the PA, rather than in Jordan.[122] Thus, while entrepreneurs were accusing especially the Netanyahu government of hindering Jordanian-Palestinian co-operation, some actually hoped that trouble between the Palestinians and the new hard-line government in Israel would cause local and foreign investors to choose Jordan, rather than the PA, and that Israel would remain keen to please its warmest Arab friend.[123] While Jordanians demanded free access to the Palestinian market, they remained reluctant to grant reciprocity to Palestinian merchants and manufacturers; instead, they simply desired a share in the Israeli dominance over the Palestinian market.[124]

The Business Community in the Palestinian Territories

Political and Economic Independence

Palestinian businesspeople exhibited a very sober attitude towards potential co-operation almost from the beginning of the peace process on. As Tareq Maayah, who returned to Ramallah from the United States in the hope that the peace process would open up business opportunities and set up the Palestinian Siemens-branch, put it, 'it is not the economy that will bring peace; only a peaceful solution of the conflict will allow the economy to kick off.'[125] Similarly, Tareq Sous, a textiles manufacturer, said, 'you cannot separate politics and economics; if you ask me how is the business, I will tell you, as good or bad as the political situation.'[126] The views of the Palestinian business community were often conflicting and contradictory. On the one hand, Palestinian businesspeople wished for independence, the development of a national economy and more balanced, equal economic relations with Israel. On the other hand, many entrepreneurs also relied on raw material imports from Israel, acted as subcontractors or agents for Israeli companies, depended on the Israeli market and continued ties to the Israeli economy and therefore opposed a separation of the two economies. Mazen Sinokrot, Chairman of the Sinokrot Global Group and of the Palestinian Food Industries Association, for example, pointed out,

> It is our right as Palestinians to set up our own state, with full control over the borders to our neighbouring countries. For me, as a businessman, there

should be some form of co-operation, but it should be based on an equal footing, where each side has its own laws and regulations.[127]

In 1993, a short-lived optimism prevailed. A survey conducted among 195 Palestinian companies with 15 or more employees – representing more than half of the largest Palestinian establishments – found that 92 per cent of the companies expected the Oslo Accords to have a positive effect on economic growth. 89 per cent of the firms expected an increase in their sales to Israel. 76 per cent of the Palestinian establishments surveyed favoured co-operation with Israeli firms, preferably in the form of joint ventures. 53 per cent had a direct or indirect subcontracting arrangement with Israeli firms. Those establishments involved in subcontracting, usually smaller enterprises, however, expected large losses during the interim period. Nearly all of these, or 95 per cent, considered themselves to be in competition with Israeli firms, and 23 per cent believed that ending subcontracting would force many local factories to close down. A clear majority favoured the maintenance of subcontracting arrangements.[128]

The fear among Palestinian businessmen that they stood to lose, rather than win, soon came to dominate their attitude towards business relations with Israel and wore out the initial optimism. Within one year, Palestinians seemed to be reluctant to enter into new business relationships with Israelis. In another survey, carried out in 1994, 75 per cent of the 52 surveyed businesspeople opposed normal economic ties with Israel, while more than 50 per cent said that if an Israeli contacted them to do business, they would refuse. Nearly 85 per cent believed that from a nationalist perspective, it was wrong to do business with Israel. More than 80 per cent agreed with the statement that Israel was only interested in using Palestinian traders to sell to the Arab world.[129] The study concluded that 'Palestinians display great concern regarding the timing of joint ventures, and the vast majority of them feel that this form of normalization is premature.'[130] Samir Huleileh, the West Bank economist who was first part of the Palestinian negotiating team, then a high-ranking official at the Ministry of the Economy and Trade, and Marketing Director of Nassar Investments, too, argued that Palestinians should not indulge in joint ventures until the final status was agreed on, and that the priority was the development of a national economy in the Territories, independent from Israel.[131] Likewise, Samir Abdullah, General Manager of the Palestinian Trade Centre (Paltrade), a business association promoting private sector development, pointed to the Palestinian dependence on Israeli imports and infrastructure and demanded that Palestinians be given room to develop their own industries.[132]

Closures, Boycotts and Public Protests

The reluctance to establish business relations with Israel and the wish for separation and an autonomous economic policy, despite the continued dependence on Israel, were furthered by the disappointment over the first two years of trade and industrial co-operation under the Paris Protocol. As Saeb Bamieh, Director-General at the Palestinian Ministry of the Economy and Trade saw it, 'within one year after the PA took over, it became clear that Israel would not allow the PA and the Palestinian private sector to succeed.'[133] At a first official meeting between members of the Palestinian and Israeli Chambers of Commerce in the summer of 1995, the Palestinian representatives pointed out that despite the Oslo Accords, their situation had worsened, with the Israelis placing tough restrictions on exports and transportation between the West Bank and Gaza.[134] Mahmoud Farrah, a textiles producer from Al-Ram near Jerusalem, said at the beginning, with the breakthrough of the Oslo Accords, people thought there would be real peace, but with the experiences of closed borders and the restricted freedom of movement, people became disillusioned.[135]

Talal Nasruddin, Chairman of the Palestinian Federation of Industries and of the Birzeit Palestine Pharmaceuticals Company, a leading pharmaceuticals manufacturer, illustrated the ongoing limitations Palestinian entrepreneurs faced. Under occupation, Israel had dominated the Palestinian market and restricted the potential for industrial development and exports. As he explained, 'when we wanted to export, we were considered as Israelis and subjected to the Arab boycott, so we had to rely on the Israelis, both for imports and as a potential market for exports.' The largest Israeli health service, Kupat Holim, preferred to prescribe Israeli pharmaceutical products, rather than Palestinian ones. While the establishment of the PA changed this policy and enabled Palestinian manufacturers to increase their market share, they could still not import pharmaceutical products from abroad. Partially, this protected the local industry, but since most pharmaceutical companies were also acting as importers and distributors for products the industry could not manufacture locally, these goods had to be registered in Israel, too, thus restricting especially cheaper foreign imports that could undermine the market position of Israeli pharmaceuticals. In terms of international exports, Palestinian products also lagged behind Israeli goods, since these were more sophisticated and could rely on better marketing and distribution networks. The reliance on raw materials coming through Israel exposed manufacturers to closures and other barriers, such as security and health inspections.[136]

The closures that were regularly imposed on the Territories in the wake of terrorist attacks inside Israel strongly shaped the attitude of Palestinian entrepreneurs. A 1996 report from the Orient House claimed that despite the provisions of the Paris Protocol, which gave Palestinian businesses free access to the Israeli market, numerous administrative, logistical, and de facto non-tariff barriers existed, while Israeli products continued to enjoy 'unimpeded and sometimes facilitated access to the Palestinian market.' Due to the closures, the West Bank was de facto cut into half, and Palestinian companies were compelled either to have two headquarters or risk having their operations diminished due to their inability to access either of the sections of the West Bank. In the case of Gaza, the absence of a safe passage for individuals and goods between the PA areas left Israel as the only possible route of access to the West Bank. Entry permits were mandatory, but often impossible to obtain. Most companies cited their inability to obtain travel permits for their employees as the major constraint on their work. Permits were required for travel between Gaza and the West Bank on the one hand, and Jerusalem and Israel on the other, even when total closures were not in force. Permits were required for vehicles and trucks that transported goods between the West Bank, Jerusalem, Israel and Gaza. Transportation costs increased drastically, since Israeli trucks had to be rented by West Bank traders for $300 to deliver goods just to the Erez checkpoint into the Gaza Strip. From there, traders had to rent a truck with a Gaza licence plate at the additional cost of $250 per delivery. Lengthy security procedures and checks were imposed on all goods imported into the Palestinian Territories, causing additional costs for storage. The checks also often resulted in the destruction of goods, especially agricultural produce. In addition to all those measures, which at least rendered Palestinian products uncompetitive because of high additional costs, the Israeli authorities at first refused to comply with measures necessary to set up successful industrial estates, such as delegating powers to the PA for zoning, licensing and taxation, and other such actions.

Consequentially, Palestinian businessmen questioned the viability of exercises aimed at fostering regional co-operation.[137] 350 textile shops in Gaza, one-third of the Palestinian textiles industry, were forced to shut down until 1996. One West Bank trading company almost closed down because 70 per cent of its trade was dependent on Jerusalem, which was cordoned off from the West Bank. Muhammad Alami, Deputy General Manager of the Jerusalem Cigarette Company (JCC), said that 60 of his 130 employees were on unpaid leave, while sales were barely 60 per cent of normal, and expressed his dismay with schemes of regional integration: 'The Israelis are dreaming if they think they can develop ties with the Arab world while their Palestinian neighbours are hungry.'[138]

Due to the negative experiences Palestinian entrepreneurs had during the first two years after the signing of the Oslo Accords, the Palestinian Businessmen Association (PBA), a 200 member-strong organization representing the biggest Palestinian establishments, decided to boycott the 1995 MENA conference in Amman. PBA President Ibrahim Abdel Hadi said, 'we protest against the obstacles practiced by the Israeli authorities against Palestinian businessmen and against the Palestinian economy in general.'[139] With the persistence of closures and the stalemate in the political process, the business community then also boycotted the Cairo MENA conference in 1996 and the Doha meeting in 1997.[140]

Pragmatism and Dependence on Israel

While the Palestinian business community suffered under the provisions of the Paris Protocol and publicly boycotted 'normalization,' privately, many Palestinians said survey results of their business attitude should not be taken at face value.[141] Because of their dependence on Israeli raw materials and trade relations, Palestinians did not really favour a severing of the ties to the Israeli economy. Samir Huleileh, as well as Mazen Sinokrot, pointed out that there ran a divide among Palestinian businessmen in their attitude towards business ties with Israel both between small and big business and between manufacturers and merchants. Thanks to the 1996 'agency law,' which required Israeli manufacturers and merchants to operate through Palestinian agents, and to give up or share their distributorships for international goods in the PA with Palestinian agents, direct imports increased strongly. The number of registered importers grew from only 56 in 1994 to over 2,000 in 1997. The newly emerging commercial stratum favoured a higher degree of independence from Israel. Smaller businesses, especially in sectors such as food or pharmaceuticals, also preferred protection for local industries and a separation from the Israeli economy, while those sectors depending on Israel were strongly opposed to a separation, such as the textiles or stone and marble industries.

This interest was only strengthened by the fact that Jordan and Egypt, the most likely alternative export destinations, were reluctant to open their markets to Palestinian goods, and that other alternatives remained off-limits.[142] Thus, for example, despite Paltrade's publicly stated wish for more independence and its emphasis on developing the national economy autonomously, its clear geographic focus in the promotion of Palestinian exports was the Israeli market, where, according to Samir Abdullah, the Palestinian market share could easily be doubled or tripled. While businessmen seemed divided in their interest towards co-operating with Israel, Abdullah argued, effectively, the entire Palestinian business community depended on Israel in one way or another, and few Palestinians really desired a full separation.[143] Hassan Kassem, President and CEO of Arab Technology Systems (ATS), for example, said it was impossible to sever the ties between the Israeli and Palestinian economies. Palestinians could not just boycott Israel since the links were too close. Even if the PA decided to separate itself from the Israeli economy, this could not be done in a day; both sides stood to lose.[144]

Nakhleh Jubran, Chairman of the Arab Industrial Co. (AIC), pointed out that the important question was not what the terms of an agreement were, but how it was actually implemented, reflecting on the partial implementation of the Paris Protocol. Palestinian producers, he said, had learned in the past not to rely on regulations and agreements, but to be as flexible as possible and to always adapt to new circumstances. Thus, many entrepreneurs simply did not have any preference for a final status arrangement; instead, entrepreneurs were preparing for the worst case.[145] Tareq Sous mirrored this attitude. According to him, 'we cannot even think about tomorrow [...] Our future is made by others.' Sous pointed out that for most Palestinians, the question was less integration or separation – both solutions would be fine – but simply to overcome the status quo. Either one separated the two economies and the Palestinians would be free to establish closer links with the Arab world, or one had an integrated solution, but on an equal footing.[146]

As a result of the continued dependence on Israel, Paltrade organized a trade fair in Haifa in 1999, in which 45 Palestinian firms participated and which attracted 10,000 visitors. Maroun Yacoub, the Israeli adviser to Paltrade, said the exhibition was 'aimed at boosting sales of their products to Israeli consumers in general and Israeli Arabs in particular and also attracting the interest of [Israeli] business concerns and possibly leading to future joint ventures.'[147] Several Palestinian high-tech companies also participated in the Comdex fair in Tel Aviv in September 2000, only a few days before the outbreak of the Al-Aqsa Intifada. They were sponsored by the US-company Oracle, whose Israeli branch was trying to enter the Palestinian market at that time, and the organizers of the fair, the Peres Centre for Peace and the Israeli Ministry of Regional Co-operation.[148]

Palestinian high-tech companies were particularly pragmatic in their attitude towards dealing with the Israelis, and many seized the opportunity to participate in the fair. Jihad al-Wazir, son of Abu Jihad and President of a Gazan computer company, for example, said: 'There's a peace process, and, unless we actualize it, it won't become a reality [...] Through discussions about technological co-operation and development of sources of employment, we will build the elements that can make the peace process a reality.'[149] Siemens CEO Maayah pointed out that since opportunities in high-tech in the Territories were limited and the Palestinians depended on Israel anyway, co-operation at least gave young Palestinians the chance to gain experience in challenging projects, but he also stressed that the Palestinian business community wanted to be treated on an equal footing. Thus, he rejected the concept of the joint Khaddourie high-tech industrial park, which was merely about using cheap labour and having Palestinian engineers doing the labour-intensive but unchallenging work for Israeli companies; instead, Palestinians should focus on developing their own companies with authentic products and on finding their own markets.[150] Issa Eways, CEO of Rama International, a multimedia and web design company, voiced a similar attitude; Israelis, according to him, had contacted him several times regarding joint ventures, and he only rejected the offers because he did not want to engage in subcontracting, but be treated as an equal business partner.[151]

As a result of the continued dependence on Israel and the wish for a balanced and equal economic relationship, Paltrade came to lobby for a free trade agreement (FTA) between Israel and the PA for the final economic status negotiations, on the basis of a free market economy, with the private sector as growth leader, in the PA; close links with the Israeli economy, constituting a source of business opportunity for the Palestinian private sector; and the establishment and reinforcement of economic ties with the Arab states.[152] These three principles were the outcome of the 'National Economic Dialogue Project,' initiated by the PA and implemented by Paltrade in 1999, 'to activate the participation of the private sector in developing economic policies.' Two workshops were held in Ramallah and Gaza, involving some 250 representatives from the PA and the private sector, and resulted in the drafting of recommendations, formulated as White Papers, which were discussed and ratified in the National Economic Dialogue Conference in May 2000. The Second White Paper dealt with the 'Palestinian Future Economic Relations with Israel,' and reiterated the wish for a more independent course of action. A final status arrangement should

> guarantee Palestinians freedom to strengthen their economic relations with the Arab states and develop an independent Palestinian trade policy [...] It should provide opportunities that would allow for a variety in both Palestinian exports and in the markets importing them. Moreover, the door should be open for a variety in the means of production, with high quality and low cost, in order to increase the competitive capability of the Palestinian economy in the Israeli market. [...] It should improve the conditions of trade with Israel in a manner that will ensure the elimination of any monopoly or

protection on the part of Israeli companies in their relationship with the Palestinian economy.

Significantly, the private sector version of the White Paper then explicitly demanded the conclusion of a free trade agreement (FTA), a wish that was omitted from the final version of the recommendations, which were agreed on by the private sector and the PA.[153]

Difficult Relations with Jordan

Paltrade's geographical focus only changed with the outbreak of the Al-Aqsa Intifada in September 2000, shifting away from Israel towards the Arab countries and overseas markets. During 2001, Paltrade organized the Palestinian participation in trade fairs in Algeria, Jordan, Dubai, and Saudi Arabia.[154] Overall, the Palestinian relationship to the Israeli economy overshadowed, impacted on, and often determined the interests and attitudes of the Palestinian business community towards co-operation with their Arab neighbours, and specifically, Jordan. There was a clear general interest in the Jordanian market and in co-operation with Jordan, but little actual attention was devoted to Jordan in the context of closures and other obstacles to trade and industrial development. Trade with Jordan was seen by the PA as a strategy to diversify Palestinian trade, and Jordan was considered a bridge to the Arab world. As Saeb Bamieh, Director-General at the Palestinian Ministry of the Economy and Trade, said, 'for us, it is not only Jordan, but Palestinian exports to other Arab countries through Jordan.' At the same time, Bamieh pointed out, it was crucial that trade relations be based on reciprocity, in order to avoid additional competitive pressure.[155]

Tareq Maayah, CEO of the Palestinian Siemens-branch, said while Israelis and Palestinians would work with one another, Jordan represented both a potential market and a potential competitor.[156] Rama CEO Eways, who bought a Jordanian high-tech firm at the beginning of the Al-Aqsa Intifada, pointed out that the Palestinian efforts to develop the IT sector into a main pillar of the economy were similar to the vision King Abdullah promoted in Jordan. Jordanians and Palestinians could work together with their inexpensive, high quality workforces, who could even compete against such developed high-tech nations as India and Ireland, specifically in the outsourcing of jobs from European and American firms.[157] Jordanian competition was an issue of concern in particular to smaller businesses. Palestinian textile industrialists were unanimous in their complaint that Israeli-Jordanian joint ventures in textile manufacturing, facilitated and encouraged by the QIZ agreement, were established at the expense of Palestinian workshops.[158] Abdel Malik Jaber, General Manager of PIEDCO, the PADICO subsidiary that was developing the Palestinian industrial parks, on the other hand, as a representative of big business, said, while there existed potential competition, Palestinian products could withstand the pressure of rivalry. In addition, he argued, the Jordanian and Palestinian economies were so small that there was enough cake for all parties; the Palestinians also had the advantage of closer ties to Israel.[159]

Thus, in the Palestinian Territories, as in Israel and, to a certain extent, in Jordan, it was mainly the larger business conglomerates that maintained an interest in co-operation. In both Jordan and the Palestinian Territories, co-operation was a politically sensitive issue, which was often rejected in public, yet explored in secret. On the Israeli side, the peace process as such had been important because it opened up new overseas markets, while the regional markets were largely irrelevant. At the same time, Israelis were highly interested in preserving their economic dominance in the Palestinian Territories and the beneficial labour-sharing arrangement, which was now also extended to Jordan. Since both Jordanians and Palestinians desired to gain a share in the potential benefits from collaboration, the formula for co-operation was found in industrial joint ventures capitalizing on Israeli know-how and technology in combination with cheap but skilled Jordanian and Palestinian labour. It was this formula that set the stage for the evolution of co-operative ties, which mainly developed in industrial collaboration and subcontracting. Trade meanwhile remained hindered by many barriers, manifesting the Israeli desire to preserve the status quo and the Jordanian and Palestinian interest in protection for the domestic industries.

4

Business Ties between Israel, Jordan and the PA

Co-operation amongst Israelis, Jordanians, and Palestinians was characterized by unequal relations. Israelis took advantage of their superior technology and know-how and made use of cheap Jordanian and Palestinian manual labour in projects of industrial co-operation in joint industrial parks and the designated Qualifying Industrial Zones (QIZ) in Jordan. Israeli security inspections and other non-tariff barriers made the transportation of goods difficult and expensive and hindered the trade between the parties. Insufficient and dysfunctional agreements also disproportionally favoured large conglomerates with contacts to the political establishment and political actors engaged in business. Industrial co-operation and trade both came to be dominated by the elite of Israeli, Jordanian, and Palestinian businessmen. Large segments of all three societies, however, hardly benefited and often suffered under the consequences of regional collaboration.

Israeli-Jordanian Co-operation

The Failure of Government-Driven Co-operation

Inter-governmental and government-driven co-operation between Jordan and Israel hardly developed beyond the initially enthusiastic rhetoric. Private sector ties developed slowly and only really took off in three main areas after 1998: co-operation under the QIZ agreement, which created jobs in Jordan and enhanced cross-border trade and exports; co-operation in textiles manufacturing as part of a general Israeli movement to cheaper manufacturing locations; and co-operation in programming and high-tech, fuelled by Israel's shortage of skilled manpower.

King Hussein's chief motivation in concluding peace with Israel had been his hope for a generous peace dividend, but most government-driven projects of co-operation were cancelled or did not make it beyond the planning stages.[1] Both governments placed obstacles in the way of co-operation. The Regional Economic Development Working Group (REDWG) of the multilateral track established a monitoring secretariat in Amman and supervised the organization of the annual MENA conferences, but did not achieve much else. The Middle East Bank for

Reconstruction and Development (MEBRD), planned since 1994, was announced closed in 1998 after only Jordan but not Israel, Egypt, and the PA, had ratified it.[2] Both the Israeli and the Jordanian government promoted ambitious lists of investment projects at the MENA conferences, but had to scale these down in subsequent years. Despite lengthy and expensive feasibility studies, most projects were not implemented.[3] Political issues aside, many were not viable economically.[4] Jordanian officials increasingly voiced their disappointment: 'Were you to give me ten dinars for every Israeli plan that's been presented to us, we wouldn't need any more investments in Jordan.'[5]

One such project was the 1995 proposal from the US Enron Corporation and its partners, the Jordanian Near East Energy Company (NEEC) and an Israeli consortium comprising Mashav, the Dankner Group, and Delek, on the Israeli side, to export Qatari natural gas via Aqaba to Israel. It was called off at the 1997 MENA conference in Doha. Also frozen in the planning stages were the engagements of two Israeli companies in the field of oil shale development in Jordan and the proposal of the government-owned Israel Electric Corporation (IEC) to construct a joint wind farm, despite involvement of the Israeli and Jordanian Energy Ministries. Similarly, a joint border tourism project, the Desert Kingdom, was finally re-located fully to Jordan, despite the engagement of several Israeli governmental agencies and a signed joint resolution between the governments.[6] The two government-controlled telephone providers, Bezeq and the JTC, cut links with one another in September 1998, less than four years after the introduction of direct phone connections, in a payments dispute.[7] After long negotiations with Dead Sea Works, a member of the Eizenberg Group-owned Israel Chemicals Ltd., the Jordanian Dead Sea Industries, a subsidiary of the governmental Arab Potash Company (APC), announced a $120 million deal with the US company Albemarle on a joint bromine factory.[8] APC had also unsuccessfully held talks with Dead Sea Works over a joint water storage facility in 1995 and considered another $60 million joint venture with Haifa Chemicals during 1996.[9]

Because of all the difficulties, delays, and failures of these highly publicized projects with governmental involvement, the focus of co-operation increasingly moved towards the private sectors, despite initial problems in Jordan with the 'aggressive nature' of Israeli business.[10] By September 2000, there were at least 35 joint ventures operating in Jordan. Even during the Al-Aqsa Intifada, most projects continued smoothly.[11]

The Century Investment Group and Qualifying Industrial Zones (QIZ)

A small circle group of entrepreneurs with ties to the respective governments dominated industrial co-operation between Israelis and Jordanians. Co-operation took place mainly in textiles and revolved around the Qualifying Industrial Zones (QIZ), which brought investments to Jordan but benefited in particular foreign companies from third countries. Jordanian entrepreneurs acted as intermediaries providing manual labour, while much of the financial gains went to Israelis and foreign businesspeople, who even employed non-Jordanian skilled labour alongside Jordanian workers.

Industrial co-operation between Jordanians and Israelis began with a meeting between IMA President and Delta Galil Chairman Dov Lautman and Omar Salah in the summer of 1994, which led to the establishment of the first Israeli-Jordanian joint venture between Delta and the Century Investment Group in the al-Hassan Industrial Estate in March 1996.[12] 'Centurywear' produced underwear for designer brands, exported via Israel under the Israeli-American FTA, and provided hundreds of jobs.[13] As a consequence, Delta achieved its best results ever in the following years; Century soon became the single largest employer in Jordan after the government.[14] The group dominated Israeli-Jordanian co-operation and shaped the nature of co-operation significantly with its provision of cheap labour for manual manufacturing operations outsourced by Israeli firms. It ran the largest number of joint ventures, and in 2000, even bought a bankrupt textiles manufacturing plant in the Israeli development town Ofakim.[15]

Established in 1995, the Century Investment Group was owned by the Salah family, known for its contracting business in Saudi Arabia, but also relied on other investors, among them the Arab Bank, the former Commander-in-Chief of the Jordanian Air Force and Chairman of Royal Jordanian Ihsan Shurdom, the government-owned Social Security Corporation (SSC), the Housing Bank, and the Jordan National Bank.[16] Most of its projects were registered abroad and involved nominally international partners, which covered the Israeli engagements in the ventures. Thus, for example, Century's software venture with the MLL (Malam) Group, initiated by Amiram Shor, its Chairman and Chairman of the Israeli Software Houses Association in 1998, was registered in the Netherlands, featured three international partners, and was managed by a former officer in the Jordanian army.[17] After a company review in 1999, Century's management decided not to focus entirely on Israeli partners anymore, but the majority of projects remained joint ventures with Israelis.[18] Omar Salah, calling himself 'the poster child for normalization,' had so many business contacts in Israel that he rented an apartment in Tel Aviv.[19]

Salah's contacts in Israel also led to a variety of other projects. For example, the Israeli businessman, who had initiated Century's joint venture with the jewellery producer Paz Chen in 1995 and acted as Century's agent in Israel since 1998, was involved in three further joint ventures, among them a company that provided third-country companies operating in the QIZ in Irbid with the necessary Israeli input to qualify for export to the United States.[20] Century also planned a $100 million manufacturing facility in Jordan with the Israeli branch of the Jewish-owned multinational high-tech company Vishay until the outbreak of the new Intifada.[21] Century's internal review of 1999 led to an increased interest in information technology, and Salah had a number of IT projects in the pipeline.[22] Reports in 2000 also claimed that Century was planning a multimillion-dollar venture, together with Yossi Vardi, the Israeli high-tech 'godfather,' AOL, Koor, the IDB Holding Co., and several Israeli venture capital funds.[23]

Even the agreement on the Qualifying Industrial Zones (QIZ), the most significant initiative to further Jordanian-Israeli industrial co-operation, was a result of Salah's lobbying efforts.[24] The agreement was formally initiated by the United

Table 6: Portfolio of the Century Investment Group, 2000

Name	Partner	Industry	Location	Operations	Remarks	Jobs
Centurywear, Centurywear Ladies	Delta Galil (ISRAEL), 1996	Textiles	Al-Hassan Industrial Estate	Brand-name underwear; exports under Israeli-US FTA	Largest garment manufacturer in Jordan	1,850
Centurywear Rusaifa Plant (Saltex)	Cannon Country Knitting Mills (USA), 1999	Textiles	Rusaifa	Outerwear casual garments, exports under QIZ agreement	Largest number of disabled employees in Jordan	800
Century Dutch Dairy Dessert	Koor (ISRAEL), registered in the Netherlands with partner Balton, 1995	Dairy	Al-Hassan Industrial Estate	Koor pulled out in 1995 due to difficulties, project was taken over by Century (value: $6 Mio.)	n/a	800
Century Dutch Canning Industries	Caniel (ISRAEL), registered in the Netherlands with Caniel subsidiary as partner, 1998	Tin cans	Al-Hassan Industrial Estate	Went bankrupt in 2000 (value: $8 Mio.)	Rumours about half-hearted commitment by Caniel	n/a
Century Gold Industries	Paz Chen (ISRAEL), registered in the Netherlands, 1998	Jewellery	Al-Hassan Industrial Estate	Imports raw material from Israel, exports under Israeli FTAs with USA and EU	Sole facility of its kind in Jordan	100
Century Shopping Mall	International investors, including Koor-parent company Shamrock (USA/ISRAEL), 1999/2000	Shopping mall	n/a	n/a	n/a	n/a
Century Batteries	Tadiran (ISRAEL), 1997	Consumer batteries	Al-Hassan Industrial Estate	Consumer batteries for Israeli market, was fully taken over by Century after difficulties	Salah: 'Tadiran sold us a lemon,' difficulties with old machinery and half-hearted commitment by Tadiran	n/a

Table 6: Portfolio of the Century Investment Group, 2000, continued:

Name	Partner	Industry	Location	Operations	Remarks	Jobs
Malam Software Design Centre	Malam (MLL) Ltd. (ISRAEL), November 1997	Software	Amman	Programming for the Israeli software firm (value: $4 Mio.)	n/a	n/a
Motorola Electronics	Motorola Israel Ltd. (ISRAEL), February 1998	Electronics	Al-Hassan Industrial Estate	Assembly for the Israeli company	n/a	80
Medical Textiles	Standard Textiles (USA, owned by a US-Israeli)	Textiles	Al-Hassan Industrial Estate	n/a	n/a	164
Delta Programming	Delta Galil (ISRAEL)	Software	n/a	Programming for the Israeli textiles company	n/a	n/a
Industrial Plastic Bags	Palrig (ISRAEL)	Plastics	Al-Hassan Industrial Estate	Subcontracting for the Israeli plastics producer	n/a	160
Century Men's Suits	Bagir (ISRAEL), 1998	Textiles	Al-Hassan Industrial Estate	Men's suits for Bagir, indirectly led to QIZ Agreement due to hole in Israeli-US FTA that excludes suits	Largest suit manufacturer in the Middle East	442
Metal Blinds	Holis (ISRAEL)	Metal blinds	n/a	n/a	n/a	450
n/a	Yee Tung Group (HONG KONG)	Textiles	Al-Hassan Industrial Estate	Manufactures sweaters and shirts	Largest foreign garment manufacturer in the QIZ	1,650
New Horizon	Yee Tung Group (HONG KONG), 2000	Textiles	Ofakim, Israel	Manufactures sweaters and shirts (value: $2 Mio.)	Century and Yee Tung bought the bankrupt 'New Horizon' plant in the Israeli development town	n/a

Source: Compiled from data provided by Omar Salah, the Century Investment Group, and various other sources[25]

States, in order to stimulate economic growth and provide Jordan with a tangible peace dividend. Thanks to the agreement, Jordan became, together with Israel and Egypt, one of only three countries worldwide to obtain unreciprocal duty-free access to the US market. Signed at the MENA conference in Doha on 16 November 1997, the agreement stipulated that any good produced in designated industrial zones could qualify for unrestricted access to the US market if it contained at least 35 per cent of value added from the QIZ. Of these 35 per cent, at least one-third (i.e., 11.7 per cent) had to be added by the Jordanian manufacturer in the QIZ and one-third by an Israeli manufacturer. The latter requirement was reduced to 8 per cent and 7 per cent in high-tech, respectively, for a period of five years in February 1999, again due to Salah's lobbying efforts.

Most operations under the QIZ arrangement were located in the al-Hassan Industrial Estate near the northern Jordanian town of Irbid, established in 1991. The estate's designation as the first QIZ on 6 March 1998 more than doubled the number of jobs and significantly boosted the investment volume in the park in less than two years.[26] However, according to Salah, the original agreement mainly benefited companies from third countries, rather than furthering Israeli-Jordanian co-operation.[27] Several Asian and American companies established their presence without local partners, such as Jordache, which had initially planned a large joint venture with Century.[28] Until November 1999, only one company had four of its products qualified and exported to the United States under the QIZ agreement, and this company was not a Jordanian-Israeli venture, but a subsidiary of the Hong Kong-based company Boscan International, which bought zips from Israel and employed skilled Chinese workers alongside unskilled Jordanian labour. QIZ products were also subjected to the Arab boycott, and the benefits of technology transfer and foreign currency generation remained restricted to the QIZ.[29]

Foreign Investments in Jordan and the Textiles and High-Tech Industries

Actual co-operation between Israelis and Jordanians under the QIZ agreement remained limited, but Jordan nevertheless benefited from a boom in foreign investment and exports through the establishment of manufacturing operations in the kingdom by foreign companies following the example of Boscan International. Twenty companies were reported to be in the process of setting up factories in the al-Hassan Estate in August 2000. Six additional QIZs were designated during 2000, among them the Israeli-planned Jordan Gateway Zone, the private Tajammu'at zone, a governmental zone in Kerak, the private al-Dalil Estate near Zarqa, the 'Cybercity' near Irbid, and the private Qastal QIZ, owned by a Palestinian who also ran an Irbid-based textile company.[30] Jordan's overall exports and exports to the United States grew significantly. In the first seven months of 2000, QIZ exports increased more than threefold over the same period in 1999. Total exports to the US rose by 63 per cent in 1999 and quadrupled during the first four months of 2000, compared to the corresponding period in 1999.[31] Total Jordanian QIZ exports for 2000 amounted to $172 million, of which 33 per cent went to Israel and 32 per cent to the USA.[32] A clear majority of those exports were in clothes, illustrating an increasing concentration in textiles manufacturing.[33]

Boscan International was the first foreign firm to establish operations in the al-Hassan Estate. It soon became the biggest venture there and for two years remained the sole company to take advantage of the QIZ agreement. The company had been brought to Jordan by an Israeli who established business contacts and several ventures in the kingdom on the basis of a former political role close to Prime Minister Rabin and through his friendship with King Hussein.[34] Charlie Chang, the head of the group, and Abdallah Tayyeh, Boscan's Vice-President for operations, were crucial in lobbying the Jordanian government to allow companies to employ up to 50 per cent of foreign labour, which was more productive and enhanced competitiveness.[35] Tayyeh himself started his own company in April 2000, providing seven out of 18 foreign garments manufacturers with the necessary Israeli input.[36] Similarly, Emad al-Shamma', the erstwhile General Manager of Howard Brykes, a subsidiary of the Israeli branch of the garments manufacturer Sari International, which became the third company to have its products qualified under the QIZ arrangement, established his own consulting firm in 2000 to advise foreign companies on QIZ operations in Jordan.[37]

The foreign companies moving to Jordan in order to take advantage of the QIZ arrangement were part of a general reinvigoration of Jordan's textiles industry, which had suffered immensely from the UN embargo against its natural market, Iraq, and high customs imposed on machinery and raw material imports. By early 1998, the Jordanian industry employed 11,000 workers, but most factories were operating at a mere 20-30 per cent of capacity.[38] Later that year, Salah claimed: '90 per cent of local textile operations are subcontracting for Israeli companies working with international buyers based in Israel.'[39] The trend started by Delta soon exerted pressure in particular on smaller Israeli companies to re-locate manufacturing operations to Jordan, where labour costs were cheap enough for them to remain competitive. Under the Jordanian-Israeli trade agreement, there were no barriers to shipping half-finished products back and forth, and Israeli supervision in Jordan was easy. Many Israeli textile companies had so far entertained subcontracting arrangements in Galilean Arab villages, the West Bank or Gaza, but now moved to Jordan.[40]

For most Jordanian manufacturers, subcontracting for Israeli firms was the only way to survive in business, although many resented the lack of alternatives and the control the Israelis exerted.[41] According to the Israeli embassy in Amman, by 1998, there were 30 Jordanian textile companies co-operating with 17 Israeli firms. Hilik Cohen, Operations Manager in Jordan for Lodzia, said: 'Many Jordanians who own factories that are out of operation have been approaching us since we came to Jordan. There is a high demand; these people do not care about the political situation in the region.'[42] According to a Jordanian lawyer engaged in brokering deals at the al-Hassan Industrial Estate, at least nine factories were wholly Israeli-owned, possible under the 1995 Investment Law and a complementary second law passed in 2000. The al-Hassan Industrial Estate housed 68 companies in 2000, al-Dalil already employed 600 local and 1,000 foreign workers in QIZ-facilitated joint ventures, and the private Tajammu'at Estate had as many as 8,000 workers employed in its factories.[43] Most Israeli companies were not operating under the QIZ arrangement, but exported garments via Israel to the United States, taking advantage of a unique clause in the US-Israeli FTA, which stipulated that only 35 per cent of value added had to originate in Israel in order to qualify as an Israeli product under the rules of origin. Only the foreign companies exported under the QIZ arrangement, thus gaining unrestricted access to the US market.[44]

The losers of Israeli-Jordanian co-operation in textiles and of the QIZ arrangement were the Palestinians, many of whom had earlier provided cheap labour in subcontracting arrangements.[45] Likewise, ordinary Jordanians gained employment, but little else; working conditions were bad, wages low, and the prospect for advancement limited. The clear winners of co-operative schemes and projects were Israeli manufacturers, foreign entrepreneurs and workers, as well as those Jordanians collaborating closely with both. The government also benefited from the boom in foreign investment and exports. It thus supported and protected those Jordanian entrepreneurs engaged in and around QIZ business.

Thanks to the success of the al-Hassan Estate and the general formula of combining cheap Jordanian labour with foreign investment and know-how, a second industrial estate was designated as both a QIZ and a Free Economic Zone (FEZ) by the Jordanian government and made headlines. A consortium involving the US-Israeli Safra Group, which also held the First International Bank, and the Jordanian Dajani family, which had earlier held talks on co-operative projects with the Israeli companies Tadiran, Elite, and Africa Israel Investments, developed the Jordan Gateway Industrial Park.[46] The park, originally the idea of Gili Deckel, a former security official who had participated in the Israeli-Jordanian negotiations on civil aviation, was to generate $300 million in direct investment in Jordan alone, as well as employment for thousands in both Israel and Jordan. However, the zone was only approved in Israel in August 2000 – five years after its initiation and four years after the United States had approved it as a QIZ – after long delays and drastic revisions due to the protests of environmentalists and the Israeli Ministry of the Environment.[47] A third QIZ was the Cybercity, a joint venture between Boscan International and the Irbid-based University of Science and Technology, which was to focus on information technology and expected more than $100 million in investments.[48] The mutual interest in collaboration in high-tech was based on Israel's lack of software engineers by the late 1990s, while Jordan had engineers, but few employment opportunities. Thus, joint ventures such as the one between the Israeli start-up Visuality Systems, managed by Sam Widerman, the former General Manager of Siemens Israel (Siemens Data Communications, SDC), and the Jordanian software market leader were highly successful and attracted funding from the US-Israeli-Jordanian governmental fund TRIDE or from the Israeli venture capital fund Apex Mutavim.[49]

One rare example of co-operation beyond textiles, IT, and other sectors that took advantage of cheap Jordanian labour and Israeli know-how, was the Israeli-Jordanian-Palestinian venture, which sold Dead Sea products under the 'Sea of Life'-brand name. On its website, the company stated that 'the company name symbolizes the unprecedented co-operation between peace-loving businessmen in Jordan and Israel.'[50]

Delays and Obstacles in Trade and Transportation

Trade between Jordan and Israel remained limited and was hindered by agreements, which imposed many restrictions on trade and the transportation of goods. Nevertheless, trade ties developed, mainly helped by co-operation in garments manufacturing, with raw materials transported from Israel to Jordan, and the finished goods exported back to Israel, from where they were re-exported to overseas markets. The Israeli side protected its own merchants and forwarders, who were the main beneficiaries of trade relations.

Although trade had taken place before the signing of the peace treaty, Israeli-Jordanian trade did not begin officially before mid-1996.[51] While Israel strongly favoured a future FTA, Jordan's refusal to commit itself to free trade in the context of fears that competition would undermine the already weak domestic industrial sector delayed trade negotiations repeatedly.[52] Agreements on trade and transportation were only signed in the autumn of 1995, with ratification delayed until mid-1996.[53] According to a representative from the Israeli Ministry of Transportation, 'both security considerations and preservation of economic interests' had postponed the transport agreement. For example, Israel had insisted that for the protection of Israeli truckers, a maximum of 180 Jordanian trucks would only be allowed into Israel at a time.[54] After the trade volume amounted to a meagre $10 million during 1996, the agreements were amended; Israeli customs on Jordanian goods were unilaterally cut, and the transportation agreement was modified in December 1996.[55]

Table 7: Truck Traffic between Jordan and Israel

	Departures from Jordan to Israel				Arrivals to Jordan from Israel			
Year	Haifa Port	Back-to-Back	Door-to-Door	Total	Haifa Port	Back-to-Back	Door-to-Door	Total
1996	18	355	-	373	106	952	-	1058
1997	299	39	1270	1504	118	40	1108	1266
1998 (January-July)	33	111	1100	1244	407	199	1122	1728

Source: UNDP and RSS, Peace Follow-Up Unit, Follow-Up Report on the Transportation Agreement between Jordan and Israel in the Peace Process, Report No. 10, February 1999

Until the modification, goods were transported under the back-to-back rule, i.e. had to be unloaded at the border and were then transported on in other trucks. From 1997 on, door-to-door transportation was generally introduced except for goods from third countries, which had to be delivered back-to-back. Despite the door-to-door rule, however, a convoy system was maintained and a wide range of restrictions applied. Trade was significantly reduced compared to pre-peace levels and was hindered by the difficulties to obtain visas, the limited working hours and high fees and taxes at the borders as well as lengthy procedures and checks. A merchant had to inform border authorities at least 24 hours prior to the date of crossing; empty Jordanian trucks could not enter Israel to transport goods back, although Israeli trucks were allowed to do so in Jordan.[56]

Table 8: Jordanian and Israeli Exports, 1997

Jordanian Exports to Israel		Israeli Exports to Jordan	
Good	Value (Mio. JD)	Good	Value (Mio. JD)
Clothing and textile products	7.2	Cloth and garment	9.2
Minerals and chemical materials	1.2	Industrial and agricultural machinery	2.7
Paper and paper products	0.9	Iron and iron products	2
Electrical appliances and metric tools	0.8	Parts of laboratory equipment	1.5
Construction materials	0.5	Gold and jewellery	1.2
Fertilizers	0.4	Fertilizers and fodder	0.6
Food stuff	0.3	Primary materials	0.4
Oils and fat	0.2	Paper, paper products, plastics	0.4
Cleaning materials	0.1	Spare parts, cars	0.2
Furniture and wood	0.1	Food stuff	0.2
Other	1.9	Other	2.8
Total	13.6	Total	20.5

Source: UNDP and RSS, Peace Follow-Up Unit, Follow-Up Report on the Transportation Agreement between Jordan and Israel in the Peace Process, Report No. 10, February 1999

The implementation of the agreement on trade and economic co-operation, effective from April 1996 on, faced similar obstacles. Non-tariff as well as tariff barriers hindered the flow of goods. Yarn and textile products, the raw material for the re-located Israeli textiles manufacturing industry, dominated imports from Israel to Jordan. Exports were mainly the finished garments, which were re-exported to Israel and on to western markets. Jordanians attempting to export other goods to Israel faced not only customs tariffs, but also a multitude of internal Israeli taxes that affected the price of a good. The re-negotiation of the agreement in December 1996 reduced customs, and the number of goods exempted from customs was increased from 41 to 64; 48 goods enjoyed a 50 per cent customs reduction, and 36, instead of initially 19, goods enjoyed a 30 per cent tariff reduction.[57] Yet, only 64 out of a total of 1,266 exporting Jordanian companies, or 5 per cent, were actively engaged in exporting to Israel and the PA by mid-1998, according to the Jordanian Ministry of Trade and Industry, of which a majority agreed that customs barriers and transportation problems were the main obstacles hindering trade with Israel.[58]

Given the multitude of barriers and obstacles, it was not surprising that during 1996, exports from Jordan to Israel amounted to only 0.4 per cent of total Jordanian exports; imports equalled only 0.067 per cent of Jordan's total imports. Due to the larger size of the Israeli economy, Jordan's relative contribution to Israel's foreign trade balance was even smaller. Although Israeli officials kept pushing for a further liberalization of trade between the two countries, especially since the initial trade agreement was poised to expire in October 1998, the development of trade remained contingent upon the expansion of the QIZ arrangement, with textile imports and exports between Israel and Jordan, and a rapid increase in Jordanian exports to the United States.[59] During the last three quarters of 1999, trade between Jordan and Israel amounted to $27.5 million, of which $14.5 million were Israeli exports to Jordan, hardly a substantial portion of Israeli foreign trade and actually down 10 per cent compared to the corresponding period a year earlier. Jordanians complained that Israel kept the border customs station open for only eight hours a day, and about technical and security difficulties. Israel, on the other hand, demanded that Jordan open a customs station on the border, instead of sending every truck entering the kingdom in a convoy to Amman to undergo customs checks.[60] The customs station was erected in September 2000; and Israeli businessmen were also issued visas on the border from then on.

Even though not all issues were fully resolved before the eruption of the Al-Aqsa Intifada in the Territories, trade recovered and expanded during 2000. According to the Israel-Jordan Chamber of Commerce, Israeli imports of Jordanian goods grew by 79.8 per cent from 1999 to 2000, and Israeli exports increased by 82.8 per cent. Imports of textiles grew by 1,139.2 per cent and became the single largest import good with a 21.76 per cent share of total Israeli imports from Jordan; exports increased by 1,209.2 per cent and also represented the single largest export good with a share of almost 30 per cent. These trends continued well into 2001, when during the first three months of the year, textile imports continued to grow by 269.9 per cent, and remained the most traded good. The Intifada raging in the Occupied Territories did not affect Israeli-Jordanian trade negatively, with imports growing by 108.4 per cent, and exports rising by 244.3 per cent, during the first three months of 2001 over the same period in 2000.[61]

Apart from the increase in direct trade, Jordanians also increasingly used Israeli ports for their imports and exports, especially for those goods manufactured for export to the US under the QIZ arrangement. According to a report published in the Jordanian daily Al-Ra'i in October 1999, Jordanian importers preferred the port of Haifa to Syrian or Lebanese ports, because it was nearer, more efficient, and had lower haulage costs. Some cargo bound for Jordan also arrived via Haifa from the Far East, instead of using the port of Aqaba. Jordanians also imported goods via El Al cargo planes to Ben-Gurion Airport near Tel Aviv, from where they were transported by truck to Jordan.[62]

Despite the overall disappointing level of trade until the increase in the flow of goods due to QIZ operations, the interest in trade relations yielded some success very early after the signing of the peace treaty. Camel Grinding Wheel Works Sarid Ltd. (Gamal) of Kibbutz Sarid was one of the first Israeli companies to expand sales into Jordan in 1995 and was promptly awarded the 'Industry Prize for Outstanding Exporter' for its accomplishments in multiplying export turnover.[63] The Jordanian Petra Engineering Industries won a $20 million order to supply chillers and air handling units for Ben-Gurion Airport in Israel in 1996, the first significant sale of Jordanian goods to Israel to be publicized. Petra Engineering also announced an agreement with its Israeli agent to provide 120,000 air-conditioning units to the Israeli market in a $120 million deal between 1996 and 2000. Petra remained the most successful example of Jordanian sales in Israel, although the company encountered difficulties in the context of the new Intifada from 2000 on.[64]

Israeli freight forwarders became active in Jordan following the establishment of the first joint ventures, which necessitated the transportation of goods between both countries. Agish, an Israeli forwarding company that had worked for Delta in the past followed the textiles manufacturer to Jordan. Thanks to its ties to Delta and the subsequent takeover of all forwarding operations for Century and its joint ventures, Agish held about 70 per cent of the market, with an office in Amman that also handled shipments from Jordanians to international destinations.[65] Transclal, one of Agish's main competitors, was also mainly involved in transporting raw materials and cut fabrics for ventures operating under the QIZ arrangement or in subcontracting between Israel and Jordan. Transclal co-operated with a Jordanian agent in Amman, Deeb Shaheen of Rum & Golf Co., since May 1996. According to Gideon Wolff, Transclal's export manager, the engagement in forwarding between Israel and Jordan was an extension of the domestic competition among Israeli forwarders, much as the engagement of Israeli industrialists in joint ventures in Jordan was a result of pressures in terms of the domestic and global competition.[66]

On the Jordanian side, the forwarding business with Israel was mainly in the hands of smaller companies. However, almost every competitor had at least a fraction of trade going to Israel or leaving through the port of Haifa, including such prominent companies as Amin Kawar & Sons, the business of an influential Christian Jordanian family, or Aramex, the courier service whose founder Fadi Ghandour was appointed a member of King Abdullah's Economic Consultative Council.[67] Rum & Golf Co., the Jordanian agent for Transclal, controlled about 85 per cent of the trade flow between Jordan and Israel. Deeb Shaheen also engaged in trade under his own name, when Jordanians or Israelis merchants did not want their name to be openly involved in deals. Thus, under Shaheen's name, the JCFC sold cement to its Israeli counterpart, Nesher, since Israel had restricted JCFC's direct cement sales to the Palestinians. Nesher then sold the Jordanian cement to the PA, under a deal with the monopolistic Palestine Cement Co., controlled by the PCSC, which was run by Arafat's economic advisor, Muhammad Rashid (Khaled Salam). Cement accounted for about half of the total Jordanian export volume to Israel.[68] A similar deal under Shaheen's name was the daily export of 100 tonnes of salt by the APC subsidiary, Safi Salt, to Israel. According to Shaheen, Jordan also exported sand, stone, and fish from a project of the Inter-Arab Investment Fund and from a private fish farm, Jordan Valley Co., run by a member of the important tribal Tarawneh family from Kerak.[69]

Under the cloak of secrecy, Israeli companies even managed to establish trade links to Iraqi firms via Jordan. In February 1998, the Wall Street Journal reported that Israel maintained unofficial trade relations with Iraq, with goods going to Iraq via Jordan, and Iraqi oil passing the same way.[70] Dead Sea Works, with the help of the Tel Aviv contractor Mordehai Yona, tried to sell salt to Iraq in 1995, in violation of the UN embargo, according to the Hebrew daily Ma'ariv. According to another Israeli involved in the deal, Israel sold thousands of tonnes of salt to Iraq in 1995 with the involvement of Jordanian and Palestinian businesspeople and a former member of an elite Israeli commando unit.[71] This example illustrated how Israeli entrepreneurs managed to take advantage of the given circumstances, despite all existing restrictions and difficulties relating to trade and transportation. Only a few allied Jordanian and Palestinian businesspeople likewise benefited from the ties.

Israeli-Palestinian Co-operation

The Politics of Co-operation and Joint Industrial Parks

Industrial co-operation and trade between Israelis and Palestinians were similarly hindered by insufficient and dysfunctional agreements, which led to the dominance of a community of interests among Israeli entrepreneurs and the Palestinian political-economic elite. Israelis continued to take advantage of Palestinian labour, while trade came to be dominated by Israeli big business firms and Palestinians, who either entertained close ties to the PA or were officials in the Authority. Political intermediaries and contacts brought many deals underway, while both governments obstructed co-operation and trade.

Given the pre-existing ties between the Israeli and Palestinian economies, Israeli-Palestinian peace negotiations had an important 'official' economic dimension from their very beginning. This was further enhanced by the fact that the PLO had partially opted for peace due to its near-bankruptcy following the Gulf War. A 1991 PLO paper on prospective regional co-operation had played a role in the establishment of the Oslo channel.[72] Thus, the economic aspects of peace between Israel and the Palestinians were highly politicized, but already after the second MENA conference in Amman in 1995, many business leaders concluded that, 'the biggest obstacle to development in the region may be the governments themselves.'[73] Very illustrative of the mix of politics and business was the two-year long saga of negotiations between the Histadrut and Palestinian union leaders over repayments of wage deductions to Palestinian labourers. Overshadowed by political demands and closures, the signing of an agreement was cancelled four times. In the face of Palestinian demands of up to NIS 700 million, the Histadrut leadership only under pressure agreed to negotiate at all and paid NIS 4 million by the end of 1995.[74]

The meshing of political and economic issues also made it easier for the PA to assume a major role in Israeli-Palestinian business ties. The casino in Jericho, in which the PA held a 35 per cent-stake, was so popular with Israeli customers (gambling was illegal in Israel) that it remained one of the most successful peace projects until it was damaged and closed during the Al-Aqsa Intifada.[75] Most large-scale peace projects were taken over by the PA or the private businesses of PA officials, inviting corruption, which deterred investors and prevented further projects.[76] Despite the PA's declared support for private sector development, it entertained a number of monopolies controlling Israeli imports into the Territories and became a competitor to local private business.[77] In fact, the PA allowed only two Israeli firms to register in the Territories until the end of 1996.[78]

The most significant initiative in industrial co-operation between Israelis and Palestinians, however, were the joint border industrial estates, intended to create more than 160,000 direct and indirect jobs. Estates were to be located in Jenin, Nablus, Tulkarem, Jericho, and Hebron. Three more zones were to be created in the Gaza Strip, among them the Gaza Industrial Estate (GIE) at Karni and the Rafah/Keren Shalom border park, a high-tech estate jointly developed by the Israeli ISCAR and Dankner groups. Only the GIE began operating before the Al-Aqsa Intifada. The high-tech park Khaddourie near Tulkarem, supposed to assume operations in May 2001, never opened. On the eve of the Intifada, six industrial parks were under construction, with investments totalling $250 million. Israeli companies were attracted to the estates by the promise of cheap labour, as well as the tax exemptions available to investors under the 1995 Investment Promotion Law, updated in 1998, and a top corporate tax rate of 22per cent.[79]

Initially, the estates were to be developed by the two governments. Israel, however, proposed the establishment of Israeli-controlled enclaves making use of cheap labour such as the Erez Industrial Park. After lengthy debates, in response, the PA decided to pursue the establishment of the parks alone and handed over development of most of the estates to the Palestinian Industrial Estates Development Company (PIEDCO), a PADICO-subsidiary.[80] PIEDCO developed the Gaza Industrial Estate (GIE) and held shares in other developers, such as the Nor-

Table 9: Projected Employment in Palestinian Industrial Parks

Industrial Park	Direct Jobs	Indirect Jobs
Jenin Industrial Estate	8,000	12,000
Nablus Industrial Estate	7,500	11,200
Khaddourie IT Industrial Park	1,300	2,000
Jericho Industrial Estate	8,000	12,000
Tarqoumiah Industrial Estate/Hebron	11,500	17,200
Gaza Industrial Estate (GIE)/Karni	8,000	12,000
Rafah/Keren Shalom Industrial Park	20,000	30,200
Total	64,300	96,600

Source: PIEFZA Document ANR20008, Dated 2000/12/11.

thern International and Industrial Company (NIIC), which developed the Jenin and Nablus estates. Other major shareholders in NIIC were the APIC conglomerate, the Arab Bank, and the Jenin-based Fakhoury family, related to the family active in QIZ business in Jordan.[81]

In November 1995, development of the GIE began, but the quarrels between Israelis and Palestinians and internal debates on both sides repeatedly delayed its inauguration.[82] The GIE should have begun operating by late 1996; it officially opened in December 1998. Only two Palestinian-Israeli joint ventures were among the signed 13 contracts.[83] Numerous Israeli companies had expressed their interest but were deterred by the lack of a 'closure-safety' guarantee. Although Israel secured $55 million for a political risk insurance fund, closure-related losses were not covered. In addition, as in Jordan, the EU did not extend its rules of origin to the parks – the United States did – and the resulting impossibility to export duty-free to the EU also deterred investors.[84] Despite this, by March 2000, 34 factories, primarily in textiles, and two distribution warehouses were operating, employing 1,500 workers.[85] According to PIEDCO Assistant General Manager for International Relations, Bunmi Ayeni, almost all projects featured some form of Israeli involvement.[86] Israelis also initiated the construction of bonded warehouses to serve the traffic flowing through the Karni border crossing, although the project was not realized before the Intifada.[87] The crossing itself had been modernized, which raised the cost of transporting goods across the border, leading to a boycott and a ten-day closure of the crossing, after which fees were reduced by 30 per cent in April 1999.[88] On the eve of the Intifada, development of the second phase of the GIE had just been completed, and the Palestinian Industrial Estates and Free Zones Authority (PIEFZA) had moved to encourage investments by taking over half of the wages paid to workers in the GIE.[89] Four companies had begun building their own factories. All foreign ventures, however, closed with the onset of the Intifada.[90]

The delays the GIE had faced also confronted the other industrial zones. The 300ha Jenin Industrial Estate was not approved until December 1999 and construction work did not begin until February 2000, despite plans to open the park in October 1997 and appeals to the Israeli authorities and the IMA from the developing NIIC.[91] A feasibility study for the zone found that there was considerable potential investor demand: 28 interested companies had registered with NIIC by March 1998, but only three of them were Israeli.[92] The $81 million Nablus Industrial Estate (NIE) received approval in April 1999 and attracted interest from 41 mostly domestic companies that wished to re-locate from their locations in residential areas. As was the case with the GIE and the Jenin estate, the NIE feasibility study also explicitly pointed out that 'the QIZ in Irbid and the other QIZs to be designated within Jordan and Egypt will be direct competitors.'[93] Other industrial parks, such as the ones near Hebron and Qalqiliya, seemed to be more attractive to Israeli and foreign investors, but were only in the conceptual stages by September 2000.[94] The development of all zones, however, was overshadowed by the political stalemate. At a business conference in Tel Aviv in July 1998, an investment consultant specializing in the Territories pointed out: 'The last two years have poisoned the atmosphere for investment.'[95]

Joint Ventures

Despite delays and the bad atmosphere, co-operative projects emerged. One of the first was a 1995 joint Israeli-Palestinian detergent manufacturing plant built in the Israeli Erez Industrial Park in the Gaza Strip.[96] In tourism, the Israeli Arava Development Corporation and the Union of Local Authorities each sought to establish tourist trails on ancient caravan routes through Israel and the Territories.[97] The Peaceworks, Inc., a venture founded by the Mexican-Israeli Daniel Lubetzky, successfully marketed Palestinian agricultural produce overseas under names such as 'Moshe Pupik' (Hebrew for 'belly-button') and 'Ali Mishmumken's World Famous Gourmet Foods' ('mishmumken' meaning 'impossible' in Arabic dialect).[98] The Dankner Group, together with General Electric, won the bid to construct the Gaza power plant for the Palestinian Electricity Company in March 1999.[99] However, while some large-scale projects made progress, smaller companies on both sides refrained from co-operation. A business start-up project, co-ordinated by the German Agency for Technical Assistance (GTZ), yielded only one concrete joint venture in IT, which the Palestinian partner terminated before its completion in July 2000.[100]

But high-tech was the field in which investors and entrepreneurs alike showed the greatest interest. In early 1998, the International Finance Corporation (IFC) and the Peres Centre for Peace founded the Technology for Peace Fund to encourage joint ventures. The $100 million fund was managed by the Israeli firm

Evergreen and the Capital Management Corporation, owned by Palestinian businessman Hani Masri, who also represented the PA in Washington.[101] Among the successful examples of co-operation between Palestinians and Israelis in high-tech was the establishment of a Palestinian Siemens branch under Tareq Maayah in Ramallah. Initiated by the Israeli Siemens branch SDC and its general manager, Sam Widerman, in 1997, Maayah, SDC, and the German parent company jointly owned Siemens Ramallah, but collaboration was discontinued when Widerman left SDC in 1998 and Maayah co-ordinated his activities only with the German headquarters henceforth. Widerman's new venture, Visuality Systems, and Maayah's Siemens Ramallah, however, maintained their collaboration.[102]

The Peres Centre for Peace, as well as the Centre for Jewish-Arab Economic Development, was also involved in the development of the Khaddourie park. At the Peres Centre's Economic Peace Conference, held in Tel Aviv in September 2000, just before violence flared in the Territories, eight Palestinian start-ups expressed their interest to establish operations in the zone.[103] Naftali Moser, technology director at the Peres Centre, pointed out that every year some 10,000 Palestinian computer specialists graduated, most of them fluent in English and Hebrew: 'This is where the real potential is.' As a result, Israeli companies such as Oracle or MLL (Malam) were active in the Territories; the latter worked with the Palestinian company Samco and provided hardware for PA offices.[104] ATS, the largest Palestinian IT establishment, represented Oracle in the Territories and carried out its first joint venture with the Israeli Oracle branch on a project for the Israeli Migdal Insurance in 1998. While relations between Israelis and Palestinians were hampered by the facts that most IT engineers were banned from entering Israel and that a breakthrough in IT joint ventures was only pending following the participation of Palestinians in the 2000 Tel Aviv Comdex fair, ATS President Hassan Kassem agreed with Hanan Maoz from the Israeli Oracle branch that 'nothing can harm the business politically.'[105] Ibrahim Barham, Chairman of the Palestinian IT Association (PITA) and employer of 40 engineers in his company, Safad Electrical and Electronics Ltd, represented HP and 3com in the Territories, but in contrast to Kassem, rather competed with the Israeli branches of the international brands since he also sold in Israel.[106]

Several initiatives aimed at training and consolidating collaborative ties underlined the significance of high-tech co-operation. The Palestinian Ministry of Education and the Peres Centre initiated a programme to establish a joint computer education programme in Israeli and Palestinian high schools. The private Global Catalyst Venture Capital Fund, a spin-off of a global initiative undertaken by an American, initiated Schools Online at Middle East (SOLAM) to enhance computer skills of children in 100 Israeli, Israeli Arab, and Palestinian schools until the end of 2000.[107] But high-tech co-operation was only in its initiation phase, when the Al-Aqsa Intifada disrupted most projects and contacts. Close to the Khaddourie Park in the industrial area in Tulkarem, Palestinians torched four Israeli factories that had employed 300 Palestinians. The economic advisor to the Israeli government's co-ordinator for the Territories said that it would 'now be more difficult to persuade Israeli and foreign investors to invest in the high-tech plants in the Tulkarem industrial area.'[108] But mainly it was Palestinian industry which suffered. According to the Palestinian Minister of Industry, Sa'adi al-Kronz, 75 factories in the West Bank and Gaza were destroyed until May 2001. Losses amounted to $20 million.[109]

The Paris Protocol and its Consequences

In trade, the customs union consolidated with the Paris Protocol continued to determine Israeli-Palestinian relations. The Paris Protocol hindered trade and led to the monopolization of trade in the hands of political-economic elites on both sides, increasing consumer prices in the Territories and exacerbating Palestinian dependence on Israeli imports and the Israeli market. Palestinian external trade became totally dependent on Israel. Only in 1998, imports from Israel for the first time decreased significantly, while the share of exports to Israel had risen from 76 per cent of total exports in 1993 to 94.8 per cent in 1998. In contrast, imports from Jordan remained low; exports even decreased. Palestinian exports to Israel dropped in absolute terms in the first two years after 1994. The trade volume of $2 billion was almost entirely directed from Israel to the PA. The Paris Protocol had been expected to introduce some aspects of an independent Palestinian trade policy, to open the Israeli and other regional markets, and to 'provide an immediate stimulus to the Palestinian economy.'[110] However, as an UNCTAD study argued, 'with the advent of the PA and the entry of other countries such as Jordan into trade relations with Israel (and other factors such as border closures), previous conditions of Israeli-Palestinian trade are eroding.'[111] Another UNCTAD study found: 'The difficulties facing the Palestinian economy today result in part from a framework for integration that is deficient, especially insofar as it has inhibited openness to the rest of the world promised by the accords.'[112]

According to Abdel Hafiz Noufal from the Palestinian Ministry of the Economy and Trade, the Joint Economic Committee only met four times in seven years; problems and obstacles were resolved, if at all, on an individual and personal basis.[113] As a result of the difficulties related to the Paris Protocol, attention focused on developing an alternative arrangement as part of the final status negotiations, expected to lead to the conclusion of a FTA.[114] On the ground, however, the situation hardly changed. In retaliation for Israeli closures, the PA instituted an embargo against 20 Israeli products in August 1997, although the ban remained largely ineffective.[115] Israel, on the other hand, refused to allow Palestinian trucks into Israel via the Erez crossing, in response to the Palestinians' refusal to let Israeli trucks enter Gaza via Karni in the dispute over high fees imposed at the modernized crossing. Since Israeli merchants also suffered from the quarrel, FICC Director-General Yossi Shustak intervened and criticized the move.[116] Israel then allowed Palestinian merchants to rent warehouses near the port of Ashdod in an effort to boost imports through the port, possibly in order to ensure the Palestinians' continued dependence on Israeli ports and to undermine the PA's project of building its own seaport at Gaza.[117]

Another result of the dysfunctional Paris Protocol, the Palestinian desire for more economic independence, and the many quarrels between Palestinians and

Israelis, were the new marketing policies in the Territories, introduced in mid-1996 and aimed at strengthening the Palestinian business sector and presenting some peace dividend to the public. The new regulations required all foreign, including Israeli, companies to have a Palestinian marketing agent and their products to be labelled in Arabic. Although the FICC at first protested vehemently and appealed to the Israeli authorities, it soon adapted and helped Israeli companies to implement the new policies. In a meeting between FICC President Gillerman and PA officials, it was agreed that the PA would encourage the establishment of agencies in the form of joint ventures, although the PA insisted that at least 51 per cent of the ventures would be Palestinian-owned. Leading Israeli companies, among them Tnuva, Osem, Tambour, and Elite, quickly appointed Palestinian agents.[113]

The Palestinian agency law also aimed to encourage direct Palestinian imports and to increase the PA's tax revenue.[119] Under the Paris Protocol, import and purchase taxes went to the Israeli Ministry of Finance if an Israeli importer distributed goods in both Israel and the PA; in the case of direct Palestinian imports, customs accrued to the PA. As a result of the new policy, not only did Israeli importers and agents lose market shares, Palestinian merchandise and goods imported to the Territories also began substituting Israeli products, even affecting the Israeli market, since so many Israelis bought goods on the cheap Palestinian border markets. According to an estimate prepared by the Israeli Civil Administration, this trade amounted to over NIS 1.3 billion annually, more than 2 per cent of private consumption in Israel and roughly the equivalent of total official Palestinian exports, which illustrates the inherent threat for Israeli merchants.[120]

Table 10: Palestinian Trade with Israel and Jordan, 1990-1998

	1990	1991	1992	1993	1994	1995	1996	1997	1998
Total Imports (Mio. $)	843	1,139	1,260	1,173	1,075	1,690	2,017	2,164	2,723
Imports from Israel (%)	84.7	85.7	87.7	86.5	85.6	90.0	86.4	83.3	69.0
Imports from Jordan (%)	1.1	0.8	0.8	0.8	0.6	0.5	0.4	1.4	1.4
Total Exports (Mio. $)	231	247	292	234	243	326	340	381	444
Exports to Israel (%)	78.4	76.9	85.2	76.0	84.3	93.9	93.8	93.9	94.8
Exports to Jordan (%)	13.9	15.6	10.0	22.4	12.8	4.5	5.3	4.9	4.9

Sources: UNCTAD, Palestinian Merchandise Trade in the 1990s: Opportunities and Challenges, UNCTAD/GDS/SEU/1, 23 January 1998.

Three categories of Palestinian businessmen secured agencies: firstly, manufacturers who could distribute products through established distributive networks and knew the domestic market well. Secondly, newcomers to the market, who represented international brands in other regional markets, such as the shareholders of PADICO or APIC, secured the most prestigious and lucrative agencies, quickly capturing large market shares. The biggest number of representations, however, went to smaller entrepreneurs who had collaborated with Israelis before. Many of these were only sub-agents for Israeli importers or partners in joint Israeli-Palestinian trading companies. Other Israeli importers simply ignored the law and continued distributing their goods in the Palestinian Territories, which remained possible since Israel controlled the borders and imposed few restrictions on the flow of goods from Israel into the Territories.[121]

The Monopolization of Imports and Subcontracting
The agency law, with its objective to enhance tax revenue for the PA, favoured the larger conglomerates and establishments close to the PA and led to the monopolization of imports and corruption. Israeli customs authorities began investigating the Koor-subsidiary United Steel Mills and Transclal on suspicion of tax fraud by declaring goods imported to Israel as bound for the PA in 1999. PA officials as well as a Gazan businessman were also involved in the deal.[122] Similarly, PA officials and a Palestinian importer sold large quantities of Gillette razor blades in Israel, without the consent of the Israeli importer and without transferring customs taxes to the Israeli authorities. In 1997, Jamil al-Tarifi, PA Minister for Local Government Affairs, worked with his Israeli counterparts to have the border between Jordan and the PA closed for two weeks so that a company owned by his son could proceed to the exclusive non-stop import of cement into the Territories. Muhammad Jerada, adviser to the Minister of Finance, was accused of monopolizing the import of flour through his companies, in collaboration with the Ministry of Supply.[123]

Most such deals involved the Palestinian Commercial Services Co. (PCSC), a government-owned company run by Muhammad Rashid (Khaled Salam), Arafat's economic adviser, which held monopolies in cement, fuel, and tobacco. The PCSC's cement import business began in 1994 with one truckload and soon achieved a market share of 70 per cent in the Territories, where the company marketed the Israeli Nesher cement, although much of it was actually imported from the Jordanian Cement Factories Co. (JCFC). Muhammad Rashid had negotiated the deal with Yossi Ginossar, former head of interrogations of the Israeli General Security Service (GSS) and a businessman who also acted as envoy between Barak and Arafat. Asked about the role of mediators such as Ginossar, PCSC general manager Hassan Salameh declined to confirm Ginossar's involvement but said, 'It is legitimate; this is the way people do business [...] The occupation corrupts the occupier [...] Government deals are special, discreet, and only special people are involved.'[124] Nesher executives repeatedly refused to outline their deal with the PCSC, surrounded by allegations of corruption of PA officials and unfair business practices towards competitors.

A similar deal was struck between the PCSC and the Dankner Group-member Dor Energy over the supply of fuel. Under occupation, the Pedasco consortium of Israel's large fuel companies, Paz, Sonol, and Delek, had held the largest market share, supplying petroleum and equipment directly to gas stations in a contract valid beyond 2000. However, in October 1994, even though no official tender had been issued, Jibril Rajoub's Preventive Security Forces informed all station owners that Dor Energy was now the exclusive supplier and blocked the entry of all Pedasco trucks two days later. The new agreement had been signed by Dor CEO Joseph Antverg and Muhammad Rashid, with the involvement of Yossi Ginossar, the alleged co-ordinator of Rashid's business affairs in Israel, and Shmuel Goren, former Israeli Co-ordinator of Activities in the Territories and director at Dor Chemicals, against both of whom Pedasco requested investigations. Another Israeli go-between was Ovadia Koko, senior partner in the Shefer and Levy fuel transport company, which shared the transportation of Dor's supplies to the PA with the Yiftah Co., whose director pointed out: 'It is Middle Eastern economics. Nothing works without baksheesh [...] Business there runs smoothly, everyone gets a piece; the people in power receive percentages.'[125] Although Dor's contract was renewed twice in 1997 and in 2000, however, the Dankner Group had to sell the company under orders from the Israeli Cartels Authority in 2000. Dor Energy as well as Dor Gas became part of Delek, after legal proceedings were opened against Dor Energy senior executives over allegations of forged invoices over NIS 12 million. In January 1999, a Tel Aviv court had already rejected Dor's claim that its relations with the PA rested on 'legitimately bribing top PA officials.'[126]

Unipal, controlled by APIC and the PCSC, received a favourable import licence from the PA so that it could compete against the Israeli cigarette producer Dubek, hitherto the main supplier. An Israeli importer claimed that Rashid had approached him in order to establish a joint import monopoly, with Ginossar receiving a 5 per cent share from both sides. Dubek later agreed upon an arrangement with the PCSC, by which the PCSC imported Dubek cigarettes from Greece. Other PA officials winning tenders and import licences included Nabil Shaath, whose Egyptian company Team, run by his son, imported computers and won 92 per cent of all commissions from his Ministry of Planning and International Co-operation, or Yasser Abbas, the son of Abu Mazen, and Sami Rablawi, one of the top officials in the Palestinian Ministry of Finance, whose joint company Paltech imported consumer electronics.

In Gaza, the equivalent to the PCSC was Sharikat al-Bahr (Sea Co.), run by Hashen Hussein Hashem Abu Nada, another economic adviser to Arafat, and Ramzi Khoury, Arafat's office director, which operated on receiving commissions for import deals with Israelis.[127] As Hussam Khader, PLC representative from Nablus, said:

> They cut up the pie among themselves. The Palestinian leaders thought that our economy was some sort of inheritance due them and their children. Every honcho got himself a fat slice of the imports into the Authority. One got the fuel, another got the cigarettes, yet another the lottery, and his crony

the flour. Gravel is a monopoly belonging directly to the security apparatuses, and they earn a fortune from it that finances their operations.[128]

As the involvement of Ginossar and others clearly illustrated, Israelis in both politics and business benefited from the centralization of economic power in the PA and from monopolistic deals. According to Housing and Construction Holding Co. (HCH) Deputy CEO Amit Segev – the HCH subsidiary Lime and Stone Production had a virtual monopoly in the PA market – there were 'certain ways of doing business in the PA: You need to get the blessing for a deal from the PA; they tell at what price you sell, to whom to sell.'[129]

Beyond the large-scale trade operations controlled by the PA, most of the trade between Israel and the PA was merchandise in the form of semi-finished products manufactured in subcontracting arrangements. The Palestinian industries engaged in subcontracting were usually the larger establishments and those active in the more advanced sectors, but their financial capacities were too limited to market goods directly in Israel. With the shift of Israeli manufacturing operations to Jordan, it was these potential industrial leaders and exporters who suffered most or adapted by moving to Jordan themselves.[130] Many of the smaller Palestinian establishments were also forced into trade and subcontracting relations with Israelis as their only choice for survival. Thus, Palestinian stone and marble factories, one of the most important Palestinian industries with a 3 per cent contribution to GDP, sold 25 per cent of their production to Israelis, supplying the materials for the expansion of settlements.[131]

The most significant sector of subcontracting was the textiles industry, which employed 65,000 workers and contributed 15 per cent of the Palestinian manufacturing output in 1999. However, only six Palestinian companies exported abroad, while most establishments worked for Israeli companies.[132] Shoe manufacturing, for example, was located mainly in Hebron, and supplied half of the entire production for the Israeli market in arrangements such as the one between the Israeli Kibbutz firm Dafna-Harlata and the Tossetti Shoe Factory.[133] In the Gaza Strip and other West Bank towns, textiles manufacturers sew clothes for Israeli firms. The main problem facing these companies was less the impact of the peace process than the concurrent liberalization of the Israeli market, with increasing competition from cheap Asian imports since the protectionist Israeli trade regime was gradually dismantled after 1995.[134] Those companies manufacturing for export under subcontracting arrangements with Israelis were harmed by the move of many Israeli companies to Jordan after the establishment of QIZ operations there.[135] Palestinians from inside the Green Line, who had previously worked in subcontracting arrangements, often moved their operations to West Bank towns such as Jenin or Tulkarem after 1993, although many of them subsequently either closed down under the impact of closures or moved on to establish factories in Jordan.[136] Thus, while co-operation in industry and trade favoured the large conglomerates and the political-economic elites on both sides, smaller Palestinian companies in particular suffered from the consequences of the unequal relationship between the Israeli and Palestinian economies.

Palestinian-Jordanian Co-operation

Three Dimensions of Palestinian-Jordanian Relations

Palestinian-Jordanian business relations involved three dimensions. Firstly, the big Jordanian merchant and business families – many of them of Palestinian origin – were engaged in the large conglomerates set up to further economic development in the Territories. The Palestinian G7 resident in Jordan, for example, dominated PADICO. The Jordanian-Palestinian Consolidated Contractors Co. (CCC) likewise took part in many projects in the PA. Another Jordanian-Palestinian company set up by the G7 was the Jerusalem Development and Investment Company (JEDICO), which tried to prevent purchases of Arab property by Israelis and American Jews in East Jerusalem.[137] Similarly, a joint Palestinian-Jordanian marketing company was to be formed in 1998, working towards increasing the volume of trade and developing new prospects for collaboration.[138] In mid-2000, there were even plans to set up a joint Palestinian-Jordanian industrial zone in Jericho, after a delegation of Jordanian businessmen had participated in an industrial fair and conference in Hebron. The project, however, was then stalled due to the new Intifada.[139]

Secondly, trade relations between Palestinian and Jordanian companies and exports to the respective other market were often entertained by smaller enterprises. Jordanian firms considered the Territories their natural market and a supplement, if not an alternative, to the Iraqi market. Palestinian companies saw Jordan alongside Egypt as the most likely destinations for their products beyond the Israeli market. Most of these companies, similarly to the large business families, had family ties across the river Jordan, which made a cross-border engagement a natural enterprise. Trade here involved mainly Jordanian imports of stone from Bethlehem and Hebron and exports of textiles, foodstuff, cleaning materials, and plastics.[140] An exception rather than the rule were engagements such as the involvement of the multimedia company Rama International in Jordan. After its success in the Territories, Rama shifted its attention to Jordan following the outbreak of the new Intifada and bought a start-up in Amman. On the basis of his conviction that Palestinians and Jordanians could complement each other and attract outsourcing programming contracts, Rama founder Issa Eways soon also teamed up with another Jordanian company.[141]

Thus, it was the third dimension of Palestinian-Jordanian relations that achieved the greatest success. Jordanian government-controlled companies engaged in trade deals, exporting to the Palestinian Territories, often making use of their contacts to Israeli authorities and companies alike and involving them. Most significant in this field was the export deal the Jordanian Cement Factories Company (JCFC) entertained in collaboration with the Israeli Nesher cement producer and the Palestinian Commercial Services Co. (PCSC). After a trade agreement between the PA and Jordan had been signed in May 1995, the first shipments were in steel and cement. Both goods were exempted from customs under the pact, although Israel immediately imposed a limit of 15 truckloads a day on non-Israeli cement imports to the Territories, in order to protect Nesher, which had hitherto held a virtual monopoly in the Palestinian market.[142] Transportation across the river Jordan was problematic and expensive. The bridge could only hold 25 tonnes at a time, and the back-to-back transportation rule applied at first. Nevertheless, the JCFC benefited greatly from a construction boom in the West Bank and in 1996 concluded an agreement with the PA over the export of 400,000 tonnes annually until 2001.[143] In 1998, the JCFC incurred a loss of $2.6 million, after a 12 per cent drop in local construction activity and Israeli restrictions on exports. In the context of the company's partial privatization and modernization, and thanks due to its exports to the PA, however, the JCFC then realized a net profit of JD 12.7 million for the first six months of 1999, a 167 per cent improvement over the same period the preceding year. Exports rose by more than 50 per cent.[144]

The PCSC, which imported Nesher cement from Israel exclusively, became the Palestinian agent for the JCFC as well. The calculation was simple. While the PA had a demand of 2.3 million tonnes of cement annually, it did not produce any. Nesher met the demands of the Israeli market with a supply of 5.5 million tonnes. The JCFC needed only 2.3 million tonnes to meet local demand, so that it could export the remainder of its total production of 4.5 million tonnes. A deal was struck between the three companies, by which Nesher's virtual monopoly in the Palestinian market was preserved in that it bought and re-sold JCFC cement in the Territories. All three companies benefited considerably. By the outbreak of the Al-Aqsa Intifada, the JCFC was selling 400,000 tonnes annually each to the PCSC and directly in the Israeli market.[145]

Trade Relations

Trade negotiations between Jordan and the PA in 1995 aimed high, with talks about the creation of a free zone in the Jordan Valley and the conclusion of an eventual free trade agreement (FTA). However, the Jordanian authorities failed in their attempt to involve Israel in the talks and to conclude a pact consistent with both sides' separate agreements with Israel.[146] Apart from the JCFC's success in the Palestinian market, trade between the two entities hardly evolved and remained hindered by a number of obstacles and difficulties. During a visit of a Palestinian delegation to Amman in November 1996, Said Haifa, director of the Palestinian Trade Promotion Corporation (PTPC), said that the corporation had issued $20 million worth of import licences. However, only $3 million worth of goods had actually been imported from Jordan. Both he and FJCC President Haidar Murad called for closer co-operation and co-ordination between the private sectors in both countries.[147]

Vested interests often favoured Israeli over Jordanian exporters; and Jordanian manufacturers lacked adequate marketing techniques. The main problem, however, was that Israel remained a central player in trade relations between Jordan and the PA, imposing tariffs, standards, and other barriers.[148] Regular talks between Jordanians and Palestinians were held, seeking to alleviate the obstacles merchants faced, but the outlook of trade remained unchanged.[149] In July 1998, the Jordanian-Palestinian Economic Committee, comprising the presidents of the Jordanian and Palestinian Chambers of Commerce and Industry, called on Israel to remove all

Table 11: Jordanian-Palestinian Trade, 1995-1998

Year	Jordanian exports (Mio. JD)	Jordanian imports (Mio. JD)
1995	1.7	10.4
1996	6.8	25.1
1997	13.1 (Jordanian origin) 4.3 (transit/other origin)	18.1
1998 (January-July)	8.3 (Jordanian origin) 2.1 (transit/other origin)	9.8

Source: UNDP and RSS, Peace Follow-Up Unit, Follow-Up Report on the Transportation Agreement between Jordan and Israel in the Peace Process, Report No. 10, February 1999.

impediments hindering the flow of goods. It also called for further co-ordination and the implementation of signed agreements between the two parties, after a successful first trade exhibition of Jordanian products in Gaza.[150]

Israeli obstacles were considered to be aimed at keeping the Palestinian market under Israeli control. The difficulties related to trade reinforced the widespread feeling in Amman that the anticipated peace dividend had not materialized. According to JTA Chairman Kamal Kakish, Israel was aware that 'any exporting from Jordan will decrease the size of Israel's exports' and thus introduced a variety of trade barriers. These discouraged exporters such as the Amman-based Metalco Heating Systems, whose export manager said the prospect of inspections for all 48 models of its boilers was 'a deterrent.' In addition, as Rashed Dawarzah from El-Zay Readywear pointed out, 'No one has adequate information concerning tariffs and what it takes to export the product.' A 1998 report from the Jordanian Ministry of Industry indicated that Jordanian exports to the PA totalled only $7 million for the first seven months of 1998, which was already a 28 per cent-increase over the same period the previous year.[151]

Israel kept emphasizing that the real problem were the similarities between the Palestinian and Jordanian economies and the competition between them. As a result, in 1998, Israel finally gave in and exempted about 3,000 products from customs, 75 per cent of those goods for which Jordan had requested exemptions.[152] Despite the approval, Jordan was held waiting until the expansion of the so-called A1 list until 2000, although the United States harshly criticized Israel for not implementing the exemptions, which should have been approved and put into practice as early as 1996.[153] Similarly, it was only in 1999 that Israel agreed to negotiations over the introduction of door-to-door transportation between Jordan and the PA. Only for a few days in 2000 just before the new Intifada, direct deliveries actually took place.[154] A new agreement was signed between Israel and the PA, which further expanded the A1 list to include 1,300 items and set a ceiling for the value of each item imported at a total of $20 million a year.[155]

According to one Jordanian businessman, virtually 'everybody' at some point tried to enter the Palestinian market. However, only those Jordanian entrepreneurs, who also had ties to Israel or were engaged in exporting to overseas destinations, were successful. The reason for this lay in the fact that Jordanians had to choose between the Iraqi and the Palestinian markets due to the continued Iraqi boycott of the Palestinian economy. Only those exporters who did not depend on the Iraqi market because of their overseas ties or their relations to Israel could afford the risk of trying to enter the Palestinian market and could hope to successfully obtain entry permits and licences from the Israeli authorities.[156] Those merchants also represented less of a threat to Palestinian manufacturers. The latter were reluctant to allow competing Jordanian products of similar quality into their domestic market and were often active alongside Palestinian agents for Israeli companies in maintaining trade barriers between Jordan and the PA over fears of Jordanian competition, according to JEDCO Assistant Director-General Moayyad Samman.[157]

In meetings, however, Jordanian and Palestinian businessmen alike called for the removal of Israeli obstacles hindering the flow of goods. ACI President Abu Hassan, for example, said during a meeting in April 2000, 'we should not succumb to Israeli policy which put obstacles and hampers the flow of goods between Jordan and the Palestinian Territories. The government should intensify its efforts to remove all obstacles that weaken the flow of goods between the two sides.' Hashim Natsheh, Deputy Director of the Palestinian Chambers of Trade and Industry, echoed his demands.[158] However, as Gadi Sassower, a forwarder active in both Israel and Jordan and a participant in the negotiations of the Israeli-Jordanian transportation agreement, pointed out, the Jordanian authorities had in fact always been glad to keep their dealings with Israel and the PA apart. In doing so, the Jordanian government could use its influence on Israel directly in order to increase its market share in the Territories, without having to grant reciprocity to Palestinian merchants and exporters.[159] In fact, while the Jordanians often argued that apart from Israeli trade barriers, it was the Palestinians who feared competition, Jordanian manufacturers alike preferred not to open their domestic market to Palestinian competitors.

Competition and Transportation

Competition between Palestinian and Jordanian producers hindered trade between the two entities in many sectors. For example, before the peace process, Palestinian pharmaceutical manufacturers had not been able to enter Arab markets, and the Arab boycott had often been used as a pretext to protect local industries. Following the establishment of the PA, the Palestinian Ministry of Health permitted Egyptian companies to enter the Gaza and wanted to similarly allow

Jordanian manufacturers to export to the West Bank. Jordan, however, did not grant reciprocal entry to its market to the Palestinians. As a result, the issue of mutual pharmaceutical exports was postponed indefinitely. An attempted merger of the Palestinian market leader, Jerusalem Pharmaceuticals, with the leading Jordanian al-Hikma, owned by the Jordanian-Palestinian Dawarzah family, also failed.[160]

In detergents, Jordanian companies managed to enter the West Bank market, but Palestinians failed to capture a share of the Jordanian market. As AIC Chairman Nakhleh Jubran said, Jordanian producers benefited from lower production and delivery costs.[161] In food, Israeli companies imported Jordanian products alongside Egyptian and Turkish goods and sold those in the Territories. Consequentially, the Israeli-Jordanian list of tradable goods even included some products, which could not be directly exported from Jordan to the PA but were clearly intended for the Palestinian market. Mazen Sinokrot called this a 'joint effort by Jordanians and Israelis to suffocate the Palestinians.' Jordan at the same time refused to permit Palestinian products to enter its market. At a 1998 meeting between the Palestinian Food Producers Association and its Jordanian counterpart, Sinokrot as association chairman offered to lobby the PA for free trade in foodstuffs, if the Jordanian manufacturers agreed to do the same in Jordan; the Jordanians declined.[162] Overall, Jordanian products coming into the West Bank and Gaza under the guise of Israeli-Jordanian trade threatened to replace Palestinian goods and undermine domestic industries.[163] Despite the difficulties, the actual volume of trade surpassed $200 million, a significant share of which was unofficial merchandise through smuggling and tourist purchases.[164]

But this was not enough to achieve the market diversification, which could have increased competition and trade efficiency for the Palestinians and opened up further markets. Jordan was considered a potential 'gateway for the Palestinian economy to the Arab Mashriq and the Gulf states.' But official Palestinian exports had dropped from $182 million in 1982 to $32 million in 1990 and were down to $20 million in 1997 and 1998. Imports meanwhile increased from a level historically below $10 million to $38 million in 1998. The main difficulty facing Palestinian exporters was transportation. From Gaza, exports went through the Erez checkpoint and after that in a convoy accompanied by Israeli security patrols. The only commercial vehicles allowed to carry goods from the PA to Jordan were the 'green trucks,' 'a fleet of ageing, bare-backed and stripped trucks [...] with Israeli security clearance to cross into Jordan.' Exports from the West Bank had to undergo three security and customs inspections by the Israeli, Palestinian, and Jordanian authorities and were similarly subjected to back-to-back transportation. Due to the complex procedures, imports were far more frequent than Palestinian exports. In 1998, a monthly average of 2,822 truckloads was exported through all crossing points, compared to 14,476 imported. Both imports and exports, however, faced lengthy inspections, adding to costs and sometimes damaging the good transported. Only trade in cement enjoyed several advantages with regard to transportation, which contributed to the flourishing cement trade and explained the overall significance of cement in Jordanian-Palestinian trade.[165]

Table 12: Truck Traffic between Jordan and the PA, 1997

Crossing Point	Type of Good	Number of Trucks
King Hussein Bridge	Jordanian exports: cement	4,103
	Jordanian imports: other goods	1,375
Prince Muhammad Bridge	Jordanian imports: vegetable oil	357
	Palestinian imports: various goods	8,393

Source: UNDP and RSS, Peace Follow-Up Unit, Follow-Up Report on the Transportation Agreement between Jordan and Israel in the Peace Process, Report No. 10, February 1999.

Some of those obstacles were remnants from the military occupation. Most measures hindering the Palestinian external trade with Jordan, however, were only introduced with the signing of the peace accords and the Paris Protocol and clearly favoured Israeli importers over Palestinian merchants.[166] The Israeli-Jordanian transportation agreement superseded the regulations of the Palestinian-Jordanian transportation agreement, signed in June 1995. A follow-up study concluded that despite the clarity of the regulations, most had not been implemented properly.[167] Among the difficulties, which hindered the flow of goods between the PA and Jordan, were the difficulties to obtain visas; high taxes and fees at the borders, where working hours and days were restricted; the general limitations of back-to-back transportation; and the specific instructions to transport goods only on open trucks and to use crates with specific measures. The 'green trucks,' in total only 350, all dated from before 1967 and could only cross into Jordan once a week. On the Jordanian and Palestinian sides, obstacles had their origin chiefly in the lack of co-ordination and information.

Trade between Jordanians and Palestinians, despite the great interest both sides showed publicly, thus remained 'extremely limited.' The reasons lay both in the competition between Jordanian and Palestinian manufacturers as well as in Israeli obstacles and barriers particularly relating to traffic.[168] Co-operation clearly favoured the large Jordanian-Palestinian businesses involved in investments in the Territories and the Jordanian government-controlled companies, which enjoyed advantages over smaller private enterprises and could thus dominate exports. The Jordanian-Palestinian competition in trade as well as Israel's control over the borders and its involvement in all agreements, at the same time, ensured that Israel could not be sidelined and that Israeli entrepreneurs preserved their dominance over the Palestinian market as well as their market position in Jordan.

Table 13: Costs of Palestinian Imports from Jordan

Description	Amount charged incl. VAT (NIS)	Amount charged incl. VAT (NIS)
Jordanian side		
Transportation to King Hussein Bridge (JD 70)	406	
Clearance formalities of KHB (JD 70)	406	
Palestinian/Israeli side		
Coordinating fees (PA)	120	
Allenby Bridge entry fees (Israel)	139	
Allenby Bridge entry fees (PA)	125	
Allenby Bridge usage fees (PA)	117	
Off landing/loading charges of Allenby Bridge	292	
Bank charges	29	
Clearance formalities		486
Inland transportation		700
Attendance charges		324
Total	1,634	1,510
17% VAT	256	1,766
Grand Total NIS ($1 = NIS 4)		3,400

Source: UNCTAD, Cooperation Between the Palestinian Authority, Egypt and Jordan to Enhance Subregional Trade-Related Services, UNCTAD/GDS/SEU/3; 14 February 2000.

Overall, thus, business co-operation amongst Israelis, Jordanians, and Palestinians, clearly favoured Israeli businesspeople in the regional equation and large enterprises with political contacts in all three entities. Dysfunctional and insufficient agreements as well as the obstructive policies of all three governments hampered industrial co-operation and trade. Trade relations, in particular, were dominated by the large conglomerates and helped by former or current government officials, inviting corruption and mismanagement. In industry, co-operation also favoured the Israeli side and the larger companies in Jordan and the Palestinian Territories. Israeli entrepreneurs contributed know-how, technology, and management, their Jordanian and Palestinian counterparts, cheap manpower. The Palestinians were the big losers of Israeli-Jordanian industrial collaboration, as were most ordinary

Palestinians and Jordanians, for whom prices increased and who shared little of the promised and eagerly awaited peace dividend. Political connections and the tight interrelations between political and economic elites in all three entities significantly contributed to the evolution of business ties favouring these elites.

5

Business Leaders and Political Elites

This chapter outlines the connections between economic and political elites in Israel, Jordan, and the Palestinian Territories. In all three countries, inter-elite relations were extremely tight and played a significant role in the overall development of economic and political affairs in each of the three entities during the peace process. In Israel, entrepreneurs played an important part in preparing the ground for the peace process, but were hardly involved in pursuing the process further once the overarching objective of gaining access to new overseas markets had been achieved. Both in Jordan and under the PA, a new stratum of economic elites emerged, which established close ties to the political leadership. Political and economic elites were united in their taking advantage of the peace process and of the new business opportunities.

Israel

Business, Politics and the Military

Three dimensions of the tight inter-connections between political, military, and economic elites characterized the Israeli 'peace' economy: firstly, the generally fluid structure of inter-elite movements, with many retired government officials and army generals moving into business, as businesspeople moved into politics; secondly, the role businesspeople took on as emissaries for Israeli governments; and thirdly, formal and informal mechanisms and institutions involving entrepreneurs in the peace process. Despite the concurrent liberalization of the economy and the demise of the Histadrut's influence, inter-elite ties remained close, although they grew shadowier at the same time. Between 1996 and 1999, one in ten Knesset delegates was interrogated by the police over suspicions of corruption-related crimes, among them Prime Minister Netanyahu and Arieh Deri, leader of the third-strongest Shas party. In Transparency International's 'Corruption Perception Index,' Israel continuously slipped from rank 14 in 1996 to rank 22 in 2001.[1]

One good example of elite movements between business and politics was Netanyahu's mentor, Moshe Arens. A former Foreign Minister and Minister of

Defence, he became Deputy Chairman of the Israel Corporation after the Labour victory in the elections of 1992. Arens then returned to politics as Acting Chairman of the Likud in 1997.[2] Moshe Shahal, Labour Minister of Energy under Rabin and Peres, began managing a $400 million investment fund for joint Middle East economic projects for Merrill Lynch, the Peres Centre for Peace, and Clal, after his retirement from politics in 1996. In addition, Shahal was allegedly engaged in a venture to set up a private power plant in Jordan, while serving as an adviser to Minister of Public Security Ben-Ami. He was also involved in a deal whereby the PA would become a partner in one of the Israeli fuel companies.[3] Shlomo Ben-Ami himself had earlier chaired Koor's 'peace enterprise' and had advocated 'open-minded co-operation with Palestinian businessmen' in this function.[4]

Not only on the top-level were movements from politics into business and vice versa frequent. Otniel Schneller, who had participated in the negotiations over the Israeli-Jordanian transportation agreement as a representative from the Ministry of Transportation, became General Manager of Comgro Ltd. This import and export firm operated trade offices in Amman and participated in infrastructural joint ventures in Jordan. Yoram Katz, employed in the Advisory for Arab Affairs in the Prime Minister's Office from 1963 until 1982 and responsible for the Labour party's electoral promotion efforts among Israeli Arabs in 1992, established a small firm engaged in trade with both Palestinians and Jordanians following his political career.[5] Yoram Gabbai, head of the Israeli negotiating team on fiscal issues in Paris and former head of the state revenue administration, became chairman of Bank Ha'Poalim's portfolio management subsidiary. Overall, most members of the Paris Protocol negotiating team had been drawn from Israel's universities and public institutions, although the Paris Protocol advisory team co-ordinated closely with the IMA.[6]

The traditionally close ties between the army and politics, especially the Labour party, was illustrated in the movement of several former chiefs of staff into politics, most prominent among them Prime Ministers Yitzhak Rabin and Ehud Barak, or Amnon Lipkin-Shahak, Minister under Barak and his special emissary. Oded Tira, IMA President since 1999, had been a Brigadier-General prior to his career in industry. Gili Deckel, General Manager of Jordan Gateway Projects, had formerly also been a senior military official and had participated in the Israeli-Jordanian negotiations, during which he developed the idea to establish a joint industrial park.[7] David Kolitz, CEO of the Elul Group, FICC Vice-President, and a former member of the IMA presidency, had earlier been a special assistant to the Minister of Defence during the Camp David negotiations with Egypt. In addition to Kolitz, five out of seven leading executives of his group had formerly been high-ranking officers in the Israel Defence Forces (IDF).[8] Kolitz described himself as a close personal friend of Prime Ministers Rabin and Peres and said he had always been very active on the 'political side of Israeli business'; he had also participated in all MENA conferences. Together with Yossi Maiman, Director of the investment group Merhav, Kolitz and another friend of Rabin's, who had worked with him in a political function and was later active in co-operative ventures in Jordan, acted as emissaries for Prime Minister Rabin. The group was sent to Amman several times both before and after the signing of the peace treaty. According to Kolitz, the group's task was purely political, and although many business ideas were floated, none yielded any concrete results. Elul later re-oriented itself and expanded especially in Asia.[9]

Delta Chairman Dov Lautman acted as a special envoy for regional economic development under Prime Ministers Rabin and Peres from 1993 to 1996. He also became Chairman of the Peres Centre for Peace. According to Lautman, who had been IMA President at the beginning of the Oslo peace process, he, FICC President Gillerman and Koor CEO Gaon were particularly active in the pro-peace movement. Like Kolitz, Lautman considered himself very active on the 'public side of business,' first as IMA President, then as one of the leading proponents of peace in his role as one of the foremost actors in Israeli-Jordanian co-operation.[10] Lautman had also been touted as a potential leader of the Israeli delegation to the Paris economic talks with the Palestinians. Eli Hurwitz, Director of Teva Pharmaceuticals, Israel's largest drug company, and another former IMA President, was actually offered the job, but declined 'due to the extensive time commitment it required.'[11]

Benny Gaon, Koor CEO until the conglomerate's transformation, was one of the most active businesspeople promoting links with the Arab worlds. He not only repeatedly attempted to bring together leading Israeli executives with PA President Arafat, but also became Chairman of the Israel-Jordan Chamber of Commerce and chaired a special commission on links with the Arab world as a member of the IMA presidency from 1999 on. Gaon also openly supported Shimon Peres during the 1996 elections, in which Peres lost to Netanyahu.[12] Michael Yungreis, director of the Israel-Jordan Chamber of Commerce, had previously been an official at the Ministry of Finance, where he had been involved in negotiations with the Palestinians. Yungreis pointed out that he met many businesspeople and government officials during the Milu'im, the annual army reserve duty. Here, and during the regular conscription service, many friendships were bolstered that were maintained for a lifetime, thus strengthening inter-elite connections between politics and business.[13]

Gadi Sassower, J. Sassower managing director, pointed out that every Israeli forwarder, if not every Israeli private sector entrepreneur, had personal contacts to relevant government officials, often originating in common military service, family connections, or neighbourly relations. Sassower himself, a former President of the Haifa Chamber of Commerce and long-standing President of the Israeli Shippers Association, was closely acquainted with the Director-General of the Ministry of Transportation. During a phone call to his friend, Sassower complained that the Israeli negotiating team on transportation with Jordan involved only one 'private sector' representative from the government-owned Zim shipping company. He was promptly nominated to participate in the negotiations.[14]

Alon Dankner, brother of Shmuel Dankner, the head of the family-owned Dankner Group, and himself involved in the business of one of Israel's richest families, played a role in a number of political affairs, including the incorporation of the Gesher party into the Likud. He also cultivated a friendship with the then-head of the Jordanian Special Forces and eldest son of King Hussein, Abdullah, who acceded to the throne in 1999. The two had met through one of Dankner's Jordanian friends and business associates.[15] Oded Ben-Haim, responsible for the international relations of the Dankner Group, joined the group in early 2000 after a career in the Foreign Ministry. In his last position there, he had been head of the Israeli trade office in Qatar, which was opened as an outcome of the peace process and the MENA conferences.[16] Stef Wertheimer, Chairman of the ISCAR Group, was one of the most influential private businessmen in the country and owned a significant share in the IDB Holding Co. He had been a member of the Knesset from 1977 to 1981 for the Dash party, a party of the liberal left, and remained active in promoting a greater export-orientation of the Israeli economy. His economic adviser, Avraham Asheri, had formerly been CEO of the Israel Discount Bank, and a Director-General of the Ministry of Finance. Yossi Vardi, known for his involvement in many Israeli IT projects, had been economic adviser to Shimon Peres when the latter was Foreign Minister under Rabin. Vardi had collaborated with Rafi Benvenisti, then a special advisor to the Minister of Finance, Avraham Shohat, and later a special adviser to the Minister of Regional Co-operation, Shimon Peres, in the preparation of Israel's official publications for the MENA summits.

Businessmen as Envoys and Mediators

Several of the aforementioned businesspeople were linked to one another in initiatives such as their common membership in the Minister for Regional Co-operation's Advisory Council, created alongside the Ministry after Barak's electoral victory in 1999. Members included Dov Lautman, Benny Gaon, Avraham Asheri, Oded Tira, and Yossi Vardi. Other members of the council were Intel Chairman Dov Fruman, Bank Leumi President and CEO, Galia Maor, El Al Chairman Yosef Chechanover, ex-IMA President Dan Propper, as well as further representatives from large private sector groups, Bank of Israel-governor Yaacov Frenkel and Uri Savir, a Labour member of the Knesset and President of the Peres Centre for Peace. A very similar group of top executives had taken part in Gaon's efforts to organize a meeting with Yasser Arafat. Likewise, high-profile delegations frequently visited Jordan. Gaon, FICC President Gillerman, and Yossi Vardi, for example, attended the Jordanian Dead Sea IT conference in March 1999.[17] Lautman, Gillerman, Jonathan Kolber, Gaon's successor as Koor CEO, and several others were also represented on the board of the Peres Centre for Peace.

Even more influential, however, were businessmen acting behind the scenes. Daniel Abraham, a Jewish-American millionaire and the largest donor to US President Clinton, had his business interests in Israel, including shares in Koor and Teva, looked after by the law firm of former Israeli President Haim Herzog's son. He was so well-acquainted with many Israeli and regional politicians that he managed to organize a private meeting between Ehud Barak and Yasser Arafat in Barak's house in September 2000. Abraham was one of the main contributors to a European fund that underwrote Yossi Beilin's meetings with Abu Mazen and the secret conferences that paved the way for the Oslo Accords, and became the main contributor to the Peres Centre for Peace. Abraham also supported Rabin, Peres, and Barak in their bids to become Prime Minister. In 1998, his 'Centre for Middle East Peace and Economic Cooperation' published a proposal for the establishment of desalination plants in Hadera and Gaza, which was promptly introduced as a bill in the Knesset by Yossi Beilin and Likud MK Meir Shitrit. Further than that, Abraham had conveyed messages between Hafez al-Assad and Yitzhak Rabin. Some analysts, however, viewed his involvement sceptically: 'When Ehud Barak wants to send an important message to Arafat, he goes to Yossi Ginossar not Daniel Abraham.'[18]

Abraham's role mainly on the left of the Israeli political spectrum was mirrored by businessman Ron Lauder's involvement on the right. However, Yossi Ginossar and his Israeli colleagues were indeed more influential. Several former officials from the Civil Administration, the army, and the security services had business interests in the Territories and were involved in political contacts between Israel and the PA. Among these were the former Co-ordinator of the Civil Administration's Activities in the Territories, David Kimche, who also had a seat on the board of the Peres Centre, and the former head of the Civil Administration, General Danny Rothschild. Ginossar's ties with Arafat and the PCSC, for which Ginossar acted as its Israeli agent and mediator on the fuel and cement deals, were widely known. He was also involved in the establishment of the Jericho casino and helped his former colleagues from the General Security Service to gain a concession to design the security facilities for the casino.

According to PA Minister and negotiator Saeb Erekat, the connection was established when Prime Minister Rabin first sent Ginossar as his official liaison to Arafat in 1994. Weekly meetings between Ginossar and Arafat took place until Rabin's assassination. Ginossar, also Chairman of the public building company Amidar, was one of only five senior Israeli officials involved in private meetings with PA President Arafat. Contacts had first been made through Daniel Abraham's associate, Steve Cohen, the director of the Centre for Middle East Peace and Economic Cooperation, during the 1980s. Ginossar maintained the link not only for Prime Minister Rabin, but also for Barak and Sharon, playing a 'very crucial role in the liaison between the Barak government and the PA.' He also joined the Israeli negotiating team at Camp David shortly before the new Intifada in 2000, albeit officially as an American delegate. Ariel Sharon, with whom Ginossar had maintained contact since the 1970s, sent him with a message to Yasser Arafat. Ginossar then introduced to Arafat Sharon's most trusted aide, his son Omri. Besides Ginossar, the businessman and former Co-ordinator of the Civil Administration's Activities in the Territories, Shlomo Gazit, also acted as personal envoy for Shimon Peres. Gazit, however, claimed that he did not have any business interests in the PA.[19] Another businessman carrying messages from Prime Minister Barak to Arafat was Yitzhak Segev, a retired military governor. In August 1999, Arafat agreed to receive Segev because of the latter's business interests in the Territories, according to Palestinian officials, while he declined to meet Israeli Minister of the Environment Dalia Itzik.[20] The only Prime Minister, who did not have any businessman as his liaison, was Binyamin Netanyahu.

Formal Mechanisms of Influencing Peace

Within the political arena, it was Shimon Peres who was engaged most in furthering the peace process and its economic dimension. Apart from his 1993 book on the 'new Middle East' and his role as Foreign Minister and Prime Minister until 1996, Peres founded the Peres Centre for Peace and became Minister of Regional Co-operation following Barak's electoral victory in 1999. This ministry was specifically created for Peres, whom Barak tried to prevent from influencing the overall direction of the peace process.[21] It was located in Tel Aviv, far away from the centres of power in Jerusalem, and had only about 15 officials. Revolving entirely around Peres' personality and vision, most of its regional co-operation projects did not make it beyond the conceptual stages by the time Peres left the ministry after Ariel Sharon became Prime Minister in 2001. The ministry drew on the resources of the Peres Centre as well as on an inter-ministerial committee, which had been formed in 1993. This committee involved Rafi Benvenisti, then adviser to Minister of Finance Avraham Shohat and later Peres' adviser at the Ministry of Regional Co-operation; Peres' former economic adviser Yossi Vardi; private consultant June Dilevsky; Mayor Admon and Dan Catarivas from the Ministry of Finance; and Gabby Bar, head of the Middle East and North Africa desk at the Ministry of Trade and Industry. The committee had originally prepared Israel's publications and lists of projects for the MENA conferences. Like the ministry, however, it remained without much influence and was particularly sidelined under Netanyahu between 1996 and 1999.[22]

The Peres Centre, established after the 1996 elections, was somewhat more successful in its efforts. Its most tangible activities, supervised by Prof. Samuel Pohoryles, a long-time senior official at the Ministry of Agriculture, were in agriculture. The Centre's most publicized initiative, however, was the Peace Technology Fund, which invested in joint ventures and Palestinian projects in high-tech. Yet, until 2000, the only meaningful investments were in Paltel, the PADICO-subsidiary providing telephone services in the PA. Like the Ministry of Regional Co-operation, the Peres Centre remained a co-ordinating agency without much influence. There were also considerable animosities between the Peres Centre and other, grassroots, peace-advocating institutions in Israel. Businesspeople engaged in co-operation, peace activists, and even Foreign Ministry officials alike criticized the Centre for 'doing virtually nothing to promote regional co-operation, apart from holding conferences and seminars.'[23]

The Economic Cooperation Foundation (ECF), established in 1991 by the architects of the Oslo channel, Yair Hirschfeld and Ron Pundak, played a similar role in facilitating dialogue and promoting co-operation, albeit without much influence on the ground. It was involved in preparing the 1995 MENA conference in Amman and helped overcome deadlocks in the official channels especially after Netanyahu took power in 1996. Overall, however, the ECF focused on creating a favourable legal and political environment for co-operation and co-ordinated little with the business sector.[24] Indeed, most governmental and non-governmental institutions were only involved in promoting Israel's perspective on regional co-operation through conferences and workshops.

In contrast, the Ministry of Industry and Trade was by nature of its work involved in the everyday dealings of Israeli businessmen with their Arab counterparts. Concerned exporters and the IMA always issued recommendations and had a say in the negotiations of economic agreements. The QIZ agreement, for example, was refined into its final form thanks to input from Moshe Nahum, responsible for international trade relations at the IMA. Initially, it was proposed to determine qualification for unrestricted access to the US market on the basis of joint equal investments of Israelis and Jordanians in a project. Nahum, however, pointed out that Jordanians could simply establish a subsidiary in Israel, then engage in a project in a QIZ and thus have their products qualified for unrestricted access to the United States, without actually co-operating with any Israeli company. The final conditions were agreed upon at an informal meeting between government officials and private sector representatives, most notably from the IMA. This committee was an informal, yet regularly meeting, decision-making body.[25]

Another institution represented at the informal committee was the Israel Export Institute (IEI), a joint private sector-governmental institution promoting exports and representing 90 per cent of all Israeli exporters. Avi Sofer, director of a newly created Middle East desk since 1999, participated in preparatory discussions for final status negotiations with the Palestinians alongside Gabby Bar, Moshe Nahum, and Mendy Barak, head of the FICC's Middle East desk. According to Sofer, the government and the business sector hardly ever advocated contradictory positions. Lobbying was usually a harmonious process of co-ordination.[26]

The most influential business sector institution, however, remained the IMA. Doron Tamir, Global Wires CEO, IMA Vice-President under Dov Lautman and Dan Propper, and Oded Tira's contender for the presidency in 1999, stressed that the majority of business leaders had supported Prime Ministers Rabin and Peres. There had almost been no communication at all with Netanyahu, who admitted later that one of his biggest mistakes had been his strained relationship with the IMA and the business community.[27] Moshe Nahum similarly pointed out that no economic agreement could be negotiated without the IMA's involvement. The IMA presented its preferences, and in most cases, the government would pursue those in the negotiations. As Nahum said, 'agreements are not for the government, but for the people, for business, and that's us.'[28]

Despite the IMA's influence, many of those entrepreneurs who actually engaged in co-operative efforts were disappointed by the lack of governmental support and the bureaucratic barriers they faced. Their complaints also signify the difference between the interest of big business, which needed a peace process in order to expand abroad but not necessarily within the region, and the smaller businesses, who tried to take advantage of the new regional opportunities. Dov Rochman, formerly Benny Gaon's right hand for Koor's peace projects, said that the parties had not done enough to encourage business across the borders prior to the new Intifada. Politicians had left the business side of peace to the private sector without any encouragement. In addition, those Israelis, mostly from big business companies, who had only half-heartedly engaged in highly publicized peace ventures, had damaged the image of Israeli business and its relations with the Arab world considerably.[29] Gili Deckel from the consortium developing the Jordan Gateway Industrial Zone felt equally disappointed with the government. He claimed that it had been 'ineffective in assisting the private sector' in the effort to develop peace economically. Deckel had secured the personal support of Shimon Peres, yet felt disillusioned by the hurdles created by the Israeli bureaucracy.[30]

Hence, most institutions merely served to link political and economic elites and reflected the limited interest of Israeli businesspeople in promoting the discourse of peace and regional economic co-operation. Most of these institutions and organizations did little to advance actual co-operation. The government and most associations left those entrepreneurs interested in enhancing ties between Israel and its neighbours without much support.

Jordan

Decline of the Old Elites

Similar to the processes in Israel, the Jordanian political economy underwent drastic transformations during the 1990s concurring with the peace process. These changes led to a demise of formerly influential elites and the emergence of a young business generation. Newly founded business associations supported reform and the normalization of relations with Israel. The moderate representatives of this group, often simply a new generation from the traditionally influential families, were drawn into a new core elite group around the new king, Abdullah, in the years after his accession to the throne in 1999. Thus, the old system of rule under the Hashemite regime in Jordan was preserved, albeit with new players. Both old elites opposed to reform and those too openly engaged in co-operative projects with Israelis were left out of the new circles of power.

Until the 1990s, the elite stratum of 'Big 7' managers had, albeit without much influence on economic policy-making, dominated the traditional 'private sector' associations, such as the Amman Chamber of Industry (ACI), the Amman Chamber of Commerce (ACC), the Federation of Jordanian Chambers of Commerce (FJCC), and the Jordan Businessmen Association (JBA). Rotations between politics and business were frequent.[31] But the old elites decayed in the context of persistent economic crisis and subsequent reform. Power shifted in favour of a new generation. When the pragmatist Abdul Karim Kabariti became Prime Minister in 1996, JBA Chairman Tabba'a welcomed the liberalization promises made by the new government. The associations jointly proposed the formation of a consulting council with the Prime Minister. However, when Kabariti's successor, Abdul Salam Majali, tried to accelerate the pace of reform and privatization, all associations protested and called for a higher degree of protection.[32]

The JBA had been founded in 1985 as a voluntary association – membership in the ACI and FJCC was compulsory – but essentially remained a club of the big business representatives loyal to the monarchy. Among its founding members were Mamduh Abu Hassan, Chairman of the Jordan Ceramic Industries Co. (JCIC), former board member of the Central Bank of Jordan (CBJ) and the Jordan

Phosphate Mines Co. (JPMC), and former Senator; Hamdi Tabba'a, who had been ACC President, Minister of Industry and Trade, and Jordan Cement Factories Co. (JCFC) Chairman; and Issam Bdeir, a former ACI President. The remaining six board members also came all from prominent families.[33] The JBA's influence, as much as the power of the ACI and the ACC, had always been limited, but their joint rejection of the normalization of ties with Israel deprived them further of their political standing.[34] The ACC had been transformed from the exclusive club of the merchants most loyal to the palace into a mass organization. By the mid-1990s, under President Haidar Murad, the ACC had already lost its influence first to the ACI, then to the JBA, both of which had espoused reform more willingly than the ACC during the early 1990s. All three associations, however, failed to live up to their own demands: They could play a meaningful role neither in the formulation of a 1994 law introducing a sales tax, nor in the preparation of the 1995 MENA conference in Amman.[35] The ACC lost further ground when during the 1998 election campaign for a new board, two blocs of candidates, one under incumbent President Haidar Murad, the second under Vice-President Riyad Saifi, competed in the ferocity of their rejection of any ties with Israel.[36]

The ACI, meanwhile, under pressure from among its own ranks, achieved some degree of reform. The new regional Irbid Chamber of Industry in particular, thanks to its efforts at the al-Hassan Industrial Estate, gained increasing prominence.[37] During the presidential elections in 2000, long-term ACI President Khaldoun Abu Hassan lost to Othman Bdeir, who was considered more open towards reform. Abu Hassan claimed that the government had interfered in favour of Bdeir and that 'our position against normalization with Israel and our pro-Iraqi stances were the reasons behind the campaign against us.'[38] Following his victory, Bdeir said he would maintain the ACI's anti-normalization stance, but added he would not 'block any businessman who wants to deal with Israel.' This effectively ended the boycott and ensured a continued role in politics for the ACI.[39]

In addition to their internal quarrels and their attitude towards normalization, the traditional elites had also been weakened during the years of economic crisis. Several of the Big 7 had faced financial troubles. A number of government-owned industries had gone bankrupt. Despite the opposition of many of the old guard, the pace of privatization was accelerated during the last two years of King Hussein's reign and under King Abdullah. Large chunks of the Jordan Telecommunications Company (JTC) and the JCFC were sold to foreign strategic partners.[40] The Jordan Electric Power Company was split into three firms in January 1999, two of which were to be privatized. The drilling arm of the Jordan Petroleum Refinery Co. (JPRC) was separated into the Petra Drilling Co., which was also to be privatized, as was Royal Jordanian. Although privatization still moved slowly, less of the prestigious managerial positions on the boards of government-owned companies were now available. The people who used to fill them became increasingly irrelevant in the political arena.

New areas of economic activities and new actors emerged, in particular once King Abdullah strengthened his position from 2000 onwards. A new economic plan outlined the king's vision to develop IT into Jordan's third-largest sector after mining and tourism. In his speech at Jordan's first IT forum in March 2000, Abdullah put a strong emphasis on the role of the private sector in realizing his vision, including through 'qualifying industrial zones.'[41] The forum was an outcome of the REACH initiative presented by some thirty, mostly young private sector representatives to the king in June 1999. REACH aimed to create 30,000 IT-related jobs until 2004, generating $550 million in annual exports and attracting $150 million in FDI.[42] The Young Entrepreneurs Association (YEA) and 26 other business associations presented the similar 'Jordan Vision 2020' initiative in June 2000.[43] The two initiatives followed the even more significant First Economic Forum, held at the Dead Sea in November 1999, where under the direct supervision of the king, 160 public and private sector representatives had deliberated economic reform. Less than three weeks after the meeting, King Abdullah formed a new Economic Consultative Council (ECC), which was, according to the royal decree, to follow up on the country's economic policies and to focus on boosting the role of the private sector to spur economic growth.[44]

New Economic and Political Elites

The ECC brought young businesspeople to the front, who were content to limit themselves to promoting economic reform without concurring political measures. Effectively, King Abdullah co-opted these new elites and thus cemented his reign over the country, while pushing ahead with the programmes needed to ensure Jordan's economic survival.[45] The ECC's main task was to recommend economic, legislative, and administrative reforms. Of its 20 members, 14 were private entrepreneurs, only six were public sector representatives. For the first few months, however, despite a flood of suggestions from the ECC to the government, Prime Minister Abdul Raouf Rawabdeh avoided acting on the proposals. His attempt to preserve the interests of the traditional elites prompted an unprecedented petition from a majority of parliamentarians to the king outlining their complaints against the Prime Minister and his inactivity. Two months later, Abdullah dismissed Rawabdeh, whose government included some prominent opponents of normalization, and appointed a business-oriented government under the ECC member Ali Abul Ragheb.[46]

All ECC members were known for their reformist tendencies. Fadi Ghandour had founded the forwarding service Aramex, which in 1997 had become the first Arab company to be listed on the NASDAQ. He had also been among a group of businessmen advising King Abdullah before the creation of the ECC.[47] Ghassan Nuqul, Vice-Chairman of the family-owned Nuqul Group, a Palestinian G7 enterprise, was included in the council as a strong supporter of reform, as was Fawaz Zou'bi, a founding member of the Young Entrepreneurs Association (YEA).[48] Karim Kawar, the 33-year-old founder of the Ideal Group and President of the Jordanian IT association, INTAJ, was one of the conceptual heads of the REACH initiative.[49] He was one of the leading high-tech specialists in Jordan and a close personal friend of King Abdullah. The Kawar family held a forwarding business headed by Karim's cousin, Amin, who was also Vice-President of the Jordanian-American Business Association (JABA), another reformist new business association.[50] Two other family members had served in Parliament from 1989 to 1993. Samir Kawar had been a JBA founding member and Minister of Transportation in 1995.

Salaheddin Bashir was another ECC member. A 33-year-old graduate from Harvard Law School, whose tuition fees King Hussein had personally paid, he had advised the government on the negotiations over Jordan's WTO accession. Bashir was also known for his criticism of the government's protection of the domestic industry.[51] Anwar Battikhi, head of the Hashemite University in Zarqa, was chosen for his proposal to launch private QIZs in joint ventures with American companies to attract high-tech firms and foreign investments.[52] Muhyieddin Touq had been Minister of Administrative Reform from 1995 to 1996 under Prime Minister Kabariti and was head of UNRWA's Education Department. Khaled Touqan, the President of the governmental Balqa Applied University, and Samih Dawarzah, the 70-year-old JTA Chairman and President of the market leader Hikma Pharmaceuticals, were two further members from traditionally influential families. Dawarzah's relative Rashed headed the El-Zay Readywear firm, which operated under the QIZ agreement.[53] Fuad Abu Zayyad had returned from the United States to Amman in 1995 in order to head the Inter-Arab Investment Fund under the auspices of the US-governmental Overseas Private Investment Corporation (OPIC). He said that the ECC had been created in order to bring in fresh ideas, after 'the old guard had had their chance.'[54]

Another observer remarked that all ECC members had been picked for their role in the new dynamics in the private sector, which marked the shift from the old generation to a new one. The transformation process had its roots in the economic crisis of the late 1980s, but was fuelled by the emergence of a new generation from the elite families and the return of businesspeople from the Gulf following the war in Kuwait. King Abdullah's surprising accession to the throne and his determination to push through economic reform also contributed to the changes.[55] That the new elite was not only in favour of economic reform in Jordan, but was also pragmatic and open towards Israel, was illustrated in the involvement of several ECC members in business relations with Israel. The ECC also recommended the development of the Aqaba Special Economic Zone (SEZ). The new Prime Minister, Ali Abul Ragheb, who had headed the committee on Aqaba, admitted that interested investors in the zone came mainly from Israel. Emad Fakhoury, the former commercial attaché at the Jordanian embassy in Israel and CEO of the Century Group, became Royal Commissioner for Investment and Economic Development, another sign that Israel was considered a top priority in the promotion of the SEZ.[56]

Fakhoury, although not a member of the ECC, was part of the new elite as a close personal friend of the king. He had earlier been involved in all negotiations concerning economic ties between Israel and Jordan. His younger brother Kamil worked for the company developing the private Tajammu'at QIZ near Amman. Kamil co-ordinated closely with Emad al-Shamma', the former manager of a joint venture in the al-Hassan Industrial Estate and a private consultant advising on QIZ operations. Both Kamil Fakhoury and al-Shamma', as well as Abdallah Tayyeh, the former Boscan International manager and private QIZ consultant, agreed that ties between the new business leaders and the political elite were close. Fakhoury pointed out that at least seven of his former fellow students and friends in the United States had assumed key positions in the Royal Palace.

Al-Shamma' and Fakhoury emphasized that common experience abroad provided the connection between businesspeople and the government and palace. The young generation in both business and politics had often studied together. Fakhoury and al-Shamma' themselves, for example, knew 'half the government and half the royal palace on a first name basis.' This new group did not include more than twenty or thirty people and involved those dealing with Israel or other international markets. The examples of al-Shamma', the Fakhoury brothers, and Tayyeh demonstrated that business relations with Israel were one of the factors linking the new elite. The average businessman with ties mainly to Iraq was excluded from this circle. At the same time, however, it was the moderate reform-minded businesspeople, which became part of the King Abdullah's new elite, while aggressive 'normalizers' such as Omar Salah were excluded from this circle.[57]

New business associations, such as the YEA and JABA, played an important role in holding the network of political and economic elites together. Another association that played an important role in transforming Jordan's economy under the new king was INTAJ, the Jordanian IT association, whose President Karim Kawar was a member of the ECC and which had presented the REACH initiative. Several leading INTAJ-members co-operated with Israelis. Its focus, according to one founding member, lay on implementing King Abdullah's vision of turning Jordan into a regional IT hub. The new generation was working to realize the king's vision.

It was therefore no coincidence that even in the public sector, a younger generation increasingly came to the fore, many of whom had earlier worked in the private sector.[58] The leading examples here were Prime Minister Abul Ragheb and Foreign Minister Abul Elah Khatib, a former JCFC general manager, who had directed Jordan's negotiations with the WTO. Other representatives of the younger generation could also increasingly found in key positions. Samer Tawil, for example, a former business consultant in the United States, became Secretary-General of the Ministry of Industry and Trade and the Jordanian Joint Chairman of the QIZ Committee in 2000. Tawil pointed out that the consolidation of the new elite came in the context of a diversification of Jordan's options with its WTO accession and the conclusion of the FTA with the United States. By 2000, as Tawil explained, there were three groups within the business sector. The conservative entrepreneurs focusing on Iraq increasingly lost their influence. Young, aggressive normalizers favoured a full and immediate opening of the economy. The third group of moderates advocated Jordan's integration into the regional and global economy without disrupting domestic stability. This implied that relations with Israelis were tolerable as long as they did not attract the attention of the anti-normalization movement. Tawil maintained that 'the future belongs to the moderates,' who worked closely with the new king.[59]

Pro-Peace Business Associations and Anti-Normalization

The Young Entrepreneurs Association (YEA) and the Jordanian-American Business Association (JABA) were the two organizations most visibly associated with the new elites. Eight young entrepreneurs, among them Century Chairman Omar Salah, founded the YEA in November 1998, in order to support young entrepreneurs and push ahead with reform in the kingdom. By end-1999, its membership base had grown to 165, despite exclusivist entry conditions such as a recommendation from an established member. The YEA became an influential player through its Jordan Vision 2020 initiative. In contrast to the traditional business associations, the YEA did not participate in the anti-normalization movement. Most of the young entrepreneurs engaged in trade and joint ventures with Israelis became members of the new association.[60]

JABA was similarly founded in 1998 and officially launched in early 1999. It grew from 24 founding members, including Omar Salah, to about 250 members by the end of 2000. Even more so than the YEA, JABA was explicitly established as an association for those businesspeople, who did not feel represented in the traditional organizations. Vice-President Amin Kawar described the ACI and the ACC as 'very bureaucratic institutions, without much member participation.' In contrast, JABA attracted those progressive entrepreneurs who represented American companies in Jordan or had a substantial interest in the American market. Among them were many businessmen who were engaged in manufacturing operations and exports under the QIZ agreement. JABA maintained close links to the YEA and INTAJ, but also to the Jordan Trade Association (JTA) and the ACI. The latter became more open towards reform under its new President Othman Bdeir and displayed a less hostile attitude towards Israel since 2000. JABA was considered more moderate than the YEA. Although it did not have any representative on the ECC, JABA President Fawaz Sha'lan and board member Maher Mu'asher had been instrumental in one member's appointment to the council.[61]

Despite his initial involvement in both associations, the man most active in promoting ties with Israel, Omar Salah, remained on the margins within the new political-economic elite under King Abdullah. Salah had been proposed as a presidential candidate during the first YEA board elections, but a majority of the members opted for Laith al-Qassem, the son of a former Chief of the Royal Court. The political situation was not conducive to having an outspoken 'normalizer' as association president. Salah became Vice-President but resigned from the board in 2000. Despite the success of the Century Group and its economic weight as Jordan's single largest employer after the government, Salah was not appointed to the ECC, and he felt excluded from the elite network around King Abdullah. Salah had also not been invited to the Economic Forum chaired by Abdullah, which had preceded the establishment of the ECC. According to him, Abdullah's economic advisor, Bassem Awadullah, told him the invitation had been delayed. Salah interpreted this as a clear sign that the king did not want to include the most prominent proponent of normalization within the new elite circle. Salah also pointed out that although Century still enjoyed excellent relations with the new Prime Minister and Foreign Minister Khatib, his lobbying efforts for a FTA with Israel did not yield any success. As a result of the government's failure to support him, Century would re-orient itself and operate more globally in the future.[62]

In the face of the domestic hostility towards Israel, the influence of the anti-normalization movement, and the stalled peace process, Salah had tried to remain out of the limelight. During 1997, after Netanyahu's election as Israeli Prime Minister, Salah had repeatedly claimed not to deal with any Israelis directly. When the Intifada broke out, he left the country and spent several months in the United States.[63] The power of the anti-normalization movement was particularly strong in the period of transition between King Hussein and King Abdullah, while Hussein underwent cancer treatment during 1998 and 1999 and until Abdullah had established himself firmly in power by 2000. In 1998, the Lower House publicly debated the dangers emanating from Israeli ownership of factories in Jordan.[64] Growing poverty and unemployment in Jordan were attributed on the popular level to the false promises of peace with Israel and strengthened the anti-normalization movement as much they weakened the monarchy. Normalization was the issue dominating the political agenda and thus played an important role in the formation and consolidation of the new ruling elites, which had often made money through its ties with Israelis. Thus, the move against the anti-normalization opposition was a logical step in the consolidation of Abdullah's reign. At the same time, stability concerns dictated that a moderate position would prevail and outspoken normalizers such as Salah be excluded from the positions of influence, at least publicly.[65]

Once, however, Abdullah dismissed his first Prime Minister, Abdul Raouf Rawabdeh, a powerful member of the traditional elite, the new government acted and cracked down on the anti-normalization movement. Seven leading activists were put into prison following the publication of two 'blacklists' in February 2001. With the support of a new generation of business leaders and consolidated ties between political and economic elites, Abdullah's reign was secure and stable. Even before that, however, the anti-normalization movement had had little influence beyond exerting pressure through the public discourse. Most co-operative projects had never been endangered, and most businessmen engaged in co-operation pointed out that they did not feel threatened by the movement's activities.[66]

The Palestinian Territories

The New Alliance, Corruption and the 'Slush Fund'

Like the Israeli and Jordanian economies, the Palestinian economic and political-economic system underwent drastic changes during the 1990s. Economic and political power became centralized in the hands of a core elite stratum. Many of the 'Tunisians,' those PLO officials, who arrived in Gaza and the West Bank following the creation of the PA, established their own companies monopolizing imports in deals with Israelis. The Palestinian Diaspora, most prominent among them the Jordanian G7, invested in large conglomerates such as PADICO. The alliance between the two groups personalized interest politics and gave rise to monopolization, mismanagement, and corruption. The PA emerged as the central player not only in politics, but also in the economy. Only after 1997, when international donors officially reprimanded the PA, did interest politics become gradually more transparent, albeit without much impact on the centralized system of economic power.

Before the establishment of the PA, a power struggle had taken place between the PLO and those West Bank capitalists and G7 members, which mostly had their origins in the town of Nablus. Following the Gulf Crisis, Abdel Majid Shouman, who opposed the Oslo Accords, had suspended his payments to the PLO. Most of the G7 remained critical of the PA. Abdel Muhsin Qattan resigned from the Palestinian National Council (PNC) because of a dispute over the PA's uncompromising attitude towards the MENA summits. Only the Masri brothers, Subih and Munib, successfully advocated a rapprochement and coalition with the PA. They became particularly close to the moderate members of the PA leadership, Ahmad Qurei (Abu Ala), former head of the PLO's Economic Department, and Mahmoud Abbas (Abu Mazen), Arafat's right hand and one of the most important actors in the Oslo negotiations. Thanks to the Masris, who played leading roles in PADICO, relations between the PA and the G7 were mended. Maher Masri became head of the Palestinian Economic Council for Development and Reconstruction (PECDAR) and later, Minister of the Economy and Trade.[67]

PECDAR, where Muhammad Shtayyeh, a long-term PLO official, soon took over as head from Masri, became the central institution cementing the PA's power. The council administered and disbursed donor funding and thus became the controlling authority of all ministries, effectively supervising their budgets. As Shtayyeh put it, PECDAR was the 'airport, on which the PLO arrived from Tunis in the West Bank and Gaza.' It also administered the PLO's finances outside the PA's institutional framework, thus maintaining the PLO's grip over the Palestinian proto-state institutions. However, PECDAR ran only a few programmes geared towards private sector development. Although it claimed to issue tenders for construction and infrastructure works, most of these were actually awarded to international companies, often under the conditions set out by donor countries.[68]

Nablus remained one of the centres of opposition to the PA, not only as a stronghold of the Islamist opposition forces, but also as a commercial town. In 1997, Palestinian business leaders from Nablus challenged the PA to streamline bureaucracy and to institute a system of law in order to attract foreign investments. Mu'ath Nabulsi, Chairman of the Nablus Chamber of Commerce, also demanded: 'Give the private sector the freedom it requires.'[69] Similar claims emanated from the second Palestinian Expatriate Businessmen's Conference, held in the West Bank town in July 1998.[70] The owners of smaller enterprises in Nablus as well as in Jenin, in particular, despite their nationalist aspirations, had feared that the PA's takeover of both towns in 1995 would lead them to lose their traditional clients, Palestinians from inside Israel.[71] In the face of the opposition originating in Nablus against the PA, Arafat adopted a strategy of coercion in order to bring the town under control. Against the usual procedure of recruiting security forces locally, patrols were sent from Gaza.[72]

At the same time, the PA leadership fully mended fences with the large and influential families when the PA awarded the PADICO-subsidiary Paltel the exclusive right for telecommunications services in the PA. An exclusive deal had previously been signed with ITI and AT&T, but was now abrogated despite an April 1996 law that required competition and protected earlier agreements. The official excuse was that Arafat had not fully understood the terms of the contract because of his poor English. The link between the PA and the G7 remained the Masri family: Not only were Maher Minister of the Economy and Trade and Munib PADICO Chairman, the family also dominated most subsidiary boards as well as PADICO's main investors, such as the Cairo Amman Bank. It was also involved in the Shouman-owned Arab Bank. Hani Masri, owner of Capital Investment Management, was not only Arafat's envoy in Washington, but also one of the major investors and actors in the Peres Centre's Peace Technology Fund. In addition, the family owned the newspaper Al-Ayyam. The Masris thus provided the connection between the 'Tunisians' and the Diaspora. They personified the interconnections between the new political and economic elites and the centralization of economic power.[73]

PADICO, due to the favourable PA concessions, gained dominance over key strategic sectors of the Palestinian economy. In violation of its own by-laws, the company owned more than 49 per cent of the shares in four of its eight subsidiaries. It held 70 per cent of the Palestine Securities Exchange (PSE). On the PSE, PADICO itself and Paltel were the two most traded companies. The major shareholders in Paltel were PADICO, APIC, and the PCSC. No regulatory authority supervised trading on the exchange. Paltel meanwhile proceeded to make profits for its investors, charging international rates for phone calls from the PA to Israel, including for calls within the same area code and calls to Jerusalem. A public outcry ensued and forced the company to adjust its tariffs in 1998. In an illustration of the PA's close ties to Paltel, Palestinian Minister of Telecommunications Emad Elfalugi had backed the high rates for calls to Israel, saying that the money was needed to develop infrastructure. Other Palestinian sources claimed that Arafat had authorized Paltel's decision.[74] Similarly, PADICO's subsidiary, PIEDCO, coordinated closely with the governmental Palestinian Industrial Estates and Free Zones Authority (PIEFZA). In fact, PIEDCO's General Manager, Abdel Malik Jaber, had been PIEFZA's first Managing Director. The PA also held a direct 10 per cent-stake in PIEDCO, which in turn had a seat on PIEFZA's board.[75]

Because of the close personal ties between the PA, PADICO, and APIC, the two conglomerates did not participate in interest politics through the Palestinian business association and private sector organizations. Rather, they pursued their interests in personal meetings with Arafat.[76] Favourable concessions from the PA and the monopolistic nature of the conglomerates' operations also cemented the alliance of the G7 and Diaspora Palestinians with PA officials and Tunisian profiteers. All of these had a vested interest in maintaining the status quo, with economic and political power centralized in their hands. PADICO, APIC, the PCSC and Sharikat al-Bahr dominated the economy. In addition, according to Paltrade General Manager Samir Abdullah, the core of the Palestinian political economy further included those medium-sized companies, which secured contracts from the PA. The PA became the largest purchaser in the Territories, accounting for 25 per cent of national consumption, following its establishment. PA officials, again, held most of those companies, thus further strengthening the alliance and the vested interest in sustaining the rule of the PA.[77]

But the PA not only became the single largest employer in the Territories, profits were also used directly to buy loyalty. Thus, monopolies were handed to organizations such as the Veteran Warriors Association, an organization comprised of former Fedayeen loyal to Arafat. It held 40 per cent of the monopoly for sand.[78] According to PCSC General Manager Hassan Salameh, not even he knew where the profits from the company's cement deal went. Only Muhammad Rashid was in charge of investments and accounts. Salameh added, however, that Arafat had his own way of ruling the 'jungle.' He thus implicitly confirmed that the benefits from the PA's commercial activities were used to create jobs, pay the numerous security services, and support PLO loyalists.[79] In 1997, Rashid had confirmed the existence of a secret bank account in Tel Aviv, to which only he and Arafat had access. The so-called 'Fund B' (Al-Sunduq al-Thani) was used to pay martyr allowances to widows and orphans as well as the casualties of the Sabra and Shatila massacre and to finance PA operations that donor countries refused to support. Hisham Awartani, head of the Nablus Centre for Palestinian Research and Studies, said: 'Arafat needs these people as a political power base, and therefore he pays the salaries out of the slush fund.' Allegations that money disappeared into private pockets, however, were frequent.[80]

Coercion, Public Protest and External Pressure for Reform

Apart from aligning itself with the wealthy Diaspora entrepreneurs and buying loyalty through the provision of employment and welfare, the PA also resorted to coercion. It pushed those who refused to collaborate out of the market, or forced them into working with or for the PA. Thus, the manager of the Palestinian International Bank, Issam Abu Issa, a Qatari citizen from one of the richest Palestinian families in the Gulf, was accused of having misappropriated $20 million from the bank. Abu Issa denied the allegations and claimed the PA wanted to take over the bank. This assertion seemed to be confirmed when the PA appointed a new board of directors made up entirely of PA officials. The incident caused a diplomatic uproar due to the Qatari government's involvement as a shareholder in the bank and the close personal ties between the Abu Issas and the Qatari ruling family.[81]

Local entrepreneurs from smaller businesses were less lucky. PA security agents tortured Ibrahim Mahmoud Shawahin, a Hebronite quarry industrialist, over accusations of tax fraud. He was released only against paying a large sum. Numerous other small business owners from Hebron and Nablus suffered the same fate in 1996 and 1997.[82] Mahmoud al-Fara, one of the wealthiest businessmen in the Gaza Strip and involved in the construction of the Palestinian airport there, said that PA security forces compelled him to buy cement from the PCSC, despite his agreement with an Egyptian company to import cement at a much lower price. The 32-year-old construction worker Yusuf al-Baba died from torture in an illegal arrest over his refusal to pay protection money. Omar al-Baba, who wanted to build a petrol station in Nablus, was told he would be granted a licence 'if only I would be kind enough to give them 30 per cent of the profits.'[83] Said Kanaan, one of the leading entrepreneurs in the town, was similarly refused a licence to operate a $500,000 petrol station. He had failed to invite Muhammad Rashid and the PCSC into the project.[84] But the practices of the PA did not remain without reaction and resentment against the monopolies grew, as a Gazan merchant made clear:

> We live in amazing, shameful times. But you should know that every revolution has its fighters, thinkers, and profiteers. Our fighters have been killed, our thinkers assassinated, and all we have left are the profiteers. These don't think primarily of the cause, they don't think about it at all. They know that they are just transients here, as they were in Tunis, and, as with any regime whose end is near, they think only of profiting from it while they can.[85]

Taxi drivers went on strike over increasing taxes in 1999. At the same time, there were fears of violent riots in protest against the high prices of cement and flour, the import of which were controlled by the PCSC.[86] Reports from human rights organizations and the public protests over corruption and high consumer prices fuelled investigations against the PA, which had begun in 1997, but were now taken to the international level. In 1997, a newly set up auditing office found that the PA had misused $326 million – nearly half the annual budget – during 1996. Several companies had not paid taxes. Others had won tenders from the PA due to their personal ties with officials.[87] A second commission of enquiry confirmed the charges of widespread corruption in all ministries.

An ensuing cabinet re-shuffle, however, brought only minor changes in the summer of 1998. Critics such as the Palestinian delegate Hussam Khader said: 'By giving a vote of confidence to this government, the PLC has legalized corruption.' A poll conducted by the Jerusalem Media Communications Centre found that more than 70 per cent of Palestinians believed that PA corruption would not decrease under the new government. About half of those predicted it would further increase. According to a second poll from the Arab Studies Society, Arafat's approval rating had dropped from 78 per cent at the beginning of 1998 to only 48 per cent at the time of the re-shuffle.[88]

Public discontent as well as increasing protests from donor countries finally forced the PA to conduct its affairs more transparently. The annual donor conference in Tokyo in 1999 forced the PA to publish the PCSC's holdings for the first time. During that year, the company made a net profit of $77 million, $18 million of which alone were in the cement trade. The PCSC was to be split and privatized, although this did not happen until the new Intifada.[89] The PA's report, prepared with help from the IMF, was presented to the following donor conference in Lisbon in June 2000. Funds from the secret account in Tel Aviv as well as PCSC profits were officially included in the PA's budget for the year and helped offset a $600 million deficit.[90]

Table 14: PCSC Holdings, 1999

Equity Holdings (End-1999)	Est. Market Value (Mio. $)	Equity (%)
Jericho Resort (Hotel & Casino)	60.0	30.0
Cement Company	50.0	100.0
Palcell	50.0	35.0
Paltel	32.2	8.0
Arab Palestinian Investment Co. (APIC)	16.0	20.0
PADICO	15.0	8.0
Various Real Estate	14.0	100.0
Bioniche Life Sciences Inc.	9.0	10.0
United for Storage and Refrigeration	8.5	30.0
Peace Technology Fund	6.2	34.0
Qaser Jaser Hotel (Intercontinental)	5.0	25.0
Palestinian Flour Mills Co.	4.1	47.0
Palestinian Electricity Co.	2.6	6.0
Palestinian Investment Bank	2.3	8.0
Bethlehem Convention Centre	2.0	45.0
Coca-Cola	1.5	15.0
Gaza Insurance Co.	1.5	14.0
Al-Ahlia Co.	1.4	50.0
National Aluminium Profile Co. (NAPCO)	1.3	16.0
Grand Park Hotel	1.2	25.0
Steel Co.	1.2	15.7
Vegetable Oil Company	1.0	7.0
Palestinian-Qatar Fund	0.9	33.0
Al-Moutkhasea Investment	0.9	15.0
College and School	0.7	40.0
Al-Ahlia Industrial Company	0.7	15.0
Al-Salam International Co.	0.5	5.0
Al-Marie Co.	0.5	--
Glass Cutting	0.4	40.0
Palestinian Cigarettes Co.	0.3	28.0
Logo Company	0.3	28.0
Al-Takenion Engineering Co.	0.2	50.0
Jordanian Specialized Co.	0.2	50.0
First Choice Management	0.1	30.0
Subtotal	**291.6**	
Other Assets (End-1999)		
Cash and Cash equivalent	11.0	
Receivables and other debit balance	32.0	
Property and Land	10.0	
Total	**344.6**	

Source: Seitz, 'PA Commercial Holdings Made Public;' published on the website of the Jerusalem Media Communications Centre (JMCC), www.jmcc.org/media/report/2000/Jun/4b.htm.

Private Sector Associations and Interest Politics

On the level below the alliance of political and economic elites from abroad, liaison between the public and private sector involved both formal mechanisms and informal contacts. The latter took place between the resident business elite and PA ministerial officials. One of the most important players within this network was Samir Huleileh, Marketing Director of the Nassar Investment Company since 1997. Huleileh had helped prepare the negotiations with Israel and had participated in all talks relating to economic affairs. He had then worked at PECDAR and the Ministry of the Economy and Trade. In May 1997, Huleileh resigned from the post of Assistant Deputy Minister for Trade due to the corruption within the PA. Through his contacts, however, Huleileh continued to promote the private sector in a number of meetings and talks between the public and private sectors. He also remained a member of the negotiating team and the Joint Economic Committee (JEC). According to him, the private sector had been consulted informally prior to the Paris talks, for which the managers of the larger firms had formulated a consensual opinion.

Business associations were only established after the talks. The Palestinian Chambers of Commerce, Industry, and Agriculture were re-structured in order to represent merchants. A General Federation of Industries was founded, as were Paltrade and the PBA.[91] Interest politics, however, remained personalized. Within the PA ministries, the officials most directly involved in the liaison with the private sector were the director-generals, such as Saeb Bamieh, the Director-General responsible for trade co-operation, or Abdel Hafiz Noufal, responsible for trade in the West Bank. Both had been worked under Abu Ala in the PLO's Economic Department and had participated in the Paris negotiations. Bamieh was also in charge of the technical team preparing the Paris talks and the final status negotiations, which for the first time involved formal consultations with the private sector.[92]

Most of the entrepreneurs resident in the West Bank, however, had an ambivalent attitude towards lobbying and their ties to the PA. According to Mazen Sinokrot, chairman of the largest Palestinian food manufacturer and head of the Palestinian Food Producers Association, the private sector was heard with regard to internal issues, but had largely been excluded from the negotiations with Israel and Jordan. The private sector had played a successful role in providing input for the formulation of the Palestinian agency law, the investment law, and the tax income law. However, the creation of two ministries, one for the economy and trade, and one for industry, which was an outcome of the pressure on the PA to provide employment, made lobbying more difficult and less transparent. Personal contacts retained their significance.[93] Similarly, Nakhleh Jubran from the AIC and Chairman of the Association of Palestinian Chemical Industries, pointed out that 'the whole concept of lobbying, how to establish associations, how to work in a political environment and so on, started only very recently.' Private sector influence on policy-making was also hindered by the fact that 'people here do not understand what there is and what would be good for them.' As Jubran said, many political interests were involved in bilateral talks. Private sector concerns were therefore rarely taken into account. As a result of both the occupation and the arbitrary economic policy of the PA, Palestinian entrepreneurs had learned not to rely on regulations and agreements, but to be as flexible as possible.[94]

Despite their criticisms, both Sinokrot and Jubran were part of a second-tier elite that at least had access to decision-makers and could exert some influence on policy-making. Other members of this stratum were Muhammad Masrouji and Talal Nasruddin, the chairmen of the two leading pharmaceutical manufacturers, Jerusalem Pharmaceuticals and the Birzeit Palestine Pharmaceutical Co. According to Masrouji, ministry officials were not informed well and did not listen to the private sector.[95] Nasruddin, who was also Chairman of the General Federation of Industry, said that frequent meetings had taken place between officials from the Ministry of the Economy and Trade and private sector representatives from 1995 until 1999. In these, it was co-ordinated which goods should be added to the list of tradable products between Jordan and the PA. The outcome of those negotiations, however, did not always reflect the interests of the Palestinian industrialists.[96]

ATS President Hassan Kassem similarly pointed out that businesspeople had only very limited influence on policy-making, although almost every entrepreneur had direct access to decision-makers.[97] The President of the Palestinian IT Association (PITA), Ibrahim Barham, said the association had at first concentrated on sector-specific issues, but later turned to the broader sphere of public-private sector relations. Its efforts were recognized when it joined the PBA, Paltrade, the General Federation of Industries, and the Chambers of Commerce, on the board of the Palestinian Investment Promotion Authority (PIPA) and in the 'Private Sector Co-ordinating Body.' This council was created in 2000 to increase private sector influence.[98] At the same time, PITA remained without much influence on the actual decision-making on economic policy, where wider political considerations played a larger role than private sector concerns.[99]

Smaller Palestinian companies had even less influence on policy-making, since the private sector associations were all dominated by the big local companies. The Farrah brothers, who ran a small textile factory in Al-Ram, for example, were satisfied neither with the achievements of the PA, nor with the limited role of the Union of Palestinian Textile Industries. Public criticism, however, was rare. As Mahmoud Farrah said: 'If we say that we are satisfied with the PA, we deceive ourselves; if we say we are not, people would accuse us of undermining the authority.' Smaller companies not only suffered most from Israeli barriers against industrial development and trade, but also from the centralization of economic power in the hands of PA officials and large conglomerates.[100] The sole association catering to the needs of smaller Palestinian companies, which represented the overwhelming majority of establishments in the Territories, was the European-Palestinian Chamber of Commerce. Hana Siniora, the former head of the Israel-Palestine Centre for Research and Information (IPCRI) and publisher of the Jerusalem Times, had established it in 1989. The Chamber had unsuccessfully lobbied for the establishment of a Small Business Authority. According to Siniora, Paltrade and the European-Palestinian Chamber represented the Palestinian commercial sector, while the Palestinian Chambers of Commerce, in contrast, were largely dysfunctional.[101]

Paltrade was the most successful private sector institution. Founded in September 1998, it brought together all the leading Palestinian establishments.[102] Its Chairmen were Mazen Sinokrot and later Nassar Nassar, owner of the Nassar Investment Company. Jaber Nabahin of the Gazan Nabahin Industry and Trading Co. was Vice-Chairman; Khaled Qutoub of the National Bottling Co. was Secretary; and Fuad Muhammad Oudeh, head of one of Gaza's largest textiles manufacturers, was Treasurer. By 2000, the association had 105 full and 100 associated members. As an independent private sector institution, however, Paltrade faced financial difficulties, since it could not rely on PA sponsorship.

Paltrade maintained good relations with the Ministry of the Economy and Trade, which was the most influential PA body with regard to economic affairs. The Ministry of Industry remained rather ineffective, competed with Paltrade, and favoured a protectionist economic regime. Co-ordination between PA institutions and the private sector was inadequate. Accordingly, one of Paltrade's most important initiatives aimed at unifying private sector efforts, co-ordinating the public and private sectors, and discussing PA relations with Israel and Jordan. The 'National Economic Dialogue' resulted in the formation of the Private Sector Co-ordinating Body in December 2000, although this council did not properly come into existence until 2001. Members appointed by the PA dominated not only the Chamber of Commerce, but also the General Federation of Industries. Those private sector associations remained dysfunctional and served to reward businesspeople with prestigious positions, in return for political loyalty, which made issue-focused work difficult.[103] The National Economic Dialogue also achieved the adoption of a unified position towards final status negotiations. It recommended a free trade agreement (FTA) with Israel, in line with Paltrade's preferences. The 'White Papers' accepted jointly by the PA and the private sector during the dialogue stated:

> The private sector should participate in the formulation of laws through suitable representation in the various bodies so as to establish firmly the foundation of a free market economy by having laws such as the Encouragement of Competition.

Further than that, co-ordination between the public and private sectors was to be improved. Trade agreements were to be reviewed in co-ordination with the private sector. In addition, the private sector also affirmed 'its opposition to the emergence of monopolies, private or governmental [...] It is recommended that a law regarding monopolies and privileges be established with the participation of the Palestinian private sector.'[104]

But despite the inroads Paltrade made with the National Economic Dialogue, recommendations were not implemented by the time the Intifada interrupted all talks within the PA as well as between the PA and Israel. Interest politics had just begun moving towards greater transparency, when the outbreak of violence interrupted the development of a successful public-private sector partnership. The Intifada also harmed in particular those companies, which had already continuously suffered under both the Israeli occupation and the rule of the PA.

In all three entities, hence, interest politics functioned less according to an institutionalized, transparent pattern, but were contingent upon personal access to decision-makers. The large conglomerates and managers of public and quasi-public sectors firms were clearly advantaged. In Israel, political, military, and economic elites were closely connected, and there was a high degree of mobility between the three fields. Institutions were dominated by big business and promoted the vague discourse of regional economic co-operation and peaceful existence yet did little to advance actual business ties beyond seeking to preserve Israel's economic dominance in the relationship with Jordanians and Palestinians. In Jordan, the old vanguard sustaining Hashemite rule was replaced by new business elites, which were often the sons of the old economic and political elites or at least part of a socio-economically and politically favoured stratum. These new elites formed an alliance with King Abdullah and secured his reign and his quest for economic reform and development, although peace turned lukewarm in the context of the popular opposition to normalization. Under the PA, the large expatriate conglomerates and PA officials formed a coherent elite stratum, which marginalized most ordinary Palestinians, including small-scale entrepreneurs. Corruption and mismanagement characterized the PA, while business associations were largely without influence. The tight interrelations between economic and political elites, thus, both provided the basis for the nature of business co-operation, which favoured the large conglomerates, and were reinforced by the evolution of business ties, which, in particular in Jordan and the Palestinian Territories, represented the foundation for the centralization of economic and political power. The close ties between economic and political elites thus also contributed to growing political and socio-economic inequality in all three entities, which contributed to the failure of the peace process.

6

Peace, Social Equality and Democracy

Israeli entrepreneurs had considerable influence on the course of the peace process and most importantly, Israel's economic relations with Jordanians and Palestinians. However, the consolidation of the alliance between 'big business' and the government saw a backlash in the 1996 election, when a majority of the electorate voted for Netanyahu and thus, against the peace process. Democratization suffered setbacks in Jordan and under the PA, where the new alliances of economic and political elites disillusioned large segments of the population with peace. In Jordan, this resulted in a reversal of the process of political liberalization and the consolidation of the Hashemite regime ruling with a mixture of integrationist and oppressive policies. In the PA, mismanagement and corruption discredited not only the Palestinian leadership, but also the Oslo process at large, and were an important factor in the outbreak of the new Intifada in 2000.

Israel

Objectives of Peace: Outward Expansion and Foreign Investment

Two dimensions characterized the involvement of the Israeli business sector in the peace process. Firstly, the interest and active engagement of entrepreneurs in paving the ground domestically for peace negotiations was fuelled by the need to expand economically. Secondly, their engagement in negotiations and as mediators, both in the role of political emissaries and as entrepreneurs engaged in trade and industrial joint ventures reflected their desire to preserve economic interests and influence in Israel's relations with Jordanians and Palestinians. Taken together, the interests, actual engagement, and political role of Israeli businesspeople in the peace process reflected the limitations of the Israeli conception of peace. These limits led to the ultimate failure of the economic underpinnings of peace and, despite major changes within the Israeli political economy, increasing economic and political inequality, which in turn negatively affected the peace process. In this sense, the involvement of Israeli entrepreneurs in the peace process demonstrated that Shimon Peres' four pillars of the 'new Middle East' – democratization, political stability, regional security, and regional economic development – were indeed interrelated, while it also illuminated the shortcomings of the Oslo process in all four spheres.

The Israeli involvement in the peace process was a result not only of security considerations after the Gulf War, but also originated in the interests of the business sector following the economic crisis of the 1980s. Economic expansion, a diversification of business opportunities, and the attraction of foreign investment were necessities recognized by Israeli business. The end of the Arab boycott, which could only be achieved in the context of a regional peace process, was crucial to the successful realization of these objectives. Peace negotiations were a precondition for Israel's acceptance as a legitimate business partner and a destination for foreign investments. The political discourse of the Oslo process disguised these considerations as a concern for 'regional economic development.' However, as Emma Murphy correctly asserted,

> Although Israel has outlined its commitment and desire for regional economic development, that is not the basis of its own development strategy. Israel seeks to utilize the results of its liberalization programme and its high-tech, skilled labour force economy to engage fully and advantageously in the present process of globalization. The achievement of peace in the region is the essential step towards opening global as opposed to simply regional markets.[1]

As a result of the desire for peace and outward expansion, business leaders began exerting pressure on the Shamir government during the late 1980s to enter into negotiations with the Palestinians. In 1989, Eli Hurwitz, Teva director and a former IMA President, had expressed the new consensus among Israeli businessmen by stating: 'The future is problematic without peace.'[2] IMA Director-General Yoram Blizovsky even argued: 'Palestinian industrialists view us, industrialists, as a more credible partner than the government.'[3]

Politicians began to react to the demands voiced by the business community.[4] The Chug Mashov (feedback circle) faction within the Labour party, founded in 1982 by Yossi Beilin and other members of the younger generation within the party, first reflected them in its political platform. A resolution adopted at Mashov's 1991 May Conference stated: 'The chance to successfully address the challenges of the Israeli economy, and especially mass immigration and the necessity of growth, depends on our ability to take the path of peace.' The Meretz party's 1992 election manifesto similarly stated:

> Peace agreement with our neighbours and a policy consistent with the values and interests of the democratic world will enable Israel to integrate into the world economy and into a stronger and expanding European Community, to become the recipient of investments and credit and to possess a progressive and exporting economy.[5]

As soon as the Labour party under Rabin won the 1992 elections and formed a government including Meretz, the two factions set to turn their programmes into reality. Big business executives such as Lautman, Gaon, and Gillerman, openly favoured the new political platforms of the Labour and Meretz parties and became readily involved, promoting peace publicly through the media and as emissaries and envoys. They had strongly supported Rabin during the election campaign and equally backed Peres during the 1996 elections. However, the discourse revolving around regional economic development and co-operation remained vague.[6]

The involvement of the Israeli business sector in promoting peace at home and abroad was not so much fuelled by its interest to engage in trade and industrial co-operation with Palestinians and Jordanians. Rather, it had its origins in the wish to preserve economic interests in the Occupied Territories, which Israeli business dominated under the status quo and which provided one of Israel's most important markets. Equally important was the interest to open up new markets overseas and to strengthen relations with new trade partners and those which had hitherto sought to maintain a low profile. The target of Israel's peace process was not the Middle East, but East and South East Asia, Europe and the former Soviet Union, the United States, and Japan. Thus, the actual objective of re-defining the Israeli-Arab conflict from a geo-strategic and political dispute into a multidimensionally resoluble issue was the Israeli ambition to expand overseas and to attract foreign investment.

The transformation of the Israeli political economy through the re-structuring of the Histadrut, Koor, and the large Israeli banks, had its roots in the deep economic crisis of the mid-1980s, but was fully resolved only through the initiation of the peace process, which brought overseas investors to Israel. In retrospect, it was no coincidence that the level of foreign direct investment peaked at $3.6 billion in 1995. Foreign direct investment had only increased threefold over a period of ten years until 1990, but then went up from $686 million in 1991 to $3.6 billion in 1995.[7] As a result of the stalemate in the peace process, but also the successfully completed transformation, foreign investment then decreased until 1999 to $2.4 billion. Similarly, Israeli exports more than doubled between 1990 and 1999. The Israeli economy grew faster than any world economy between 1991 and 1996, and the business sector achieved a constantly increasing growth rate and share in GDP.

It was further unsurprising that all the leading conglomerates attracted foreign investors or raised capital through their own investments overseas and domestically.[8] Koor was first taken over by Shamrock, then by Claridge. Delta Galil attracted a 22 per cent-investment from Sara Lee. Telrad sold 20 per cent of its shares to Nortel. Arison Investments bought 18 per cent of Bank Ha'Poalim and a 35 per cent-stake in HCH. Nestlé took over 40 per cent of the leading food manufacturer, Osem, while Unilever acquired 50 per cent in Strauss, one of the two leading dairy producers.[9] The Israel Corporation was taken over by the Eizenberg Group, which had considerable investments in the United States. Similarly, the IDB Holding Co. and the DIC achieved re-structuring involving foreign capital under the Recanati family. The Dankner Group, another family-owned conglomerate, also raised capital through its engagements overseas and later sold part of its business, Dor Energy and Dor Gas, to one of the local petroleum companies. The emergence of new sectors such as high-tech, which boosted economic growth and exports alike, similarly, was an outcome of the transformation. The changes had only become possible in the context of the ongoing liberalization, the end of the Arab boycott, and a re-orientation of the military-technological companies towards a peaceful application of their know-how.

Peace Business and the Limited Nature of Influence

In his article, 'Peace, Interdependence, and the Middle East,' Steve Yativ argued that Israel's increased economic interaction with extra-regional actors would not only benefit it materially, but also increase its sense of security. As a result, Israel would be 'more likely to co-operate with Arab states for joint economic gains.'[10] In fact, however, the Israeli business sector restricted itself to reaping the 'peace dividend' overseas. Regional co-operation did not figure prominently on its agenda. These limitations to the business community's interest in peace were reflected in the restrained involvement of entrepreneurs in negotiations and political relations as well as in the nature of their engagement in trade and industrial co-operation. Most big business firms explored the prospects for trade and industrial joint ventures at the height of the euphoria surrounding the peace agreements, but little came out of those preliminary talks. Commitment was often a mere lip service and remained half-hearted. At the same time, Israeli entrepreneurs quickly realized the formula for success in both Jordan and the PA: Israeli know-how, management, and marketing, plus Jordanian and Palestinian labour, often in combination with governmental support from both sides.

Textiles manufacturing and high-tech, especially software programming, stood out as those sectors, in which skilled labour in Israel was short in supply and expensive, while abundant in Jordan and the Territories. In the context of Israel's opening to world markets, the competitiveness of its labour-intensive industries decreased due to high labour costs. Jordanians and Palestinians were in dire need of employment opportunities in the face of closures, the substitution of Palestinian workers with Asian immigrants in Israel, and the economic crisis and unavailability of Jordan's most important export destination, the Iraqi market. In both sectors, however, Israelis had a huge competitive advantage in terms of experience, know-how, technology, and marketing so that control over a project while outsourcing manufacturing and thus saving expenses was simple.

In this sense, co-operation between Israeli, Jordanians, and Palestinians evolved less as a direct consequence of peace agreements on the basis of a genuine economic interest in co-operation, but rather as an indirect result of peace. The peace process had fuelled the transformation of the Israeli political economy and the liberalization of the business sector, which in turn exposed sectors to increased competition both domestically and abroad and necessitated a reduction of production costs. Jordan and the Territories offered many advantages as manufacturing locations, required foreign investment, and were pressed hard to provide employment opportunities. Thus, the two most successful sectors of co-operation, textiles and high-tech, were the only areas of collaboration, which were fuelled by a genuine business interest and economic potential. However, they were also characterized by a strong asymmetry.

In addition, business engagements were often facilitated by direct contacts to the respective governments on the other side. Where governmental contacts, more often than not on an informal basis, existed prior to the actual establishment of a project, success was almost guaranteed. Those entrepreneurs seeking governmental assistance in the course of realizing a deal often complained that their own government failed to support them. Business interests and pre-existing ties to the Jordanian palace or government or the PA also enabled entrepreneurs to fulfil a political role, although this rarely went beyond an indirect involvement. Yossi Ginossar, who participated in the Camp David talks, was a rare exception. Dov Lautman or Benny Gaon, the most prominent pro-peace businesspeople, for example, never participated directly in negotiations, although Lautman had been considered a potential leader of the Israeli delegation to the Paris talks.

The political engagement of businesspeople remained limited to publicly promoting peace. Otherwise, Israeli entrepreneurs became politically active only indirectly by lobbying to ensure a preservation of their business interests. The Israeli-Jordanian transportation and trade agreements, the Paris Protocol, and the course of the preparatory negotiations for a final status arrangement with the Palestinians, as well as even the Jordanian-Palestinian trade protocol, over which Israel retained critical influence, all reflected their interests. Similarly, Israeli businesspeople were ardent supporters of the QIZ agreement, which complemented the US-Israeli free trade agreement (FTA) and ensured that Israelis would reap some benefits from Jordanian exports to the US market. They however strongly lobbied against the US-Jordanian FTA, which was considered to potentially deprive Israeli entrepreneurs of their profits from the Jordanian efforts to open up new export destinations, as well as a reduction in the required Israeli share in QIZ operations.

Both the initial public involvement of Israeli entrepreneurs in promoting peace as well as their later lobbying efforts in shaping the agreements and the course of relations between Israel and its neighbours were ultimately manifestations of their business interests, rather than a commitment to lasting peace. Despite the business community's strong support for Peres in the 1996 elections, their political and public engagement in favour of peace cooled down considerably during the years of the Netanyahu government. The status quo of relations, which had been achieved by 1996, was good enough for the Israeli business community. It now focused on reaping the benefits from asymmetrical trade agreements in the region and even more so, the fruits of the Israeli economy's opening towards new markets. The election of Ehud Barak as Prime Minister in 1999, generally heralded as the beginning of a new and promising phase in the peace process, did not seem to move the business community particularly. Benny Gaon, for example, pointed out during a meeting between King Abdullah and Israeli businessmen in August 2000 that it was 'difficult to say there is overly openness or enthusiasm for business ties with Jordan, mainly due to political circumstances and the state of the peace process. This has led to acceptance of the existing situation, except for a few very dedicated persons.'[11] Only the lobbying efforts were intensified in order to ensure a preservation of Israeli economic interests under a final status arrangement with the Palestinians.

In fields beyond their immediate economic interest, Israeli businesspeople did not play a particular role in the peace process and did not adopt a unified position, but left those issues to the politicians. What was relevant was a preservation of economic interest, which necessitated a peace process along with economic agreements ensuring that businesspeople would not stand to lose much in an eventual overall settlement. The precise course this peace process took was less important than that a peace process evolved at all and ensured the opening up of new markets and opportunities. In this sense, as regards the Israeli business community, both the arguments put forward by Wright – that businesspeople in the Middle East had a vested interest in conflict continuation – and by Çarkoğlu, Eder, and Kirişci – that the mobilization of domestic constituencies in favour of peace and the creation of regional business ties would be the keys to peace – were undermined by the experience of the Oslo peace process.[12] Israeli businesspeople did have a vested interest in the initiation of a peace process and pursuing a settlement with Israel's Arab neighbours. However, this vested interest remained limited to the preservation of economic interest, which dictated a transformation of the domestic economy in order to open up new markets and business opportunities overseas. The business community's interests and its engagement in co-operation did not further the peace process. In fact, the nature of its interests and engagement contributed to the decline of peace and its ultimate failure.

Peace, Inequality and Democracy

In contrast to what Shimon Peres and the supporters of the functionalist approach to peacemaking in the Middle East had expected, the transformation of the Israeli political economy and the course of the peace process did not strengthen democracy and political stability in Israel. On the contrary, the transformation and the nature of the Israeli involvement in particular in industrial co-operation, while benefiting the elites that instigated them, negatively affected the lower echelons of society. Sammy Smooha rightly argued:

> The transition to a peace economy and economic growth will benefit in particular the elite and upper middle class of professionals, managers, businessmen, and industrialists, who are well equipped to seize the new opportunities [...] On the other hand, these economic transformations will inflict a serious blow on the working class and the poor.[13]

Inequality in Israel increased with the onset of the peace process. A new stratum of top wage earners emerged, which received annual salaries of several million shekels. At the same time, privatization, the decrease of the public sector, and equally important, the migration of traditional industries such as the re-location of textiles manufacturing to Jordan, contributed to a decrease in average labour wages and employment opportunities. The share of income of the lower three-tenths of the population declined to less than 5 per cent during the mid-1990s. Another factor further enhancing the marginalization of the socio-economically disadvantaged segments of Israeli society was the import of foreign labour, which began substituting Palestinian workers from 1991 onwards. By the end of the 1990s, the share of those foreign workers equalled 10 per cent of the labour force, the number of unemployed Israelis. Foreign labourers, however, were considerably cheaper.[14]

Growing inequality as a result of the peace process and the transformation of the domestic political economy in Israel contributed to a growing political schism, which in turn negatively affected the peace process. The 1996 elections, in which Netanyahu ousted Peres as Prime Minister, 'demonstrated that the losers from liberalization can crystallize into a substantial political force.' Those segments of the population suffering from the increasing openness of the Israeli economy effectively voted against the peace process.[15] Uri Ram rightly argued that growing inequality 'reinforces the already existing overlap between political preference and social status in Israel.' The upper echelons of society

> Identify with the tie between Israeli economic growth and peaceful coexistence in the Middle East. The translation between their status and their politics is evident, and finds expression both in political behaviour and in public opinion polls. In the elections for the fourteenth Knesset (1996), in the wealthy neighbourhoods and well-established locations, Labour won 60 per cent of the votes and Likud won only 27 per cent, whereas in development and immigrant towns, Labour won only 26 per cent and Likud won 57 per cent.[16]

In this sense, the peace process and the associated changes within the Israeli economy and society exacerbated the growing political schism and contributed to the domestic failure of peace. Although Ehud Barak won a remarkable majority of the vote in 1999, his arrogant and elitist style of policy-making quickly made him unpopular among the electorate. Ariel Sharon won the 2001 elections with the highest margin ever, in the context of the Intifada and a growing national sentiment that the peace process had failed. Another important factor in Sharon's victory was also the electoral boycott of Palestinians living inside Israel. The lower segments of Israeli society had turned towards Netanyahu and the Likud in 1996 because of their suffering from the domestic economic consequences of the peace process. Similarly, the Arab population in Israel had become increasingly disillusioned with the peace process, which finally resulted in their participation in the violent riots of October 2000 and their boycott of the 2001 elections.

By that time, however, unemployment in many Arab towns and villages had reached record highs, compounded by problems in education, housing, illegal building, health and welfare services, municipal budgets, and development projects.[17] In addition, the Arab population living in Israel had become a double victim of the peace process. The Oslo process not only failed to resolve the Israeli-Arabs' struggle for identity, but also deprived them of job opportunities due to the re-location of the labour-intensive industries from Israel to the Territories or Jordan, a process, which had begun before Barak's tenure. In fact, an opinion poll carried out among Palestinians living in Israel found that their attitude towards the government did not change considerably between 1999 and 2001, but confirmed that resentment had strongly increased between 1995 and 1999.[18] The subsequent boycott of many Palestinians living in Israel of the 2001 elections contributed to Sharon's electoral victory and a further deterioration of the peace process.

Israeli entrepreneurs focused on preparing the ground for a peace process and took advantage of the new opportunities opened up as a result of that process. They were unable, or had no interest in maintaining or furthering the momentum of the peace process through collaborative projects beyond preserving their own economic concerns. Thus, they contributed to growing socio-economic inequality not only regionally, but also domestically. This increasing imbalance enhanced the political and economic schisms evident in Israeli society, which further undermined the peace process with the resulting electoral victories for the Likud party in 1996 and 2001. The interests, attitudes, and engagement of Israeli entrepreneurs in the peace process, as well as the nature of realized co-operative business ties, failed to fulfil the positive role assigned to them by a majority of writers in the years preceding and following the Oslo Accords. In fact, they contributed to undermine that very same process, in addition to endangering domestic political stability and democracy by undercutting the pre-existing social contract. The economic dimension of the Oslo process not only failed to cement peace, but also exacerbated regional and domestic inequalities and thus contributed to the overall failure of peace.

Jordan

The Passive Role of Jordanian Business

Similar to Israel, Jordan's participation in the peace process was based on economic considerations. However, in contrast to Israel, the kingdom's decision to opt for peace was not driven by the business sector, but by King Hussein, in the face of considerable reluctance among the population and even within the government. The involvement of the Jordanian business community in the peace process featured two distinguishable phases. The first phase, from 1994 until early 1998, saw a constant deterioration in bilateral relations between Jordan and Israel. It was fuelled by the lack of progress in inter-governmental projects; affairs such as the attempted assassination of a leading Hamas member in Amman by Mossad agents or the shooting of seven school children by a member of the Jordanian border patrol in 1997; the overall stalemate in the peace process after 1996; and Jordan's worsening economic situation.

The business sector, by and large dependent on Jordan's main trading partner, Iraq, publicly rejected all efforts aimed at normalizing relations with Israel. A majority of entrepreneurs had at first believed in the potential for economic co-operation and explored projects behind the façade of public rejection. The palace deliberately fostered expectations of a large 'peace dividend.' As the promised benefits did not materialize, however, both the average Jordanian and a majority of the business community increasingly snubbed the warm peace King Hussein promoted. Entrepreneurs grew disillusioned with the Israeli business attitude and became increasingly vocal in rejecting ties with Israel. As a result, many joined the political opposition, which thrived on the unpopularity of normalization. The leading business associations, clubs of the executives in government-owned companies and of heavily state-dependent enterprises, joined all other professional associations in their anti-normalization stance and with an increasing openness boycotted the MENA conferences. The business associations avoided taking part in the preparations for the 1995 conference in Amman. Only a few attended the 1996 meeting in Cairo, and the associations officially boycotted the 1997 Doha conference. The anti-normalization movement, including the business associations, achieved its greatest success when it managed to all but cancel the Israeli trade fair in Amman in 1997, unhindered and therefore almost encouraged by the government and the palace.

The 1997 MENA conference in the Qatari capital, however, heralded the beginning of the second phase of the business community's involvement and engagement in the peace process. This phase fully began with the inauguration of the al-Hassan Industrial Estate as Jordan's first Qualifying Industrial Zone (QIZ) in the spring of 1998. Until the conference, a sole businessman had relatively openly promoted the benefits of peace. Omar Salah, however, educated abroad, stood outside the traditional circles of influence and the business associations. His family, engaged in the construction business in Saudi Arabia, hardly had any political or economic interests to preserve in Jordan. Nevertheless, Salah was a crucial actor in the conclusion of the Israeli-Jordanian QIZ agreement, which became the basis of the new political economy in Jordan. He recognized the potential for outsourcing manufacturing operations from Israel to Jordan and established a range of joint ventures with leading Israeli firms in the al-Hassan Estate near Irbid, close to the Israeli border and far away from the Jordanian centres of power in Amman. The Century Investment Group soon became the single largest employer after the government. The QIZ agreement benefited Jordan in creating employment opportunities, attracting foreign investment, and boosting the kingdom's exports through an extension of the Israeli-US FTA. It simultaneously ensured, however, that Israeli companies profited from Jordan's economic growth.

The benefits of the QIZ agreement were debated controversially in Jordan, but soon saw the emergence of young, pragmatic, largely foreign-educated business leaders, who quickly grasped and capitalized on the potentials of co-operation. The palace protected this new stratum, which was also connected to the government, often through long-standing family ties. The anti-normalization movement could not intimidate those young businesspeople engaged in co-operation. Several government-owned companies such as the Jordan Cement Factories Co. (JCFC) now also concluded deals with Israelis. These were kept secret, as were most deals involving entrepreneurs with lesser political standing, in the face of the growing popular opposition to the king's warm peace. In the context of the political mood, the government did not play a large role in promoting the QIZ agreement, which probably guaranteed the success of operations. Most were kept secret until the overall success of the al-Hassan Industrial Estate was undeniably established in 1999.

At the same time, those business leaders engaged in co-operation with Israeli companies were flexible and pragmatic enough not to openly promote warm peace. The anti-normalization movement had particular influence over public opinion in 1997 and 1998. Thus, the entrepreneurs engaged in the al-Hassan Industrial Estate, if their involvement was publicized at all, made it clear that they did not like dealing with Israel, but that they sought to strengthen the Jordanian economy on the basis of the available opportunities. Abdallah Tayyeh, the former Vice-President of Boscan International, for example, said:

> If you ask me whether I like dealing with Israel – no. I would rather be in a stronger position and a less dependent role. I am very loyal to Jordan and want to see it strong. But the [necessary Israeli input to attain QIZ status] 8 per cent have been imposed, so we use it.[19]

It was these moderates who entertained ties with the palace and entered into a political-economic alliance with the new king, Abdullah II. Omar Salah, in contrast, exhibited a much less accommodating political opinion and therefore found himself excluded from the circles of power around Abdullah. However, most members of the new business generation passively took advantage of the opportunities peace offered, but did not seek to advance the peace process further. Instead, other options were equally explored and resulted in Jordan's WTO accession and the conclusion of a FTA with the United States.

From Rentierism to Patrimonial Capitalism

The business community played a passive role in the peace process at best. During the first phase, this passive engagement remained a public rejection of normalization and ties with Israel. During the later phase, businesspeople took advantage of the opportunities that emerged in the context of peace. Entrepreneurs rarely sought to advance and solidify the peace process and Jordanian relations with Israel any further. Instead, the moderate elements of the new business elite dominated. These favoured economic reform, but also sought to avoid an open break with the traditional elite and the established system of rule, which was based on integrationist policies. Peace was simply an exogenous given.

The Jordanian political economy was transformed significantly. The older elites opposed King Hussein's decision to make peace. The young generation of business leaders established itself as a potent force in the Jordanian economy and politics on the basis of its collaboration with Israeli companies. Reforms had begun before peace. However, the peace process and Jordan's rehabilitation in the eyes of the international community following its unpopular neutrality during the Gulf War, which attracted foreign aid under the cover of reform, enhanced the economic transformation. In this sense, the changes in the political economy in Jordan, as in Israel, were a direct result of the peace process. The new elite of young business leaders cemented its ties to the palace and the government, often through their ties to young officials from a similar social background.

Under King Abdullah, this new elite became the central force in Jordanian politics. The influence of traditional elites declined. The internal quarrels of established business associations and the slow, but steady progress made on privatization deprived the old elite of their role in politics. Business associations established by the younger generation gained influence through their role in developing reform initiatives such as REACH or the Jordan Vision 2020 document. Both the Young Entrepreneurs Association (YEA) and the Jordanian-American Business Association (JABA) grew quickly and entertained close ties to the palace and the government. In addition, young business leaders were called on to serve in the new Economic Consultative Council (ECC), which was not only an instrument of economic policy-making, but was de facto the king's personal think tank on all issues associated with economic reform. The new elite also took on the responsibility in complementing the government in the allocation of resources in the kingdom. Hitherto, the public sector had provided most employment opportunities. Now, the new enterprises created a growing number of jobs, often through their ties to Israel and in QIZ manufacturing operations, which increased exports to the United States and hence yielded foreign reserve.

While external capital inflows accruing directly to the state were still essential for Jordan's economic survival, the kingdom did not exhibit the characteristics of a rentier system as strongly as it had in the past. Economic transition, however, did not lead to the emergence of a proper market economy. Instead, while the Jordanian legislative framework now resembled a western market economy, sociopolitical action and interaction continued to follow the same pattern as under the rentier system. The new elites enjoyed privileged access to the palace and the government, most noticeably through the formation of the ECC, which was critically termed an unelected quasi-government. They continued to rely on personal interest politics and upheld King Abdullah's rule in the kingdom through the provision of employment and public support for the monarchy. As Oliver Schlumberger observed: 'Relying on private capital accumulation, but at the same time determined by patrimonial socio-political relations, this hybrid economic order can best be grasped as *patrimonial capitalism*.'[20] Schlumberger rightly added, 'political and economic elites in Jordan have proven to be extremely flexible and highly capable of adapting to changing local, regional or international circumstances.' The best examples for this adaptability were the changes following from Jordan's peace treaty with Israel, and the subsequent transformation of the Jordanian political economy. However, the new business elite, more often than not the 'progeny of the men who served, or continue to serve, in some of the highest state posts,' was interested in economic reform, not political change.[21]

The new system of patrimonial capitalism, thus, did not advance economic liberalization and reform to such a degree that the political system of rule was transformed. While employment opportunities were created, large segments of the society remained dependent on the state and the enterprises of the new elites. In most textile factories located in Irbid, for example, rudimentary training was provided, but wages remained low, and opportunities to advance one's prospects remained limited. Skilled labour was imported from abroad under a new law, which allowed up to 50 per cent of foreign workers to be employed. These workers were better qualified than their Jordanian counterparts. The new system thus ensured that the Jordanians remained satisfied to be employed at all, rather than demanding further benefits.

King Abdullah was part of the same generation as the young business leaders and formed a strategic political-economic alliance with them. Reforms suited those entrepreneurs in positions to take advantage of them. Dealing with Israel was tolerated and encouraged, although members of the new elite had to refrain from statements too openly in favour of normalization. In return for the creation of a favourable business environment, the young new leaders of the business community supported Abdullah and provided a new elite circle sustaining Hashemite rule in the kingdom. Peace in Jordan accelerated the economic transition the country had begun during the late 1980s and contributed to the emergence of a new, pragmatic business generation. This young generation developed a vested interest in peace, albeit in a different way than the original Functionalist writers on the peace process had envisaged. Instead of openly promoting peace, those entrepreneurs took advantage of the opportunities dealing with Israel offered, while refraining from advancing or even supporting the peace process publicly. The new pragmatism led to a re-orientation and re-assessment of Jordan's warm peace. Warm peace cooled down and became lukewarm. While the business community dealt with Israel, it cast its eyes on the advantages the kingdom's WTO accession and the conclusion of a FTA with the United States offered. Instead of full economic and political liberalization, a new system of patrimonial capitalism came into existence.

The End of Democratization

As the economic benefits from Jordan's engagement in co-operation with Israel only accrued to the elites, a new social contract based on the consent of those co-opted into the system of patrimonial capitalism did not emerge. Instead, the measures of political liberalization that King Hussein had first introduced in 1989 were increasingly reversed after 1993. The king made clear that 'expressions of popular discontent relating to peace and normalization with Israel would not be permitted to disrupt' the peace process.[22] Although the palace pursued a cautious strategy and tolerated the popular protests against the Israeli trade fair in 1997, when the anti-normalization was at the peak of its power, Jordan remained committed to peace. King Hussein made the choice between democratization and peace in favour of the peace process.

In 1992 and 1993, the government cracked down on the Islamist opposition, which at the height of the Gulf Crisis had been included in the government. The election law was changed for 1993 in order to limit the influence of the Muslim Brotherhood. The regime's determination to resort to oppression manifested itself again in 1996, when in the context of new riots King Hussein went on television and threatened to use an 'iron fist' to restore order.[23] Back in 1989, after the first such incident, King Hussein had opted for liberalization. This time, as well as during further clashes in 1998 and early 2002, the government resorted to force. Laurie Brand rightly pointed out that by 1996 already, the 'episode of regime transition and re-consolidation' had ended. After a period of free elections and significant widening of public freedoms, the pre-1989 boundaries and practices had gradually been re-asserted.[24]

During the last year of King Hussein's reign, when the king was undergoing treatment for cancer in the United States, and during the first year of King Abdullah's reign, uncertainty surrounded the Hashemite monarchy again. However, through its alliance with the new economic and political elites, the regime re-asserted itself and Abdullah successfully mastered the apparent power struggle with Prime Minister Rawabdeh over the pace of reform. When the transition towards the rule of the moderates and pragmatists under Abdullah was completed, less than two years after the young king had acceded to the throne, political liberalization suffered further setbacks. The ECC sidelined the government. The anti-normalization movement was repressed forcibly. The Jordanian Lower House was dissolved and elections repeatedly delayed.

Thus, economic co-operation created a vested interest in the continuation of the peace process, while domestic political stability dictated a re-orientation towards a lukewarm or cool, instead of warm, peace and diminished the prospects for democratization in Jordan. Although the new elites and their king spoke the discourse of political and economic liberalization, it was clear by 2002 that the new system of patrimonial capitalism was no liberal market economy. Political opposition was once again treated with a mixture of integration, co-option, and repression. In addition, the old elites on the right, possibly the most potent force of opposition, had even less interest in increasing the level of political liberalization and in a re-distribution of resources or wealth. The forces on the left side of the political spectrum remained powerless and unorganized. As one observer commented, 'the hopeless battles against the politics of normalization and the economic reform programme have led to a virtual stagnant situation for the opposition and confrontations with the regime have simply become unproductive political spectacles.'[25]

But not only democratization suffered a setback as a result of the dynamics of peace in Jordan. The new system of patrimonial capitalism, while substituting public sector employment with mainly blue-collar jobs in the private sector, did little to stem the tide of increasing inequality in Jordan. By the end of 1997, 26 per cent of the Jordanian population lived in absolute poverty. 45 per cent of all families lived on a monthly salary of at most JD 150.[26] By 1999, a third of the population lived in poverty. The unofficial, but widely recognized, unemployment rate had risen to 27 per cent. The economic reforms implemented favoured the economic elite. Thus, consumers, not producers, paid the new sales tax, which the kingdom introduced in 1994. It was a '"regressive tax" that favoured merchants and large businessmen, and was therefore a socially unjust tax that disproportionally impacted on the poor.'[27] Violent riots broke out, especially in the south of the country, which shook Jordan in 1996, 1998, and again in early 2002, as a result of rising poverty and inequality. The protests illustrated that the new system would continue to be dominated by the overriding policy objective, which had also characterized King Hussein's long rule. Regime security and political stability were achieved with a mixture of integrationist policies and repression, to which the government resorted during these three instances of political protest.

In this sense, the peace process further accelerated rising inequality – a consequence of economic reform – and led to the reversal of democratization, which had begun in 1989 but was now undermined in the context of the regime's choice for peace. Both rising inequality and the reversal of political liberalization were thus results of the peace process. Peace benefited only a small elite stratum around the palace and the government and strengthened the rule of a new alliance of political and economic elites under a system of patrimonial capitalism. Peace was thus not a peace of the king anymore, but still a peace of the elites. As it did not yield widely distributed benefits, a consensual social contract could not come into existence, and thus, the process of liberalization or democratization could not be sustained under the given circumstances. At the same time, peace turned lukewarm a few years into the normalization of relations with Israel. Although political stability seemed to be ensured during the Intifada, the Jordanian monarchy and its economic elites failed to fulfil the role assigned to them in cementing peace.

Business co-operation, especially on the basis of the opportunities the QIZ agreement had opened up, created a vested interest in the maintenance of peace, but only among the ruling elite. In this sense, Jordan was the most successful example of a creation of vested interests in peace, of the mobilization of domestic actors in favour of peace, and of economic transition. The old elites with a possible interest in conflict continuation – on the basis of their interests in the Iraqi market – lost power. Political stability was achieved, albeit for the price of a growing divide between the moderate proponents of peace and reform and the majority of the population, which suffered from rising poverty and unemployment and which was deprived of political influence. Jordan continued to walk the tightrope that King Hussein had been walking during most of the four decades of his reign. The kingdom re-oriented itself cautiously with its accession to the WTO and its conclusion of a free trade agreement (FTA) with the United States. Jordan's economic elites gained a vested interest in maintaining peace, but under the condition of an unequal division of the peace dividend, peace remained necessarily lukewarm.

The Palestinian Territories

The Economic Dimension of Peace

Peace for the Palestinians involved an important economic dimension. It was as much about achieving development and prosperity as it was about realizing the Palestinians' nationalist aspirations. However, ordinary Palestinian entrepreneurs played only a limited role in the political direction of the peace process and exerted little influence on the economic agreements the PLO and later the PA, concluded with Israel and Jordan. This was due to the underdeveloped nature of the business sector and the economy at large, and the fact that a movement from outside the Territories was largely driving and directing the nationalist struggle. At the same time, however, the economic dimension of peace had significant effects on the domestic political economy. It enabled the PA to impose itself as the central political and economic actor and marginalized the local business community. Diaspora businesspeople acquired leverage through their involvement in investment projects in the Territories and formed an alliance with the political elites of the PA.

Resident entrepreneurs in the West Bank and Gaza were largely excluded from political and economic negotiations. Although negotiators later often became involved in business affairs, this followed from their political engagements and their contacts and understanding of the opportunities opened up by agreements. The local business community exhibited a sober attitude towards peace and especially, the potential dividends from co-operation and trade. While Palestinians in general supported a peace deal with Israel – which was hoped would fulfil the nationalist aspiration for independence – entrepreneurs had struggled for a long time with the 'de-developing' policies of the Israeli authorities. The trade volume was large, but mainly one-way, from Israel into the Territories. The years after the 1993 Declaration of Principles quickly proved that the scope for an independent economic policy or for indigenous development was limited. Most entrepreneurs remained utterly dependent on Israel, for raw materials, imports and exports, and as a market destination. From 1994 onwards, the initially optimistic attitude of many businesspeople turned into disillusionment due to the closures the Israeli government imposed.

The closures were the most decisive element in shaping the Palestinian economy during the Oslo process, harming the local business sector even further, while forcing and allowing the PA to impose itself as the major actor in the economy. Mazen Sinokrot, for example, said in 1996 that because of the closures, he had to lay off workers and cut back production when sales dropped by 60 per cent, as trucks were not permitted to enter his company's major market, Gaza.[28] As a result of such lay-offs, firstly, the PA was forced to create job opportunities in the context of growing unemployment and spreading dissatisfaction with the peace process. The distribution of resources through the provision of employment, at the same time, increased the dependence of many Palestinians on the proto-state and created a quasi-rentier system. Secondly, the provisions of the Paris Protocol and the difficulties related to trade, together with the PA's desire to centralize revenue, resulted in the Palestinian agency law. This law increased the PA's economic and political leverage but did not benefit the resident business community. Together, the closures, the Paris Protocol, and the resulting domestic legislation, marginalized the local business community while it propelled the PA into the position of the dominant force in politics and the economy. Closures deprived local entrepreneurs of business opportunities and all but ended Palestinian employment inside Israel, hitherto one of the most important sectors of the Palestinian economy. The wealthy Diaspora, however, was hardly affected by the closures, since its conglomerates focused on internal Palestinian projects. PA officials took advantage of the conditions the closures and the 1995 agency law created and established monopolistic trade operations. These did not only push local merchants out of the market, but also increased consumer prices and thus harmed the Palestinian population at large.

As a result of the closures and the dysfunctional Paris Protocol, Palestinian entrepreneurs quickly became disillusioned with their hopes for improved business prospects. The agency law was intended to promote the local private sector by restricting the scope for the direct engagement of Israeli companies in the Palestinian market. However, this instrument turned out to benefit the PA, its officials, and those entrepreneurs close to it, disproportionally. Bigger manufacturing companies often managed to obtain representations for products that they did not produce themselves, thus solidifying and enhancing their market positions. The large Diaspora conglomerates secured agencies for international brand name goods, the most prestigious and lucrative form of representations. The latter, in particular, harmed domestic industries through the entry of competitive products into the market. Smaller companies and small-scale entrepreneurs often represented Israeli companies, but the bulk of smaller manufacturing enterprises came under increasing pressure.

The PA gained increasing revenue, which enabled it to create more job opportunities and tie an increasing number of Palestinians to the proto-state. Loyalty was also rewarded by granting favourable concessions to the friendly conglomerates, such as PADICO. Most importantly, PA officials established their own trade companies and struck deals with Israeli officials and businesspeople, importing certain goods under monopolistic conditions. Some of the benefits the PA accrued from these deals formed a second, secret budget, which was specifically used to buy and reward loyalty and to finance the various security and intelligence services sustaining the PA's authority. Local businesspeople were drawn into a dependent relationship with the PA. Alternatively, they found themselves disadvantaged and under strong competitive pressures, in addition to the difficulties related to trade and transportation. As a result, the business community began to boycott all regional initiatives from the 1995 MENA conference in Amman onwards. The meetings were considered hypocritical exercises in regional economic development rhetoric, while the process of de-development continued unmitigated.

Given the conflicting interests of the vast majority of small-scale businesspeople in the Palestinian Territories – favouring independence on the one hand, while depending on Israel economically – the private sector in the end came out in favour of a free trade agreement. This arrangement would have enhanced the PA's economic policy-making authority with regard to external trade and industrial policy, but would have left Palestinian-Israeli relations de facto unchanged. Although Israel would potentially have faced increased competition from Palestinian producers in its domestic market, the goods concerned would have lacked the necessary quality in order to compete successfully. Subcontracting arrangements, the most significant form of collaboration under occupation, would have continued. Thus, the arrangement the private sector lobbied for was in accordance with the preferences of the PA, which at the moment when efforts were made to institutionalize interest politics further had already consolidated its grip economically and politically.

The alliance between the PA and the Diaspora entrepreneurs established a new dimension in Palestinian-Israeli economic relations. For most local businesspeople, however, conditions deteriorated during the peace process. Hence, the majority of Palestinian entrepreneurs neither actively engaged in co-operation nor supported the Oslo process politically and economically. Instead, Palestinian businesspeople were hindered in developing or expanding their entrepreneurial activities and boycotted those initiatives, which accompanied and represented the economic dimension of the peace process publicly.

Marginalization of Local Entrepreneurs and Neo-Patrimonialism

The Palestinian political economy was completely transformed as a direct result of the peace process. The nature of the process, its economic dimension, and the almost exclusive support from the international community for the PA, all contributed to the emergence of new dominant elites. These new elites were expatriate Palestinians. Local businesspeople were left without much influence. A growing schism emerged between the PA, the Diaspora business community, and local entrepreneurs, although they came to be active in different fields. The PA dominated trade; the Diaspora engaged in large-scale infrastructure and industrial ventures, while the majority of small-scale businesses remained active mainly in subcontracting.[29] A new economic and political order emerged in the Territories, under which the PA came to establish itself as the dominant player in the economy.

This new political-economic system was a result of the peace process, the economic agreements it entailed, and the political and economic power it bestowed on the PA. It was characterized by the centralization of political and economic power in the hands of the elites. The political role of the PA led to its increasing involvement in the economy. The failure to achieve real economic development and growth, however, led those suffering most under the given circumstances to increasingly oppose the peace process. Like in Israel, where the lower segments of society voted against the peace process in the 1996 elections, large segments of the Palestinian population grew increasingly radicalized. Approval rates for Arafat and the number of Fatah supporters declined continuously. Radical movements such as Hamas and the Islamic Jihad enjoyed growing popularity.[30]

In many ways, the marginalization of local entrepreneurs and the monopolization of newly created business opportunities in collaboration with Israeli companies, contributed to a growing rejection of peace among the population. This discredited not only the PA leadership, but also the political process it pursued. As Hussam Khader, the Nablus representative in the Palestinian Legislative Council (PLC), said:

> We are, in fact, talking about a mafia that began to operate in parallel with the conducting of the negotiations with Israel. The same men who talked politics and Oslo tried at the same time to forge ties with Israeli companies."[31]

The neo-patrimonial, or patrimonial-capitalist, order that was emerging under the PA perpetuated the economic weakness of the Palestinians further. It was thus only a temporarily stabilizing mechanism, not a sustainable model of state-society relations. Christopher Parker rightly argued in 1999:

> A corporatist, neopatrimonial dynamic is clearly emerging as a major pillar of stabilization in the relationship between the PA and society in the self-rule areas. It is, however, a model that arises from and is likely to perpetuate the fundamental structural malaise that threatens Palestinian acceptance of the emerging order [...] At an immediate and practical level, factionalism and neopatrimonialism are unlikely to create an environment conducive to the kinds and degree of economic growth that will satisfy expectations and demands associated with self-rule. On the contrary, the neopatrimonial framework is likely to encourage non-productive forms of social competition, which neither advance the cause of nation-building nor promote national political and economic integration over the long-term.[32]

Thus, the new political-economic order actually contributed to undermine the stability of the PA's rule, since it did not do much to induce sustainable growth. The majority of the population found itself marginalized and deprived of the benefits from peaceful co-operation, trade, and indigenous economic development, and turned towards other means. One positive side effect of this disillusionment, at first, was a strong movement towards the formation of civil institutions, such as NGOs and associations. However, the PA quickly repressed those voices too critical of its own performance, while it ensured that the moderates became dependent on funds and co-ordination with PA institutions. The negative side-effect was the growth in support for the radical nationalist and Islamist organizations, which further undermined the peace process. This also damaged the Palestinians' image in the eyes of the international community and reduced the willingness of international donors to maintain their efforts for peace and their support for Palestinian development initiatives.

Local entrepreneurs were drawn into a dependence on the PA, or else, were completely marginalized. The difficulties to even survive in business then also meant that entrepreneurs could not afford to engage in political initiatives. The spiral set in motion with the creation of the PA, the Paris Protocol, the agency law, corruption, and monopolization, fully deprived the vast majority of resident entrepreneurs in the West Bank and Gaza of any meaningful political and economic role. In this sense, Palestinians not only suffered economically, but also politically. Instead of realizing their nationalist aspirations in the establishment of a liberal, democratic state, Palestinians found themselves under the condition of the new patrimonial capitalism revolving around the PA. Prospects for democratization, economic development, and thus also political stability, remained bleak.

Arafat's popularity rates decreased almost continuously and fell to only 39 per cent in April 2000, the lowest since 1994. Support for his Fatah party also declined. Hamas gained growing support, although the largest increase in numbers was found among those Palestinians not associating themselves with any political faction. In July 1998, only 31 per cent of Palestinians thought their economic conditions had worsened over the previous three years. By April 2000, 53 per cent believed they had been better off economically before the peace process. Attitudes towards the PA hardly changed throughout 1999 and 2000, prior to the Intifada. About 70 per cent of Palestinians believed that corruption existed in the PA. Around 60 per cent believed the level of corruption would remain the same or even increase.[33] In this sense, opinion polls confirmed Parker's argument that 'the structural underpinnings at the social, political, and economic nexus [of PA rule] were not transformed in ways capable of sustaining pluralist developments in Palestinian society.'[34]

Thus, the transformation of the Palestinian political economy towards a neopatrimonial order pushed a majority of Palestinian businesspeople out of the market and deprived them of political participation. Even though the business associations, under Paltrade's leadership, initiated the National Economic Dialogue in 1999, the outcome of the conference remained vague until the outbreak of the Intifada in September 2000. As in Israel and Jordan, businesspeople in the Palestinian Territories failed to fulfil the positive role assigned to them by Çarkoğlu, Eder and Kirişci.[35] Their failure, however, did not originate in their interest in conflict continuation, as Wright claimed, but in the political-economic dynamics of the peace process itself.[36] Those elites who did engage in co-operation did not advance the peace process, but undermined it by enhancing domestic and regional inequality. Like the 1996 elections in Israel, the 2000 Intifada was as much a backlash against the peace process pursued by a corrupt leadership, as it was triggered by the failure of this peace process to deliver the anticipated Palestinian statehood.

The Oslo Process and Palestinian Democracy

Instead of solidifying the peace process, business ties between Palestinians and Israelis undermined the credibility of the Palestinian leadership, which had opted for peace and pursued the negotiations, and thus, the peace process itself. The second Intifada in the Occupied Territories has generally been explained with reference to the unsuccessful Camp David negotiations and Ariel Sharon's controversial visit to the Haram al-Sharif (Temple Mount) in Jerusalem. In fact, the Intifada was a direct consequence of the neo-patrimonial order emerging under the PA and political and economic deprivation. Almost prophetically, Parker argued in 1999, that the neo-patrimonial social order failed to induce support for peace and, in fact, would potentially lead to greater social unrest:

> The new order in the 'Palestinian areas' has proved unable to allow tensions arising in a time of economic hardship and political change to be mitigated either by grassroots innovation or through the legislative and executive efficacy of the PA. That this has not led to even greater social unrest in the OT than has already been seen is in large measure due to an artificial decoupling of political and economic developments – a situation that has been made possible by massive donor funding.[37]

Until the Tokyo conference of donors in 1999, the international community had gone along with what then came to be labelled corruption. It was generally assumed that only Arafat and the PA could bring about peace. The conduct of domestic political affairs seemed of minor importance until that time. As Hiba Husseini, Vice-Chairman of the PSE and a leading private sector advocate, put it, 'everybody was very happy to deal with only a few people and to know who to give the money to.'[38] But when the donors finally forced the PA to introduce a greater degree of transparency into its management of economic and political affairs, large segments of the population and the business sector had become dependent on the proto-state.

As a result, the PA could not provide the resources necessary to steer political developments anymore. Even before, economic decline could not fully be met by donor assistance, and consequently, poverty had risen substantially.[39] Living standards in the Palestinian economy had already steeply declined during 1993-97.[40] The Intifada was hence the consequence of the overall economic and political frustrations that most Palestinians had suffered from throughout seven years of the peace process. The monopolies, corruption, the high unemployment rate, and the restrictions on trade and other business opportunities for the average population inspired the belief that most people did not stand to lose anything anymore. The result was the desperate armed struggle against the Israeli occupation led by militarized and radicalized armed factions, whom the PA sought to direct but increasingly failed to control. The business sector, again, did not play any significant role during the Intifada. Some of the monopolistic operations continued as they had before the Intifada. For most small-scale businesses, conditions grew even worse. In this sense, the Palestinian business sector had little interest in conflict continuation, but had little influence over political developments, either.

The PA leadership, which had opted for peace and pursued the negotiations, had created a political and economic order, in which political association with the leadership entailed economic gain, both domestically and in collaboration with Israel. Through its monopolistic and corrupt practices, it discredited itself, the 'economy of peace,' and ultimately the peace process itself. Politically, at the same time, the corruption prevailing within the PA demonstrated that the hopes of many Palestinians for a democratic order in the Territories were not to be satisfied. Instead, with the onset of the Intifada, most Palestinians, including most businesspeople, found themselves between a rock and a hard place. On the one hand, the PA and its leadership under Arafat had discredited itself and lost credibility. On the other hand, the alternatives seemed even worse. Hamas and the Islamist organizations gained support and threatened to establish a strict political order in accordance with their interpretation of Islam. The young militants loomed large during the Intifada but had no clear political agenda other than ending the occupation militarily. The result was the widespread disillusionment with all political factions.

As in Jordan, the peace process and associated processes such as the establishment of the PA, its conclusion of economic agreements and the substance and implementation of those agreements, as well as its domestic economic legislation, induced a major transformation of the domestic political economy. Instead of economic and political liberalization, however, the peace process and the economic dimension it involved saw the creation of an alliance of political elites within and around the PA and economic elites. Most important amongst these were the Jordanian G7 and other wealthy expatriate Palestinians, but the network also included some resident entrepreneurs. It was these elites which engaged in the establishment of new collaborative ties with Israelis. For most Palestinians, cooperation with Israel hardly changed, unless relations were hindered and ended because of closures, obstacles in transportation, and trade barriers, or because Israeli textile manufacturers moved to Jordan. Through the allocation of resources on the basis of its administration of donor funds, the creation of employment, and even simple force, the PA established itself as the dominant force in politics and the economy. The patrimonial-capitalist, or neo-patrimonial, order that was established during the first seven years of the peace process, however, was not sufficiently stable to produce and distribute enough economic resources to guarantee political stability. Due to the increasing dissatisfaction with the PA's financial mismanagement, corruption, and repression, as well as the failure to bring about the anticipated Palestinian state over seven years of negotiations, both the PA and the peace process lost credibility. The Intifada, which broke out in September 2000, was merely a natural consequence.

7

The Regional Failure of the Peace Business

The engagement of Israeli, Jordanian, and Palestinian businesspeople and politicians-turned-entrepreneurs in the peace process contributed to the emergence of a regional elite united in a community of interests. Each of these elites established itself as the dominant force in the domestic economy and politics. Yet, the regional elite community of interests failed to grant enough concessions to the disadvantaged both regionally and domestically in order to co-opt them successfully. Thus, the elites failed to successfully form a regional hegemonic bloc and ultimately led the peace process into its failure. In addition, the elites, at least in Israel and the Palestinian Territories, undermined their own domestic hegemony based on the political consent of the ruled through economic concessions.

Business and Co-operation

Diverging Business Interests in Peace

Israeli, Jordanian, and Palestinian businesspeople all had a strong interest in peace, yet exhibited diverging conceptions of the economic dimension of peace. To the Israeli business community, peace was a necessary precondition for opening up new markets overseas. The second Israeli interest focused on a preservation of the economic status quo in the region, which favoured Israeli entrepreneurs due to their dominance over the Palestinian market. In contrast, Jordanian entrepreneurs were mainly interested in achieving indigenous development for the weak domestic business sector. Many rejected the normalization of ties with Israel. Even for the pragmatic young business elites engaged in co-operation, collaboration with Israel was only one beneficial aspect of the new circumstances the peace treaty created. The QIZ agreement, Jordan's WTO accession, and the conclusion of a free trade agreement (FTA) with the United States were equally important. Similarly, for a majority of the Palestinian business community, the main interest in peace lay in the realization of independence, not only politically, but also economically. However, only a few entrepreneurs could afford not to engage in co-operation due to their dependence on Israel. At the same time, the new elite alliance of PA officials and wealthy Diaspora businesspeople established its hegemony over Palestinian society through its control over revenue, on the one hand from the international community in the form of financial aid, on the other through the engagement in monopolistic trade deals with Israeli firms.

The Israeli business community exerted its influence domestically in order to pave the way for the peace process, which opened up extra-regional markets. The associated process of economic liberalization did not weaken the economic elites but was in fact an expression of their adaptability and the preservation of their domestic dominance. Regionally, the Israeli business elite did not have much interest in co-operation for the sake of cementing peace. Instead, the Israeli business community sought to preserve the status quo with regard to relations with the Palestinians. Jordan was discovered as a convenient manufacturing location. Industrial subcontracting and outsourcing in the kingdom replaced many such operations in the Palestinian Territories. Israeli dominance was thus not only preserved, but in fact enhanced. Employing a discourse of regional economic co-operation and development, Israeli businesspeople even managed to blame the Palestinian side for the poor evolution of new business ties on top of the pre-existing relations. Thus, for example, Uri Menashe, CEO of Cargal and Chairman of the IMA's Autonomy Committee, attributed the slow start of business co-operation to the PA's boycott of collaborative ties with Israel in June 1994.[1] In fact, however, industrial co-operation beyond the existing pattern of subcontracting was not in the Israeli interest anyway. Already before the conclusion of the Oslo Accords, the Israel Manufacturers Association (IMA) had warned that competition from Palestinians was hurting Israeli industry. It further claimed that if the IMA's concerns were not heard, 'Israel could easily find itself with 10,000 more unemployed workers,' according to Ze'ev Fink, Chairman of the General Industry Sector at the IMA.[2]

Thus, the Israeli business community prepared the ground for the peace process through its control over the evolution of the discourse surrounding economic relations between Israel and its neighbours and determined the nature of economic co-operation with Palestinians and Jordanians. Israeli entrepreneurs promoted co-operation rhetorically, without engaging in much actual collaboration beyond exporting to the Territories, subcontracting, and the re-location of manufacturing operations. Palestinians and Jordanians could hardly afford rejecting collaboration, despite their reluctance. They faced many Israeli obstacles and barriers and were thus left complaining. This made it easy to portray them as the parties which rejected the normalization of relations and a development of co-operative ties. An illustrative example of the diverging attitudes towards co-operation and peace among the three business communities was the 'Taste of Peace' regional culinary conference, the fifth such industry-based meeting organized by the Centre for Jewish-Arab Economic Development in 1996. Out of 100 participants, 60 were Israelis, 25 were Palestinian, and only nine were Jordanian. Only a dozen Israelis and one Jordanian exhibitor displayed their products at the conference. Jordanians and Palestinians seized the opportunity to air their grievances regarding obstacles to trade. The Jordanian Food Manufacturers Association complained that it was 'virtually impossible' to sell its products in Israel. Palestinian entrepreneurs said that security procedures made it hard to sell goods in Israel or to even transport them from the West Bank to Gaza.[3]

The differing attitudes and interests of businesspeople from Israel, Jordan, and the Palestinian Territories were a result of the pre-existing political and economic balance of power between the three entities and business communities. They also laid the ground for co-operation in trade and industrial joint ventures among them, which further enhanced the regional imbalance and thus perpetuated the negative attitudes of many Palestinians and Jordanians.

Unequal Regional Economic Relations

Regional economic co-operation between Israeli, Jordanian, and Palestinian entrepreneurs was characterized by unequal engagement and unequal benefits. Trade and industrial collaboration among the business communities disproportionally benefited the stronger side in the regional equation and effectively enhanced the pre-existing regional and domestic imbalances. Despite their optimism with respect to the beneficial impact of regional business ties, even Çarkoğlu, Eder and Kirişci pointed out in their work: 'Although trade and other forms of co-operation will benefit both sides, relative gains will not be shared equally.' They also had to concede:

> Technologically stronger economies typically dominate weaker ones, and dependent relations with the stronger economy tend to surface after regional co-operation arrangements. The fact that the weaker as well as the stronger sides are mutually aware of this possibility will constitute a serious barrier to regional economic co-operation. Being in an advantageous position, stronger economies will be much more willing to co-operate whereas the weaker sides will be reluctant to engage in a potentially dependent relationship with the stronger side.[4]

Thus, it was unsurprising that Palestinians and Jordanians seemed much more reluctant to enter into trade and industrial co-operative ties with Israelis than vice versa, although the main interest on the Israeli side lay in opening up extra-regional markets. In Jordan, public reluctance dominated. Only with the signing of the agreement on the Qualifying Industrial Zones (QIZ) in 1997, did ties begin to develop. The agreement opened up the path to pragmatic co-operation. Israelis sold the required input to Jordanian and foreign manufacturers, who were the main beneficiaries of co-operation. Direct collaboration between Israelis and Jordanians focused on the outsourcing of manufacturing operations in the textiles industry and in high-tech manufacturing. Here, the Israelis retained control, contributed capital, know-how, technology, and marketing, while the Jordanians provided cheap labour. Effectively, the young entrepreneurs in Jordan, who formed a new elite stratum under the similarly pragmatic King Abdullah, were drawn into a community of interests and an elite alliance with the Israeli entrepreneurs, as were PA officials and Palestinian Diaspora businesspeople.

Industrial co-operation between Palestinians and Israelis revolved around the same formula as Israeli-Jordanian ties: Israeli know-how, technology, and marketing, and Palestinian manual labour. The joint industrial border parks were the most significant initiative in the field of industrial co-operation, but failed to convince entrepreneurs on both sides. Until the outbreak of the new Intifada, only the Gaza Industrial Estate (GIE) assumed operations and involved a number of smaller co-operative projects. Overall, the Palestinian business community benefited least from co-operative ties. Most entrepreneurs remained dependent on Israel for raw materials and as a market. In addition, the re-location of Israeli manufacturing operations to Jordan often deprived Palestinian businessmen of their only source of income, since many smaller establishments depended on the subcontracting arrangements with Israeli firms.

The nature of industrial co-operation between Israelis, Jordanians, and Palestinians confirmed Laura Drake's prediction that industrial co-operation 'might threaten to develop in an unbalanced manner in favour of Israel as the only developed country in the region.' Israel would exploit the existing complementarities in the factors of production, providing 'capital, technology, and managerial experience in exchange for cheap Arab labour.' Co-operation, moreover, according to Drake, would most likely not take place within Israel, as 'this would be unacceptable for security and "demographic" reasons.' Rather, collaborative industries, or industrial parks, would be located near Israel's borders instead of within them. On the basis of the success of this pattern, co-operation would then expand into the larger Arab world, 'beginning most probably with Jordan.'[5] In fact, the re-location of such manufacturing enterprises to Jordan turned out to be such a convenient solution, that outsourcing industrial operations there often replaced industrial collaboration with Palestinian firms in the West Bank and Gaza Strip as well as within Israel. In addition, Israeli entrepreneurs also benefited disproportionally from trade. They retained their dominance over the Palestinian markets. The Jordanians, despite frequent complaints, captured a slice of the cake for themselves. Corrupt Palestinian officials exploited their control over imports and their contacts to members of the Israeli authorities successfully.

While the elites proceeded making the profits, the lower segments of all three societies suffered. However, similar to the unequal sharing of the benefits among the elites, the lower segments also suffered unequally. While some Israelis lost their jobs in manual labour, Dov Lautman, whose company Delta had re-located manufacturing operations to Jordan, claimed that this enabled him to avoid the laying off of Israeli workers:

> That's what is keeping 3,000 jobs here in Israel. Maybe if we hadn't taken advantage of the peace process and the opportunity to work in the region, we would have had to lay off some people here.[6]

Overall, the suffering of the lower echelons of the three societies fed similar backlashes in all three entities, differing only in the extent of anger and despair. In Israel, the rejection expressed itself in the 1996 and 2001 elections as well as the violent riots of the 'Israeli-Arabs' at the beginning of the Intifada. In Jordan, the unequal distribution of shares fuelled the anti-normalization movement and later the re-orientation towards a lukewarm peace. In the Occupied Territories, the indigenous population increasingly resented both Israelis and the Palestinian elite alliance of PA officials and Diaspora businesspeople. The anger found its expression in the new Intifada from September 2000 onwards. The regional elite community of interests thus failed to consolidate its hegemonic grip over the three societies. It also failed to cement the peace process it had a vested interest in, although the existing status quo during seven years of peace-making benefited them significantly and was possibly good enough itself. The business opportunities opened up through the peace process were far more important than the achievement of an endurable peace.

The Failure to Build a Regional Hegemonic Bloc

Although united in a community of interests in profits and business opportunities, Israeli, Jordanian, and Palestinian businesspeople failed to successfully build a regional hegemonic bloc. They thus failed to consolidate the peace process. Insufficient concessions both domestically and regionally generated resentment, envy, and ultimately, the rejection of normalized economic relations and of peace.

The concept of hegemony employed here draws on the writings of Antonio Gramsci. Gramsci had originally applied the concept of hegemony to the leadership of the bourgeoisie in European countries, distinguishing between successfully consolidated hegemonies and non-hegemonic societies. As he had argued during the early 1930s, the bourgeois hegemony was most complete in northern European countries, where capitalism had first become established. This hegemony

> necessarily involved concessions to subordinate classes in return for acquiescence in bourgeois leadership, concessions which could lead ultimately to forms of social democracy which preserve capitalism while making it more acceptable to workers and the petty bourgeoisie.[7]

Gramsci's concept of hegemony involved not only the realm of the economy, but also the ideational sphere. Of primary significance, however, was the originality of his approach to explain the persistence of social democracy in those countries, where hegemony had been established most successfully. Concessions to the demands of workers established and guaranteed the leadership of the bourgeois elites. Hegemony was not achieved and maintained through coercion, but through co-option and consensus in a form of social contract.[8]

In this sense, the elites failed in their project to consolidate a regional hegemony and cement the particular peace process they pursued, because they failed to make enough concessions to co-opt those opposing the process. Domestically, the hegemonic project failed in all three entities. Regionally, the alliance of businesspeople making profits under the given circumstances of the peace process also failed in its attempts to establish hegemony, as it failed to co-opt the weakest part of the chain, Palestinian entrepreneurs and Palestinian society at large.

The economic dimension of the peace process among Israelis, Jordanians, and Palestinians saw the transformation of the domestic and regional political economies. In Israel, this transformation began with the liberalization and globalization of the Israeli economy and was driven by the business community following the crisis of the 1980s. Expansion necessitated an end to the conflict with Israel's neighbours and most importantly, the Arab boycott. The domestic initiation of the peace process by the business community was a manifestation of its hegemony in terms of both its control over discourse and its influence on politics. However, since the lower echelons of society did not gain equal benefits from the domestic transformation, and were now also faced with the loss of job opportunities due to the re-location of manufacturing operations, the pre-existing hegemony of the Israeli business elite eroded and resulted in a non-hegemonic state of affairs. This led to what Gramsci called 'caesarism,' the rule of a strongman, which could be both progressive and reactionary, although the latter was more likely to emerge.[9] In the Israeli case, the first strongman to take over was Binyamin Netanyahu, in the context of the electoral backlash against the enterprise of peace. Ehud Barak, who followed him, was almost as autocratic yet more progressive (i.e., pro-peace). He was then ousted by the reactionary Ariel Sharon.

In Jordan, the ruling elites achieved a mixture between caesarism under King Abdullah and the hegemony of the new elite stratum of young entrepreneurs, without whom the new king might not have established his reign successfully. Under King Hussein, Jordan had been a classical example of modern-day caesarism, which was, in Robert Cox's words, 'particularly apposite to industrializing Third World countries.'[10] The business elite did not exert much influence and by and large opposed peace and the normalization of economic relations with Israel. However, with the opening up of business opportunities, in particular through the conclusion of the QIZ agreement, a new stratum of business leaders emerged. This new Jordanian elite not only began to dominate the economy, but was increasingly also found in government positions. The members of King Abdullah's Economic Consultative Council (ECC) became a decisive factor in policy-making. Concessions were made to those who opposed the peace treaty and normalization by adopting a more moderate position, which emphasized Jordan's economic development over regional co-operation and promoted a lukewarm concept of peace, rather than King Hussein's warm peace. The moderates and King Abdullah thus consolidated their joint grip over Jordanian society. However, this political-economic system of rule remained fragile, and instead of relying on integrationist policies and co-option solely, King Abdullah, like his father, increasingly resorted to coercion and repression. The economic benefits the elites gained from their engagement in collaboration with Israeli entrepreneurs were not distributed widely enough for them to establish themselves as the decisive force. The result was a mixture of a domestic hegemony of the young entrepreneurs and King Abdullah's caesarist rule.

In the Palestinian Territories, the Palestinian Authority (PA) managed to achieve hegemony through its alliance with the wealthy Diaspora only for a short while. Some of the economic benefits were used to reward loyalty and create employment. Overall, however, the PA failed to make enough concessions to ordinary Palestinians, including the vast majority of small-scale entrepreneurs, in order to consolidate a consensus in favour of the peace process the PA was pursuing. At the same time, and more importantly, regionally, the elites with a vested interest in this particular peace process failed to grant enough concessions to the Palestinians at large on a regional scale. Israeli obstacles and barriers to trade, industrial development, and investment alienated large segments of Palestinian society, including many businesspeople. Jordan pursued its own interest of gaining access to the Israeli and Palestinian market, and was largely disinterested in opening up its domestic market to Palestinian produce. As a result of corruption, unfavourable agreements, and disadvantaging policies on a regional level, Palestinian society witnessed a deterioration of socio-economic conditions. Thus, the endeavour to build and maintain hegemony failed not only domestically, but also regionally. The least privileged of the three societies, which had the clearest interest in a radical transformation of the status quo, was not ready to accept and submit to the existing and increasing economic inequality on the domestic and regional levels. The Intifada was the resulting reaction against the exploitation and socio-economic deprivation of the Palestinian population on both the regional (through the interests of Israeli entrepreneurs) and domestic levels (by the PA and the Diaspora).

Business, Peace, Policy-Making and Democracy

Business, State, Society and Foreign Policy-Making

Israeli, Jordanian, and Palestinian business elites influenced the course and direction of the peace process both directly and indirectly. Directly, businesspeople influenced policy-making and the course of the peace process through their access to negotiators or direct involvement in negotiations. Most importantly, they shaped the economic agreements accompanying the peace process. IMA policy recommendations and demands effectively translated directly into policies adopted by the Israeli government in most cases. Omar Salah and Dov Lautman played a crucial role in the conclusion of the QIZ agreement. Businesspeople such as Yossi Ginossar or Dov Lautman had direct access to policy-makers – in Ginossar's case in both Israel and the PA, – and took advantage of their contacts in order to conclude business deals. The wealthy Palestinian Diaspora elite, which invested in the conglomerates such as PADICO and APIC, had direct access to the Palestinian political elite, or was part of it itself like the Masri family, and received favourable licences.

Indirectly, business elites shaped the development of the peace process through their engagement in the public sphere and indirect involvement in negotiations. In addition, their engagement in trade and industrial co-operation enhanced the pre-existing regional imbalance, served to perpetuate the regional balance of economic power, and were hence also a form of indirect influence on the foreign policy-making process. Thus, the indirect influence of businesspeople on the course and direction of the peace process, both in terms of shaping the discourse of peace and economic development as well as with regard to the evolution and nature of collaborative business ties, was even more important than their direct involvement.

The significance attributed to indirect influence here is in accordance with Gramsci's definition of state-society relations under the condition of a successfully established hegemony. Gramsci's concept of hegemony was not confined to economic determinism, but also involved ideational and political dimensions. Indeed, Gramsci's main contribution to understanding the interplay of state and social forces was the illumination of how a hegemonic class dominated not only on the basis of its control over the means of production, i.e. economically, but also, and more importantly, through its influence over the discursive sphere. As a result, Gramsci did not understand state and society as separate concepts, but pointed out: 'The general notion of the state includes elements which need to be referred back to the notion of civil society.' He thus defined the state as 'the entire complex of practical and theoretical activities with which the ruling class not only justifies and maintains its dominance, but manages to win the active consent of those over whom it rules.'[11] Hegemony was achieved when the worldview of the dominant class was diffused into every aspect of daily life so that this prevailing consciousness was internalized by the broad masses to become part of their 'common sense.' The discursive and economic spheres formed a 'historic bloc,' in which the ideational superstructure of state and civil society reflected the social relations of production.[12]

As a result, under the condition of hegemony, policy-making reflected the interest of the hegemonic elite, whether the latter directly formulated policy, influenced it, or only had an indirect impact on the policy-making process. In the northern European countries, where hegemony was most complete, the power of the bourgeoisie was consolidated to such an extent that the bourgeoisie needed not run the state itself: 'Landed aristocrats in England, Junkers in Prussia, or a renegade pretender to the mantle of Napoleon I in France, could do it for them so long as these rulers recognized the hegemonic structures of civil society as the basic limits of their action.'[13] It followed that the distinction between civil society and the state, or between economic and political elites, became blurred, if not meaningless altogether.

Business elites in Israel, Jordan, and the Palestinian Territories played a crucial role in shaping the peace process indirectly and in leading it into its failure. State policies domestically and foreign policy in all three entities were a reaction to the hegemonic struggles within the three societies, and sometimes a manifestation of the established hegemony of the political-economic elites, as Gramsci had outlined the process. In Israel, hegemony had been established and maintained successfully for decades until the 1990s. An elite alliance of government officials, industrialists, and the managers of Histadrut-owned conglomerates had dominated not only the economy, but also society at large. The discourse that unified Israeli society was the language of the Zionist labour movement, which incorporated both workers' and business interests in the Histadrut.[14] This hegemonic arrangement survived the economic crisis of the 1980s, but then underwent drastic transformations. As a result of the crisis, the Histadrut lost power, and the business elite gained even more influence. The entrepreneurial elite prepared the ground for the peace process due to its interest in economic expansion. Under the condition of a consolidated hegemony at the beginning of the peace process, the Israeli business elite could successfully steer the evolution of a societal discourse in favour of peace on the basis of its discursive power and its public engagement in favour of peace.

In many ways, the governments of Rabin and Peres were manifestations of the hegemony exercised by the business elite. The ruling Labour and Meretz parties adopted their wish for peace as a policy platform. But the influence of the hegemonial elite went further, in that they managed to shape societal discourse. A 1993 pamphlet from the Peace Now movement, for example, reflected the discursive link between peace and prosperity in its declaration: 'From the seed of peace your economic growth will flourish.'[15] Thus, both state policies and societal discourse followed the interests of the Israeli business elite in the initial phase of the peace process. With their declared openness towards regional co-operation and integration, Israeli business leaders similarly shaped the regional discourse surrounding the economic dimension of peace.

Israel's initiation of the peace process was certainly also grounded in the evolution of societal discourse in favour of peace ever since the Israeli invasion into Lebanon in 1982. However, the business elite's push for a resolution of the conflict with Israel's neighbours was crucial and led the Labour and Meretz parties to adopt a pro-peace platform for their successful election campaign in 1992. The Rabin and Peres governments co-ordinated closely with the entrepreneurial elite, managed the transformation of the domestic political economy in accordance with the interests of the business community, and implemented the peace programme favoured by the economic elites. The first few years of the Oslo process opened up opportunities for Israeli entrepreneurs. The parallel tracks of domestic changes liberalizing the Israeli economy and of the conclusion of economic agreements with Israel's neighbours gave Israeli industry time to adapt to the new competition. They also ensured Israeli dominance over the Palestinian market. As a result of the interplay of both factors, collaborative ties especially with Jordanian firms emerged, which guaranteed Israeli competitiveness and saved costs. All this was accompanied by a societal consensus that peace was necessary for the security, stability, and prosperity of the country. The regional discourse emphasized regional development and integration. The business elite thus exercised influence over the course of the peace process not only through the involvement of business associations and individual businessmen in negotiations and the formulation of economic agreements. It also influenced policy-making indirectly and ensured that policies were in accordance with its interests, while, under the condition of the pre-existing hegemony, these policies secured the consent of society at large.

Yet, the benefits of the new opportunities were distributed unevenly. While a new stratum of top-salary earners emerged, the divide between rich and poor grew during the 1990s. Co-operation and the re-location of manufacturing operations to Jordan were an important factor in creating resentment amongst the lower echelons of society. The backlash followed in Binyamin Netanyahu's electoral victory in 1996. It was a manifestation of the erosion of hegemony that Netanyahu entertained almost no ties to the business community. Likewise, Barak and Sharon maintained much looser links to the entrepreneurial elite than Rabin or Peres had. In this sense, the domestic hegemonial arrangement in Israel unravelled. The direct election of the Prime Minister since 1996 thus was also a decoupling of politics and business. Increased space for manoeuvre and the breakdown of the domestic political-economic hegemony resulted in increased autonomy for the government, or at least the Prime Minister, with regard to the overall conduct of peace negotiations. Netanyahu, Barak, and Sharon all pursued the peace process with a lesser economic dimension than Rabin and Peres. Simultaneously, the unity of the Israeli societal discourse broke up and fully ended with the outbreak of the Intifada, which saw the deterioration of the Israeli peace-camp on the left side of the political spectrum. While the peace process initially strengthened the hegemonic elites, they failed to grant enough concessions both domestically and regionally to the disadvantaged segments of society and parties of the process. This undermined not only peace, but also the Israeli domestic hegemonial arrangement.

In Jordan, the 'state' had been an almost autonomous actor during King Hussein's rule, which relied on a mixture of co-option and repression. The king alone decided on foreign policy in the beginning of the peace process. He was the strongman who ruled in the absence of a domestic hegemony. Business elites were part of the monarchical system of rule and sustained it. Yet, when the king opted for peace, the business community, together with a majority of the population, rejected his conception of a warm peace and a normalization of economic relations with Israel. As a result of their rejection of peace, the traditional elites lost the little influence and power they had enjoyed previously. The domestic political economy was transformed significantly. A new stratum of pragmatic young entrepreneurs emerged, which capitalized on the opportunities peace opened up. The moderate 'normalizers' among them, who pragmatically accepted the limits to political discourse and action, formed an alliance with the new king, Abdullah, and established a quasi-hegemonic system. Peace, to them, was a given, as was Hashemite rule in the kingdom. State policies favoured these new elites and allowed them to take advantage of the new business opportunities. The new elites were also directly involved in the policy-making process, either through the newly established business associations, or through the inclusion of entrepreneurs in the ECC and in the government. Policy-making thus reflected the almost hegemonic influence of the new business elites both indirectly and directly.

The discursive struggle in Jordan followed this pattern closely. While King Hussein and leading politicians at first spoke the language of a warm peace, large segments of the society and the business community opposed peace and normalization on principle. The compromise that sustained the moderate new business leaders and King Abdullah in power rhetorically was a focus on reform and Jordan's indigenous economic development. Instead of discussing normalization, the new discourse emphasized Jordan's integration into the global economy through its WTO accession and the free trade agreement (FTA) concluded with the United States. Co-operation with Israel was merely one option amongst many. At the same time, the sensitivity of the issue of normalization dictated that under the con-

condition of growing poverty, unemployment, and inequality, peace necessarily had to turn lukewarm. Although co-operation continued almost unhindered by the Intifada, the new domestic political-economic system of rule was consolidated at the expense of solidifying the regional hegemonial order. The new elites harvested the fruits from co-operation but otherwise did not advance or defend peace. Although King Abdullah reacted with repression to the publication of a first blacklist of companies involved in co-operation in 2001, it also appeared likely that peace would turn cooler yet again, and that more attention would be paid to exploiting Jordan's other options.

In this sense, under the non-hegemonic condition prevalent in Jordan, King Abdullah emerged as the strongman to take advantage of the situation, much as his father had done during his reign. Those strongly in favour of full normalization and a warm peace among the business leaders, like Omar Salah, were not numerous enough and did not gain access to political decision-makers in order to achieve hegemony. The political influence of the moderates, in contrast, was a manifestation of the non-hegemonic system, which dictated a lukewarm peace for the sake of domestic political stability. Thus, foreign policy became a compromise between the rejection of normalization by large segments of the population and the interests of the young entrepreneurs and the king. It was conditioned by the domestic struggle for hegemony and was a manifestation ultimately of the regime's desire to survive. Economic reform and development were crucial to the survival of the Hashemite monarchy, and led the moderate reformers and business executives into an important role in politics. At the same time, the general societal resentment of normalization and peace dictated that peace had to cool down considerably.

In the Palestinian Territories, like in Jordan, the Palestine Liberation Organization (PLO) made foreign policy at the beginning of the peace process without any participation of societal forces and actors. Under the condition of an almost complete political vacuum, the PLO, which then filled the ranks of the Palestinian Authority, decided on foreign policy. However, the PA co-opted political and economic elites resident in the Territories and achieved an almost fully consolidated hegemony over the Territories economically and politically. Local entrepreneurs were marginalized and exerted little influence on the course of negotiations, economic agreements, and the peace process. In contrast, PA officials and the wealthy Diaspora businesspeople achieved dominance over all spheres of political, economic, and social life in the Territories. The result was the establishment of hegemony based on the assent of the ruled, which however lasted only a short while. The neo-patrimonial system of rule in the Territories rested on concessions and consensus achieved through the creation of jobs and the allocation of resources received from abroad.

As long as revenue in the form of import tax and donor aid flowed and was distributed through the PA, as support for 'martyr's' families, employment, direct bribes and other forms of payments, and even financial resources for non-governmental organizations (NGOs), the dominance of the new alliance remained almost unchallenged. PA officials both made policies and capitalized on them. The PA also managed to contain the radical organizations opposing the peace process, such as Hamas or the Islamic Jihad, and enjoyed the support of society. In terms of policy-making, the business associations even promoted an economic final status arrangement with Israel in line with the preferences of the PA, the Diaspora business community, and the largest resident entrepreneurs. This was a manifestation of the short-lived hegemony not only over the economy, but also in terms of the discourse surrounding the peace process in the Palestinian Territories.

When revenue became scarcer, however, and the peace profits worsened socio-economic conditions for large segments of Palestinian society, the PA faced increasing resentment. Consumer prices had increased not only due to Israeli policies, but also due to the misconduct of PA officials, reports about which increasingly surfaced and fuelled resentment. Instead of re-distributing the benefits from monopolistic trade deals, which the PA defended as in the interest of the Palestinian people until 1999, PA officials pocketed the money and commissioned themselves as contractors and suppliers. Yet, in the context of increasing resentment due to worsening socio-economic conditions and the constant delays in the attainment of nationalist objectives, the PA increasingly lost its influence over society. The hegemonic order eroded. The PA could move neither forward, nor back. Due to the interests of the political and economic elites, the PA could not opt out of the Oslo process, yet it could not afford to conclude a peace agreement, which would not have secured the approval of the domestic population. Hence, the Camp David negotiations had to fail. Arafat's acceptance of a deal at Camp David in the summer of 2000 would have undermined the PA's legitimacy. Under the given circumstances, the PA could do little but follow popular opinion, which revolted against both the enduring Israeli occupation and the Palestinian leadership itself. It came to support the Intifada despite the damage that would inevitably be inflicted on the authority, its infrastructure, and on the business interests of political and economic elites. Foreign policy in the Palestinian Territories, therefore, like in Jordan, followed the interests of political and economic elites, but was conditioned by the state of domestic hegemony. As hegemony increasingly broke down, Palestinian foreign policy had to follow the course set by popular opinion.

The Intifada, therefore, was a struggle against both the domestic and the regional quasi-hegemonial systems of domination. It was directed both against the Palestinian leadership and the Israeli occupation and exploitation, although the PA quickly re-emerged by riding the wave of popular opinion and adopted the Intifada as a means of resistance against Israel and its policies. The Palestinian political and economic elite failed to consolidate its hegemony domestically by granting enough concessions to the underprivileged segments of society. The result was a backlash against the dominant elites, as it also occurred in Jordan and Israel. The Intifada was the ultimate manifestation of the elites' failure to consolidate a regional hegemony. The business communities in all three societies did play an important role in the peace process, but ultimately undermined it by not granting enough concessions to the disadvantaged segments of the societies. Although the new elites successfully invested in co-operation and reaped the benefits, they undermined the very peace process opening up such opportunities through their failure to re-distribute, domestically and regionally.

Peace, Co-operation and Economic Liberalization

The domestic failure of the peace process in Israel, Jordan, and the Palestinian Territories also undermined the argument put forward by Çarkoğlu, Eder and Kirişci that economic liberalization as such would advance peace. It also disproved the related argument that economic liberalization would lead to political liberalization and democratization, which would further strengthen peace.[16] Economic liberalization and peace were intrinsically linked to one another. Indeed, the peace process was made possible by, if not a direct outcome of, the Israeli and Jordanian economic reform agendas. However, economic reform furthered inequality and thus ultimately undermined peace in the domestic political arena. The Israeli and Jordanian moves towards economic reform and liberalization were part of a worldwide emergence of a neo-liberal paradigm during the late 1980s and early 1990s. The reason for the new consensus on economic liberalization in Israel, Jordan, as well as elsewhere, lay in the crises of the 1980s. As Gerd Nonneman observed:

> The new consensus noted the failure of state interventionism in the style prevalent for over two decades, and of public enterprises more specifically. The model did not produce a viable economy; the enterprises did not generate revenues and had in fact proved, on the whole, a drain on the state's resources; even in terms of social equity and structural change of the economy the results were meagre. The deciding factor was that the whole system by the 1980s was simply no longer affordable.[17]

In the Israeli case, in addition, the isolation of the economy due to the Arab-Israeli conflict and the Arab boycott necessitated not only domestic reform, but also an opening up of new markets in order to achieve expansion. Peace, therefore, was a necessarily concurrent development to domestic economic liberalization. Similarly, in Jordan, King Hussein decided to opt for peace in the hope for a massive peace dividend, directly through co-operation with Israel and indirectly through foreign investment in the kingdom. Peace, therefore, was the consequence of the economic crisis of the late 1980s and was conditioned by the economic survival of the country, which in turn guaranteed the monarchy's security. As Etel Solingen summed up, 'coalitions advancing economic liberalization have more often than not embraced the peace process for both economic and domestic political reasons.'[18]

However, economic liberalization, as Emma Murphy and Tim Niblock pointed out, 'generally widens the gap between rich and poor, at least in the short term.'[19] Alan Richards and John Waterbury elaborated on the negative effects on, in particular, the lower echelons of society in more detail:

> The process is inevitably painful. Standards of living for people on fixed incomes and/or low- and middle-income urbanites may decline; privileged labour unions may find their wages and benefits eroding; educated and skilled youth may face an economy generating very little employment. Short-term

contraction, it may be argued, is the price that must be paid to assure future sustained growth, but getting from the short to the longer term often proves politically perilous, if not fatal.[20]

Both the Israeli and the Jordanian experiments with economic reform and liberalization proved prime examples for the growing gap between rich and poor, and for the political pitfalls of liberalization. Reform and liberalization, which concurred and accompanied the peace process in both countries, increased inequality. This fed a backlash against not only the process of reform, but also peace, which was associated with liberalization by those suffering from its consequences. The Israeli Arab population, Israeli blue-collar workers, and parts of the Jordanian rural population in underdeveloped areas all resorted to protest. The first violent riots had occurred in Jordan in 1989 and were repeated in 1996, 1998, and 2002. The Palestinian population living inside Israel resorted to violent protests in October 2000. The Israeli working class voiced its resentment against liberalization and peace in the 1996 and 2001 elections. Indeed, in this respect, Israel and Jordan were also representative examples for many countries, in which economic liberalization provoked popular protest.[21]

Another common consequence of these political pitfalls of economic liberalization has been considered the limited nature of reform and liberalization.[22] It therefore fitted into the picture that Jordanian reform progressed very slowly, in particular with regard to privatization, or that the Israeli banks resurfaced as major investors towards the late 1990s. In addition, the Israeli core conglomerates did not lose their economic and political influence, either. The limited pace and scope of liberalization, however, may be seen in conjunction with one frequent criticism levelled against the neo-liberal consensus in favour of economic liberalization. Shapiro and Taylor pointed out: 'Historically, no country has entered into modern economic growth without the state's targeted intervention or collaboration with large-scale private enterprises.'[23] The Israeli and Jordanian cases appeared to confirm this observation. Economic reform and liberalization was driven not against the Israeli core conglomerates, but in their interest and through collaboration with them. Similarly, the emergence of a new Jordanian political economy favouring the moderate reformers and 'normalizers' illustrated that the state drove reform not against the business elite, but in co-operation with at least the new entrepreneurial elites. Thus, economic reform in Jordan did not yield a liberal market economy, but a system of patrimonial capitalism.

However, since peace was only part of the economic adjustment both Israel and Jordan underwent during the 1990s, it was no coincidence that it was considered in a pragmatic fashion at best and turned lukewarm, if not cool. Domestic reform and economic growth were much more important than peace as such. In other words, neither Jordan nor Israel had an interest in a warm peace and close neighbourly relations as such, but pursued the self-interest of economic development and expansion. The negative side-effects of the programmes of economic reform and liberalization, however, undermined the domestic political-economic arrangements and, by extension, the peace process. In addition, economic liberalization dented political reform and the movement towards greater transparency and democracy in both countries. Thus, Solingen was correct in his assertion that 'economic restructuring is central to the connection between peace in the Middle East and democratization,' although the effects were negative, rather than positive as he predicted.[24]

Peace, Political Liberalization and Democracy

The relationship between economic and political liberalization has been widely discussed in recent years among scholars of the Middle East and other regions of the world. It is a complex field of analysis, which cannot be dealt with comprehensively here, yet a few preliminary conclusions can be drawn from the Israeli and Jordanian experiences. Emma Murphy and Tim Niblock asserted that the purely economic aspects should not be viewed in isolation when assessing the contribution economic liberalization can make to a country's development. Rather, the social and political dimensions of the economic liberalization process, which can be of crucial importance, need to be taken into account as well.[25] Scholars have increasingly been united in their agreement that the interaction of economic and political liberalization is a complex and dynamic one. Most have agreed that there can be no clear answer to the question whether political liberalization inevitably follows economic liberalization.[26] Yet, some authors suggested that political liberalization, at least to some degree, would follow economic reform. Gerd Nonneman, for example, argued:

> Almost everywhere, the contrast between increasing economic burdens and political aspirations on the one hand, and regimes' relatively declining resources and international pressures and influences on the other, would seem to hold out the prospect of further, if perhaps very gradual, liberalization.[27]

Çarkoğlu, Eder and Kirişci made a similarly optimistic argument with regard to the interrelations of economic liberalization, democratization, and peace in the Middle East, following Shimon Peres and other proponents of the functionalist approach to peace.[28] Indeed, the Jordanian experience appeared to confirm these optimistic expectations, at least prior to the peace process, when economic crisis led to both economic and political reform.[29] However, the experience of the peace process demonstrated forcefully that reform, peace, and participatory politics in Jordan were not compatible. Political liberalization was increasingly reversed after 1993. Thus, Jordan's experience confirmed David Pools' conclusions about the links between economic and political liberalization in the Middle East:

> Presidents and kings remain in charge of a state-controlled process of partial liberalization, which has its origins in strategies of economic reform and regime survival. The assertion of a civil society, autonomous of the state and organized through political parties, is not yet part of the picture, although continuing economic reforms and an electoral process might bring about that. It is more likely, however, that the more full-blooded and intense eco-

nomic liberalization becomes (and the privatization of state-owned concerns could be a pivotal issue here), the stronger the tendency will be for a retreat to a stricter authoritarianism.[30]

The Jordanian experience also undermined the optimistic expectations, which Richards and Waterbury had with respect to the positive effects of peace on democratization. Less inter-state conflict, they had argued, would diminish the common governmental justification for repression and control and enhance the prospects for democratization.[31] The Palestinian case also illustrated the negative relationship between the peace process and participatory politics. Instead of strengthening civil society, the PA's dominance over politics and the economy, and the concurrent containment of the political opposition, was justified with the necessities of peace. Peace, however, in both Jordan and the Palestinian Territories, only benefited a small elite stratum and furthered these elites' power and influence.

Similarly, if one defined political liberalization so as to signify the extent and success of democracy and participation, the Israeli experience during the peace process confirmed that economic liberalization would not necessarily broaden political participation and strengthen the democratic system. On the contrary, party politics in Israel were weakened. Since 1996, no government has completed its full term in power. In addition, the Palestinian minority living inside Israel responded to rising inequality and its increasing marginalization with the boycott of the 2001 elections, effectively the cancellation of Israeli-Arab efforts aimed at integration. At the same time, policy-making remained a domain of the political and economic elites, which were closely connected with one another and often overlapped. This equally applied to the Jordanian and Palestinian cases.

One should not overestimate the significance of elite dominance in the political arena, as Tim Niblock argued, since most liberal democracies are in fact managed by elites.[32] Yet, the peace process, as an extension and manifestation of economic liberalization and reform pursued in Israel and Jordan, turned out to be counterproductive to the advancement of political liberalization and participation in all three entities. Economic liberalization and reform in Israel and Jordan provided the foundations for peace. This peace, however, necessarily turned lukewarm, if not cool, since it remained a peace of the elites, which pocketed the benefits, while inequality, poverty, and unemployment rose. Similarly, the direction of the peace process by the Palestinian Authority hugely benefited PA officials and associated economic elites, yet undermined both economic and political freedom for the majority of the Palestinian population. Liberalization contributed to the increase in inequality, which in turn led to a breakdown of domestic assent to peace. In this sense, one could consider the breakdown of the peace process a re-assertion of social forces in the domestic and regional political arenas.

The functionalist conception of peace in the Middle East, however, failed. Businesspeople did not play a key role in advancing peace, but created a peace of the elites, which failed, because it undermined the domestic social contract in the context of an uneven distribution of the benefits. As a result of increasing inequality and poverty, and a worsening of the socio-economic conditions of the lower echelons of society, the elites endangered and sacrificed a domestic political-economic hegemony based on consensus and concessions. The respective social contracts unravelled, and as a result, political participation decreased or had to be restricted.

In this sense, democracy suffered in all three entities. In Israel, democracy was weakened. The Arab minority's boycott of the 2001 elections illustrated the shortcomings of the Israeli democracy more visibly than ever before. In Jordan, the palace decided that peace and democracy would not go together, and instead formed an alliance with an elite stratum, whose sole interest lay in reaping the benefits from the newly opened up business opportunities. In the Palestinian Territories, the conduct of the PA of economic and political affairs undermined hopes for a participatory liberal-democratic system and significantly contributed to the outbreak of the new Intifada, which was directed both against the Israeli occupation and against the PA leadership. Peace in the Middle East, therefore, did not fulfil the positive expectations with regard to the evolution of business ties, which would advance peace, and with it, economic liberalization and reform as well as the movement towards greater transparency, political liberalization, and participator politics in a democratic fashion. Peace among Israelis, Jordanians, and Palestinians failed in all these spheres. It was largely due to the self-interested involvement and engagement in the peace process of the respective elites, that the peace process undermined liberalization, domestic stability, and ultimately, peaceful coexistence itself.

Conclusion

This study has investigated the role private entrepreneurs and business communities in Israel, Jordan, and the Palestinian Territories played in the peace process until its disruption through the Al-Aqsa Intifada in September 2000. It has tried to test the widely-held belief that businesspeople promote and consolidate peace in the light of the empirical evidence on the three entities. On a more abstract level, this study has considered the interrelations between domestic political economy, regional economic co-operation, and Middle East peace.

The main finding of this study is that the engagement of businesspeople in the peace process, as well as the resulting nature of business ties between Israelis, Jordanians, and Palestinians, failed to strengthen and advance peace in the Middle East. Instead, they weakened political and economic stability both domestically and regionally and thus contributed to the failure of the peace process. The economic dimension of peace also had a seriously negative impact on the development of participatory politics in all three entities and must consequently be considered as one of the chief reasons for the eruption of the Al-Aqsa Intifada in September 2000. These findings support the theoretical assumption of this study, namely, that the specific configuration of state-society relations is one of the principal determinants of foreign policy and co-operation among societies and states. The realm of domestic political economy, hence, must be taken into account as a basic influence on the relations between states.

Peace, Co-operation and Inter-Elite Ties

The economies of Israel, Jordan, and the Palestinian Territories were all characterized by a dualism between the state and large business enterprises on the one hand, and small and medium-sized enterprises on the other, which overshadowed the conventional distinction between the public and private sectors. All three economies were highly politicized, with a large role assigned to the government and political roles played by the large conglomerates. In all three entities, during the years of the peace process, both the dualistic and the political nature of the economies grew more pronounced and set the stage for the nature of the evolving business ties between them.

The peace process itself was largely driven by the influential business elites. Thanks to their access to politicians and their control over discourse, Israeli businesspeople paved the way for and drove the peace process, eager to end the Arab boycott and open up new overseas markets. Jordanian businesspeople remained reluctant in public, but a new elite stratum of young entrepreneurs emerged, which engaged actively in industrial co-operation with Israelis. Palestinians were similarly sceptical about the potential benefits of peace, yet they remained largely dependent on Israel. The resulting nature of regional economic co-operation between Israelis, Jordanians, and Palestinians reflected Israeli dominance and disproportionally benefited the stronger side in the regional equation.

Co-operation also enhanced inequality both on the regional level and in the domestic arenas. On all sides, collaborative ties were hampered by insufficient and dysfunctional agreements as well as obstructive government policies. There was a wide gap between the publicly declared commitment of the governments to advance economic ties between the entities and the reality on the ground. Trade came to be dominated by large conglomerates and was characterized by the involvement of intermediaries with political contacts. In industry, co-operation similarly favoured Israeli businesspeople on the regional plane and the larger companies on the domestic level. Israeli entrepreneurs took advantage of their superior technology, know-how, and marketing and distribution channels while outsourcing manufacturing operations, making use of cheap Jordanian and Palestinian manual labour.

The tight interrelations between politics and business in all three entities both provided the foundations for the evolution of business ties and grew closer due to the transformations of all three domestic political economies during the years of the peace process. Political and economic elites in Israel, Jordan, and the Palestinian Territories were also united in their interest to capitalize on the potentials for co-operation regionally. Israeli businesspeople initiated the peace process and drove it forward until their primary objectives – the lifting of the Arab boycott and the opening up of extra-regional markets as well as the preservation of Israeli interests in particular in the Palestinian Territories – had been achieved. In both Jordan and the Palestinian Territories, new political-economic elites built up their power and influence by capitalizing on the business opportunities opened up by the peace process. In Jordan, the moderate 'normalizers' formed an alliance with King Abdullah and gained increasing political influence, while the public resentment against peace in the context of rising poverty and unemployment at the same time dictated that peace had to turn lukewarm, if not cool. In the Palestinian Territories, PA officials and Diaspora entrepreneurs centralized economic and political power in their own hands. Meanwhile, the majority of ordinary Palestinians and most resident Palestinian businesspeople were marginalized politically as well as socio-economically and suffered under both the enduring Israeli occupation and the corruption and misconduct of their own leadership.

Thus, in all three entities, the economic dimension of the peace process strengthened the political and economic elites, while, at the same time, increasing inequality and fuelling resentment against the peace process itself. Most ordinary

Jordanians and Palestinians gained no share in the peace dividend they had been promised earlier. The Palestinians at large also suffered from the development of industrial co-operation between Israelis and Jordanians, which replaced their own subcontracting arrangements with Israel. On the Israeli side, in addition, blue-collar jobs were cut, creating resentment against economic liberalization and the peace process. The resulting gap between elites and the rest of society in Israel, Jordan, and the Palestinian Territories undermined the peace process and endangered the dominant domestic position of all three elites.

The Failure of Elite Peace

Peace among Israelis, Jordanians, and Palestinians remained a peace of the elites and as such, it was bound to fail because it led to rising poverty and unemployment among the lower echelons of all three societies and accentuated both economic and political inequality. Although democracy as such may not be a necessary pre-condition for the attainment and consolidation of peace, the economic marginalization of wide segments of society in the pursuit of peace and the associated processes of economic reform undermined the social contract, which would otherwise have secured the political assent of most Israelis, Jordanians, and Palestinians. As peace remained a peace of the elites economically, it also remained an elitist phenomenon politically, and as such had to fail.

Israeli business elites played a significant role in initiating the peace process and in shaping the economic agreements with Jordanians and Palestinians in accordance with their own interests. Within Israel, an increasing socio-economic gap fuelled a backlash against peace in the 1996 elections. Shimon Peres, who was supported by a majority of business executives, was defeated by the populist leader Binyamin Netanyahu. Similarly, the Palestinian population living inside Israel grew increasingly disillusioned with its socio-economically disadvantaged position and rebelled in solidarity with the Palestinians of the West Bank and Gaza Strip in the riots of October 2000. Jordanian businesspeople likewise reaped the benefits opened up by economic co-operation yet did little to address the increasing poverty and the growing gap between rich and poor in Jordan. They were also content to limit themselves to promote economic reform for their own benefit, instead of pursuing parallel political change. A new political-economic order of neo-patrimonial capitalism emerged, which allowed economic co-operation to take place, but made it a public taboo. Since the benefits were distributed only among a tightly-knit new elite in politics and business, peace grew cold and generated disillusion in Jordanian society.

In the Palestinian Territories, the political economy was completely transformed under the conditions the peace process created. A new alliance came to dominate Palestinian politics and the economy and to monopolize economic and political power. At the same time, due to a combination of Israeli policy, dysfunctional and insufficient agreements, and the malpractices of the PA, living standards in the Palestinian Territories deteriorated. In addition, the new political-economic order of neo-patrimonial capitalism under the PA decreased prospects for democracy in the Palestinian Territories. As a result, both the Palestinian leadership, and the peace process it pursued, lost credibility and support among most ordinary Palestinians. Large segments of Palestinian society increasingly opposed the Oslo process, which provided the basis for the corrupt, undemocratic, and socio-economically disadvantaging new order in the Palestinian Territories. The upshot was the outbreak of the new Intifada, which was directed not only against the enduring Israeli occupation, but also against the new Palestinian elites. For these elites had largely destroyed popular faith in their own leadership and in the peace process they pursued and could no longer sustain the social contract based on co-opting ordinary Palestinians through the re-distribution of foreign financial aid.

On a regional level, Israeli, Jordanian, and Palestinian businesspeople and politicians-turned-entrepreneurs engaged in the peace process were united in a community of interests. However, the elites did not manage to establish and consolidate their hegemony regionally, since they failed to successfully co-opt the populations into the new order. A more even distribution of the benefits from regional interaction domestically could have gained the assent of the populations for the peace process. This was particularly true of Palestinian society, the weakest element in the regional triangle. Instead, insufficient concessions and the experience of worsening socio-economic and political conditions led large segments of Israeli, Jordanian, and Palestinian society to resent the dominance of the elites, the domestic political-economic orders, and the peace these elites pursued. The Intifada, therefore, was an expression of dissatisfaction not with peace as such, but with the specific, exclusivist form it took on during seven years of peace-making.

Peace failed both domestically and regionally in the Middle East. While the elites reaped the economic benefits of the peace process, the lower segments of all three societies suffered, and their anger found its expression in backlashes against peace. The failure to build a regional hegemonic bloc by co-opting the weakest side in the regional equation led to a radical rejection and, ultimately, the collapse, of the very process that had benefited the elites. Overall, the business elites in Israel, Jordan, and the Palestinian Territories played a crucial role in preparing the ground for the Middle Eastern peace process and in shaping its course. However, their interests, their engagement in trade and industrial co-operation, and the repercussions of these interests and engagements in the domestic political economies, ultimately contributed to the breakdown of the peace process. It was largely due to the self-interested engagement of the respective elites, that the peace process undermined liberalization, domestic stability, and finally, peaceful co-existence itself. The peace process faltered because, as Laura Drake rightly pointed out, 'a lasting process of whatever kind, peaceful or otherwise, must involve populations and not only leaders.'[1] The peace process between Israelis and Palestinians, in particular, failed because it remained limited to interaction among elites, while large segments of both societies did not benefit from peace and eventually came to oppose it. Jordanian-Israeli peace, despite its success in establishing a transnational community of interests among political and economic elites, had to compensate for growing inequality and popular opposition to a 'warm' peace by cooling down.

On a theoretical level, the findings of this study confirm that the nature of state-society relations and, more specifically, the domestic struggle for hegemony play an important role in shaping foreign policy. The pre-existing hegemonic order in Israel had provided the basis for the initiation of the peace process. The growing inequality, which resulted from that process, however, weakened this domestic hegemony, as the consent of the electorate to the pursuit of this process waned. In Jordan, the new elite established itself as the central force in politics and the economy. At the same time, its vulnerability dictated a slow-down in the pursuit of peace and normalization. The peace process became a taboo in public discourse and was thus not further consolidated in Jordan. The PA and its allies in the big business conglomerates managed to establish a hegemonic order, but this was short-lived because it did not distribute enough benefits to a majority of the population. Increasing poverty and diminished prospects for political participation thus discredited not only the Palestinian leadership, but the entire Oslo process.

It can therefore be concluded that the relations between Israel, Jordan, and the Palestinian Territories were conditioned to a large extent by the respective configurations of state-society relations and the domestic struggle for hegemony. In all three entities, foreign policy was crucially affected by the nature of state-society relations. Driven by the interests of political and economic elites, the peace process generated popular resentment at home against worsening socio-economic conditions. This popular backlash against peace made it increasingly difficult for the political and economic elites to maintain hegemony in their respective societies. They failed in this endeavour because they put profits above peace.

The international relations between Israel, Jordan, and the Palestinian Territories with regard to the peace process, therefore, cannot be understood in the framework of most conventional theories of international politics or foreign policy decision-making. It is essential to consider the configuration of state-society relations within the realm of the domestic political economy at any given time as an important determinant not only of foreign policy, but also of the nature and extent of co-operation and conflict among states and societies.

Epilogue: The Intifada and Prospects for Counter-Hegemony

This study has illustrated the processes within the domestic political economies of Israel, Jordan, and the Palestinian Territories, which shaped the peace process and ultimately, led to its breakdown and the eruption of the Al-Aqsa Intifada. Peace in the Middle East was driven by political-economic elites, which exploited the opportunities that it opened up yet failed to mobilize behind it the support of large segments of all three societies. As a result, not only peace itself was undermined, but the configuration of the social forces competing for the establishment of a new hegemony was altered as well.

In consequence, the findings of this study also provide insights into how peace among Israelis, Jordanians, and Palestinians may be established and maintained in the future, in line with the critical-theoretical framework grounded in the writings of Robert Cox and Antonio Gramsci.[2] Cox had famously pointed out theory was 'always *for* someone and *for* some purpose.' Conventional theory, which Cox called problem-solving theory, took the world as it was as its framework for enquiry, aiming to make the prevailing social and power relationships and institutions work more smoothly. In contrast, reflectivist, or critical, theory did not take these social and power relationships for granted, but questioned them by 'concerning itself with their origins and how they might be in the process of changing.' In doing so, critical theory was inherently concerned with change, emancipation and the achievement of social equity among humanity. As Cox further pointed out, while periods of stability favoured an engagement in problem-solving theory, 'a condition of uncertainty in power relations beckons to critical theory as people seek to understand the opportunities and risks of change.' As such, the disruption of the peace process through the Al-Aqsa Intifada allows for a critical-theoretical assessment of the prospects for change and a new peace among Israelis, Jordanians, and Palestinians.

The peace process was driven in its form as it existed prior to the Intifada by the political-economic elites in Israel, Jordan, and the Palestinian Territories. The decline in socio-economic equality and political influence for the lower segments of all three societies undermined that very process. The Intifada has shifted the focus back from the inter-state process of peace-making or maintaining peace to questions of domestic reform, economically and politically. This points to the fact that full peace in the Middle East can only be achieved and maintained in 'warm' co-existence if societal peace is advanced and inclusive policies implemented. These need to address and end the existing socio-economic and political inequalities in all three societies. On a regional scale, co-operation needs to focus on the difficulties and disadvantages of Palestinian society at large.

The challenge to the peace process manifested in the Intifada undermined the existing Palestinian leadership, but has also called into question the Israeli political, economic, and military leadership and the legitimacy of the Jordanian monarchy. New social forces have emerged, which should seek to build new historical blocs within their respective societies, in order to establish new forms of hegemony. Antonio Gramsci had theorized about the possible path to social re-structuring, rejecting the path of revolution as a 'war of movement,' which rarely yielded success. Instead, Gramsci argued, an alternative strategy was a 'war of position,' which 'slowly builds up the strength of the social foundations of a new state' by 'creating alternative institutions and alternative intellectual resources within existing society:'[3]

> Only a war of position can, in the long run, bring about structural changes, and a war of position involves building up the socio-political basis for change through the creation of new historic blocs. The national context remains the only place where an historic bloc can be founded.[4]

Thus, the new social forces, which have emerged during the peace process and through the Intifada – ranging from Palestinian intellectuals critical of suicide-bombings, the PA, and peace in its current form, to those Jordanian entrepreneurs who have so far shunned a greater political role – need to create their own vision of peace, on the basis of social justice, economic reform, and democracy within their respective societies. This vision would sow the seeds for a true transformation of the region into a 'new Middle East.' Peaceful regional co-existence would follow from justice and equality on the domestic level. The Intifada, despite all the bloodshed and terror on both sides, and the peace that has grown necessarily cold in Jordan, have propelled new social forces to the fore. These may yet be able to establish a counter-hegemonic historic bloc, domestically and regionally, to build real peace in the Middle East. Tareq Sous, a textiles entrepreneur from Bethlehem – like most of his colleagues – suffered under the political and economic conditions the peace process created as much as under the impact of the Intifada. In spite of all the negative experiences, he said, 'we are still looking forward to deal with Israelis, as friends, partners, clients, as equal partners and neighbours in peace.'[5]

Notes

Introduction:

[1] Edgar Feige, 'The Economic Consequences of Peace in the Middle East,' *Challenge*, New York, January-February 1979; Henry J. Burton, *The Promise of Peace: Economic Cooperation between Egypt and Israel* (Washington D.C.: Brookings Institution Staff Paper, 1980); Ruth Arad, Zeev Hirsch, and Alfred Tovias, *The Economics of Peacemaking: Focus on the Egyptian Israeli Situation* (London: Macmillan, 1983).

[2] Stanley Fisher, Dani Rodrik, and Elias Tuma, eds., *The Economics of Middle East Peace: Views from the Region* (Cambridge: MIT Press, 1993), p 4.

[3] Gideon Fishelson, 'Regional Economic Cooperation in the Middle East', in Steven L. Spiegel, ed., *The Arab-Israeli Search for Peace* (Boulder: Lynne Rienner, 1992), p. 104. See also Gideon Fishelson, 'The Peace Dividend: Regional Trade & Cooperation,' *Israel-Palestine Journal*, Vol. 1. No. 1 (Winter 1994); and Michael Porter, Yagil Weinberg, and Noreena Hertz, 'Making Real Progress in the Middle East: The Bottom-Up, Economic Solution,' *Financial Times*, 16 September 1997.

[4] Meir Merhav, ed., *Economic Cooperation and Middle East Peace* (London: Weidenfeld & Nicholson, 1989); Gideon Fishelson, ed., *Economic Cooperation in the Middle East* (Boulder: Westview Press, 1989).

[5] Jawad Anani, 'Areas of Potential Economic Cooperation in the Context of the Middle East Peace Process,' in Spiegel, *Arab-Israeli Search*, p. 121. See also Maen Nsour, 'Economic Interdependence and Peace,' *Jordan Times*, 30 May 1999, and Mohammad Shtayyeh, *Israel in the Region: Conflict, Hegemony or Cooperation*, Palestinian Economic Council for Development and Reconstruction (PECDAR), 1998.

[6] Tayseer Abdel Jaber, 'The Impact of the Israeli Economy on the Neighbouring Arab Countries in Time of Peace: An Arab Viewpoint,' in Louis Blin and Philippe Fargues, eds., *L'Economie de la Paix au Proche-Orient/The Economy of Peace in the Middle East* (Luisant: Maisonneuve et Larose/CEDEJ, 1995), Vol. 1: Strategies.

[7] Stanley Fisher et al, eds., *Securing Peace in the Middle East: Project on Economic Transition* (Cambridge: MIT Press, 1994).

[8] Shimon Peres, *The New Middle East* (Shaftesbury: Element, 1993), p. 62.

[9] Joel Peters, *Pathways to Peace: The Multilateral Arab-Israeli Peace Talks* (London: The Royal Institute for International Affairs, 1996), pp. 5-6.

[10] World Bank, *Developing the Occupied Territories: An Investment in Peace* (Washington, D. C.: International Bank for Reconstruction and Development [IBRD]/World Bank, 1993); *Middle East Peace Talks, Regional Co-operation and Economic Development: A Note on Priority Regional Projects* (Washington, D. C.: IBRD/World Bank, 1993); *Emergency Assistance Program for the Occupied Territories* (Washington, D. C.: IBRD/World Bank, 1994); *The West Bank and Gaza. The Next Two Years and Beyond* (Washington, D. C.: IBRD/World Bank, 1994); *Peace and the Jordanian Economy* (Washington, D. C.: IBRD/World Bank, 1994).

[11] Axel J. Halbach et al, *Regional Economic Development in the Middle East: Potential Intra-Regional Trade in Goods and Services Against the Background of a Peace Settlement* (Munich: Weltforum Verlag, 1995; ifo Institut für Wirtschaftsforschung München, ifo research reports, Department for Development and Transformation Studies 84); Axel J. Halbach et al, *New Potentials for Cooperation and Trade in the Middle East: An Empirical Analysis* (Munich: Weltforum Verlag,

1995; ifo Institut für Wirtschaftsforschung, ifo research reports, Department for Development and Transformation Studies 85).
[12] Michel Chatelus, 'Economic Co-operation Among Southern Mediterranean Countries,' in Roberto Aliboni, Tim Niblock, and E. G. H. [George] Joffé, eds., *Security Challenges in the Mediterranean Region* (London: Frank Cass, 1996), pp. 99-100.
[13] Joseph Ginat and Onn Winckler, eds., *The Jordanian-Palestinian-Israeli Triangle: Smoothing the Path to Peace* (Brighton: Sussex Academic Press, 1998).
[14] Ofira Seliktar. 'The Peace Dividend: The Economy of Israel and the Peace Process,' in Ilan Peleg, ed., *The Middle East Peace Process: Interdisciplinary Perspectives* (Albany: State University of New York Press, 1998).
[15] Lori Plotkin, 'The Doha Conference: A Post-Mortem,' *Peacewatch*, No. 149 (Washington, D. C.: The Washington Institute for Near East Policy, Special Reports on the Arab-Israeli Peace Process, 21 November 1997).
[16] Hisham Awartani and Efraim Kleiman, 'Economic Interaction Among Participants in the Middle East Peace Process,' *Middle East Journal*, Vol. 51, No. 2 (April 1997), p. 216. See also Ishaac Diwan and Michael Walton, 'Palestine between Israel and Jordan: The Economics of an Uneasy Triangle,' *The Beirut Review*, No. 8 (Fall 1994), special issue on The Economics of Middle East Peace, p. 22, and the so-called Harvard Report, R. Z. Lawrence, *Towards Free Trade in the Middle East: The Triad and Beyond* (Cambridge: Institute for Social and Economic Policy in the Middle East, Harvard University, 1995).
[17] Markus Bouillon and Olaf Köndgen, 'Jordaniens Friedensdividende 1994 – 1998. Eine Bestandsaufnahme', *KAS-Auslandsinformationen*, No. 9/1998.
[18] Sara [M.] Roy, 'De-Development Revisited: Palestinian Economy and Society since Oslo,' *Journal of Palestine Studies*, Vol. 28, No. 3 (Spring 1999).
[19] Nicholas Guyatt, *The Absence of Peace: Understanding the Israeli-Palestinian Conflict* (London: Zed Books, 1998), pp. 180-181; Edward Said, *Peace and its Discontents: Gaza-Jericho, 1993-1995* (London: Vintage, 1995).
[20] Mahmoud Abdel Fadel, 'The Middle Eastern Free Trade Area: A Sceptical Note,' in Blin and Fargues, *L'Economie de la Paix*.
[21] Laura Drake, 'Arab-Israeli Relations in a new Middle East Order: The Politics of Economic Cooperation,' in J. W. Wright, ed., *The Political Economy of Middle East Peace: The Impact of Competing Trade Agendas* (London: Routledge, 1998), p. 22. See also Ali Kadri and Malcolm MacMillen, 'The Political Economy of Israel's Demand for Palestinian Labour', *Third World Quarterly*, Vol. 19, No. 2 (1998), pp. 297-311.
[22] Eberhard Kienle, 'Middle East Peace and Normalization: The Political Consequences of Unequal Solutions,' in Blin and Fargues, *L'Economie de la Paix*, pp. 67-69.
[23] Zima Flamhaft, *Israel on the Road to Peace: Accepting the Unacceptable* (Boulder: Westview Press, 1996); Curtis R. Ryan, 'Jordan in the Middle East Peace Process: From War to Peace with Israel,' in Peleg, *Middle East Peace Process*. Recent examples include Myron J. Aronoff and Yael S. Aronoff, 'Domestic Determinants of Israeli Foreign Policy: The Peace Process from the Declaration of Principles to the Oslo II Interim Agreement' and Adam Garfinkle, 'The Transformation of Jordan, 1991-1995,' both in Robert O. Freedman, ed., *The Middle East and the Peace Process: The Impact of the Oslo Accords* (Gainesville: University Press of Florida, 1998).
[24] World Bank, *Developing Middle East Peace Talks; Emergency Assistance; The West Bank and Gaza; Peace*; Halbach et al, *Regional Economic Development; New Potentials for Cooperation*.
[25] Drake, 'Arab-Israeli Relations in a new Middle East Order', p. 33.
[26] Fredrik Barth and Unni Wikan, 'The Role of People in Building Peace,' in Ginat and Winckler, *The Jordanian-Palestinian-Israeli Triangle*.

[27] Ali Çarkoğlu, Mine Eder, and Kemal Kirişci, *The Political Economy of Regional Cooperation in the Middle East* (London: Routledge, 1998), pp. 113 and 54. A similar argument is made by Shaul M. Gabbay and Amy J. Stein, 'Embedding Social Structure in Technological Infrastructure: Constructing Regional Social Capital for a Sustainable Peace in the Middle East' in Wright, *Political Economy of Middle East Peace.*
[28] J. W. Wright, 'Competing Trade Agendas in the Arab-Israeli Peace Process: A Case Studies Approach,' in Wright, *Political Economy of Middle East Peace*, p. 42.
[29] Çarkoğlu, Eder, and Kirişci, *Political Economy of Regional Cooperation*, p. 185.
[30] Ibid, p. 232.
[31] Some writers would include Egypt, Syria, and sometimes even Lebanon in this core region. Yet, Egypt's separate peace agreement with Israel has not yielded significant economic interaction, while neither Syria nor Lebanon have progressed significantly in their talks with Israel.
[32] Laurie A. Brand, *Jordan's Inter-Arab Relations: The Political Economy of Alliance Making* (New York: Columbia University Press, 1994), pp. 8-9.

Social Forces, Politics, and International Relations:

[1] David Mitrany, *The Functional Theory of Politics* (New York: St. Martin's Press, 1975), p. 102.
[2] Ernst B. Haas, *Beyond the Nation-State: Functionalism and International Organization* (Stanford: Stanford University Press, 1964).
[3] Ernst B. Haas, *The Uniting of Europe: Political, Social, and Economical Forces, 1950-1957* (London: Stevens, 1958).
[4] Andrew Hurrell, 'Regionalism in Theoretical Perspective,' in Louise Fawcett and Andrew Hurrell, eds., *Regionalism in World Politics: Regional Organization and International Order* (Oxford: Oxford University Press, 1995), pp. 59-61.
[5] Alan S. Milward, *The European Rescue of the Nation-State* (London: Routledge, 1992).
[6] Timothy Dunne, 'Realism,' in John Baylis and Steve Smith, eds., *The Globalization of World Politics* (Oxford: Oxford University Press, 1997).
[7] Scott Burchill, 'Realism and Neo-Realism,' in Scott Burchill et al, *Theories of International Relations* (Houndmills: Palgrave, 2nd ed., 2001), p. 70.
[8] Joseph M. Grieco, *Cooperation Among Nations: Europe, America, and Non-Tariff Barriers to Trade* (Ithaca: Cornell University Press, 1990), pp. 3-4.
[9] Hans Morgenthau, *Politics Among Nations: The Struggle for Power and Peace* (New York: Knopf, 1949); and E. H. Carr, *The Twenty Years' Crisis: An Introduction the Study of International Relations* (London: Macmillan, 1939).
[10] Kenneth N. Waltz, *Theory of International Politics* (New York: McGraw-Hill, 1979), pp. 104-105.
[11] O. R. Holsti, 'International Relations Models,' in Michael J. Hogan and Thomas G. Paterson, eds., *Explaining the History of American Foreign Relations* (Cambridge: Cambridge University Press, 1991).
[12] Kenneth N. Waltz, 'Realist Thought and Neo-Realist Theory,' *Journal of International Affairs*, Vol. 44, No. 1 (1990), p. 29.
[13] Waltz, *Theory of International Politics.*
[14] Robert O. Keohane, *International Institutions and State Power: Essays in International Relations Theory* (Boulder: Westview, 1989), pp. 7-9.
[15] Kenneth A. Oye, ed., *Cooperation Under Anarchy* (Princeton: Princeton University Press, 1986). See also Scott Burchill, 'Liberalism,' in Burchill et al, *Theories of International Relations*; and Timothy Dunne, 'Liberalism,' in Baylis and Smith, *Globalization of World Politics.*

[16] See Robert O. Keohane, ed., *Neorealism and its Critics* (New York: Columbia University Press, 1986); and David A. Baldwin, ed., *Neorealism and Neoliberalism: The Contemporary Debate* (New York: Columbia University Press, 1993).
[17] Robert O. Keohane, *After Hegemony: Cooperation and Discord in the World Political Economy* (Princeton: Princeton University Press, 1984), pp. 85-109.
[18] Charles P. Kindleberger, *The World in Depression, 1929-1939* (Berkeley: University of California Press, 1973); Robert Gilpin, *The Political Economy of International Relations* (Princeton: Princeton University Press, 1987).
[19] Keohane, *After Hegemony*.
[20] Hurrell, 'Regionalism in Theoretical Perspective,' p. 53.
[21] Christian Reus-Smit, 'Constructivism,' in Burchill et al, *Theories of International Relations*, p. 213.
[22] Robert O. Keohane, 'Institutional Theory and the Realist Challenge After the Cold War,' in Baldwin, *Neorealism and Neoliberalism*, p. 294.
[23] Waltz, *Theory of International Politics*, pp. 121-122. Barry Buzan defended Waltz's claim, while Andrew Linklater emphasized this inherent inconsistency; see Barry Buzan, 'The Level of Analysis Problem in International Relations Reconsidered,' and Andrew Linklater, 'Neo-realism in Theory and Practice,' both in Ken Booth and Steve Smith, eds., *International Relations Theory Today* (Cambridge: Polity Press, 1995).
[24] Richard K. Ashley, 'Untying the Sovereign State: A Double-Reading of the Anarchy Problematique,' *Millennium*, Vol. 17, No. 2 (1988). See also Richard K. Ashley, 'Living on Border Lines: Man, Post-Structuralism, and War,' in James Der Derian and Michael J. Shapiro, eds., *International/Intertextual Relations: Post-Modern Readings of World Politics* (New York: Lexington, 1989); R. B. J. [Rob] Walker, *Inside/Outside: International Relations as Political Theory* (Cambridge: Cambridge University Press, 1993); and Richard K. Ashley and R. B. J. [Rob] Walker, 'Reading Dissidence/Writing the Discipline: Crisis and the Question of Sovereignty in International Studies,' in Richard K. Ashley and R. B. J. [Rob] Walker, eds., *Speaking the Language of the Exile: Dissidence in International Studies*, special issue of *International Studies Quarterly*, Vol. 34, No. 3 (1990).
[25] Robert O. Keohane, 'International Institutions: Two Approaches,' *International Studies Quarterly*, Vol. 32, No. 4 (1988); Richard Devetak, 'Postmodernism,' in Burchill et al, *Theories of International Relations*; Mark Neufeld, *The Restructuring of International Relations Theory* (Cambridge: Cambridge University Press, 1995); and Nick Rengger and Mark Hoffman, 'Modernity, Post-Modernism and International Relations,' in Joe Doherty, Elspeth Graham, and Mo Malek, eds., *Post-Modernism and the Social Sciences* (London: Macmillan, 1992); and Andrew Linklater, 'The Question of the Next Stage in International Relations Theory: A Critical-Theoretical Point of View,' *Millennium*, Vol. 21, No. 1 (1992).
[26] Richard K. Ashley, 'The Poverty of Neorealism,' in Keohane, *Neorealism and its Critics*, p. 276.
[27] John Gerard Ruggie, 'Continuity and Transformation in the World Polity: Toward a Neorealist Synthesis,' in Keohane, *Neorealism and its Critics*.
[28] Alexander Wendt, *Social Theory of International Politics* (Cambridge: Cambridge University Press, 1999), p. 4.
[29] Alexander Wendt, 'Anarchy is What States Make of It: The Social Construction of Power Politics,' *International Organization*, Vol. 46, No. 2 (Spring 1992), pp. 394-395.
[30] Martha Finnemore, *National Interests in International Society* (Ithaca: Cornell University Press, 1996), p. 2.
[31] See, in particular, Hedley Bull, *The Anarchical Society* (London: Macmillan, 1977).
[32] Wendt, *Social Theory of International Politics*, pp. 10-15. See also Finnemore, *National Interests in International Society*, p. 2.

[33] Alexander Wendt, 'The Agent-Structure Problem in International Relations,' *International Organization*, Vol. 41, No. 3 (Summer 1987); and David Dessler, 'What's at Stake in the Agent-Structure Debate?' *International Organization*, Vol. 43, No. 3 (Summer 1989). See also Finnemore, *National Interests in International Society*, pp. 14-22.

[34] Gilpin, *Political Economy of International Relations*, p. 38.

[35] Andre Gunder Frank, *Latin America: Underdevelopment and Revolution: Essays on the Development of Underdevelopment and the Immediate Enemy* (New York: Monthly Review Press, 1969) and *Capitalism and Underdevelopment in Latin America: Historical Studies of Chile and Brazil* (New York: Monthly Review Press, 1967).

[36] Andrew Linklater, *Beyond Realism and Marxism: Critical Theory and International Relations* (Houndmills: Macmillan, 1990), pp. 105-107. See also Andrew Linklater, 'Marxism,' in Burchill et al, *Theories of International Relations*.

[37] Immanuel Wallerstein, 'The Rise and the Future Demise of the World Capitalist System,' *Comparative Studies in Society and History*, Vol. 16, No. 4 (September 1974); Immanuel Wallerstein, *The Modern World-System: Capitalist Agriculture and the Origins of the European World Economy in the Sixteenth Century* (New York: Academic Press, 1974).

[38] Richard Little, 'International Relations and the Triumph of Capitalism,' in Booth and Smith, *International Relations Theory Today*, p. 79.

[39] Linklater, *Beyond Realism and Marxism*, p. 98.

[40] Keohane, *After Hegemony*, pp. 41-46. See also Gilpin, *Political Economy of International Relations*, p. 42.

[41] Gilpin, *Political Economy of International Relations*, pp. 42-43. See also Linklater, *Beyond Realism and Marxism*, p. 108.

[42] Little, 'International Relations and the Triumph of Capitalism,' p. 82.

[43] J. David Singer, 'The Level-of-Analysis Problem in International Relations,' in Klaus Knorr and Sidney Verba, eds., *The International System: Theoretical Essays* (Westport: Greenwood Press, 1961), p. 81.

[44] Graham Allison and Philip Zelikow, *Essence of Decision: Explaining the Cuban Missile Crisis* (New York: Longman, 2nd ed., 1999) p. 143.

[45] Ibid, p. 255.

[46] Robert D. Putnam, 'Diplomacy and Domestic Politics: The Logic of Two Level Games,' *International Organization*, Vol. 42, No. 3 (Summer 1988); and Peter Evans, Harold K. Jacobson, and Robert D. Putnam, eds., *Double-Edged Diplomacy: International Bargaining and Domestic Politics* (Berkeley: University of California Press, 1993).

[47] Stephen D. Krasner, *Defending the National Interest: Raw Materials Investments and US Foreign Policy* (Princeton: Princeton University Press, 1978), p. 13 and p. 33.

[48] Peter B. Evans, Dietrich Rueschemeyer, and Theda Skocpol, eds., *Bringing the State Back In* (Cambridge: Cambridge University Press, 1985).

[49] Stephen Hopgood, *American Environmental Foreign Policy and the Power of the State* (Oxford: Oxford University Press, 1998).

[50] Neera Chandhoke, *State and Civil Society: Explorations in Political Theory* (London: Sage, 1995), p. 11. See also Roger Owen, *State, Power, and Politics in the Making of the Modern Middle East* (London: Routledge, 1992), pp. 50-52.

[51] Peter J. Katzenstein, 'Introduction: Domestic and International Forces and Strategies of Foreign Economic Policy, in Peter J. Katzenstein, ed., *Between Power and Plenty: Foreign Economic Policies of Advanced Industrial States* (Madison: University of Wisconsin Press, 1978), p. 4.

[52] G. John Ikenberry, David A. Lake, and Michael Mastanduno, 'Introduction: Approaches to Explaining American Foreign Economic Policy, in G. John Ikenberry, David A. Lake, and Michael Mastanduno, eds., *The State and American Foreign Economic Policy* (Ithaca: Cornell University Press, 1988), p. 7.

53 Stephen D. Krasner, 'Review Article: Approaches to the State, Alternative Conceptions and Historical Dynamics,' *Comparative Politics*, Vol. 16, No. 2 (January 1984), pp. 226-227.
54 Andrew Moravcsik, 'Taking Preferences Seriously: A Liberal Theory of International Politics,' *International Organization*, Vol. 51, No. 4 (Autumn 1997), p. 513.
55 Krasner, *Defending the National Interest*, p. 29.
56 Michael W. Doyle, 'Kant, Liberal Legacies, and Foreign Affairs,' *Philosophy and Public Affairs*, Vol. 12, No. 3 (1983); Michael W. Doyle, 'Liberalism and World Politics,' *American Political Science Review*, Vol. 80 (1986); W. J. Dixon, 'Democracy and the Management of International Conflict,' *Journal of Conflict Resolution*, Vol. 37, No. 1 (1993); Bruce M. Russett, *Grasping the Democratic Peace: Principles for a Post-Cold War World* (Princeton: Princeton University Press, 1993).
57 Çarkoğlu, Eder, and Kirişci, *Political Economy of Regional Cooperation*, p. 185.
58 Brand, *Inter-Arab Relations*.
59 Markus Bouillon, 'Walking the Tightrope: Jordanian Foreign Policy from the Gulf Crisis to the Peace Process and Beyond,' in George [E. G. H.] Joffé, ed., *Jordan in Transition: 1990-2000* (London: Hurst, 2000).
60 Peter Calvert, *The Foreign Policy of New States* (Brighton: Wheatsheaf, 1986), p. 14.
61 Robert W. Cox, 'Social Forces, States, and World Orders: Beyond International Relations Theory,' in Keohane, *Neorealism and its Critics*, p. 205.
62 Cox, 'Social Forces, States, and World Orders,' p. 205.
63 Ibid, p. 206
64 Robert W. Cox, 'Gramsci, Hegemony and International Relations: An Essay in Method,' in Stephen Gill, ed., *Gramsci, Historical Materialism and International Relations* (Cambridge: Cambridge University Press, 1993), p. 51. The essay referred to was first published in *Millennium*, Vol. 12, No. 2 (Summer 1983), pp. 162-175.
65 Ibid, pp. 56-57.
66 Cox, 'Social Forces, States, and World Orders,' p. 219.
67 Robert W. Cox, *Production, Power, and World Order: Social Forces in the Making of History* (New York: Columbia University Press, 1987).
68 Anthony Brewer, *Marxist Theories of Imperialism: A Critical Survey* (London: Routledge, 1980), p. 272.
69 Linklater, 'Marxism,' p. 143.
70 Robert W. Cox, 'Towards a Posthegemonic Conceptualization of World Order: Reflections on the Relevancy of Ibn Khaldun,' in Robert W. Cox with Timothy J. Sinclair, *Approaches to World Order* (Cambridge: Cambridge University Press, 1996), p. 151.
71 Cox, 'Gramsci, Hegemony and International Relations,' pp. 59-62.
72 Cox, 'Social Forces, States, and World Orders,' p. 225. See also Cox, 'Gramsci, Hegemony and International Relations,' pp. 61-62, and Cox, *Production, Power, and World Order*, p. 7.
73 Quoted in Cox, 'Gramsci, Hegemony and International Relations,' p. 58.
74 Robert W. Cox, 'Realism, Positivism, and Historicism,' in Cox with Sinclair, *Approaches to World Order*, p. 56.
75 Cox, *Production, Power, and World Order*, p. 6.
76 Linklater, *Beyond Realism and Marxism*, p. 29.

The Economy, Business, and Politics:

1 Ira Sharkansky, *The Political Economy of Israel* (New Brunswick: Transaction, 1987), p. 33.
2 Michael Bruno, *Crisis, Stabilization, and Economic Reform: Therapy by Consensus* (Oxford: Clarendon Press, 1993), p. 23.

3 Yair Aharoni, *The Israeli Economy: Dreams and Realities* (London: Routledge, 1991).
4 David Kochav, 'The Influence of Defence Expenditure on the Israeli Economy,' in Moshe Sanbar, ed., *Economic and Social Policy in Israel: The First Generation* (Lanham: University Press of America and The Jerusalem Centre for Public Affairs/Centre for Jewish Community Studies, 1990); Paul Rivlin, *The Israeli Economy* (Boulder: Westview Press, 1992); Eli Sagi, 'Peace and the Israeli Economy,' in Sara [M.] Roy and Karen Pfeiffer, eds., *Research in Middle East Economics. The Economics of Middle East Peace: A Reassessment, Vol. 3* (Stamford: Jai Press, 1999).
5 Amir Ben-Porath, *State and Capitalism in Israel* (Westport: Greenwood Press, 1993), pp. 54-55.
6 Emma Murphy, 'Structural Inhibitions to Economic Liberalization in Israel,' *Middle East Journal*, Vol. 48, No. 1, (Winter 1994), pp. 67-69. For a detailed account of the Histadrut's rise and decline, see Lev Luis Grinberg and Gershon Shafir, 'Economic Liberalization and the Breakup of the Histadrut's Domain,' in Gershon Shafir and Yoav Peled, eds., *The New Israel: Peacemaking and Liberalization* (Boulder: Westview, 2000).
7 Asher Arian, *The Second Republic: Politics in Israel* (Chatham: Chatham House, 1998), p. 49.
8 Sharkansky, *Political Economy*, p. 11.
9 Yakir Plessner, *The Political Economy of Israel: From Ideology to Stagnation* (Albany: State University of New York Press, 1994), pp. 115-117.
10 Aharoni, *Israeli Economy*, p. 161.
11 Arian, *Second Republic*, pp. 55-57.
12 Aharoni, *Israeli Economy*, p. 161.
13 Ibid, pp. 161-166.
14 Bruno, *Crisis, Stabilization*.
15 Adam Garfinkle, *Politics and Society in Modern Israel: Myths and Realities* (Armonk: M. E. Sharpe, 1997), p. 116.
16 Arian, *Second Republic*, p. 42.
17 Michael Shalev, 'Liberalization and the Transformation of the Political Economy,' in Shafir and Peled, *New Israel*.
18 CA IB Investment Bank of the Bank of Austria Group, *Economic Update Israel*, 28 June 2000.
19 This paragraph draws on the work carried out for Markus Bouillon and Ralph Stobwasser, 'Israel and the Occupied Territories,' in Sara and Tom Pendergast, eds., *Worldmark Encyclopaedia of National Economies,* (Farmington Hills: Gale Group, 2002; 4 vols).
20 Sharkansky, 'Israel's Political Economy,' p. 162.
21 Michael Shalev, *Labour and the Political Economy in Israel* (Oxford: Oxford University Press, 1992), p. 297, and Aharoni, *Political Economy*, pp. 220-221.
22 Michael Shalev, 'Have Globalization and Liberalization "Normalized" Israel's Political Economy?' *Israel Affairs*, Vol. 5, Nos. 2-3 (Winter-Spring 1999, special issue on Israel: The Dynamics of Change and Continuity), p. 126.
23 Arian, *Second Republic*, pp. 47-51.
24 Gershon Shafir and Yoav Peled, 'The Globalization of Israeli Business and the Peace Process,' in Shafir and Peled, *New Israel*.
25 Gershon Shafir, 'Business in Politics: Globalization and the Search for Peace in South Africa and Israel/Palestine,' *Israel Affairs*, Vol. 5, Nos. 2-3 (Winter-Spring 1999, special issue on Israel: The Dynamics of Change and Continuity).
26 Grinberg and Shafir, 'Economic Liberalization,' pp. 110-119.
27 Amotz Asa-El, David Harris, Galit Lipkis-Beck, and Jennifer Friedlin, 'Bridge over Troubled Waters,' *Jerusalem Post*, 19 February 1997.
28 Interview with Danny Rappaport.

[29] Plessner, *Political Economy*, p. 120, and Rivlin, *Israeli Economy*, pp. 61-62.
[30] Other major investments held by the IDBH/DIC group included NetVision, Cellcom, Tevel, Barak Lines in communications; and American Israeli Paper Mills, Kitan, Polgat, Nesher, Cargal, and Bagir in industry. Shai Shalev, 'Leon Recanati Makes IDB His,' *Globes*, 3 July 2001.
[31] Judy Maltz, 'Banks' Investment Comeback,' *Globes*, 21 June 2001.
[32] Daniel Maman, 'The Social Organization of the Israeli Economy: A Comparative Analysis,' *Israel Affairs*, Vol. 5, Nos. 2-3, (Winter-Spring 1999, special issue on Israel: The Dynamics of Change and Continuity).
[33] Shalev, 'Globalization and Liberalization,' p. 136.
[34] Aziz Haidar, *On the Margins: The Arab Population in the Israeli Economy* (London: Hurst, 1995).
[35] Eran Razin, 'Location of Entrepreneurship Assistance Centres in Israel,' *Tijschrift voor Economische en Sociale Geografie*, Vol. 89, No. 4 (1998), p. 433.
[36] Shalev, 'Globalization and Liberalization,' p. 126.
[37] Yair Aharoni, *Structure and Performance in the Israeli Economy* (Tel Aviv: Cherikover, 1976; Hebrew); quoted in Shalev, *Labour*, p. 296.
[38] Arian, *Second Republic*, p. 57-62.
[39] Gershon Shafir, 'Business in Politics,' p. 107.
[40] Shalev, *Labour*.
[41] Shimshon Bichler and Jonathan Nitzan, 'Military Spending and Differential Accumulation: A New Approach to the Political Economy of Armament – The Case of Israel,' *Review of Radical Political Economics*, Vol. 28, No. 1 (May 1996), p. 60.
[42] Shalev, 'Globalization and Liberalization,' p. 126.
[43] Jonathan Nitzan and Shimshon Bichler, 'The Impermanent War Economy? Peace Dividends and Capital Accumulation in Israel' in Wright, *Political Economy of Middle East Peace*, p. 81.
[44] Aharoni, *Israeli Economy*, p. 330.
[45] Yuval Elizur and Eliahu Salpeter, *Who Rules Israel?* (New York: Harper and Row, 1973), pp. 9-26.
[46] Murphy, 'Structural Inhibitions,' p. 85.
[47] Maman, 'Social Organization,' pp. 91-92. For a more detailed account of policy forum networks, see Daniel Maman, 'The Power lies in the Structure: Economic Policy Forum Networks in Israel,' *British Journal of Sociology*, Vol. 48, No. 2 (June 1997), and Maman's dissertation, *Institutional Linkages between the Economic Elites and the Political and Bureaucratic Elites in Israel: 1974-1988*, Doctoral Dissertation, Hebrew University of Jerusalem, July 1993 (Hebrew, *Mazavei Mifgash beyn Elitot Kalkaliyot le-Elitot Politiyot v'Menhaliyot be-Yisrael*).
[48] Yael Yishai, 'Interest Politics in a Comparative Perspective: The (Ir)Regularity of the Israeli Case,' *Israel Affairs*, Vol. 5, Nos. 2-3, (Winter-Spring 1999, special issue on Israel: The Dynamics of Change and Continuity), pp. 80-84.
[49] Gabriel Sheffer, 'Structural Change and Leadership Transformation,' *Israel Affairs*, Vol. 5, Nos. 2-3 (Winter-Spring 1999, special issue on Israel: The Dynamics of Change and Continuity), p. 64.
[50] Yishai, 'Interest Politics,' p. 79.
[51] Marcia Drezon-Tepler, *Interest Groups and Political Change in Israel* (Albany: State University of New York Press, 1990), p. 47.
[52] Yael Yishai, *Land of Paradoxes: Interest Politics in Israel* (Albany: State University of New York Press, 1991), p. 72.
[53] See the IMA website, www.industry.org.il; and Drezon-Tepler, *Interest Groups*, pp. 61-100.
[54] See the FICC website, www.tlv-chamber.org.il.

[55] This is a routine estimate, since no official figures are published, taken from the annual Economist Intelligence Unit, *Country Profile: Jordan, 1998-1999* (London: EUI, 1998), p. 18.

[56] Gilbert Anderer, *Die Politische Ökonomie eines Allokationssystems: Jordanien und die internationale Arbeitsmigration seit 1973* (Frankfurt: Peter Lang Verlag, 1991) and M. A. J [Monther] Share, 'The Use of Jordanian Workers' Remittances,' in Bichara Khader and Adnan Badran, eds., *The Economic Development of Jordan* (London: Croom Helm, 1987).

[57] Marius Haas, *Husseins Königreich: Jordaniens Stellung im Nahen Osten* (Munich: Tuduv Verlag, 1975). See also Fawzi Khatib, 'Foreign Aid and Economic Development in Jordan: An Empirical Investigation,' in Rodney Wilson, ed., *Politics and the Economy in Jordan* (London: Routledge, 1990), and Khalil Hammad, 'The Role of Foreign Aid in the Jordanian Economy, 1959-1983,' in Khader and Badran, *Economic Development*.

[58] World Bank, *Claiming the Future: Choosing Prosperity in the Middle East and North Africa* (Washington, D. C.: IBRD/World Bank, 1995), p. 15.

[59] Bryan Daves, 'Biting the Hand that Feeds You: The Dilemma of Economic Reform and Regime Stability. Jordan in Comparative Perspective,' *Politics and the State in Jordan, 1946-1996*, Collection of Papers Given at the International Symposium at the Institut Du Monde Arabe, Paris, 24-25 June 1997, p. 197.

[60] Giacomo Luciani, 'Allocation vs. Production States: A Theoretical Framework,' in Hazem Beblawi and Giacomo Luciani, eds., *The Rentier State* (London: Croom Helm, 1987), p. 69; and Michel Chatelus, 'Rentier or Producer Economy in the Middle East? The Jordanian Response,' in Khader and Badran, *Economic Development*, pp. 206-208.

[61] Brand, *Inter-Arab Relations*, p. 48.

[62] Halbach et al, *New Potentials for Cooperation*, pp. 22-24.

[63] Amatzia Baram, 'No New Fertile Crescent: Iraqi-Jordanian Relations, 1968-1992,' in Joseph Nevo and Ilan Pappé, eds., *Jordan in the Middle East: The Making of a Pivotal State 1948-1988* (Ilford: Frank Cass, 1994), p. 136.

[64] Monther Share, 'Jordan's Trade and Balance-of-Payments Problems,' in Wilson, *Politics*, p. 104.

[65] World Bank, *Peace and the Jordanian Economy*, p. 8. On Jordan's development until the late 1970s, see also Michael P. Mazur, *Economic Growth and Development in Jordan* (London: Croom Helm, 1979).

[66] Deutsches Orient-Institut, *Nahost-Jahrbuch 1988: Politik, Wirtschaft und Gesellschaft in Nordafrika und dem Nahen und Mittleren Osten* (Opladen: Deutsches Orient-Institut, 1989), pp. 95-98.

[67] Laurie A. Brand, 'Economic and Political Liberalization in a Rentier Economy: The Case of the Hashemite Kingdom of Jordan,' in Iliya Harik and Denis J. Sullivan, eds., *Privatization and Liberalization in the Middle East* (Bloomington: Indiana University Press, 1992).

[68] *Twenty Fifth Annual Report, 1990* (Amman: Central Bank of Jordan, Department of Research and Studies, 1991), p. 70.

[69] Leila G. Deeb, 'The Economic Activities of the 'Returnees' from the Gulf Countries and their Effect on Jordan's economy,' in Blin and Fargues, *L'Economie de la Paix au Proche Orient*.

[70] Bouillon and Köndgen, 'Jordaniens Friedensdividende.'

[71] United States Department of State, *Country Commercial Guide: Jordan, 2001*, www.state.gov/www/about_state/business/com_guides/2001/nea/jordan_ccg2001.pdf.

[72] This paragraph draws on work carried out for *Jordan: US Free Trade Agreement*, Oxford Analytica Daily Brief, 18 October 2001, and for 'Country Assessment: Jordan,' *International Standards Compliance Index*, Research Department, Oxford Analytica, June-July 2001.

[73] Brand, 'Economic and Political Liberalization,' p. 170.

[74] Taher H. Kanaan, 'The State and the Private Sector in Jordan' in Nemat Shafik, ed., *Economic Challenges Facing Middle Eastern and North African Countries* (Houndmills: Macmillan in

association with the Economic Research Forum for the Arab Countries, Iran and Turkey, 1998), p. 79.
[75] Brand, 'Economic and Political Liberalization.'
[76] Kanaan, 'State and Private Sector,' p. 79.
[77] Osama J. A. R. Abu Shair, *Privatization and Development* (Houndmills: Macmillan, 1997), p. 136.
[78] Kanaan, 'State and Private Sector,' pp. 79-81; and Abu Shair, *Privatization*, pp. 140-141.
[79] Kanaan, 'State and Private Sector,' p. 81.
[80] World Bank, *Jordan Privatisation Note*, Privatisation Technical Assistance Mission, 9-15 December 1995.
[81] Abu Shair, *Privatization*, p. 142.
[82] Timothy J. Piro in his study of the Jordanian political economy speaks only of the 'Big 5', comprising the APC, the JPMC, the JCFC, the JPRC, and the JFIC; however, according to Osama Abu Shair, the JGIC and the JEIC may be included in this group. See Timothy J. Piro, *The Political Economy of Market Reform in Jordan* (Lanham: Rowman & Littlefield, 1998), pp. 37-53; and Abu Shair, *Privatization*, ibid.
[83] 'General Assembly decides to bury Jordan Glass Industries Company,' *Jordan Times*, 20-21 June 1996.
[84] 'Jordan Passes Foreign Ownership Law,' *Israel Business Today*, Vol. 9, No 18 (31 December 1995), p. 23; and Haggay Etkes, 'Jordan to Allow Foreigners to Buy 100% Ownership of Jordanian Software House,' *Globes*, 23 March 2000.
[85] Tareq Ayyoub, 'Government Shuns Criticism, will Forge Ahead with Privatization,' *Jordan Times*, 21 October 1998.
[86] Abu Shair, *Privatization*, p. 143.
[87] Piro, *Political Economy*, pp. 38-39.
[88] Economic and Social Commission for Western Asia (ESCWA), *Trade Efficiency in ESCWA Member Countries: A Comprehensive Study*, New York 1999, E/ESCWA/ED/1999/6, pp. 32-33.
[89] Laurie A. Brand, 'In Search of Budget Security: A Reexamination of Jordanian Foreign Policy,' *Politics and the State in Jordan, 1946-1996*, p. 231.
[90] Lamia Radi, *L'Elite Palestinienne: Strategies de Survie et Modes d'Influence, 1967-1997*. Doctoral dissertation, Institut d'Etudes Politiques de Paris, Cycle Superieur d'Etudes Politique, 1997, pp. 92-106.
[91] Brand, *Inter-Arab Relations*, pp. 63-68.
[92] Ibid, pp. 72-73.
[93] Daves, 'Biting the Hand,' p. 203.
[94] Pete W. Moore, *Doing Business with the State: Business Associations and the Rentier State in Jordan and Kuwait*, Manuscript, March 1999. On the ACC, see also Abla M. Amawi, 'The Consolidation of the Merchant Class in Transjordan during the Second World War,' in Eugene L. Rogan and Tareq Tell, eds., *Village, Steppe and State: The Social Origins of Modern Jordan* (London: British Academy Press, 1994).
[95] Zayd J. Sha'sha, 'The Role of the Private Sector in Jordan's Economy,' in Wilson, *Politics*, pp. 82-83.
[96] Brand, *Inter-Arab Relations*, pp. 60-62.
[97] Brand, 'Economic and Political Liberalization,' p. 179.
[98] Piro, *Political Economy*, p. 81.
[99] Abu Shair, *Privatization*, p. 175.
[100] Brand, *Inter-Arab Relations*, p. 82.
[101] Abu Shair, *Privatization*, p. 176.
[102] Brand, *Inter-Arab Relations*, p. 62.

[103] Abu Shair, *Privatization*, pp. 134-138.
[104] Radi, *L'Elite Palestinienne*.
[105] Brand, *Inter-Arab Relations*, pp. 63-64.
[106] ESCWA, *Trade Efficiency*.
[107] Saad G. Hattar, 'King Forms Economic Consultative Council to Monitor Implementation of Vital Reforms,' *Jordan Times*, 14 December 1999, and Zvi Barel, 'When a King Wants a New Economy,' *Ha'Aretz*, 19 June 2000.
[108] This excludes Israeli settlements. In this definition, I follow a widely accepted view of what constitutes the Palestinian economy, based on the definition of the Israeli Central Bureau of Statistics [ICBS] used from 1968 to 1994, referring to the 'Administered Territories' or 'Judea, Samaria, and the Gaza Strip' respectively. See United Nations Office of the Special Coordinator in the Occupied Territories (UNSCO), *Quarterly Report on Economic and Social Conditions in the West Bank and Gaza Strip*, www.arts.mcgill.ca/mepp/unsco/. The Palestinian Diaspora will only be considered here in extension through its involvement in the Territories, although a considerable amount of Palestinian economic activity still takes place in the Diaspora, where a significant proportion of Palestinians live. The total Palestinian population was projected to reach 7.8 million in 2000; see Samih K. Farsoun and Christina E. Zacharia, *Palestine and the Palestinians* (Boulder: Westview Press, 1997), p. 140. See also the statistical appendix compiled by Samer Khalidi, in Michael C. Hudson, ed., *The Palestinians: New Directions* (Washington, D. C.: Centre for Contemporary Arab Studies, Georgetown University, 1990), p. 260.
[109] 1997 Census on Population, Housing and Establishment, Palestinian Central Bureau of Statistics; www.pcbs.org/english/phc_97/popu.htm.
[110] On the economic history of the Occupied Territories prior to 1967, see in particular Fawzi A. Gharaibeh, *The Economies of the West Bank and Gaza Strip* (Boulder: Westview Press, 1985), Sara M. Roy, *The Gaza Strip: The Political Economy of De-Development* (Washington, D. C.: Institute for Palestine Studies, 1995), Ziad Abu-Amr, 'The Gaza Economy: 1948-1984' and Antoine Mansour, 'The West Bank Economy: 1948-1984,' in George T. Abed, ed., *The Palestinian Economy: Studies in Development under Prolonged Occupation* (London: Routledge, 1988).
[111] A. [Arie] Arnon and J. [Jimmy] Weinblatt, 'Sovereignty and Economic Development: the Case of Israel and Palestine,' *Economic Journal*, Vol. 111 (June 2001).
[112] United Nations Conference on Trade and Development (UNCTAD), *The Palestinian Economy and Prospects for Regional Cooperation*, UNCTAD/GDS/SEU/2, 30 June 1998, p. 44.
[113] Adam Garfinkle, *Israel and Jordan in the Shadow of War: Functional Ties and Futile Diplomacy in a Small Place* (London: Macmillan, 1992).
[114] Abu-Amr, 'Gaza Economy,' p. 113.
[115] Radwan A. Shaban, *Towards a Vision of Palestinian Economic Development*, Palestine Economic Policy Research Institute (MAS), September 1996.
[116] Arie Arnon et al, *The Palestinian Economy: Between Imposed Integration and Voluntary Separation* (Leiden: Brill, 1997), pp. 12-13.
[117] Roy, *Gaza Strip*, p. 110 and pp. 135-287.
[118] Mohammad Shtayyeh, 'The Palestinian Economy in Transition: Policies and Structural Change,' in Blin and Fargues, *L'Economie de la Paix*, Vol. 2: La Palestine: Entrepreneurs et Entreprises/Palestine: Entrepreneurs and Enterprises, p. 126.
[119] Ephraim Ahiram, 'The Future of Economic Development of the West Bank and Gaza and Their Economic Relations with Israel and Jordan,' in Fisher, Rodrik, and Tuma, *Economics of Middle East Peace*, p. 262.
[120] Simcha Bahiri, 'Gaza and Jericho First: The Economic Angle,' *Israel-Palestine Journal*, Vol. 1, No. 1 (Winter 1994), p. 62.
[121] World Bank, *Developing the Occupied Territories*, Vol. 2: The Economy, pp. 11-16.

[122] Sara [M.] Roy, 'Separation or Integration: Closure and the Economic Future of the Gaza Strip Revisited,' *Middle East Journal*, Vol. 48, No. 1 (Winter 1994).

[123] Sharif S. Elmusa and Mahmoud El-Jaafari, 'Power and Trade: The Israeli-Palestinian Economic Protocol,' *Journal of Palestine Studies*, Vol. 24, No. 2 (Winter 1995).

[124] Muna Jawhary, *The Palestinian-Israeli Trade Arrangements: Searching for Fair Revenue-Sharing*, Palestine Economic Policy Research Institute (MAS), December 1995.

[125] Claus Astrup and Sebastien Dessus, *Trade Options for the Palestinian Economy: Some Orders of Magnitude*, World Bank, October 2000.

[126] Samir Huleileh and Gil Feiler, *Guidelines for Final Status Economic Negotiations between Israel and Palestine*, Israel-Palestine Centre for Research and Information (IPCRI), Commercial Law Report Series, November 1998. See also Nu'man Kanafani, 'Trade – a Catalyst for Peace?' *Economic Journal*, Vol. 111 (June 2001), p. F284; and Nu'man Kanafani, *Trade Relations between Palestine and Israel: Free Trade Area or Customs Union*, Palestine Economic Policy Research Institute (MAS), December 1996.

[127] Shmuel Amir et al, *Alternative Models of Economic Arrangements within the Framework of a Permanent Settlement between Israel and the Palestinian Authority*, Draft sponsored by the Foreign Ministry of Japan, 23 March 1999.

[128] Roy, 'De-development Revisited,' p. 69.

[129] Arie Arnon and Avia Spivak, 'Economic Aspects of the Oslo Peace Process: The Disappointing Consequences of an Incomplete Agreement,' *Israel-Palestine Journal*, Vol. 5, No. 3-4 (Autumn-Winter 1998).

[130] Samir Abdullah and Clare Woodcraft, 'Israeli Closure Policy: Sabotaging Sustainable Development,' in Roy and Pfeiffer, *Research in Middle East Economics*.

[131] Hajo Rabe, *The Political Economy of Palestine: The Transformation of Economic Elites after Oslo*, paper given at a PASSIA meeting, 30 April 1998; www.passia.org/index_pfacts.htm.

[132] Valerie Kessler, 'Palestine's External Trade Performance under the Paris Protocol: Hopes and Disillusions,' in *Evaluating the Paris Protocol: Economic Relations between Israel and the Palestinian Territories* (Draft), Study financed by the European Commission, July 1999, p. 29.

[133] Roy, 'De-development Revisited,' p. 71; and Stanley Fischer, Patricia Alonso-Gamo, and Ulric Erickson von Allmen, 'Economic Developments in the West Bank and Gaza since Oslo,' *Economic Journal*, Vol. 111, (June 2001), p. F262.

[134] Rabe, *Political Economy*.

[135] Rex Brynen, 'Buying Peace? A Critical Assessment of International Aid to the West Bank and Gaza,' *Journal of Palestine Studies*, Vol. 25, No. 3 (Spring 1996).

[136] Ora Coren [Koren], 'Unilateral Economic Separation: A Punishment that Will Increase the Violence. Assessment: $500 Million Damage to the Palestinian Economy in Three Weeks,' *Ha'Aretz*, 29 October 2000. See also 'Sanctions Suffocating Gaza's Fragile Economy,' *Washington Post*, 5 December 2000.

[137] Gharaibeh, *Economies of the West Bank and Gaza Strip*, pp. 85-87.

[138] Bakir Abu Kishk, 'Industrial Development and Policies in the West Bank and Gaza', in Abed, *Palestinian Economy*, p. 168.

[139] Gharaibeh, *Economies of the West Bank and Gaza Strip*, pp. 87-92.

[140] Rabe, *Political Economy*.

[141] Mohammad Sarsour, 'Palestinian Industry and the Peace Era,' in Blin and Fargues, *L'Economie de la Paix*, Vol. 2, pp. 202-203.

[142] Roy, *Gaza Strip*, p. 238.

[143] Ezra Sadan, 'The Best Way for Both Sides,' *Israel-Palestine Journal*, Vol. 1, No. 1 (Winter 1994).

144 Mohamed Nasr, 'Industrial Survey – 1994: Main Results, Report No. 1,' *First Reading in PCBS Statistical Report Series*, Palestine Economic Policy Research Institute (MAS), April 1997, p. 22.
145 Roy, *Gaza Strip*; Majed El-Ferra and Malcolm MacMillen, 'External Constraints on Manufacturing Development in Israeli-Occupied Gaza,' *Middle East Journal*, Vol. 36, No. 1 (January 2000).
146 Mohammed K. Shadid, 'Israeli Policy Towards Economic Development in the West Bank and Gaza,' in Abed, *Palestinian Economy*, p. 125.
147 Abu Kishk, 'Industrial Development', pp. 177-179.
148 Mohamed Nasr, *Opportunities and Potentials for Palestinian Industrialization*, Palestine Economic Policy Research Institute (MAS), September 1997, p. 16.
149 Arnon et al, *Palestinian Economy*, p. 167.
150 Gharaibeh, *Economies of the West Bank and Gaza Strip*, p. 99.
151 Roy, *Gaza Strip*, pp. 300-303.
152 Rabe, *Political Economy*.
153 Gil Feiler, 'Creating Jobs for the Palestinians,' *Israel-Palestine Journal*, Vol. 1, No. 1 (Winter 1994).
154 Radwan A. Shaban, 'Worsening Economic Outcomes since 1994 Despite Elements of Improvement,' in Ishac Diwan and Radwan A. Shaban, eds., *Development Under Adversity: The Palestinian Economy in Transition* (Washington, D. C.: IBRD/World Bank and Palestine Economic Policy Research Institute [MAS], 1999), p. 28.
155 'Palestinians Set Up Investment Firms in Areas, Jerusalem,' *Jerusalem Post*, 28 September 1993.
156 Patricia Golan, 'Building Up is Hard to Do,' *Jerusalem Post*, 17 November 1998.
157 See APIC website, www.apic-pal.com.
158 Radi, *L'Elite Palestinienne*.
159 Roy, *Gaza Strip*, p. 25.
160 Rabe, *Political Economy*.
161 Adel Samara, 'Globalization, the Palestinian Economy, and the 'Peace Process',' *Journal of Palestine Studies*, Vol. 29, No. 2 (Winter 2000), p. 22.
162 Israeli journalist Asher Davidi, quoted in Christopher Parker, *Resignation or Revolt? Socio-Political Development and the Challenges of Peace in Palestine* (London: I. B. Tauris, 1999), p. 110.
163 Roy, *Gaza Strip*, pp. 270-271.
164 Farsoun and Zacharia, *Palestine*, pp. 224-227.
165 Radi, *L'Elite Palestinienne*, pp. 133-144.
166 Ishac Diwan and Radwan A. Shaban, 'Introduction and Background,' in Diwan and Shaban, *Development Under Adversity*, p. 10.
167 Louis Blin, 'Les Entrepreneurs Palestiniens', in Blin and Fargues, *L'Economie de la Paix*, Vol. 2.
168 Farsoun and Zacharia, *Palestine*, p. 220.
169 Rabe, *Political Economy*.
170 Hillel Frisch and Menachem Hofnung, 'State Formation and International Aid: The Emergence of the Palestinian Authority,' *World Development*, Vol. 25, No. 8 (1997).
171 Roy, 'De-development Revisited,' pp. 70-71.
172 Samara, 'Globalization.'
173 Rabe, *Political Economy*.
174 Parker, *Resignation or Revolt*, p. 121.

Business Interests in Peace and Co-operation:
[1] Uri Ram, '"The Promised Land of Business Opportunities:" Liberal Post-Zionism in the Glocal Age,' in Shafir and Peled, *New Israel*, p. 228.
[2] Bichler and Nitzan, 'Military Spending,' p. 90.
[3] Kadri and MacMillen, 'Political Economy, p. 304.
[4] Shafir and Peled, 'Globalization,' p. 247.
[5] Shafir, 'Business in Politics,' pp. 114-117.
[6] Jon Immanuel, 'Economic Success in Areas a Must for Autonomy,' *Jerusalem Post*, 12 February 1993.
[7] Shafir, 'Business in Politics,' pp. 114-117. See also Shafir and Peled, 'Globalization,' pp. 257-262.
[8] Quoted from Shafir and Peled, 'Globalization,' p. 258.
[9] 'Conference Time,' *Israel-Palestine Journal*, Vol. 1 No. 1 (Winter 1994), pp. 104-105.
[10] 'Gaon Egyptian Venture,' and 'Kenny Rogers Crosses Borders,' *Israel Business Today*, Vol. 8, No. 401 (9 December 1994), p. 8.
[11] Asa-El et al, 'Bridge Over Troubled Waters.'
[12] Robbie Steinberg, 'Gaon to Help 'Privatize the Peace',' *Ha'Aretz*, 12 March 1998.
[13] Ora Koren, 'Benny Gaon: Middle East no Longer Interests World, Focus Must be Reinstated,' *Globes*, 1 February 1998.
[14] Ora Coren [Koren], 'There is Life after Koor for Benni Gaon,' *Ha'Aretz*, 16 March 2000.
[15] Allan Retzky, 'Peace in the Middle East: What Does it Really Mean for Israeli Business?' *Columbia Journal of World Business*, Vol. 30, No. 3 (Fall 1995), pp. 30-31.
[16] Interviews with Danny Rappaport and Dov Rochman.
[17] Interview with E. H. [anonymity requested].
[18] Interview with Gabby Bar.
[19] Leon Hadar, 'Israel Looks to Asia: The Lure of Business Cuts Across Culture and Religion,' *Business Times*, 17 October 1994, p. 12.
[20] Interview with Amit Segev.
[21] Interview with Badia Tannus.
[22] Interview with Doron Tamir.
[23] Interview with Gabi Roter.
[24] Jose Rosenfeld, 'Rabin, Peres Meeting Arafat in Casablanca: Economic Summit Begins Today,' *Jerusalem Post*, 30 October 1994.
[25] Steve Rodan, 'Rules of the Game,' *Jerusalem Post*, 27 October 1995.
[26] Ibid.
[27] P. V. Vivekanand, 'Cairo Conference Shrouded by Uncertainties of Peace Process,' *Jordan Times*, 16 November 1996; and Steve Rodan, 'Qatar Conference Urges 'Land for Peace',' *Jerusalem Post*, 19 November 1997.
[28] 'Industry Profile: The Textile Sector,' *Israel Business Today*, Vol. 9, No. 4 (21 April 1995), pp. 26-27.
[29] Gad Perez, 'Cut your Cloth to Suit your Coat,' *Ha'Aretz*, 9 December 1997. See also Blandine Destremau, *The Restructuring Process of the Israeli Garment Industry*, Paper presented to the ESCWA Expert Group Meeting on the Impact of the Peace Process on Selected Sectors, 23-25 June 1997, E/ESCWA/ID/1997/WG.I/22.
[30] Shira Beuer, 'High-Tech Textiles,' *Ha'Aretz*, 28 October 2000; and Haggay Etkes, 'Hayek: Quantum Leap in Cooperation with JEDCO,' *Globes*, 9 April 2000.
[31] Ora Coren [Koren], 'The Cooking Oil Industry is Emigrating,' *Ha'Aretz*, 1 September 1999.
[32] Interview with Amit Segev.

[33] Rachel Neiman, 'Gillerman: Speed up Trade Pact with Jordan,' *Jerusalem Post*, 28 October 1994.
[34] 'Study Examines Israeli and Palestinian Markets to Enlighten Jordanians,' *Jordan Times*, 3 June 1996. See also 'The City of Peace,' *Israel Business Today*, Vol. 8, No. 397 (28 October 1994); 'Alron to Build Jordanian Gas Stations, *Israel Business Today*, Vol. 8, No. 400 (25 November 1994), p. 17; 'Jordan Israel Trucking,' *Israel Business Today*, Vol. 9, No. 5 (5 May 1995), p. 18; 'Dead Sea Recreation Zone,' *Israel Business Today*, Vol. 9, No. 7 (2 June 1995), p. 20; 'Israeli Products in Amman,' *Israel Business Today*, Vol. 9, No. 8 (16 June 1995), p. 20.
[35] Ora Koren, 'Bureaucratic Delays in Implementation of Projects with Jordan,' *Globes*, 28 July 1996.
[36] Interview with Moshe Nahum.
[37] Interview with Gabby Bar.
[38] 'Industry Profile: The Textile Sector.' See also Farida Salfiti, *Israel's 'Peace Dividend:' The Jordanian Case,* Centre for Palestine Research and Studies (CPRS), Department of Strategic Analysis, March 1997.
[39] Ora Koren, 'Trade Ministry Internal Report: Another 14,000 Traditional Industries Workers to be Laid-Off,' *Globes,* 14 June 1998.
[40] Interview with Moshe Nahum.
[41] Gadi Golan, 'Kitan Management Decides to Close Israeli Sewing Factories, Transfer Sewing to Jordan,' *Globes*, 13 September 1997.
[42] Orna Raviv, 'Lautman: Changes in Jordan Won't Affect Israeli Companies Operating There,' *Globes*, 27 January 1999.
[43] Interview with Moshe Nahum. See also Keren Tsuriel, 'Manufacturers: Cooperation Endangered due to Jordan-US, EU Free Trade Zone Agreements,' *Globes*, 22 August 2000.
[44] Ora Koren, 'Jordan Calls for Reduced Israeli Share in Joint Projects with Preferential Terms,' *Globes*, 29 July 1998.
[45] Interview with Michael Yungreis.
[46] Ora Koren, 'Netanyahu in Amman: Business, not Pleasure,' *Globes*, 6 August 1996.
[47] Etkes, 'Jordan to Allow Foreigners.'
[48] Joel Bainerman, 'Peace Without Economic Ties,' *Israel Business Review*, Vol. 1, No. 1 (July 1994), pp. 40-41.
[49] Simcha Bahiri, 'Economic Separation or Integration: A Rejoinder to Dr. Samir Hazboun,' *Israel-Palestine Journal*, Vol. 3, No. 2 (Spring 1996), pp. 91-94.
[50] Samir Hazboun and Simcha Bahiri, 'Palestinian Industrial Development and Israeli-Palestinian Attitudes to Cooperation,' *Israel-Palestine Journal*, Vol. 1, No. 4 (Autumn 1994), pp. 74-81.
[51] Jacob Dallal, 'Arab Competition Worries Chicken Farmers,' *Jerusalem Post*, 28 October 1993.
[52] Arnon and Spivak, 'Economic Aspects.'
[53] Galit Lipkis-Beck, '20 CEOs to Meet Arafat in Two Weeks,' *Jerusalem Post*, 4 September 1996; and 'Gaon seeks CEOs' Meeting with Arafat,' *Jerusalem Post*, 4 October 1996.
[54] Ora Koren, 'Gaon, Lautman Offer Arafat Aid to Develop Joint Ventures in Light Industries in Territories,' *Globes*, 21 December 1996.
[55] Judy Siegel-Itzkovich, 'Peace May Fuel Software Boom,' *Jerusalem Post*, 3 October 1993.
[56] Interview with Amiram Shor. See also Keren Tsuriel, "99 Software Exports up 33per cent to $2 Bln,' *Globes*, 25 January 2000; Keren Tsuriel, 'Manufacturers Association Proposes Compromise: Import only 2,000 High-tech Workers,' *Globes*, 12 July 2000; Haggay Etkes, 'Israeli-Jordanian Company Visuality Systems Raises $1 mln from Apex Mutavim,' *Globes*, 28 March 2000.
[57] Ronny Lifschitz, 'Tul-Karem instead of Bombay,' *Globes*, 19 August 1999.

[58] Gershon Baskin and Zakaria al-Qaq, *A Reevaluation of the Border Industrial Estates Concept*, Israel-Palestine Centre for Research and Information (IPCRI), Commercial Law Report Series, December 1998; Israel Manufacturers Association (IMA), Division of Foreign Trade and International Relations, *Joint Ventures in the Karni Park: Required Conditions, Findings and Conclusions, in combination with the Findings of the Israel Export Institute*, May 1997 (Hebrew, *Agaf sahar huz v'ksharim binleumi'im, hitahdut ha-ta'asiyanim b'yisrael, Mizamim meshutafim be-Park Karni: tnayim nidrashim, mimza'im v'maskanot, b'shiluv mamza'ay makhon ha-yizu'a ha-yisraeli*).

[59] Nina Gilbert, '10 Firms Show Interest in Karni Park,' *Jerusalem Post*, 19 February 1998.

[60] Nina Gilbert, 'Strauss Wants to Enter Gaza Market,' *Jerusalem Post*, 19 February 1998; Steve Rodan, 'Forget the Big Projects,' *Jerusalem Post*, 16 October 1998.

[61] Michele Chabin, 'Stef Wertheimer: Eye on the Future,' *Lifestyles Magazine*, Summer 1994, pp. 50-51; Stef Wertheimer, 'Peace's New Priorities, *Jerusalem Post*, 4 November 1993; Robert Lenzner, 'Zionism: Phase III,' *Forbes*, 18 December 1995; Stef Wertheimer, 'Singapore as Parable, *Ma'ariv*, 8 October 1999 (English translation provided by Mr. Wertheimer).

[62] Stef Wertheimer, *Cross-Border Industrial Parks – a 'Peace Bridge'*, April 1999, Proposal for the Establishment of an Industrial Park: Egypt, Gaza, and Israel, Iscar Ltd.; Letter from Prime Minister Ehud Barak to Stef Wertheimer, 13 September 1999; Letter from Prime Minister Binyamin Netanyahu to Stef Wertheimer, 4 February 1999; Faxes from PIEDCO Director-General Abdel Malik al-Jaber and Palestinian Minister of Industry, Sa'adi al-Kronz, respectively, to Wertheimer, References 144a1917/11 February 1999, AN099076/13 March 1999, and 27 February 1999, as well as the 'Memorandum of Understanding between the Two Sides,' signed on 11 March 1999.

[63] Interviews with Avraham Asheri and Ms. Bunmi Ayeni. See also Galit Lipkis Beck, 'Wertheimer, Jordan to Build Industrial Park,' *Jerusalem Post*, 5 June 1996.

[64] Co-ordinating Bureau of Economic Organizations (CBEO), *Economic Implications of the Establishment of Autonomy in the Territories and Ways for its Integration with the Israeli Economy*, February 1993 (Hebrew, *Lishkat ha-teum shel ha-irgunim ha-kalkali'im, Bhinat ha-shlakhot ha-kalkaliyot shel hakamat ha-otonomiya b'shtakhim v'drakhey shiluva b'kalkalat yisrael*). See also Shafir and Peled, 'Globalization,' p. 261.

[65] Israel Manufacturers Association (IMA), *Final Economic Status Between Israel and the Palestinians: The Standpoint of the Manufacturers Association*, November 1999 (Hebrew, *Hitahdut ha-ta'asiyanim, Hesder ha-keva' ha-kalkali beyn yisrael l'falestina'im: 'emdat hitahdut ha-ta'asiyanim*). See also Keren Tsuriel, 'Survey of Manufacturers: 38% of Enterprises Favour Status Quo with Palestinians,' *Globes*, 19 October 1999; Dan Gerstenfeld, 'Executives split on Palestinian Business Ties,' *Jerusalem Post*, 20 October 1999.

[66] Ora Coren [Koren], 'Manufacturers and Merchants at Odds over Final-Status Deal,' *Ha'Aretz*, 6 October 1999; and 'Israeli Businessmen Want Economic Separation from the PA,' *Ha'Aretz*, 11 August 1999.

[67] Haggay Etkes, 'Forget Separation, Long Live Trade,' *Globes*, 17 February 2000; and 'Gillerman: Free Trade Zone – First Stage of Permanent Economic Settlement,' *Globes*, 11 July 2000.

[68] Danny Rubinstein, 'Back to the Markets,' *Ha'Aretz*, 6 July 1999.

[69] Zehava Dovrat, 'Gillerman: Palestinian Authority – Brand Counterfeiting Hothouse,' *Globes*, 25 January 1999; Zehava Dovrat, 'Chambers of Commerce: Annual Forgery Industry Damage – Multi Mlns. Of Dollars,' *Globes*, 10 August 1999.

[70] Robbie Steinberg, 'Forged Products Flooding Israel,' *Ha'Aretz*, 21 July 1998; Ora Coren [Koren], 'Manufacturers Call for Tax Harmony with PA,' *Ha'Aretz*, 19 September 2000.

[71] Haggay Etkes, 'Swamped with Peace,' *Globes*, 3 November 1999.

[72] Eli Groner, 'Bottom Line on Final Status: Addition by Division?' *Jerusalem Post*, 12 November 1999.

[73] Yoram Gabbai, 'Inseparable Enemies,' *Globes*, 13 December 1999.
[74] IMA, *Final Economic Status* (my translation). See also Keren Tsuriel, 'Manufacturers: We oppose Economic Separation from Palestinians,' *Globes*, 7 December 1999.
[75] Etkes, 'Swamped with Peace.' See also Ora Coren [Koren], 'Israeli Manufacturers Want Economic Union with PA as Part of Final-Status Deal,' *Ha'Aretz*, 8 December 1999.
[76] Steve Rodan, 'Jordanian Vote is a Victory for the Economy,' *Jerusalem Post*, 12 November 1993.
[77] P. V. Vivekanand, 'More Jordanians now Support Normal Ties with Israel – Opinion Poll,' *Jordan Times*, 4 March 1996.
[78] Alia A. Toukan, '80% of Jordanians Still Believe Israel is Enemy – Poll,' *Jordan Times*, 7 January 1998.
[79] 'Jordanian Private Sector Denies Co-operation with Israel,' *The Star*, 17 September 1998.
[80] Interview with Mamduh Abu Hassan.
[81] Interview with Thabet A. Taher.
[82] 'Jordanian Businessmen, Industrialists Reject Forming Regional Business Council,' *Jordan Times*, 3-4 October 1996; and 'Restore the Warm Ties,' *Jerusalem Post*, 19 December 1996.
[83] Musa Keilani, 'Stress on Inter-Arab Economic Co-operation in Cairo, Sends Message to Israel,' *Jordan Times*, 16 November 1996; and Suleiman al-Khalidi, 'Jordan Business to Shy from Israel Ties in Cairo Summit,' *Jordan Times*, 31 October-1 November 1996.
[84] Moore, *Doing Business with the State*, pp. 280-281.
[85] Ilham Sadeq, 'Doha Summit Continues to Polarise Arabs,' *The Star*, 25 September 1997; and Suleiman al-Khalidi, 'Jordanian Businessmen Opposed to Doha Conference,' *Jordan Times*, 22 October 1997.
[86] Ilham Sadeq, 'Private Sector Calls to Boycott Israeli Delegation in Doha,' *The Star*, 30 October 1997; Tareq Ayyoub, 'Anani to Head Delegation to the MENA Conference,' *Jordan Times*, 22 October 1997.
[87] Ghalia Alul, 'Irbid's New Industrial Park Leaves Jordanians Divided,' *Jordan Times*, 16 December 1997.
[88] P. V. Vivekanand, 'Jordanians Split over Economic Impact of Possible Strain in Ties,' *Jordan Times*, 26 August 1995.
[89] 'Jordanian Industrialists to Urge Iraqis to Buy More Food and Medicine from the Kingdom,' *Jordan Times*, 6 July 1996; 'Oil-for-Food Deal: Turning Point for Jordan-Iraq Business Relations,' *The Star*, 20 November 1997; Ghalia Alul, 'Trade Level with Iraq for '98 Likely to Stay Unchanged at $225 Million,' *Jordan Times*, 26 January 1998.
[90] Tareq Ayyoub, 'Iraq to Blacklist Jordanian Businesses Dealing with Israel, PNA', *Jordan Times*, 14 September 2000.
[91] Interview with Ms. Jumana Husseini.
[92] 'Jordanians Seek Amman-Haifa Air Link,' and 'Hussein Declines High-Tech Offer,' *Israel Business Today*, Vol. 8. No. 400 (25 November 1994), p. 17.
[93] Rodan, 'Rules of the Game.'
[94] Lamia Lahoud, 'Jordan Business Community Welcomes Economic Ties with Israel,' *Jerusalem Post*, 31 July 1994.
[95] P. V. Vivekanand, 'Transport Operators Gear up to Start Jordan-Israel Traffic,' *Jordan Times*, 30 January 1996.
[96] Interview with Omar Salah.
[97] Interviews with Dov Lautman and Omar Salah. On Omar Salah's biography, see the Century website, www.centuryinvest.com/omarsalah.asp; on the beginnings of co-operation, see Patricia Golan, 'Peace Partners Turned Business Partners,' *Jerusalem Post*, 14 July 1998; Dinah Shiloah, 'Peace Dividend across River Jordan,' *The Times*, 9 April 1999.
[98] Steve Rodan, 'When Business Beats Politics,' *Jerusalem Post*, 21 November 1997.

[99] Interview with Emad al-Shamma'.
[100] Interview with Kamil N. Fakhoury.
[101] Interview with Emad Najib Fakhoury.
[102] Interview with A. Q. [anonymity requested].
[103] My translation from the Arabic original.
[104] Mariam Shahin, 'Undercover Business,' *The Middle East*, February 1997.
[105] Suleiman al-Khalidi, 'Arab Businessmen Keep Low in Secret Israel Deals,' *Jordan Times*, 9 November 1996.
[106] Ora Koren, 'Jordanian Press: Just Say No to First Israeli Exhibition in Amman,' *Globes*, 30 November 1996.
[107] P. V. Vivekanand, 'Ministry Says Israeli Fair is not its Concern; Event Delayed by 3 Weeks,' *Jordan Times*, 5-6 December 1996; and 'Government Maintains Neutral Stand in Regards to Israelis Trade Exhibition, *Jordan Times*, 31 December 1996.
[108] Alia A. Toukan, 'Peace Treaty Anniversary Far from Festive,' *Jordan Times*, 26 October 1998.
[109] See *Jordan Times*, 29 November 2000.
[110] Saad G. Hattar, 'Associations Let Fly List of 'Normalisers',' *Jordan Times*, 20 November 2000.
[111] Oula Al Farawati, 'Industrialists, Economists Say Threat to Boycott American Products Little More than Ballyhoo,' *Jordan Times*, 19 November 2000.
[112] Danny Rubinstein, 'Nobody Wants Relations with Israel, Except When They Do,' *Ha'Aretz*, 25 September 2000.
[113] Bouillon and Köndgen, 'Jordaniens Friedensdividende.'
[114] Ben Lynfield, 'Jordanians Target Palestinian Market,' *Jerusalem Post*, 19 April 1999.
[115] Suleiman al-Khalidi, 'Jordan Pins Peace Dividend on Israel Ties,' *Jordan Times*, 18 June 1996.
[116] 'First Exhibition of Jordanian Products in Ramallah, a Unique Economic Event,' *The Star*, 14 November 1996.
[117] *Al-Aswaq*, 15 September 1998, see REDWG Monitoring Committee Secretariat, *Monthly Chronologies: First Annual Issue*, May 1998-April 1999.
[118] UNCTAD, *Cooperation between the Palestinian Authority, Egypt and Jordan to Enhance Subregional Trade-Related Services*, UNCTAD/GDS/SEU/3, 14 February 2000.
[119] 'Economists Organise Impact of New Israeli Government of Jordanian Economy' [sic], *Jordan Times*, 5 June 1996.
[120] Mervat Suwadeh, 'Likud Victory Dissuades Jordanian Businessmen from Investment in West Bank, Gaza,' *Jordan Times*, 5 June 1996.
[121] Interview with Mamduh Abu Hassan.
[122] Lamia Lahoud, 'Attracting Palestinian Investments,' *Jerusalem Post*, 26 November 1993.
[123] Al-Khalidi, 'Jordan Pins Peace Dividend.'
[124] Interviews with Michael Yungreis, Saeb Bamieh, Nakhleh Jubran, and Mazen Sinokrot.
[125] Interview with Tareq Maayah.
[126] Interview with Tareq Sous.
[127] Interview with Mazen Sinokrot.
[128] Hazboun and Bahiri, 'Palestinian Industrial Development.'
[129] Bainerman, 'Peace Without Economic Ties.'
[130] Hisham Awartani and Samir Awad, *Palestinian-Israeli Joint Ventures: Constraints and Prospects*, Economics Department, Centre for Palestine Research and Studies (CPRS), www.cprs-palestine.org/economy/94/joint.html.
[131] Bainerman, 'Peace Without Economic Ties;' and Samir Huleileh, 'Crash Program for Economic Survival,' *Israel-Palestine Journal*, Vol. 1, No. 1 (Winter 1994).

[132] Groner, 'Bottom Line.'
[133] Interview with Saeb Bamieh.
[134] 'Israeli-Palestinian Commercial Talks,' *Israel Business Today*, Vol. 9, No. 9 (July 1995).
[135] Interview with Mahmoud Farrah.
[136] Interviews with Talal Nasruddin and Muhammad Masrouji.
[137] 'Israeli Impediments to Investment in Palestine,' prepared by the Economic Office at the Orient House, *Israel-Palestine Journal*, Vol. 3, No. 3-4 (Autumn-Winter 1996), pp. 152-158.
[138] Pamela Dougherty, 'Counting the Costs of Closure,' *MEED*, 12 April 1996.
[139] Raed Al Abed, 'PBA Boycotts Summit to Protest Israeli Measures,' *The Star*, 6 October 1995; and Haim Shapiro, 'Israel, Jordan Reach Transport Agreement: Peres, Hassan Agree to Split Gulf of Eilat,' *Jerusalem Post*, 19 October 1995.
[140] David Harris, 'PA Misses Out the Most on Cairo's Opportunities,' *Jerusalem Post*, 15 November 1996; and Plotkin, 'The Doha Conference: A Post-Mortem.'
[141] Bainerman, 'Peace Without Economic Ties.'
[142] Interviews with Samir Huleileh and Mazen Sinokrot.
[143] Interview with Samir Abdullah.
[144] Interview with Hassan Kassem.
[145] Interview with Nakhleh Jubran.
[146] Interview with Tareq Sous.
[147] David Rudge, 'Palestinian Companies Holding Trade Fair in Haifa Next Month,' *Jerusalem Post*, 11 November 1999.
[148] Interview with Samir Abdullah.
[149] Ora Koren, 'Magic of Israel Negotiating Joint Venture with Jordan's Century, Abu Jihad's Son,' *Globes*, 2 February 1999.
[150] Interview with Tareq Maayah.
[151] Interview with Issa Eways.
[152] Haggay Etkes, 'Palestinian Private Sector Supports Free Trade Agreements with Israel,' *Globes*, 4 January 2000.
[153] *National Economic Dialogue Conference: Conference Conclusions and Private Sector Recommendations*, Ramallah, 30 May 2000, published by Paltrade.
[154] Interview with Samir Abdullah.
[155] Interview with Saeb Bamieh.
[156] Interview with Tareq Maayah.
[157] Interview with Issa Eways.
[158] Interviews with Tareq Sous and Mahmoud Farrah.
[159] Interview with Abdel Malik Jaber.

Business Ties between Israel, Jordan, and the PA:

[1] The Royal Scientific Society published a highly optimistic report on the 'economic impact of peace on Jordan' in September 1994, a month before the peace treaty was signed, see Royal Scientific Society (RSS), *Studies About the Economic Implications of Peace in the Middle East on the Hashemite Kingdom of Jordan*, Vol. 1, September 1994 (Arabic, *Al-jam'iya al-'ilmiya al-malikiya, Dirasat hawl al-athar al-iqtisadiya li'l-salam fi al-sharq al-awsat ala al-mamlaka al-urdunniya al-hashimiya*).

[2] ESCWA, *Appraisal of the Middle East and North Africa Economic Conferences*, New York 2000, E/ESCWA/ED/1999/15, 12 November 1999.

[3] See, for example, *Building a Prosperous Peace: Amman '95*, published by the International Press Office, The Royal Hashemite Court, Amman 1995; The Jordan Rift Valley Steering

Committee of the Trilateral Economic Committee/The HARZA JRV Group, *Jordan Rift Valley Integrated Development Study Final Report: Master Plan, Description of Master Plan Projects*, August 1997; *Jordan: A Winning Business Destination*, Ministry of Planning, November 1997 (6 vols.); Government of Israel, *Development Options for Regional Cooperation*, October 1994; Government of Israel, *Development Options for Cooperation: The Middle East/East Mediterranean Region 1996*, Version IV, August 1995; Government of Israel, *Programs for Regional Cooperation 1997*, November 1996; and Government of Israel, *Partnerships in Development 1998*, November 1997. The 1994 Casablanca conference remained 'not much more than a political statement of support to public-private partnership in the region;' although the 1995 meeting in Amman was a success, the Palestinian private sector already boycotted the 1996 conference in Cairo, and nine Arab states formally boycotted the 1997 Doha meeting; ESCWA, *Appraisal*. See also Gadi Golan, 'King Abdullah in Eilat: Focus on Palestinian Track, Accelerate Economic Projects,' *Globes*, 23 April 2000; and Aluf Benn and Revital Levi-Stein, 'Abdullah Envisions an "Open Jerusalem",' *Ha'Aretz*, 24 April 2000.

[4] Interview with Gil Feiler.

[5] Zvi Barel, 'Jordanians Want Bread, Not Fruits of Peace,' *Ha'Aretz*, 22 December 1999.

[6] *Interim Progress Report on Regional Development Projects*, April 2000 (ongoing database project), Israeli Ministry of Regional Co-operation; and Yair Mendelson, 'The Profits of Peace, a Piece of the Profits,' *Ha'Aretz*, 23 June 2000.

[7] Ghadeer Taher, 'Jordanian and Israeli Phone Firms to Try to Settle Dispute, *Jordan Times*, 1 December 1998.

[8] Tareq Ayyoub, 'Dead Sea Industries Company Teams Up with U.S. Firm to Set Up $120m Bromine Factory in Jordan,' *Jordan Times*, 20 May 1998. See also Ora Koren, 'US-Jordan Bromine Plant Memorandum of Understanding; Assessment: Possibility of Co-operation with Israel Down to Zero,' *Globes*, 21 May 1998; and 'Israel Seeks to Revive Bromine Venture with Jordan,' *Jordan Times*, 12 August 1998.

[9] 'Dead Sea Works Looks at Jordanian Option,' *Israel Business Today*, Vol. 9, No. 17 (15 December 1995); and 'APC, Haifa Chemicals Study $60m Joint Project,' *Jordan Times*, 9 November 1996.

[10] Koren, 'Bureaucratic Delays;' Jamal Halaby, 'Ambassador to Jordan: Five Years of Peace with Jordan Insufficient to End Animosity,' *Jerusalem Post*, 26 October 1999; Salifiti, *Israel's 'Peace Dividend;'* and Gil Feiler and Joshua Zaretsky, 'An Unforeseen Rivalry: The Peace Process and the Jordanian and Palestinian Economies,' in Roy and Pfeiffer, *Research in Middle East Economics*.

[11] Interviews with Moshe Nahum and Michael Yungreis.

[12] Interview with Dov Lautman.

[13] Golan, 'Peace Partners Turned Business Partners.'

[14] Guy Rolnik, 'Stitched in Time, Israel's Companies are Doing Fine,' *Ha'Aretz*, 8 April 1998; Yoram Gavison, 'Delta Grows Apart from Israel,' *Ha'Aretz*, 18 February 1998; and Noga Shavit-Raz, 'Delta GM: Traditional Industry has Future; High Tech won't Solve Unemployment,' *Globes*, 10 December 1997.

[15] Orna Raviv, '"New York Times": Jordanian Employees in Delta-Owned Plant are Hostile,' *Globes*, 29 December 1996; and Shiloah, 'Peace Dividend across River Jordan.'

[16] Interview with Omar Salah.

[17] Interviews with Amiram Shor and Yoav Shaham. See also Koren, 'Magic of Israel Negotiating Joint Venture.'

[18] Interview with Lutfi A. Sayegh.

[19] William A. Orne Jr., 'Jordanian Struggles to Keep Ties to Israel,' *New York Times*, 2 November 2000.

[20] Interview with R. R. [anonymity requested].

[21] Ora Coren [Koren], 'Vishay to Explore New Jordanian Factories with Century Investment,' *Ha'Aretz*, 8 August 2000. See also Orne, 'Jordanian Struggles to Keep Ties to Israel.'

[22] Dina [Dinah] Shiloah, 'In Israel and Jordan, Talk Turns to Business,' *International Herald Tribune*, 1-2 July 2000.

[23] Ora Coren [Koren], 'Arab, Israeli Partners Aim to Introduce Web into Arab World,' *Ha'Aretz*, 21 May 2000; and Levy Morav, 'Keeping Fingers Crossed for Sallah, Barak' [sic], *Globes*, 22 May 2000.

[24] Interviews with Omar Salah, Dov Lautman, and Moshe Nahum.

[25] *MEED*, 7 June 1996; Robbie Steinberg, 'News in Brief,' *Ha'Aretz*, 5 May 1998; Ora Koren, 'Century of Jordan Negotiating with Motorola Israel to Set Up Development Centre,' *Globes*, 24 May 1997; Nina Gilbert, 'Israel, Jordan Agree to Boost Trade,' *Jerusalem Post*, 13 August 1998; and Keren Tsuriel and Gadi Golan, 'New Horizon to be Sold to Century of Jordan, Hong Kong Company for $1.78 mln,' *Globes*, 16 May 2000.

[26] *The Flow of Investments into the al-Hassan Industrial Estate During 1999*, Internal Report Obtained from the Investors Services Bureau at the al-Hassan Industrial Estate, September 2000 (Arabic, *Harakat al-istithmar fi medinat al-Hassan al-sina'iya li-'Am 1999*); and Jordan Commercial and Industrial Estates Corporation (JCIEC), *Annual Report 1998*.

[27] Interview with Omar Salah.

[28] Ghalia Alul, 'Jordache Plans to Invest at Irbid's QIZ,' *Jordan Times*, 22 April 1998.

[29] United Nations Development Programme (UNDP) and Royal Scientific Society (RSS), Peace Follow-Up Unit, *Follow-Up Report on the Qualifying Industrial Zone (QIZ)*, Report No. 14, November 1999.

[30] Interview with A. Q.

[31] Riad al-Khouri, 'Peace Dividend at Last?' *Jordan Times*, 24 August 2000.

[32] 'Irbid QIZ Exports Amounted to $172m in 2000,' *Jordan Times*, 12-13 January 2001.

[33] Irbid Chamber of Industry, *Quarterly Report: First Quarter 2001*; and Rana Awwad, 'QIZ Overcomes Aftermath of the Intifada,' *Jordan Times*, 4 December 2000.

[34] Interview with E. H.

[35] Interview with Abdallah A. Tayyeh.

[36] Interview with Fuad S. Abu Zayyad.

[37] Interview with Emad al-Shamma'.

[38] Amy Henderson, 'Customs, Taxes Seen as Main Barriers to the Development of Jordanian Textile Industry,' *Jordan Times*, 18 April 1998.

[39] 'Special Report Jordan: US Free Trade Zones Stir Controversy,' *MEED*, 29 May 1998.

[40] Interviews with Shlomi Fuchs and Yunis al-'Umri. See also Destremau, *Restructuring Process*; and Assaf Adiv, 'Israeli Textile in Crisis. No Alternative for Arab Women,' *Challenge*, No. 40.

[41] Interview with Nimer Abu Taha.

[42] Ghalia Alul, 'Dealing with Israel: Blessing or Curse?' *Jordan Times*, 10 August 1998.

[43] Interviews with A. Q., Michael Yungreis, and Gabby Bar.

[44] Interview with Michael Yungreis.

[45] Interview with Tareq Sous; see also Destremau, *Restructuring Process*; Antoine Mansour, *Subcontracting Arrangements between Israeli and Palestinian Firms*, Lecture delivered at the Palestine Economic Policy Research Institute (MAS), 3 July 1997, www.palecon.org/masdir/notes/mas13.html; and Mohamed Nasr and Bassam Badran, *The Impact of the Peace Process on the Textile and Garment Industry in Palestine*, Lectures Delivered at the Palestine Economic Policy Research Institute (MAS), 28 August 1997, www.palecon.org/masdir/notes/mas14.html.

46 Interview with Gili Deckel. See also Kirk Albrecht, 'Where is all the Business? Jordanian-Israeli Economic Ties Start Slowly,' *Middle East Insight*, Vol. 12, No. 2 (January-February 1996).
47 Zafrir Rinat, 'Greens Oppose Joint Israel-Jordan Project,' *Ha'Aretz*, 5 January 2000; Dalia Tal, 'District Committee Approves Jordan Gateway for Deposit,' *Globes*, 13 February 2000; Zafrir Rinat, 'The Eucalyptus Grove, the Bridge and the Factory,' *Ha'Aretz*, 17 September 2000; and Tamar Hausman, 'Developer Turned Off by Procedural Red Tape in Jordan-Israel Border Project,' *Ha'Aretz*, 22 September 2000.
48 Haggay Etkes, 'Israel Considering Establishment of Israeli-Jordanian High-Tech Zone at Jordanian University Campus with Hong Kong Company,' *Globes*, 5 July 2000.
49 Interviews with Sam Widerman and H. Z. [anonymity requested]. See also Ora Koren, 'Siemens and Palestinian Partner Establish R & D Centre in Ramallah,' *Globes*, 28 September 1997; Nicky Blackburn, 'Jordan, Israel and US Join Forces on High-Tech Project,' *Jerusalem Post*, 13 October 1999; Ella Jacoby-Bashan, 'Israeli-Jordanian Co. Visuality Systems Signs Partnership Agreement with Wind River,' *Globes*, 4 July 2000; and Ribhi Abu El-Haj, *The Israeli Electronics Industry*, Paper Presented to the ESCWA Expert Group Meeting on the Impact of the Peace Process on Selected Sectors, 23-25 June 1997, Amman, E/ESCWA/ID/1997/WG.I/21.
50 Interview with Issa Matalka; and www.aseaoflife.com/philosophy.htm.
51 Yehuda Lukacs, *Israel, Jordan, and the Peace Process* (Syracuse: Syracuse University Press, 1997); and Garfinkle, *Israel and Jordan*.
52 Jose Rosenfeld, 'Israel Softens Stand on Jordan Trade Pact,' *Jerusalem Post*, 27 June 1995; and 'Israel-Jordan Talks Fail,' *Israel Business Today*, Vol. 9, No. 13 (15 October 1995).
53 Shapiro, 'Israel, Jordan Reach Transport Agreement.'
54 Rachel Neiman, 'Transport Deal with Jordan Expected Soon,' *Jerusalem Post*, 27 December 1995.
55 'Restore the Warm Ties.'
56 UNDP and RSS, Peace Follow-Up Unit, *Follow-Up Report on the Transportation Agreement between Jordan and Israel in the Peace Process*, Report No. 10, February 1999 (Arabic, *Wahda mutabi'a al-salam, Taqrir mutabi'a 'an ittifaqiya al-naql bayn al-urdunn wa isra'il damn mu'ahida al-salam*).
57 RSS, Peace Follow-Up Unit, *Follow-Up Report on the Trade and Economic Cooperation Agreement between Jordan and Israel in the Treaty of Peace*, April 1998.
58 UNDP and RSS, Peace Follow-Up Unit, *Follow-Up Report on the Obstacles Exporters to Israel and the PNA Face*, July 1998 (Arabic, *Wahda mutabi'a al-salam, Al-'aqabat al-latti tuwajih al-musaddirin min al-urdunn illa isra'il wa al-salta al-wataniya al-filastiniya*).
59 Sagi Chemetz, 'Israel and Jordan to Negotiate Trade Accord,' *Ha'Aretz*, 16 September 1997.
60 Haggay Etkes, 'Make-Believe Trade,' *Globes*, 26 January 2000.
61 Statistics obtained during interview with Michael Yungreis. See also 'Israeli-Jordanian Trade May Peak this Year,' *Globes*, 22 August 2000; and Haggay Etkes, 'Jordanian Exports to Israel Continue to Rise: Exports from Irbid Industrial Estate in April $3.15 mln,' *Globes*, 2 May 2000.
62 *Al-Ra'i*, 9 August 1999.
63 'Gamal Sells to Syria,' *Israel Business Today*, Vol. 9, No. 13 (15 October 1995).
64 *MEED*, 5 April 1996; and Interview with Michael Yungreis.
65 Interview with Uri Benaim and Shlomo Shaul.
66 Interview with Gideon Wolff.
67 Interview with Amin Kawar.
68 Interviews with Deeb Shaheen and Hassan Salameh. See also 'Japanese Work to Cement Jordanian-Palestinian Trade,' *Israel Business Today*, Vol. 9, No. 10 (15 August 1995); 'Jordan to Press Israel to Deliver on Trade, Water,' *Jordan Times*, 5 August 1996; Amy Henderson, 'Gov-

ernment Decides to Sell More of its Stake in the Jordan Cement Factories Company,' *Jordan Times*, 4 November 1996; Suleiman al-Khalidi, 'Cement Company Pins Hopes on Palestinian Market,' *Jordan Times*, 12 May 1998; Y. A.-S., 'Les Echanges Commerciaux Avec Israel Toujours au Point Mort,' *The Star*, 25 February 1999; Zulkafly Baharuddin, 'Privatisation Paves Way to Success for Jordan Cement Factories Company,' *Jordan Times*, 13 October 1999.
[69] Interview with Deeb Shaheen.
[70] Ran Dagoni, 'Wall Street Journal: Israel has Unofficial Trade Ties with Iraq,' *Globes*, 15 February 1998.
[71] 'Dead Sea Works Planned to Sell Salt to Iraq in '95,' *Jerusalem Post*, 29 December 1996.
[72] Interview with Hael Fahoum. See also Emma Murphy, 'The Arab-Israeli Peace Process: Can the Region Benefit from the Economics of Globalization?' in J. W. Wright Jr. and Laura Drake, eds., *Economic and Political Impediments to Middle East Peace* (Houndmills: Macmillan, 2000), p. 47.
[73] Steve Rodan, 'Getting Down to Business in the Middle East,' *Jerusalem Post*, 3 November 1995.
[74] Michal Yudelman, 'Histadrut Won't Refund "Tax" Deducted from Palestinian Workers' Pay,' *Jerusalem Post*, 16 August 1994; 'Histadrut to Transfer NIS 3m to Palestinian Trade Unions,' *Jerusalem Post*, 30 August 1994; 'Palestinians Torpedo Signing of Pact with Histadrut,' *Jerusalem Post*, 8 December 1994; 'Palestinians Disappoint Histadrut One More Time,' *Jerusalem Post*, 13 February 1995; 'Histadrut to Transfer NIS 4m to Palestinians,' *Jerusalem Post*, 8 September 1995.
[75] Khaled Amayreh, 'Jericho Roulette,' *Al-Ahram Weekly Online*, 1-7 October 1998; and Danny Rubinstein, 'Equal-Opportunity Gambling,' *Ha'Aretz*, 23 August 1999.
[76] Interview with Gil Feiler.
[77] Samara, 'Globalization,' pp. 24-25.
[78] Feiler and Zaretsky, 'An Unforeseen Rivalry, pp. 150-152.
[79] Ben-Zion Citrin, 'The PA's Tax Paradise for Investors,' *Ha'Aretz*, 13 January 2000.
[80] Interview with Jawad al-Naji et al.
[81] Interview with Abdel Malik Jaber and Munther Ghosheh.
[82] 'PA Industrial Parks to Be Joint Ventures, *Israel Business Today*, Vol. 9 No. 16 (30 November 1995); Pinhas Inbari, 'Industrial Twilight Zones,' *Jerusalem Post*, 13 December 1995; and 'Work Starts on PA Industrial Parks,' *Jerusalem Post*, 15 February 1996.
[83] Arieh O'Sullivan, 'Karni Industrial Park Readies for December Opening,' *Jerusalem Post*, 5 November 1998; and Sagi Chemetz and Amira Hass, 'Karni Park Ready for Joint Israeli-Palestinian Business,' *Ha'Aretz*, 15 December 1998. See also Ora Koren, 'Palestinians Bar Israeli Presence at Karni Industrial Park Inauguration,' *Globes*, 13 December 1998.
[84] Patricia Golan, 'Marketing a Hard Sell Called Gaza Industrial Estate,' *Jerusalem Post*, 30 November 1998; and Nina Gilbert, 'Trade with Egypt Slides; Soars with Jordan,' *Jerusalem Post*, 16 July 1998. See also Ora Koren, 'Siemens Announces Willingness to Set Up Factory in Karni Park; Peugeot, Volkswagen Also in Negotiations,' *Globes*, 3 December 1997; and Jennifer Friedlin, 'EU Said to be Hurting Trade Between Israel and Jordan,' *Jerusalem Post*, 6 August 1997.
[85] *Interim Progress Report*, and Arieh O'Sullivan, 'Joint Industrial Zone planned near Nablus,' *Jerusalem Post*, 3 May 1999.
[86] Interview with Ms. Bunmi Ayeni.
[87] *Interim Progress Report*.
[88] Zohar Blumenkrantz, 'Merchants Worried by High Costs at Karni,' *Ha'Aretz*, 13 August 1998; and *Al-Ayyam*, 15 April 1999; see REDWG Monitoring Committee Secretariat, *Monthly Chronologies*.
[89] Amos Harel, 'It's the Economy, Stupid,' *Ha'Aretz*, 14 September 2000.
[90] Interview with Abdel Malik Jaber and Munther Ghosheh.

[91] David Zeev Harris, 'Investors Might Lose Interest in Jenin Industrial Park,' *Jerusalem Post*, 2 October 1998; and *Interim Progress Report*.
[92] Palestinian Industrial Estates and Free Zones Authority (PIEFZA), *Jenin Industrial Estate Feasibility Study*.
[93] PIEFZA, *Nablus Industrial Estate Feasibility Study*, in particular tables 3-16; *Interim Progress Report*; and O'Sullivan, 'Joint Industrial Zone Planned near Nablus.'
[94] Interview with Jawad al-Naji et al; and *Interim Progress Report*.
[95] Gil Hoffman, 'Eilat's Mayor Eyes Hi-Tech Park with Jordan,' *Jerusalem Post*, 8 July 1998.
[96] 'Israeli-Palestinian Detergent Company to be Built,' *Israel Business Today*, Vol. 9, No. 18 (31 December 1995).
[97] Mendelson, 'The Profits of Peace.'
[98] Steve Rodan, 'Behind the Scenes Trade, *Jerusalem Post*, 14 November 1997; see also the company's website, www.peaceworks.com.
[99] *Al-Quds al-Arabi*, 4 March 1999, see REDWG Monitoring Committee Secretariat, *Monthly Chronologies*.
[100] Email from the project co-ordinator, Susanne Bauer, 24 October 2000.
[101] Ran Dagoni, 'World Bank, Evergreen, Palestinian Businessman to Found Territories Investment Fund,' *Globes*, 15 January 1998; Michel Zlotowski, 'Peres, Arafat Sign Investment Fund Accord, *Jerusalem Post*, 21 January 1998; 'Peres, Wolfson, Arafat Sign Technological Foundation for Peace Agreement,' *Globes*, 19 May 1998; and Ora Koren, 'Four Multinational to Set Up Plants, Regional Distribution Centres in Gaza,' *Globes*, 11 January 1999.
[102] Interviews with Sam Widerman and Tareq Maayah. See also the Siemens website, www.siemens.com; Koren, 'Siemens and Palestinian Partner Establish R&D Centre;' and David Hayoun, 'Israeli-Palestinian High-Tech Cooperation Initiated by German Company Siemens,' *Globes*, 23 January 2000.
[103] Lifschitz, 'Tul-Karem Instead of Bombay;' and Zehava Dovrat, 'Peres Centre's Economic Peace Conference: Platini and Pele to Teach Football to Israelis, Palestinians,' *Globes*, 11 September 2000.
[104] Nicky Blackburn, 'High Hopes for Hi-Tech in the PA,' *Jerusalem Post*, 19 December 1999.
[105] Interviews with Hassan Kassem and Hanan Maoz.
[106] Interview with Ibrahim Barham.
[107] *Interim Progress Report*.
[108] Ora Coren [Koren], 'Israeli-Palestinian Industrial Parks Slowly Resume Operations,' *Ha'Aretz*, 12 October 2000.
[109] 'Israel Blasts Major Bethlehem Projects,' *Jerusalem Times*, 27 April 2001.
[110] ESCWA, *Appraisal*.
[111] UNCTAD, *Palestinian Merchandise Trade in the 1990s: Opportunities and Challenges*, UNCTAD/GDS/SEU/1, 23 January 1998.
[112] UNCTAD, *Cooperation between the Palestinian Authority, Egypt and Jordan*.
[113] Interviews with Abdel Hafiz Noufal and Samir Huleileh.
[114] Economic Cooperation Foundation (ECF) and DATA-HCIF, *The EPS Model: A Possible Set of Israeli-Palestinian Economic Understandings for Permanent Status*, June-November 1998; Ora Coren [Koren], 'Final Separation, or Cooperation,' *Ha'Aretz*, 21 October 1999; Ora Coren [Koren], 'Israel and PA Agree on a Free Trade Zone,' *Ha'Aretz*, 20 September 2000; Haggay Etkes, 'Israel, Palestinians Agree in Principle to Found Free Trade Area,' *Globes*, 10 July 2000; and Keren Tsuriel, 'The Economics of Ideology,' *Globes*, 20 July 2000.
[115] 'PA Eases Embargo on Israeli Goods,' *Ha'Aretz*, 20 November 1997.
[116] Ariza Arbeli and Zohar Blumenkrantz, 'Israel and Palestinians Cross Swords over Border Crossing,' *Ha'Aretz*, 23 March 1999.

[117] Arieh O'Sullivan, 'Israel Moves to Boost Palestinian Use of Ashdod Port,' *Jerusalem Post*, 11 November 1998.

[118] Ora Koren, 'Israeli Marketers are Lagging Behind in their Readiness,' *Globes*, 30 August 1996; and 'Palestinian Marketing Policies: First Food and Cigarettes,' *Globes*, 21 December 1996. See also David Hayoun, 'Export Institute: Palestinians Restricting Israeli Entrepreneurs' Economic Freedom in Violation of Agreements,' *Globes*, 23 August 1999.

[119] Interview with Abdel Hafiz Noufal.

[120] Haggay Etkes, 'Federation of Chambers of Commerce to Try to Stop Purchase by Israelis in Territories,' *Globes*, 11 January 2000; 'Forget Separation, Long Live Trade;' and 'The Price of Rage,' *Globes*, 16 May 2000.

[121] Interview with Mazen Sinokrot.

[122] Nicole Krau, 'Koor Group Executives Suspected of Tax Fraud,' *Ha'Aretz*, 9 June 1999.

[123] Ora Koren, 'The Primrose Path,' *Globes*, 9 August 1997.

[124] Interview with Hassan Salameh. On Ginossar, see also Sara Leibowich-Dar, 'Josef, King of the Territories,' *Ha'Aretz Magazine*, 20 April 2001 (Hebrew, *Yosef melekh ha-shtakhim*).

[125] Ronen Bergman and David Ratner, 'The Man who Swallowed Gaza', *Ha'Aretz*, 4 April 1997.

[126] Interview with Oded Ben-Haim; and Nathan Lipson and Amiram Cohen, 'Tshuva Taking Over Dankner Firm,' *Ha'Aretz*, 7 June 1999.

[127] Bergman and Ratner, 'The Man who Swallowed Gaza;' Heiko Flottau, 'Das Sonnensystem von Gaza,' *Süddeutsche Zeitung*, 29 July 1997; and Radi, *L'Elite Palestinienne*.

[128] Bergman and Ratner, 'The Man who Swallowed Gaza;' and David Hirst, 'Shameless in Gaza,' *The Guardian Weekly*, 27 April 1997.

[129] Interview with Amit Segev.

[130] UNCTAD, *Palestinian Merchandise Trade in the 1990s*.

[131] Ben Lynfield, 'Living with Contradiction,' *Jerusalem Post*, 5 November 1999. See also Paltrade's sector profile; www.paltrade.org/Sector/StoneMarble.html.

[132] See the sectoral information provided by the Paltrade, www.paltrade.org/Sector/Textile.html.

[133] Ishac Diwan, 'International Economic Relations: Access, Trade Regime, and Development Strategy,' in Diwan and Shaban, *Development Under Adversity*, p. 86. See also Jon Immanuel, 'Joining Forces in Hebron,' *Jerusalem Post*, 11 July 1997.

[134] Interview with Mahmoud Farrah.

[135] Interview with Tareq Sous. See also Nasr and Badran, *The Impact of the Peace Process*.

[136] Interview with Yunis al-'Umri. See also Mansour, *Subcontracting Arrangements*.

[137] 'Jordanians, Palestinians Set Up Jerusalem Land Firm,' *Jerusalem Post*, 17 August 1997.

[138] *Al-Aswaq*, 22 September 1998; see REDWG Monitoring Committee Secretariat, *Monthly Chronologies*.

[139] Keren Tsuriel, 'Joint Jordanian-Palestinian Industrial Zone to be Set Up in Jericho,' *Globes*, 10 August 2000.

[140] Interview with Deeb Shaheen.

[141] Interview with Issa Eways.

[142] P. V. Vivekanand, 'Cement, Steel to be Jordan's First Exports to Palestinians,' *Jordan Times*, 6 May 1995; and 'Jordan to Seek Israeli Restraints on Movement of Goods to W. Bank' [sic], *Jordan Times*, 17 June 1995.

[143] 'Japanese Work to Cement Jordanian-Palestinian Trade;' 'Jordan to press Israel to Deliver on Trade, Water;' and Henderson, 'Government Decides to Sell More of its Stake.'

[144] Al-Khalidi, 'Cement Company Pins Hopes on Palestinian Market;' A.-S., 'Les Echanges Commerciaux avec Israel;' Baharuddin, 'Privatisation Paves Way to Success.'

[145] Interview with Hassan Salameh.

[146] 'Jordanien und Palästina schliessen Abkommen,' *Nachrichten für Aussenhandel*, 7 February 1995; Jose Rosenfeld and Jon Immanuel, 'Shaath: Closure Must End Before We Can Discuss Economic Cooperation,' *Jerusalem Post*, 8 February 1995; and 'Jordan, Palestinians Draft List for Duty-Free Trade, *Jerusalem Post*, 19 February 1995.
[147] 'Israeli Restrictions Limit Palestinian Imports from Jordan to Only $3 million,' *Jordan Times*, 25 November 1996.
[148] Ghadeer Taher, 'Jordan, Israel, and the Palestinians: One Partner Too Many,' *Jordan Times*, 31 May 1998.
[149] 'Jordan, PNA Remonstrate Against Israeli-Imposed Impediments to Trade, *Jordan Times*, 11 September 1996.
[150] *Al-Aswaq*, 21 July 1998; and *Al-Ayyam*, 10 May 1998. See REDWG Monitoring Committee Secretariat, *Monthly Chronologies*.
[151] *Al-Quds al-Arabi* and *Al-Aswaq*, 30 November 1998; see REDWG Monitoring Committee Secretariat, *Monthly Chronologies*.
[152] Lynfield, 'Jordanians Target Palestinian Market; and David Makovsky, 'Jordan Gripes About Israeli Grip on Trade,' *Ha'Aretz*, 24 November 1998.
[153] Zvi Barel, 'A Tightfisted Peace,' *Ha'Aretz*, 6 March 1999; and Etkes, 'Make-Believe Trade.'
[154] Amy Henderson, 'Jordan, Israel Renew Trade Protocol,' *Jordan Times*, 13 January 1999.
[155] Moti Bassok, 'Israel-PA Economic Deal Targets Car Thieves, Bad Debt,' *Ha'Aretz*, 8 June 2000.
[156] Interviews with Issa Matalka, Emad al-Shamma', and Kamil N. Fakhoury.
[157] Interview with Moayyad Samman.
[158] Tareq Ayyoub, 'Jordanian and Palestinian Businessmen Discuss Trade Barriers,' *Jordan Times*, 5 April 2000.
[159] Interview with Gadi Sassower.
[160] Interviews with Talal Nasruddin and Muhammad Masrouji.
[161] Interview with Nakhleh Jubran.
[162] Interview with Mazen Sinokrot.
[163] See the comments by Gershon Baskin and Mahmoud Abu Samra from the Palestinian Ministry of Agriculture in Gershon Baskin and Zakaria al-Qaq, eds., *Israeli-Palestinian-Jordanian Trade: Present Issues, Future Possibilities*, Israel-Palestine Centre for Research and Information (IPCRI), Commercial Law Report Series, April 1998.
[164] Interviews with Saeb Bamieh and Abdel Hafiz Noufal.
[165] UNCTAD, *Cooperation Between the Palestinian Authority, Egypt and Jordan*.
[166] 'Israeli Impediments to Investment in Palestine.'
[167] UNDP and RSS, *Follow-Up Report on the Transportation Agreement*.
[168] Ibid.

Business Leaders and Political Elites:

[1] Heidi J. Gleit, 'Fighting Corruption,' *Jerusalem Post*, 6 July 2000; see also the work carried out for 'Country Assessment: Israel,' *International Standards Compliance Index*, Research Department, Oxford Analytica, June-July 2001.
[2] Steve Rodan, 'Back in Business,' *Jerusalem Post*, 14 May 1993; and 'News in Brief,' *Jerusalem Post*, 21 February 1997.
[3] David Hayoun, 'Energy Man,' *Globes*, 1 December 1999.
[4] Shlomo Ben-Ami, 'Koor Ready to Cooperate,' *Israel-Palestine Journal*, Vol. 1, No. 1 (Winter 1994).
[5] Interview with Yoram Katz.

[6] See Economic Cooperation Foundation (ECF) and DATA-HCIF, *The EPS Model*.
[7] Interview with Gili Deckel.
[8] Information provided on the group's webpage, www.elulgrp.com.
[9] Interviews with David Kolitz and E. H.
[10] Interview with Dov Lautman.
[11] Shafir and Peled, 'Globalization,' p. 260.
[12] Aluf Benn, Alisa Odenheimer, and Ora Coren [Koren], 'PM Favors Economic Separation from Palestinian "Entity",' *Ha'Aretz*, 18 October 1999.
[13] Interview with Michael Yungreis.
[14] Interview with Gadi Sassower.
[15] Yossi Melman, 'Hunting for Friends,' *Ha'Aretz*, 12 July 1997.
[16] Interview with Oded Ben-Haim.
[17] Etkes, 'Jordan to Allow Foreigners.'
[18] Sara Leibowich-Dar, 'Marketing Man: Danny International,' *Ha'Aretz Magazine*, 13 October 2000.
[19] Leibowich-Dar, 'Josef, King of the Territories.'
[20] Akiva Eldar, 'From Hard Lines to Shorelines,' *Ha'Aretz*, 9 August 1999.
[21] Peres, *The New Middle East*; and Amir Ben-David, 'The Sky Above, The Mud Below,' *Ha'Aretz*, 3 September 2000.
[22] Interviews with Mrs. June Dilevsky, Refael Benvenisti, Sharon Pardo, Ms. Yael Levite, Dan Cativaras, and Mayor Admon.
[23] Interview with Prof. Samuel Pohoryles; and Ben-David, 'The Sky Above, The Mud Below.'
[24] Economic Cooperation Foundation (ECF) and DATA-HCIF, *The EPS Model*.
[25] Interview with Gabby Bar.
[26] Interview with Avi Sofer; see also Ora Coren [Koren], 'Free-Trade Zone Envisioned for Border,' *Ha'Aretz*, 27 June 2000.
[27] Interview with Doron Tamir.
[28] Interviews with Moshe Nahum and Samir Huleileh.
[29] Interviews with Dov Rochman and Oded Ben-Haim.
[30] Interview with Gili Deckel; and Hausman, 'Developer Turned Off by Procedural Red Tape.'
[31] Timothy J. Piro, *Managers and Minerals in a Monarchy: The Political Economy of Mining in Jordan, 1970-1989*, Ph.D. dissertation, George Washington University, 1992.
[32] Francesca Ciriaci, 'Private Sector Gives Kabariti Policy Statement a 'Thumbs Up',' *Jordan Times*, 29 February-1 March 1996; Lamia Tabbaa, 'Tabbaa Urges Government to Include Private Sector Businessmen in Official Delegations, *Jordan Times*, 20 November 1996; and Ilham Sadeq, 'New Economic Law Arouses Controversy Among Private Sector,' *The Star*, 26 June 1997.
[33] Interviews with Mamduh Abu Hassan and Thabet A. Taher.
[34] Kirk Albrecht, 'This Peace Dividend Comes Duty-Free,' *Business Week*, 26 January 1998.
[35] Moore, *Doing Business with the State*.
[36] Tareq Ayyoub, 'Commerce Chamber Holds Elections Today,' *Jordan Times*, 17 November 1998.
[37] Ghalia Alul, 'Amman Chamber of Industry Pushed for Transformation to National Body,' *Jordan Times*, 8 February 1998; and Tareq Ayyoub, 'Govt. Decision on Chamber of Industry Membership Raises Hopes, Fears, *Jordan Times*, 13 January 2000.
[38] 'ACI Goes for Full Elections,' *The Star*, 6 April 2000; Tareq Ayyoub, 'Amman Chamber of Industry Election Campaigns Heat Up,' *Jordan Times*, 11 April 2000; and 'Abu Hassan Defeated in Amman Chamber of Industry Elections,' *Jordan Times*, 13 April 2000.
[39] Tareq Ayyoub, 'New Amman Chamber of Industry Head Strives for Unity,' *Jordan Times*, 14-15 April 2000.

[40] Ayyoub, 'Government Shuns Criticism;' and 'Sale of 33.3% of Cement Company to Lafarge to Be Concluded Sunday,' *Jordan Times*, 21 November 1998.
[41] 'Excerpts of Speech Published as King Points to Jordan's Determination to Excel in IT,' *Jordan Times*, 26 March 2000.
[42] Francesca Ciriaci, 'Toe the Line to Succeed On-Line, Industry Expert Tells Local IT Companies,' *Jordan Times*, 6 March 2000.
[43] Suha Ma'ayeh, 'Jordan Vision 2020 Sets Course for Unified Economic Strategy, *Jordan Times*, 11 June 2000.
[44] Hattar, 'King Forms Economic Consultative Council.'
[45] For a similar argument on the transformation of Jordan's political economy, see Hamid El-Said, 'The Political Economy of Reform in Jordan: Breaking Resistance to Reform?' in Joffé, *Jordan in Transition*.
[46] Barel, 'When a King Wants a New Economy;' Zvi Barel, 'Neighbours: Normalisation is Not for Public Consumption,' *Ha'Aretz*, 3 May 2000; and Haggay Etkes, 'Jordan's New Prime Minister,' *Globes*, 20 June 2000.
[47] Zulkafly Baharuddin, 'Aramex Founder Fadi Ghandour Ready to Deliver for Economic Consultative Council,' *Jordan Times*, 25-26 December 1999.
[48] Zulkafly Baharuddin, 'Nuqul Group Brings Leadership from the Shop Floor to the Boardroom,' *Jordan Times*, 30 December 1999; and 'Watering Seeds of Innovation Makes Dollars and Sense to ECC Member Fawaz Hatim Zu'bi,' *Jordan Times*, 20 January 2000.
[49] Zulkafly Baharuddin, 'Karim Kawar Targets On-Line Kingdom with Companies for the IT Age,' *Jordan Times*, 2 March 2000.
[50] Interviews with Amin Kawar and Ms. Jumana Husseini.
[51] Zulkafly Baharuddin, 'Dr. Salaheddin Al Bashir Looks Ahead to Successful, Progressive Society,' *Jordan Times*, 17 February 2000.
[52] Zulkafly Baharuddin, 'Dr. Anwar Battikhi Channels Expertise into Raising Money for Higher Education,' *Jordan Times*, 24 February 2000.
[53] Zulkafly Baharuddin, 'Khaled Toukan Seeks a Delicate Balance Between the Educational System and Potential Employer Needs,' *Jordan Times*, 23 March 2000; 'Samih Dawarzah Confidently Positions Hikma International to Seize a Bigger Slice of World Market,' *Jordan Times*, 30 March 2000.
[54] Interview with Fuad Abu Zayyad; see also Zulkafly Baharuddin, 'Dr. Fuad Abu Zayyad Ready to Help Investors Get Down to Business,' *Jordan Times*, 10 February 2000.
[55] Interview with Ms. Jumana Husseini.
[56] Fahed al-Fanek, 'The Risk of Arousing Israeli Interest in Aqaba,' *Jordan Times*, 5 June 2000.
[57] Interviews with Emad al-Shamma', Kamil N. Fakhoury, and Abdallah Tayyeh.
[58] Interview with H. Z.
[59] Interview with Samer M. Tawil.
[60] Interview with Emile Cubeisy; and Young Entrepreneurs Association (YEA), *Annual Report 1999*.
[61] Interview with Amin Kawar.
[62] Interview with Omar Salah; and Omar Salah's remarks in Baskin and al-Qaq, *Israeli-Palestinian-Jordanian Trade*.
[63] Joseph Contreras, 'A Cold Wind Blowing,' *Newsweek*, 17 November 1997; Ora Coren [Koren], 'Century Chair: Netanyahu Has Made Israeli Businessmen Unwelcome in Arab World,' *Globes*, 17 November 1997; and Catherine Cohen, 'Jordan Treads Warily in Israel,' *Ha'Aretz*, 3 November 2000.
[64] Fairouz Abu-Ghazaleh, Deputies Express Concern Over Possible Israeli-Owned Factories in Kingdom,' *Jordan Times*, 19-20 February 1998; see also Zvi Barel, 'The River is Wide and the River is Frozen,' *Ha'Aretz*, 23 May 1998.

[65] Barel, 'Neighbours: Normalisation is Not for Public Consumption;' and Daniel Sobelman, 'Jordanian PM Blasts Opponents of Relations with Israel,' *Ha'Aretz*, 30 August 2000.
[66] Interviews with Omar Salah, Abdallah Tayyeh, Fuad Abu Zayyed, and Nimer Abu Taha.
[67] Pinhas Inbari, 'Looking for Arafat's Rothschild,' *Jerusalem Post*, 3 January 1996; and Radi, *L'Elite Palestinienne*, pp. 313-319.
[68] Interview with Muhammad Shtayyeh.
[69] Steve Rodan, 'Palestinian Businessmen Challenge PA to Attract Investments,' *Jerusalem Post*, 3 July 1997.
[70] *Al-Ra'i*, 30 July 1998; see REDWG Monitoring Committee Secretariat, *Monthly Chronologies*.
[71] 'Les Commercants de Jenine Craignent de Perdre Leurs Clients Israeliens Apres l'Autonomie,' *L'Orient*, 23 March 1995.
[72] Michael Lüders, 'Der Mühsame Weg nach Palästina,' *Die Zeit*, 5 December 1997.
[73] Stacey Lakind and Yigal Carmon, 'The PA Economy – Free Market or Kleptocracy? Part I: Economic Policy,' *MEMRI (The Middle East Media and Research Institute) Inquiry and Analysis No. 10*, 7 January 1999; www.memri.org/ia/IA1099.html; see also Golan, 'Building Up is Hard to Do;' Wafa Amr, 'Arafat Moves Towards Palestinian Privatisation,' *Jordan Times*, 8 May 1995; and 'PADICO Secures Major Palestinian Telephones Project,' *Jordan Times*, 28 June 1995.
[74] Amira Hass, 'Telephone Politics: Paltel Disconnects Jerusalem from Israel,' *Ha'Aretz*, 5 May 1998.
[75] Interview with Abdel Malik Jaber and Jawad al-Naji et al.
[76] Interview with Mazen Sinokrot.
[77] Interview with Samir Abdullah. See also Radi, *L'Elite Palestinienne*.
[78] Lakind and Carmon, 'The PA Economy.'
[79] Interview with Hassan Salameh.
[80] Bergman and Ratner, 'The Man who Swallowed Gaza;' and Ronen Bergman, 'How Much is the PLO Really Worth? *Ha'Aretz*, 28 November 1999.
[81] Zvi Barel, 'An Olive Branch Sprouting Leaves,' *Ha'Aretz*, 5 January 2000; and Danny Rubinstein, 'The Investor from Qatar,' *Ha'Aretz*, 31 December 1997.
[82] Steve Rodan and Muhammad Najib, 'The Tax Man Wears Many Disguises,' *Jerusalem Post*, 21 August 1998.
[83] Bergman and Ratner, 'The Man who Swallowed Gaza.'
[84] Lüders, 'Der Mühsame Weg nach Palästina.'
[85] Hirst, 'Shameless in Gaza.'
[86] Amira Hass, 'PA Taxi Drivers Strike Over Taxes,' *Ha'Aretz*, 25 November 1999.
[87] 'Audit Reveals PNA $326 m. Corruption,' *Jordan Times*, 25 May 1997.
[88] Steve Rodan and Mohammed Najib, 'PA Legalises Corruption,' *Jerusalem Post*, 14 August 1998; and Heiko Flottau, 'Warten aufs Saubermachen im Hause Arafat,' *Süddeutsche Zeitung*, 8 July 1998.
[89] Amira Hass, 'Corruption Caused by the Peace Process,' *Ha'Aretz*, 13 October 1999; and Charmaine Seitz, 'PA Commercial Holdings Made Public,' published on the website of the Jerusalem Media Communications Centre (JMCC), www.jmcc.org/media/report/2000/Jun/4b.htm.
[90] Amira Hass, 'PA Moves on Fiscal Responsibility,' *Ha'Aretz*, 3 July 2000.
[91] Interview with Samir Huleileh.
[92] Interviews with Saeb Bamieh and Abdel Hafiz Noufal.
[93] Interview with Mazen Sinokrot.
[94] Interview with Nakhleh Jubran.
[95] Interview with Muhammad Masrouji.
[96] Interview with Talal Nasruddin.
[97] Interviews with Hassan Kassem.

[98] Interview with Ibrahim Barham.
[99] Interview with Tareq Maayah.
[100] Interview with Mahmoud Farrah.
[101] Interview with Hana Siniora.
[102] *Jordan Times*, 17 September 1998; see REDWG Monitoring Committee Secretariat, *Monthly Chronologies*.
[103] Interview with Samir Abdullah. See also Haggay Etkes, 'Palestinian Minister of Industry: Flooding Palestinian Market with Israeli Products Spreads Destruction,' *Globes*, 23 August 1999; and Ora Coren [Koren], 'PA Power Plays May Scuttle Final Economic Agreement,' *Ha'Aretz*, 1 October 1999.
[104] *National Economic Dialogue Conference*.

Peace, Social Equality, and Democracy:
[1] Murphy, 'Arab-Israeli Peace Process,' p. 61.
[2] Shafir and Peled, 'Globalization,' p. 247.
[3] Shafir, 'Business in Politics,' pp. 114-117. See also Shafir and Peled, 'Globalization,' pp. 257-262.
[4] Nitzan and Bichler argue that business leaders began promoting peace after the military, but before the politicians; see 'The Impermanent War Economy?' p. 98, and in particular their remark in footnote 72 on p. 108.
[5] Shafir and Peled, 'Globalization,' pp. 249-252.
[6] Interview with Gil Feiler.
[7] Seliktar, 'The Peace Dividend,' pp. 225-227.
[8] Nitzan and Bichler make a very similar argument in 'The Impermanent War Economy?' p. 98.
[9] See the table in Ram, '"The Promised Land",' p. 229.
[10] Steve A. Yetiv, 'Peace, Interdependence, and the Middle East,' *Political Science Quarterly*, Vol. 112, No. 1 (1997), pp. 30-31.
[11] Keren Tsuriel, 'Business Meeting with Abdullah Cancelled; Benny Gaon: All Projects Stalemated,' *Globes*, 22 August 2000.
[12] Wright, 'Competing Trade Agendas;' and Çarkoğlu, Eder, and Kirişci, *Political Economy of Regional Cooperation*.
[13] Sammy Smooha, 'The Implications of the Transition to Peace for Israeli Society', *The Annals of the American Academy of Political and Social Science*, Vol. 555 (January 1998, special issue on Israel in Transition), pp. 39-40.
[14] Ram, '"The Promised Land",' pp. 230-235.
[15] Shalev, 'Liberalization and the Transformation,' p. 150.
[16] Ram, '"The Promised Land",' p. 234.
[17] David Rudge, 'Israeli Arabs Growing Angrier, Experts Say,' *Jerusalem Post*, 6 November 2000.
[18] The Institute for Peace Research, *2001 Survey: Attitudes of the Arabs to the State of Israel*; see http://orae.fes.de:8081/fes/docs/NAHER_OSTEN/ 2001%20SURVEY.HTM.
[19] Interview with Abdallah Tayyeh.
[20] Oliver Schlumberger, 'Transition to Development?' in Joffé, *Jordan in Transition*, pp. 245-246.
[21] El-Said, 'Political Economy of Reform,' p. 272.
[22] Laurie A. Brand, 'The Effects of the Peace Process on Political Liberalization in Jordan', *Journal of Palestine Studies*, Vol. 28, No. 2 (Spring 1999), p. 65. See also Glenn E. Robinson,

'Defensive Democratization in Jordan', *International Journal of Middle East Studies*, Vol. 30, No. 3 (August 1998).
[23] Curtis R. Ryan, 'Peace, Bread and Riots: Jordan and the IMF,' *Middle East Policy*, Vol. 6, No. 2 (Autumn 1996); and 'Jordan and the Rise and Fall of the Arab Co-operation Council,' *Middle East Journal*, Vol. 52, No. 3 (Summer 1998).
[24] Laurie A. Brand, *Women, the State, and Political Liberalization: Middle Eastern and North African Experiences*, (New York: Columbia University Press, 1998).
[25] Renate Dietrich, 'The Weakness of the Ruled is the Strength of the Ruler: The Role of the Opposition in Contemporary Jordan,' in Joffé, *Jordan in Transition*, p. 145. See also Ranjit Singh, 'Liberalisation or Democratisation? The Limits of Political Reform and Civil Society in Jordan,' in Joffé, *Jordan in Transition*.
[26] Bouillon, 'Walking the Tightrope.'
[27] El-Said, 'Political Economy of Reform,' pp. 268-269.
[28] Bill Hutman, 'No Sugar to Coat the Pill of Closure,' *Jerusalem Post*, 12 April 1996.
[29] Interview with Ms. Hiba Husseini.
[30] See the monthly opinion polls conducted by the Centre for Palestine Research and Studies (CPRS); www.cprs-palestine.org.
[31] Bergman and Ratner, 'The Man who Swallowed Gaza;' and Hirst, 'Shameless in Gaza.'
[32] Parker, *Resignation or Revolt*, p. 200.
[33] See the series of opinion polls conducted by the CPRS, www.cprs-palestine.org.
[34] Parker, *Resignation or Revolt*, p. 202.
[35] Çarkoğlu, Eder, and Kirişci, *Political Economy of Regional Cooperation*.
[36] Wright, 'Competing Trade Agendas.'
[37] Parker, *Resignation or Revolt*, p. 199.
[38] Interview with Ms. Hiba Husseini.
[39] Shaban, 'Worsening Economic Outcomes,' in Diwan and Shaban, *Development Under Adversity*, p. 21.
[40] Arnon and Spivak, 'Economic Aspects.'

The Regional Failure of the Peace Business:
[1] Jose Rosenfeld, 'Palestinians Not Interested in Cooperation with Israel,' *Jerusalem Post*, 1 July 1994.
[2] Joshua Shuman, 'Industrialists Fear Peace Accord Could Harm Economy,' *Jerusalem Post*, 7 January 1993.
[3] Haim Shapiro, 'Growing Pains,' *Jerusalem Post*, 31 January 1996.
[4] Çarkoğlu, Eder, and Kirişci, *Political Economy of Regional Cooperation*, p. 125.
[5] Drake, 'Arab-Israeli Relations in a new Middle East Order,' p. 24.
[6] Golan, 'Peace Partners.' See also Shavit-Raz, 'Delta GM;' Gavison, 'Delta Grows Apart;' and Rolnik, 'Stitched in Time.'
[7] Cox, 'Gramsci, Hegemony and International Relations,' p. 51.
[8] Ibid, p. 50.
[9] Cox, 'Gramsci, Hegemony and International Relations,' pp. 54-55.
[10] Ibid, p. 55.
[11] Quoted from Nazih N. Ayubi, *Over-Stating the Arab State: Politics and Society in the Middle East* (London: I. B. Tauris, 1995), pp. 5-6.
[12] Cox, 'Gramsci, Hegemony and International Relations,' p. 56.
[13] Ibid, p. 51.
[14] Shalev, *Labour*; and Sharkansky, *Political Economy*.

[15] Ram, '"The Promised Land",' p. 228.
[16] Çarkoğlu, Eder, and Kirişci, *Political Economy of Regional Cooperation*, pp. 185-186.
[17] Gerd Nonneman, 'Economic Liberalization: The Debate,' in Gerd Nonneman, ed., *Political and Economic Liberalization: Dynamics and Linkages in Comparative Perspective* (Boulder: Lynne Rienner, 1996), p. 5.
[18] Etel Solingen, 'Quandaries of the Peace Process,' *Journal of Democracy*, Vol. 7, No. 3 (1996).
[19] Emma Murphy and Tim Niblock, 'Introduction,' in Tim Niblock and Emma Murphy, eds., *Economic and Political Liberalization in the Middle East* (London: British Academy, 1993), p. xiii.
[20] Alan Richards and John Waterbury, *A Political Economy of the Middle East* (Boulder: Westview, 2nd ed. 1996), p. 215.
[21] David Seddon, 'Austerity Protests in Response to Economic Liberalization in the Middle East,' in Niblock and Murphy, *Economic and Political Liberalization*.
[22] Gerd Nonneman, 'Patterns of Economic Liberalization: Explanations and Modalities,' in Nonneman, ed., *Political and Economic Liberalization*.
[23] H. Shapiro and L. Taylor, 'The State and Industrial Strategy,' in Charles K. Wilber and Kenneth P. Jameson, eds., *The Political Economy of Development and Underdevelopment* (New York: McGraw-Hill, 5th ed. 1992), p. 433.
[24] Solingen, 'Quandaries of the Peace Process,' p. 150.
[25] Murphy and Niblock, 'Introduction,' p. xiii.
[26] Paul Aarts, *Dilemmas of Regional Cooperation in the Middle East* (The Lancaster Papers: Current Research in Politics and International Affairs, No. 4, published by the Department of Politics and International Relations, Lancaster University, 1999), pp. 34-37.
[27] Gerd Nonneman, 'Patterns of Political Liberalization: Explanations and Modalities,' in Nonneman, *Political and Economic Liberalization*, p. 59. See also Alan Richards, 'Economic Imperatives and Political Systems,' in Tim Niblock and Rodney Wilson, eds., *The Political Economy of the Middle East*, Vol. 4: Economic and Political Liberalization (Cheltenham: Elgar, 1999).
[28] Çarkoğlu, Eder, and Kirişci, *Political Economy of Regional Cooperation*, pp. 176-191. See also Peres, *The New Middle East*.
[29] This is the verdict reached, for example, by Clement M. Henry and Robert Springborg, *Globalization and the Politics of Development in the Middle East* (Cambridge: Cambridge University Press, 2001), p. 188.
[30] David Pool, 'The Links Between Economic and Political Liberalization,' in Niblock and Murphy, *Economic and Political Liberalization*.
[31] Richards and Waterbury, *Political Economy of the Middle East*.
[32] Tim Niblock, 'Democratization: A Theoretical and Practical Debate,' in Niblock and Wilson, *The Political Economy of the Middle East*, p. 75. The essay first appeared in the *British Journal of Middle Eastern Studies*, Vol. 25, No. 2 (1998).

Conclusion:
[1] Drake, 'Arab-Israeli Relations in a new Middle East Order', p 25.
[2] Cox, 'Social Forces, States, and World Orders,' pp. 207-210.
[3] Cox, 'Gramsci, Hegemony and International Relations,' p. 53.
[4] Gramsci in his 'prison notebooks;' quoted in Cox, 'Gramsci, Hegemony and International Relations,' p. 64.
[5] Interview with Tareq Sous.

List of Interviews

Israel:

-*Mr Avraham Asheri*, Economic Adviser to the Chairman of the Board, ISCAR Group, Jerusalem, 31 October 2000.
-*Mr Gabby Bar*, Deputy Director-General, Middle East and North Africa Division, Foreign Trade Administration, Ministry of Industry and Trade, and Joint Chairman of the QIZ Committee, Jerusalem, 5 December 2000 and 10 May 2001.
-*Mr Uri Benaim*, Sales and Marketing Representative, and Mr Shlomo Shaul, General Manager, Agish International Forwarding Ltd., Tel Aviv, 19 November 2000.
-*Mr Oded Ben-Haim*, former Head, Israel Economic Mission to Oman, and Head of International Relations, Dankner Investments Ltd./Dankner Group, Tel Aviv, 19 November 2000.
-*Mr Refael Benvenisti*, Senior Adviser to the Minister, Mr Sharon Pardo, Projects Manager, and Ms Yael Levite, Projects Manager, Ministry of Regional Co-operation, Tel Aviv, 26 November 2000.
-*Mr Dan Catarivas*, Deputy Director-General International Affairs, and Mr Mayor Admon, Deputy Director International Affairs, Ministry of Finance, Jerusalem, 20 November 2000.
-*Mr Gili Deckel*, General Manager, Jordan Gateway Projects, Tel Aviv, 12 November 2000.
-*Mrs June Dilevsky*, Financial Consultant and Advisor to the Ministry of Regional Co-operation, Jerusalem, 14 November 2000.
-*Dr. Gil Feiler*, Chairman, Info-Prod Research (Middle East) Ltd., Tel Aviv, 25 December 2000.
-*Mr Shlomi Fuchs*, CFO, Ravtex 1992 Ltd., Afula, 30 November 2000.
-*Mr E. H.* [anonymity requested], Tel Aviv, 11 December 2000.
-*Mr Yoram Katz*, Owner, Yoram Katz Ltd Middle East Trade Co., Herzliya, 11 January 2001 and 10 May 2001.
-*Mr David Kolitz*, Chairman and CEO, Elul Group, Tel Aviv, 23 November 2000.
-*Mr Dov Lautman*, Chairman of the Board, Delta Galil Industries Ltd., Tel Aviv, 26 November 2000.
-*Mr Daniel Lubetzky*, CEO, The Peaceworks, Inc., 23 April 2001 (email contact).
-*Mr Hanan Maoz*, Member of the Board, Oracle Israel, 10 December 2000 (telephone interview).
-*Mr Hadas Melamed*, Chief Economist, Motorola Israel, 22 and 23 November 2000 (email contact).
-*Mr Moshe Nahum*, Division of International Trade, Middle East and North Africa, Israel Manufacturers Association (IMA), Tel Aviv, 29 October 2000.
-*Prof. Dr. Samuel Pohoryles*, Deputy Director-General, The Peres Centre for Peace, Tel Aviv, 14 December 2000.
-*Mr Danny Rappaport*, Finance Director, Koor Industries Ltd., Tel Aviv, 12 November 2000.
-*Mr Dov Rochman*, former Vice-Chairman, Peace Industrial Development and Investment Co Ltd./Koor Industries Ltd., Netanya, 20 December 2000.
-*Mr R. R.* [anonymity requested], Or Yehuda, 27 November 2000.
-*Mr Gabi Roter*, General Manager, Castro, 12 November 2000 (telephone interview).
-*Mr Gadi Sassower*, President, J. Sassower Ltd., Haifa, 29 November 2000.

-*Mr Amit Segev*, Deputy CEO, Housing and Construction Holding Co Ltd., Tel Aviv, 18 December 2000.
-*Mr Yoav Shaham*, Vice-President and Director of Marketing, Formula Systems (1985) Ltd., 9 November 2000 (telephone interview).
-*Mr Amiram Shor*, Chairman MLL (Malam) Systems Ltd., and Chairman Israeli Software Houses Association, 8 November 2000 (telephone interview).
-*Mr Avi Sofer*, Director Middle East Region, Israel Export Institute (IEI), Tel Aviv, 19 December 2000.
-*Ms Jessica Steinberg*, Journalist, Jerusalem 20 November 2000.
-*Mr Doron Tamir*, President and CEO, Global Wire Group Ltd., Petah Tikvah, 4 February 2001.
-*Mr Badia Tannus*, Chairman, and Mr Shlomo Raviv, Manager, B. S. T. Ltd., Nazareth, 29 November 2000.
-*Mr Yunis al-'Umri*, Owner, al-Umri Ltd., Afula, 29 November 2000.
-*Mr Yossi Vardi*, former Economic Adviser to Foreign Minister Shimon Peres, 18 October 2000 (email contact).
-*Mr Sam Widerman*, former CEO Siemens Israel (Siemens Data Communications, SDC) and CEO Visuality Systems, Tel Aviv, 30 October 2000.
-*Mr Gideon Wolff*, Export Manager, Transclal Trade Ltd., 30 November 2000.
-*Mr Dov Yaacobi*, Joint General Manager, Klil Industries Ltd., 15 November 2000 (telephone interview).
-*Mr Michael Yungreis*, Director, Israel-Jordan Chamber of Commerce, Tel Aviv, 30 October, 23 November 2000, and 10 May 2001.

Jordan:
-*Mr Nadim A. As'ad*, General Manager, Century Wear Co., al-Hassan Industrial Estate, Irbid, 24 February 2001.
-*Mr Abdallah A. Attieh*, Assistant Director, Research Directorate, Amman Chamber of Commerce, Amman, 6 July 2000.
-*Mr Mamduh Abu-Hassan*, Chairman, Jordan Ceramic Industries Co., Amman, 13 February 2001.
-*Mr Halim F. Abu-Rahmeh*, Managing Director, Jordan Trade Association (JTA), Amman, 6 July 2000.
-*Mr Nimer Abu Taha*, General Manager, The Eagle Shirts Factory Co., Amman Industrial Estate/Sahhab, 26 February 2001.
-*Ms Kifaya Abu-Thallam*, Section Head Research and Development, Jordan International Insurance Co., Jordan International Investment Group, Amman, 14 February 2001.
-*Dr. Fuad S. Abu Zayyad*, Chairman, Inter-Arab Investment Fund LP, and member of the Economic Consultative Council (ECC), Amman, 12 February 2001.
-*Mr Emile Cubeisy*, Account Director, Cubeisy Management Consultancy and Services Ltd., and Vice-President, Young Entrepreneurs Association (YEA), Amman, 8 July 2000.
-*Mr Emad Najib Fakhoury*, former Commercial Attaché, Jordanian Embassy, Tel Aviv, former CEO Century Investment Group, Commissioner for Investment and Economic Development, Aqaba Special Economic Zone Authority, Amman, 28 February 2001.
-*Mr Kamil N. Fakhoury*, Business Development Manager, Specialized Investment Compounds Co., Tajammu'at Industrial Estate, Amman, 15 February 2001.
-*Dr. Mustafa B. Hamarneh*, Director, Jordan Centre for Strategic Studies, University of Jordan, Amman, 14 February 2001.
-*Ms Jumana Husseini*, Business Counsellor, Euro-Jordanian Business Service Team, Amman, 18 February 2001.
-*Mr Amin K. Kawar*, Deputy General Manager, Amin Kawar and Sons Co., and Vice-President, Jordanian-American Business Association (JABA), Amman, 26 February 2001.

-*Mr Muhammad A. Khawasneh*, Head Industrial Studies, Royal Scientific Society (RSS), Amman, 6 July 2000.
-*Mr Issa Matalka*, Partner in Jordael Ltd., Amman, 17 February 2001.
-*Dr. Maen F. Nsour*, Director Economic Aid Co-ordination Unit, Ministry of Planning, Amman, 4 July 2000.
-*Mr A. Q.* [anonymity requested], Amman, 15 February 2001.
-*Mr Omar Salah*, Chairman of the Board, Century Investment Group, Amman, 17 February 2001.
-*Mr Moayyad Samman*, Assistant Director General, Jordan Export Development and Commercial Centres Corporation (JEDCO), Amman, 6 July 2000.
-*Mr Lutfi A. Sayegh*, General Manager, Century Tailoring Co., al-Hassan Industrial Estate/Irbid, 24 February 2001.
-*Mr Deeb Shaheen*, General Manager, Rum and Gulf Co., Amman, 25 February 2001.
-*Mr Emad al-Shamma'*, Consultant, GURU, Tajammu'at Industrial Estate, Amman, 15 February 2001.
-*H. E. Thabet A. Taher*, Chairman, Petra Drilling Co., and Vice-Chairman, Jordan Businessmen Association (JBA), Amman, 1 March 2001.
-*Mr Samer M. Tawil*, Secretary General, Ministry of Industry and Trade, and Joint Chairman of the QIZ Committee, Amman, 27 February 2001.
-*Mr Abdallah A. Tayeh*, Managing Director, Tracon Trade Consultant Ltd., Amman, 12 February 2001.
-*Mr H. Z.* [anonymity requested], Amman, 27 February 2001.

Palestinian Territories:

-*Dr. Samir Abdullah*, General Manager, Palestinian Trade Centre (PALTRADE), Ramallah, 8 May 2001.
-*Ms Bunmi Ayeni*, Assistant General Manager International Relations, Palestinian Industrial Estates Development Co. (PIEDCO), Tel Aviv, 8 December 2000.
-*Mr Saeb Bamieh*, Director-General, General Administration for Trade Co-operation, Ministry of the Economy and Trade, Ramallah, 13 June 2001.
-*Mr Ibrahim Barham*, General Manager, Safad Engineering and Electronics Ltd., and Chairman, Palestinian IT Association (PITA), Ramallah, 14 June 2001.
-*Ms Susanne Bauer*, Project Co-ordinator, German Agency for Technical Co-operation (GTZ), German-Palestinian Business Start-Up Project, 24 October 2000 (email contact).
-*Mr Issa Eways*, President and CEO, Rama International, Ramallah, 8 May 2001.
-*Mr Hael Fahoum*, Assistant Deputy Minister for International Relations, Ministry of Finance; Vice-Chairman, Higher Commission for Investment and Finance; Vice-Chairman, Palestinian Investment Promotion Agency (PIPA), Ramallah, 27 June 2001.
-*Mr Mahmoud Farrah*, Joint Owner, Farrah Brothers Co., Al-Ram, 14 May 2001.
-*Mr Samir Huleileh*, former Under-Secretary for Trade, Ministry of the Economy and Trade, Sales and Marketing Director, Nassar Investment Company, Jerusalem, 13 June 2001.
-*Ms Hiba Husseini*, Vice-Chairman, Palestine Securities Exchange (PSE), Jerusalem, 20 June 2001.
-*Dr. Abdel Malik Jaber*, General Manager, Palestinian Industrial Estates Development Co. (PIEDCO), and Mr Munther Ghosheh, Director, Technical and Contractual Department, PIEDCO, Ramallah, 28 June 2001.
-*Mr Nakhleh Jubran*, Chairman, Arab Industrial Co., Ramallah, 16 May 2001.
-*Mr Hassan Kassem*, President and CEO, Arab Technology Systems (ATS), Ramallah, 14 May 2001.
-*Mr Tareq Maayah*, CEO, Siemens, Ramallah, 30 April 2001.

LIST OF INTERVIEWS

-*Mr Muhammad Masrouji*, President, Jerusalem Pharmaceuticals, and Chairman, Palestinian Businessmen Association (PBA), Ramallah, 15 May 2001.

-*Dr. Jawad al-Naji*, Under-Secretary, Ministry of Industry; Mr 'Ala' Aburub, Operations Manager, Nablus Industrial Estate and Jenin Industrial Estate; Mr Abdel Rahman Shtayeh, Operations Manager, Industrial Complexes and Ramallah Industrial Estate; Mr Nabil Faris, Director, International Co-operation, Ministry of Industry, Ramallah, 20 June 2001.

-*Mr Talal Nasruddin*, Chairman, Birzeit Palestine Pharmaceuticals Co., and Chairman, Palestinian Federation of Industries, Birzeit, 2 May 2001.

-*Mr Abdel Hafiz Noufal*, Director-General, West Bank Trade, Ministry of the Economy and Trade, Ramallah, 13 June 2001.

-*Mr Hassan Salameh*, Director, Palestinian Commercial Services Co. (PCSC), Ramallah, 19 June 2001.

-*Dr. Muhammad Shtayyeh*, Director-General, Palestinian Economic Council for Development and Reconstruction (PECDAR), Al-Ram, 2 May 2001.

-*Mr Hana Siniora*, Chairman, European-Palestinian Chamber of Commerce, Jerusalem, 21 June 2001.

-*Mr Mazen T. Sinokrot*, Chairman, Sinokrot Global Group, Chairman, Palestinian Food Industries Association, and Chairman of the Board, Palestinian Trade Centre (Paltrade), Ramallah, 2 May 2001 and 15 May 2001.

-*Mr Tareq R. Sous*, General Manager, Soutex Sous Textiles Co., and Board Member, Union of Palestinian Textiles Industries, Bethlehem, 18 June 2001.

-*Mr Bassem Wazir*, CEO, Sidata Information and Communication Systems Ltd., and Vice-Chairman, Palestinian IT Association (PITA), 24 April 2001 (email contact).

Bibliography

Periodicals:
- Bulletin of the Israel-Jordan Chamber of Trade and Industry (*Hebrew*).
- Business Review Weekly (weekly, English, Israel).
- Business Times (monthly, English, international).
- Financial Times (daily, English, international).
- Forbes (monthly, English, international).
- The Guardian Weekly (weekly, English, international).
- Ha'Aretz, English (since 1997) and Hebrew Versions (daily, Israel).
- International Herald Tribune (daily, English, international).
- Israel Business Review (1994-1995) (monthly, English, Israel).
- Israel Business Today (1994-1996) (monthly, English, Israel).
- Jerusalem Post (daily, English, Israel).
- Jerusalem Times (weekly, English, Palestinian Territories).
- Jordan Times (daily, English, Jordan).
- Globes: Israel's Business Arena (daily, English, Israel).
- Ma'ariv (daily, Hebrew, Israel).
- The Middle East (bi-weekly, English, international).
- Middle East Economic Digest (bi-weekly, English, international).
- Middle East International (bi-weekly, English, international).
- The New York Times (daily, English, international).
- Palestine Business Report (monthly, English, Palestinian Territories).
- The Star (weekly, English, Jordan).
- Süddeutsche Zeitung (daily, German, international).
- The Times (daily, English, international).
- Die ZEIT (weekly, German, international).

Newspaper and Magazine Articles:
- Al Abed, Raed, 'PBA Boycotts Summit to Protest Israeli Measures,' *The Star*, 6 October 1995.
- Abu-Ghazaleh, Fairouz, Deputies Express Concern Over Possible Israeli-Owned Factories in Kingdom,' *Jordan Times*, 19-20 February 1998.
- 'ACI Goes for Full Elections,' *The Star*, 6 April 2000.
- Amayreh, Khaled, 'Jericho Roulette,' *Al-Ahram Weekly Online*, 1-7 October 1998.
- Albrecht, Kirk, 'Where is all the Business? Jordanian-Israeli Economic Ties Start Slowly,' *Middle East Insight*, Vol. 12, No. 2 (January-February 1996).
- Albrecht, Kirk, 'This Peace Dividend Comes Duty-Free,' *Business Week*, 26 January 1998.
- 'Alron to Build Jordanian Gas Stations, *Israel Business Today*, Vol. 8, No. 400 (25 November 1994).
- Alul, Ghalia, 'Irbid's New Industrial Park Leaves Jordanians Divided,' *Jordan Times*, 16 December 1997.
- Alul, Ghalia, 'Trade Level with Iraq for '98 Likely to Stay Unchanged at $225 Million,' *Jordan Times*, 26 January 1998.
- Alul, Ghalia, 'Amman Chamber of Industry Pushed for Transformation to National Body,' *Jordan Times*, 8 February 1998.

-Alul, Ghalia, 'Jordache Plans to Invest at Irbid's QIZ,' *Jordan Times*, 22 April 1998.
-Alul, Ghalia, 'Dealing with Israel: Blessing or Curse?' *Jordan Times*, 10 August 1998.
-Amr, Wafa, 'Arafat Moves Towards Palestinian Privatisation,' *Jordan Times*, 8 May 1995.
-'APC, Haifa Chemicals Study $60m Joint Project,' *Jordan Times*, 9 November 1996.
-Arbeli, Ariza, and Zohar Blumenkrantz, 'Israel and Palestinians Cross Swords over Border Crossing,' *Ha'Aretz*, 23 March 1999.
-A.-S., Y., 'Les Echanges Commerciaux Avec Israel Toujours au Point Mort,' *The Star*, 25 February 1999.
-Asa-El, Amotz; David Harris, Lipkis-Beck, Galit, and Jennifer Friedlin, 'Bridge over Troubled Waters,' *Jerusalem Post*, 19 February 1997.
-'Audit Reveals PNA $326 m. Corruption,' *Jordan Times*, 25 May 1997.
-Awwad, Rana, 'QIZ Overcomes Aftermath of the Intifada,' *Jordan Times*, 4 December 2000.
-Ayyoub, Tareq, 'Anani to Head Delegation to the MENA Conference,' *Jordan Times*, 22 October 1997.
-Ayyoub, Tareq, 'Dead Sea Industries Company Teams Up with U.S. Firm to Set Up $120m Bromine Factory in Jordan,' *Jordan Times*, 20 May 1998.
-Ayyoub, Tareq, 'Government Shuns Criticism, will Forge Ahead with Privatisation,' *Jordan Times*, 21 October 1998.
-Ayyoub, Tareq, 'Commerce Chamber Holds Elections Today,' *Jordan Times*, 17 November 1998.
-Ayyoub, Tareq, 'Sale of 33.3% of Cement Company to Lafarge to Be Concluded Sunday,' *Jordan Times*, 21 November 1998.
-Ayyoub, Tareq, 'Govt. Decision on Chamber of Industry Membership Raises Hopes, Fears, *Jordan Times*, 13 January 2000.
-Ayyoub, Tareq, 'Jordanian and Palestinian Businessmen Discuss Trade Barriers,' *Jordan Times*, 5 April 2000.
-Ayyoub, Tareq, 'Amman Chamber of Industry Election Campaigns Heat Up,' *Jordan Times*, 11 April 2000.
-Ayyoub, Tareq, 'Abu Hassan Defeated in Amman Chamber of Industry Elections,' *Jordan Times*, 13 April 2000.
-Ayyoub, Tareq, 'New Amman Chamber of Industry Head Strives for Unity,' *Jordan Times*, 14-15 April 2000.
-Ayyoub, Tareq, 'Iraq to Blacklist Jordanian Businesses Dealing with Israel, PNA', *Jordan Times*, 14 September 2000.
-Baharuddin, Zulkafly, 'Privatisation Paves Way to Success for Jordan Cement Factories Company,' *Jordan Times*, 13 October 1999.
-Baharuddin, Zulkafly, 'Aramex Founder Fadi Ghandour Ready to Deliver for Economic Consultative Council,' *Jordan Times*, 25-26 December 1999.
-Baharuddin, Zulkafly, 'Nuqul Group Brings Leadership from the Shop Floor to the Boardroom,' *Jordan Times*, 30 December 1999.
-Baharuddin, Zulkafly, 'Watering Seeds of Innovation Makes Dollars and Sense to ECC Member Fawaz Hatim Zu'bi,' *Jordan Times*, 20 January 2000.
-Baharuddin, Zulkafly, 'Dr. Fuad Abu Zayyad Ready to Help Investors Get Down to Business,' *Jordan Times*, 10 February 2000.
-Baharuddin, Zulkafly, 'Dr. Salaheddin Al Bashir Looks Ahead to Successful, Progressive Society,' *Jordan Times*, 17 February 2000.
-Baharuddin, Zulkafly, 'Dr. Anwar Battikhi Channels Expertise into Raising Money for Higher Education,' *Jordan Times*, 24 February 2000.
-Baharuddin, Zulkafly, 'Karim Kawar Targets On-Line Kingdom with Companies for the IT Age,' *Jordan Times*, 2 March 2000.

-Baharuddin, Zulkafly, 'Khaled Toukan Seeks a Delicate Balance Between the Educational System and Potential Employer Needs,' *Jordan Times*, 23 March 2000.
-Baharuddin, Zulkafly, 'Samih Dawarzah Confidently Positions Hikma International to Seize a Bigger Slice of World Market,' *Jordan Times*, 30 March 2000.
-Bainerman, Joel, 'Peace Without Economic Ties,' *Israel Business Review*, Vol. 1, No. 1 (July 1994).
-Barel, Zvi, 'The River is Wide and the River is Frozen,' *Ha'Aretz*, 23 May 1998.
-Barel, Zvi, 'A Tightfisted Peace,' *Ha'Aretz*, 6 March 1999.
-Barel, Zvi, 'Jordanians Want Bread, Not Fruits of Peace,' *Ha'Aretz*, 22 December 1999.
-Barel, Zvi, 'An Olive Branch Sprouting Leaves,' *Ha'Aretz*, 5 January 2000.
-Barel, Zvi, 'Neighbours: Normalisation is Not for Public Consumption,' *Ha'Aretz*, 3 May 2000.
-Barel, Zvi, 'When a King Wants a New Economy,' *Ha'Aretz*, 19 June 2000.
-Bassok, Moti, 'Israel-PA Economic Deal Targets Car Thieves, Bad Debt,' *Ha'Aretz*, 8 June 2000.
-Ben-David, Amir, 'The Sky Above, The Mud Below,' *Ha'Aretz*, 3 September 2000.
-Benn, Aluf; Alisa Odenheimer, and Koren [Coren], Ora, 'PM Favors Economic Separation from Palestinian "Entity",' *Ha'Aretz*, 18 October 1999.
-Benn, Aluf, and Revital Levi-Stein, 'Abdullah Envisions an "Open Jerusalem",' *Ha'Aretz*, 24 April 2000.
-Bergman, Ronen, and David Ratner, 'The Man who Swallowed Gaza', *Ha'Aretz*, 4 April 1997.
-Bergman, Ronen, 'How Much is the PLO Really Worth? *Ha'Aretz*, 28 November 1999.
-Beuer, Shira, 'High-Tech Textiles,' *Ha'Aretz*, 28 October 2000.
-Blackburn, Nicky, 'Jordan, Israel and US Join Forces on High-Tech Project,' *Jerusalem Post*, 13 October 1999.
-Blackburn, Nicky, 'High Hopes for Hi-Tech in the PA,' *Jerusalem Post*, 19 December 1999.
-Blumenkrantz, Zohar, 'Merchants Worried by High Costs at Karni,' *Ha'Aretz*, 13 August 1998.
-Chabin, Michele, 'Stef Wertheimer: Eye on the Future,' *Lifestyles Magazine*, Summer 1994.
-Chemetz, Sagi, 'Israel and Jordan to Negotiate Trade Accord,' *Ha'Aretz*, 16 September 1997.
-Chemetz, Sagi, and Amira Hass, 'Karni Park Ready for Joint Israeli-Palestinian Business,' *Ha'Aretz*, 15 December 1998.
-Ciriaci, Francesca, 'Private Sector Gives Kabariti Policy Statement a 'Thumbs Up', *Jordan Times*, 29 February-1 March 1996.
-Ciriaci, Francesca, 'Toe the Line to Succeed On-Line, Industry Expert Tells Local IT Companies,' *Jordan Times*, 6 March 2000.
-Citrin, Ben-Zion, 'The PA's Tax Paradise for Investors,' *Ha'Aretz*, 13 January 2000.
-'The City of Peace,' *Israel Business Today*, Vol. 8, No. 397 (28 October 1994).
-Cohen, Catherine, 'Jordan Treads Warily in Israel,' *Ha'Aretz*, 3 November 2000.
-'Conference Time,' *Israel-Palestine Journal*, Vol. 1 No. 1 (Winter 1994).
-Contreras, Joseph, 'A Cold Wind Blowing,' *Newsweek*, 17 November 1997.
-Dagoni, Ran, 'World Bank, Evergreen, Palestinian Businessman to Found Territories Investment Fund,' *Globes*, 15 January 1998.
-Dagoni, Ran, 'Wall Street Journal: Israel has Unofficial Trade Ties with Iraq,' *Globes*, 15 February 1998.
-Dallal, Jacob, 'Arab Competition Worries Chicken Farmers,' *Jerusalem Post*, 28 October 1993.
-'Dead Sea Recreation Zone,' *Israel Business Today*, Vol. 9, No. 7 (2 June 1995).
-'Dead Sea Works Looks at Jordanian Option,' *Israel Business Today*, Vol. 9, No. 17 (15 December 1995).

-'Dead Sea Works Planned to Sell Salt to Iraq in '95,' *Jerusalem Post*, 29 December 1996.
-Dougherty, Pamela, 'Counting the Costs of Closure,' *Middle East Economic Digest (MEED)*, 12 April 1996.
-Dovrat, Zehava, 'Gillerman: Palestinian Authority – Brand Counterfeiting Hothouse,' *Globes*, 25 January 1999.
-Dovrat, Zehava, 'Chambers of Commerce: Annual Forgery Industry Damage – Multi Mlns. Of Dollars,' *Globes*, 10 August 1999.
-Dovrat, Zehava, 'Peres Centre's Economic Peace Conference: Platini and Pele to Teach Football to Israelis, Palestinians,' *Globes*, 11 September 2000.
-'Economists Organise Impact of New Israeli Government of Jordanian Economy' [sic], *Jordan Times*, 5 June 1996.
-Eldar, Akiva, 'From Hard Lines to Shorelines,' *Ha'Aretz*, 9 August 1999.
-Etkes, Haggay, 'Palestinian Minister of Industry: Flooding Palestinian Market with Israeli Products Spreads Destruction,' *Globes*, 23 August 1999.
-Etkes, Haggay, 'Swamped with Peace,' *Globes*, 3 November 1999.
-Etkes, Haggay, 'Palestinian Private Sector Supports Free Trade Agreements with Israel,' *Globes*, 4 January 2000.
-Etkes, Haggay, 'Federation of Chambers of Commerce to Try to Stop Purchase by Israelis in Territories,' *Globes*, 11 January 2000.
-Etkes, Haggay, 'Make-Believe Trade,' *Globes*, 26 January 2000.
-Etkes, Haggay, 'Forget Separation, Long Live Trade,' *Globes*, 17 February 2000.
-Etkes, Haggay, 'Jordan to Allow Foreigners to Buy 100per cent Ownership of Jordanian Software House,' *Globes*, 23 March 2000.
-Etkes, Haggay, 'Israeli-Jordanian company Visuality Systems Raises $1 mln from Apex Mutavim,' *Globes*, 28 March 2000.
-Etkes, Haggay, 'Hayek: Quantum Leap in Cooperation with JEDCO,' *Globes*, 9 April 2000.
-Etkes, Haggay, 'Jordanian Exports to Israel Continue to Rise: Exports from Irbid Industrial Estate in April $3.15 mln,' *Globes*, 2 May 2000.
-Etkes, Haggay, 'The Price of Rage,' *Globes*, 16 May 2000.
-Etkes, Haggay, 'Jordan's New Prime Minister,' *Globes*, 20 June 2000.
-Etkes, Haggay, 'Israel Considering Establishment of Israeli-Jordanian High-Tech Zone at Jordanian University Campus with Hong Kong Company,' *Globes*, 5 July 2000.
-Etkes, Haggay, 'Israel, Palestinians Agree in Principle to Found Free Trade Area,' *Globes*, 10 July 2000.
-Etkes, Haggay, 'Gillerman: Free Trade Zone – First Stage of Permanent Economic Settlement,' *Globes*, 11 July 2000.
-'Excerpts of Speech Published as King Points to Jordan's Determination to Excel in IT,' *Jordan Times*, 26 March 2000.
-al-Fanek, Fahed, 'The Risk of Arousing Israeli Interest in Aqaba,' *Jordan Times*, 5 June 2000.
-Al Farawati, Oula, 'Industrialists, Economists Say Threat to Boycott American Products Little More than Ballyhoo,' *Jordan Times*, 19 November 2000.
-'First Exhibition of Jordanian Products in Ramallah, a Unique Economic Event,' *The Star*, 14 November 1996.
-Flottau, Heiko, 'Das Sonnensystem von Gaza,' *Süddeutsche Zeitung*, 29 July 1997.
-Flottau, Heiko, 'Warten aufs Saubermachen im Hause Arafat,' *Süddeutsche Zeitung*, 8 July 1998.
-Friedlin, Jennifer, 'EU Said to be Hurting Trade Between Israel and Jordan,' *Jerusalem Post*, 6 August 1997.
-Gabbai, Yoram, 'Inseparable Enemies,' *Globes*, 13 December 1999.
-'Gamal Sells to Syria,' *Israel Business Today*, Vol. 9, No. 13 (15 October 1995).

-'Gaon Egyptian Venture,' *Israel Business Today*, Vol. 8, No. 401 (9 December 1994).
-Gavison, Yoram, 'Delta Grows Apart from Israel,' *Ha'Aretz*, 18 February 1998.
-'General Assembly decides to bury Jordan Glass Industries Company,' *Jordan Times*, 20-21 June 1996.
-Gerstenfeld, Dan, 'Executives split on Palestinian Business Ties,' *Jerusalem Post*, 20 October 1999.
-Gilbert, Nina, '10 Firms Show Interest in Karni Park,' *Jerusalem Post*, 19 February 1998.
-Gilbert, Nina, 'Strauss Wants to Enter Gaza Market,' *Jerusalem Post*, 19 February 1998.
-Gilbert, Nina, 'Trade with Egypt Slides; Soars with Jordan,' *Jerusalem Post*, 16 July 1998.
-Gilbert, Nina, 'Israel, Jordan Agree to Boost Trade,' *Jerusalem Post*, 13 August 1998.
-Gleit, Heidi J., 'Fighting Corruption,' *Jerusalem Post*, 6 July 2000.
-Golan, Gadi, 'Kitan Management Decides to Close Israeli Sewing Factories, Transfer Sewing to Jordan,' *Globes*, 13 September 1997.
-Golan, Gadi, 'King Abdullah in Eilat: Focus on Palestinian Track, Accelerate Economic Projects,' *Globes*, 23 April 2000.
-Golan, Patricia, 'Peace Partners Turned Business Partners,' *Jerusalem Post*, 14 July 1998.
-Golan, Patricia, 'Building Up is Hard to Do,' *Jerusalem Post*, 17 November 1998.
-Golan, Patricia, 'Marketing a Hard Sell Called Gaza Industrial Estate,' *Jerusalem Post*, 30 November 1998.
-Groner, Eli, 'Bottom Line on Final Status: Addition by Division?' *Jerusalem Post*, 12 November 1999.
-Hadar, Leon, 'Israel Looks to Asia: The Lure of Business Cuts Across Culture and Religion,' *Business Times*, 17 October 1994.
-Halaby, Jamal, 'Ambassador to Jordan: Five Years of Peace with Jordan Insufficient to End Animosity,' *Jerusalem Post*, 26 October 1999.
-Harel, Amos, 'It's the Economy, Stupid,' *Ha'Aretz*, 14 September 2000.
-Harris, David, 'PA Misses Out the Most on Cairo's Opportunities,' *Jerusalem Post*, 15 November 1996.
-Harris, David, 'Investors Might Lose Interest in Jenin Industrial Park,' *Jerusalem Post*, 2 October 1998.
-Hass, Amira, 'Telephone Politics: Paltel Disconnects Jerusalem from Israel,' *Ha'Aretz*, 5 May 1998.
-Hass, Amira, 'Corruption Caused by the Peace Process,' *Ha'Aretz*, 13 October 1999.
-Hass, Amira, 'PA Taxi Drivers Strike Over Taxes,' *Ha'Aretz*, 25 November 1999.
-Hass, Amira, 'PA Moves on Fiscal Responsibility,' *Ha'Aretz*, 3 July 2000.
-Hattar, Saad G., 'King Forms Economic Consultative Council to Monitor Implementation of Vital Reforms,' *Jordan Times*, 14 December 1999.
-Hattar, Saad G., 'Associations Let Fly List of 'Normalisers',' *Jordan Times*, 20 November 2000.
-Hausman, Tamar, 'Developer Turned Off by Procedural Red Tape in Jordan-Israel Border Project,' *Ha'Aretz*, 22 September 2000.
-Hayoun, David, 'Export Institute: Palestinians Restricting Israeli Entrepreneurs' Economic Freedom in Violation of Agreements,' *Globes*, 23 August 1999.
-Hayoun, David, 'Energy Man,' *Globes*, 1 December 1999.
-Hayoun, David, 'Israeli-Palestinian High-Tech Cooperation Initiated by German Company Siemens,' *Globes*, 23 January 2000.
-Henderson, Amy, 'Government Decides to Sell More of its Stake in the Jordan Cement Factories Company,' *Jordan Times*, 4 November 1996.
-Henderson, Amy, 'Customs, Taxes Seen as Main Barriers to the Development of Jordanian Textile Industry,' *Jordan Times*, 18 April 1998.
-Henderson, Amy, 'Jordan, Israel Renew Trade Protocol,' *Jordan Times*, 13 January 1999.

-Hirst, David, 'Shameless in Gaza,' *The Guardian Weekly*, 27 April 1997.
-'Histadrut to Transfer NIS 3m to Palestinian Trade Unions,' *Jerusalem Post*, 30 August 1994.
-'Histadrut to Transfer NIS 4m to Palestinians,' *Jerusalem Post*, 8 September 1995.
-Hoffman, Gil, 'Eilat's Mayor Eyes Hi-Tech Park with Jordan,' *Jerusalem Post*, 8 July 1998.
-Hutman, Bill, 'No Sugar to Coat the Pill of Closure,' *Jerusalem Post*, 12 April 1996.
-Immanuel, Jon, 'Economic Success in Areas a Must for Autonomy,' *Jerusalem Post*, 12 February 1993.
-Immanuel, Jon, 'Joining Forces in Hebron,' *Jerusalem Post*, 11 July 1997.
-Inbari, Pinhas, 'Industrial Twilight Zones,' *Jerusalem Post*, 13 December 1995.
-Inbari, Pinhas, 'Looking for Arafat's Rothschild,' *Jerusalem Post*, 3 January 1996.
-'Industry Profile: The Textile Sector,' *Israel Business Today*, Vol. 9, No. 4 (21 April 1995).
-'Irbid QIZ Exports Amounted to $172m in 2000,' *Jordan Times*, 12-13 January 2001.
-'Israel Blasts Major Bethlehem Projects,' *Jerusalem Times*, 27 April 2001.
-'Israel-Jordan Talks Fail,' *Israel Business Today*, Vol. 9, No. 13 (15 October 1995).
-'Israel Seeks to Revive Bromine Venture with Jordan,' *Jordan Times*, 12 August 1998.
-'Israeli-Jordanian Trade May Peak this Year,' *Globes*, 22 August 2000.
-'Israeli-Palestinian Commercial Talks,' *Israel Business Today*, Vol. 9, No. 9 (July 1995).
-'Israeli-Palestinian Detergent Company to be Built,' *Israel Business Today*, Vol. 9, No. 18 (31 December 1995).
-'Israeli Products in Amman,' *Israel Business Today*, Vol. 9, No. 8 (16 June 1995).
-'Israeli Restrictions Limit Palestinian Imports from Jordan to Only $3 million,' *Jordan Times*, 25 November 1996.
-Jacoby-Bashan, Ella, 'Israeli-Jordanian Co. Visuality Systems Signs Partnership Agreement with Wind River,' *Globes*, 4 July 2000.
-'Japanese Work to Cement Jordanian-Palestinian Trade,' *Israel Business Today*, Vol. 9, No. 10 (15 August 1995).
-'Jordanians, Palestinians Set Up Jerusalem Land Firm,' *Jerusalem Post*, 17 August 1997.
-'Jordanien und Palästina schliessen Abkommen,' *Nachrichten für Aussenhandel*, 7 February 1995.
-'Jordan Israel Trucking,' *Israel Business Today*, Vol. 9, No. 5 (5 May 1995).
-'Jordan, Palestinians Draft List for Duty-Free Trade, *Jerusalem Post*, 19 February 1995.
-'Jordan Passes Foreign Ownership Law,' *Israel Business Today*, Vol. 9, No 18 (31 December 1995).
-'Jordan, PNA Remonstrate Against Israeli-Imposed Impediments to Trade, *Jordan Times*, 11 September 1996.
-'Jordan to Press Israel to Deliver on Trade, Water,' *Jordan Times*, 5 August 1996.
-'Jordanian Businessmen, Industrialists Reject Forming Regional Business Council,' *Jordan Times*, 3-4 October 1996.
-'Jordanian Industrialists to Urge Iraqis to Buy More Food and Medicine from the Kingdom,' *Jordan Times*, 6 July 1996.
-'Jordanian Private Sector Denies Co-operation with Israel,' *The Star*, 17 September 1998.
-'Jordanians Seek Amman-Haifa Air Link,' and 'Hussein Declines High-Tech Offer,' *Israel Business Today*, Vol. 8, No. 400 (25 November 1994).
-Keilani, Musa, 'Stress on Inter-Arab Economic Co-operation in Cairo, Sends Message to Israel,' *Jordan Times*, 16 November 1996.
-'Kenny Rogers Crosses Borders,' *Israel Business Today*, Vol. 8, No 401 (9 December 1994).
-Al-Khalidi, Suleiman, 'Jordan Pins Peace Dividend on Israel Ties,' *Jordan Times*, 18 June 1996.
-Al-Khalidi, Suleiman, 'Jordan Business to Shy from Israel Ties in Cairo Summit,' *Jordan Times*, 31 October-1 November 1996.

-Al-Khalidi, Suleiman, 'Arab Businessmen Keep Low in Secret Israel Deals,' *Jordan Times*, 9 November 1996.
-Al-Khalidi, Suleiman, 'Jordanian Businessmen Opposed to Doha Conference,' *Jordan Times*, 22 October 1997.
-Al-Khalidi, Suleiman, 'Cement Company Pins Hopes on Palestinian Market,' *Jordan Times*, 12 May 1998.
-al-Khouri, Riad, 'Peace Dividend at Last?' *Jordan Times*, 24 August 2000.
-Koren, Ora, 'Bureaucratic Delays in Implementation of Projects with Jordan,' *Globes*, 28 July 1996.
-Koren, Ora, 'Netanyahu in Amman: Business, not Pleasure,' *Globes*, 6 August 1996.
-Koren, Ora, 'Israeli Marketers are Lagging Behind in their Readiness,' *Globes*, 30 August 1996.
-Koren, Ora, 'Jordanian Press: Just Say No to First Israeli Exhibition in Amman,' *Globes*, 30 November 1996.
-Koren, Ora, 'Gaon, Lautman Offer Arafat Aid to Develop Joint Ventures in Light Industries in Territories,' *Globes*, 21 December 1996.
-Koren, Ora, 'Palestinian Marketing Policies: First Food and Cigarettes,' *Globes*, 21 December 1996.
-Koren, Ora, 'Century of Jordan Negotiating with Motorola Israel to Set Up Development Centre,' *Globes*, 24 May 1997.
-Koren, Ora, 'The Primrose Path,' *Globes*, 9 August 1997.
-Koren, Ora, 'Siemens and Palestinian Partner Establish R&D Centre in Ramallah,' *Globes*, 28 September 1997.
-Koren [Coren], Ora, 'Century Chair: Netanyahu Has Made Israeli Businessmen Unwelcome in Arab World,' *Globes*, 17 November 1997.
-Koren, Ora, 'Siemens Announces Willingness to Set Up Factory in Karni Park; Peugeot, Volkswagen Also in Negotiations,' *Globes*, 3 December 1997.
-Koren, Ora, 'Benny Gaon: Middle East no Longer Interests World, Focus Must be Reinstated,' *Globes*, 1 February 1998.
-Koren, Ora, 'US-Jordan Bromine Plant Memorandum of Understanding; Assessment: Possibility of Co-operation with Israel Down to Zero,' *Globes*, 21 May 1998.
-Koren, Ora, 'Trade Ministry Internal Report: Another 14,000 Traditional Industries Workers to be Laid-Off,' *Globes*, 14 June 1998.
-Koren, Ora, 'Jordan Calls for Reduced Israeli Share in Joint Projects with Preferential Terms,' *Globes*, 29 July 1998.
-Koren, Ora, 'Palestinians Bar Israeli Presence at Karni Industrial Park Inauguration,' *Globes*, 13 December 1998.
-Koren, Ora, 'Four Multinational to Set Up Plants, Regional Distribution Centres in Gaza,' *Globes*, 11 January 1999.
-Koren, Ora, 'Magic of Israel Negotiating Joint Venture with Jordan's Century, Abu Jihad's Son,' *Globes*, 2 February 1999.
-Koren [Coren], Ora, 'Israeli Businessmen Want Economic Separation from the PA,' *Ha'Aretz*, 11 August 1999.
-Koren [Coren], Ora, 'The Cooking Oil Industry is Emigrating,' *Ha'Aretz*, 1 September 1999.
-Koren [Coren], Ora, 'PA Power Plays May Scuttle Final Economic Agreement,' *Ha'Aretz*, 1 October 1999.
-Koren [Coren], Ora, 'Manufacturers and Merchants at Odds over Final-Status Deal,' *Ha'Aretz*, 6 October 1999.
-Koren [Coren], Ora, 'Final Separation, or Cooperation,' *Ha'Aretz*, 21 October 1999.
-Koren [Coren], Ora, 'Israeli Manufacturers Want Economic Union with PA as Part of Final-Status Deal,' *Ha'Aretz*, 8 December 1999.

-Koren [Coren], Ora, 'There is Life after Koor for Benni Gaon,' *Ha'Aretz*, 16 March 2000.
-Koren [Coren], Ora, 'Arab, Israeli Partners Aim to Introduce Web into Arab World,' *Ha'Aretz*, 21 May 2000.
-Koren [Coren], Ora, 'Free-Trade Zone Envisioned for Border,' *Ha'Aretz*, 27 June 2000.
-Koren [Coren], Ora, 'Vishay to Explore New Jordanian Factories with Century Investment,' *Ha'Aretz*, 8 August 2000.
-Koren [Coren], Ora, 'Manufacturers Call for Tax Harmony with PA,' *Ha'Aretz*, 19 September 2000.
-Koren [Coren], Ora, 'Israel and PA Agree on a Free Trade Zone,' *Ha'Aretz*, 20 September 2000.
-Koren [Coren], Ora, 'Israeli-Palestinian Industrial Parks Slowly Resume Operations,' *Ha'Aretz*, 12 October 2000.
-Koren [Coren], Ora, 'Unilateral Economic Separation: A Punishment that Will Increase the Violence. Assessment: $500 Million Damage to the Palestinian Economy in Three Weeks,' *Ha'Aretz*, 29 October 2000.
-Krau, Nicole, 'Koor Group Executives Suspected of Tax Fraud,' *Ha'Aretz*, 9 June 1999.
-Lahoud, Lamia, 'Attracting Palestinian Investments,' *Jerusalem Post*, 26 November 1993.
-Lahoud, Lamia, 'Jordan Business Community Welcomes Economic Ties with Israel,' *Jerusalem Post*, 31 July 1994.
-Leibowich-Dar, Sara, 'Marketing Man: Danny International,' *Ha'Aretz Magazine*, 13 October 2000.
-Leibowich-Dar, Sara, 'Josef, King of the Territories,' *Ha'Aretz Magazine*, 20 April 2001 (Hebrew, *Yosef melekh ha-shtakhim*).
-Lenzner, Robert, 'Zionism: Phase III,' *Forbes*, 18 December 1995.
-'Les Commercants de Jenine Craignent de Perdre Leurs Clients Israeliens Apres l'Autonomie,' *L'Orient*, 23 March 1995.
-Lifschitz, Ronny, 'Tul-Karem instead of Bombay,' *Globes*, 19 August 1999.
-Galit Lipkis Beck, 'Wertheimer, Jordan to Build Industrial Park,' *Jerusalem Post*, 5 June 1996.
-Lipkis-Beck, Galit, '20 CEOs to Meet Arafat in Two Weeks,' *Jerusalem Post*, 4 September 1996.
-Lipkis-Beck, Galit, 'Gaon seeks CEOs' Meeting with Arafat,' *Jerusalem Post*, 4 October 1996.
-Lipson, Nathan, and Amiram Cohen, 'Tshuva Taking Over Dankner Firm,' *Ha'Aretz*, 7 June 1999.
-Lüders, Michael, 'Der Mühsame Weg nach Palästina,' *Die Zeit*, 5 December 1997.
-Lynfield, Ben, 'Jordanians Target Palestinian Market,' *Jerusalem Post*, 19 April 1999.
-Lynfield, Ben, 'Living with Contradiction,' *Jerusalem Post*, 5 November 1999.
-Ma'ayeh, Suha, 'Jordan Vision 2020 Sets Course for Unified Economic Strategy,' *Jordan Times*, 11 June 2000.
-Makovsky, David, 'Jordan Gripes About Israeli Grip on Trade,' *Ha'Aretz*, 24 November 1998.
-Maltz, Judy, 'Banks' Investment Comeback,' *Globes*, 21 June 2001.
-Melman, Yossi, 'Hunting for Friends,' *Ha'Aretz*, 12 July 1997.
-Mendelson, Yair, 'The Profits of Peace, a Piece of the Profits,' *Ha'Aretz*, 23 June 2000.
-Morav, Levy, 'Keeping Fingers Crossed for Sallah, Barak' [sic], *Globes*, 22 May 2000.
-Neiman, Rachel, 'Gillerman: Speed up Trade Pact with Jordan,' *Jerusalem Post*, 28 October 1994.
-Neiman, Rachel, 'Transport Deal with Jordan Expected Soon,' *Jerusalem Post*, 27 December 1995.
-'News in Brief,' *Jerusalem Post*, 21 February 1997.
-Nsour, Maen, 'Economic Interdependence and Peace,' *Jordan Times*, 30 May 1999.
-'Oil-for-Food Deal: Turning Point for Jordan-Iraq Business Relations,' *The Star*, 20 November 1997.

BIBLIOGRAPHY

-Orne Jr., William A., 'Jordanian Struggles to Keep Ties to Israel,' *New York Times*, 2 November 2000.
-O'Sullivan, Arieh, 'Karni Industrial Park Readies for December Opening,' *Jerusalem Post*, 5 November 1998.
-O'Sullivan, Arieh, 'Israel Moves to Boost Palestinian Use of Ashdod Port,' *Jerusalem Post*, 11 November 1998.
-O'Sullivan, Arieh, 'Joint Industrial Zone planned near Nablus,' *Jerusalem Post*, 3 May 1999.
-'PA Eases Embargo on Israeli Goods,' *Ha'Aretz*, 20 November 1997.
-'PA Industrial Parks to Be Joint Ventures, *Israel Business Today*, Vol. 9, No. 16 (30 November 1995).
-'PADICO Secures Major Palestinian Telephones Project,' *Jordan Times*, 28 June 1995.
-'Palestinians Disappoint Histadrut One More Time,' *Jerusalem Post*, 13 February 1995.
-'Palestinians Set Up Investment Firms in Areas, Jerusalem,' *Jerusalem Post*, 28 September 1993.
-'Palestinians Torpedo Signing of Pact with Histadrut,' *Jerusalem Post*, 8 December 1994.
-'Peres, Wolfson, Arafat Sign Technological Foundation for Peace Agreement,' *Globes*, 19 May 1998.
-Perez, Gad, 'Cut your Cloth to Suit your Coat,' *Ha'Aretz*, 9 December 1997.
-Porter, Michael; Yagil Weinberg, and Noreena Hertz, 'Making Real Progress in the Middle East: The Bottom-Up, Economic Solution,' *Financial Times,* 16 September 1997.
-Raviv, Orna, '"New York Times": Jordanian Employees in Delta-Owned Plant are Hostile,' *Globes*, 29 December 1996.
-Raviv, Orna, 'Lautman: Changes in Jordan Won't Affect Israeli Companies Operating There,' *Globes*, 27 January 1999.
-'Restore the Warm Ties,' *Jerusalem Post*, 19 December 1996.
-Rinat, Zafrir, 'Greens Oppose Joint Israel-Jordan Project,' *Ha'Aretz*, 5 January 2000.
-Rinat, Zafrir, 'The Eucalyptus Grove, the Bridge and the Factory,' *Ha'Aretz*, 17 September 2000.
-Rodan, Steve, 'Back in Business,' *Jerusalem Post,* 14 May 1993.
-Rodan, Steve, 'Jordanian Vote is a Victory for the Economy,' *Jerusalem Post*, 12 November 1993.
-Rodan, Steve, 'Rules of the Game,' *Jerusalem Post*, 27 October 1995.
-Rodan, Steve, 'Getting Down to Business in the Middle East,' *Jerusalem Post*, 3 November 1995.
-Rodan, Steve, 'Palestinian Businessmen Challenge PA to Attract Investments,' *Jerusalem Post*, 3 July 1997.
-Rodan, Steve, 'Behind the Scenes Trade, *Jerusalem Post*, 14 November 1997.
-Rodan, Steve, 'Qatar Conference Urges "Land for Peace",' *Jerusalem Post*, 19 November 1997.
-Rodan, Steve, 'When Business Beats Politics,' *Jerusalem Post*, 21 November 1997.
-Rodan, Steve, and Mohammed Najib, 'PA Legalises Corruption,' *Jerusalem Post*, 14 August 1998.
-Rodan, Steve, and Muhammad Najib, 'The Tax Man Wears Many Disguises,' *Jerusalem Post*, 21 August 1998.
-Rodan, Steve, 'Forget the Big Projects,' *Jerusalem Post*, 16 October 1998.
-Rolnik, Guy, 'Stitched in Time, Israel's Companies are Doing Fine,' *Ha'Aretz*, 8 April 1998.
-Rosenfeld, Jose, 'Palestinians Not Interested in Cooperation with Israel,' *Jerusalem Post*, 1 July 1994.
-Rosenfeld, Jose, 'Rabin, Peres Meeting Arafat in Casablanca: Economic Summit Begins Today,' *Jerusalem Post*, 30 October 1994.
-Rosenfeld, Jose, and Jon Immanuel, 'Shaath: Closure Must End Before We Can Discuss Economic Cooperation,' *Jerusalem Post*, 8 February 1995.

-Rosenfeld, Jose, 'Israel Softens Stand on Jordan Trade Pact,' *Jerusalem Post*, 27 June 1995.
-Rubinstein, Danny, 'The Investor from Qatar,' *Ha'Aretz*, 31 December 1997.
-Rubinstein, Danny, 'Back to the Markets,' *Ha'Aretz*, 6 July 1999.
-Rubinstein, Danny, 'Equal-Opportunity Gambling,' *Ha'Aretz*, 23 August 1999.
-Rubinstein, Danny, 'Nobody Wants Relations with Israel, Except When They Do,' *Ha'Aretz*, 25 September 2000.
-Rudge, David, 'Palestinian Companies Holding Trade Fair in Haifa Next Month,' *Jerusalem Post*, 11 November 1999.
-Rudge, David, 'Israeli Arabs Growing Angrier, Experts Say,' *Jerusalem Post*, 6 November 2000.
-Sadeq, Ilham, 'New Economic Law Arouses Controversy Among Private Sector,' *The Star*, 26 June 1997.
-Sadeq, Ilham, 'Doha Summit Continues to Polarise Arabs,' *The Star*, 25 September 1997.
-Sadeq, Ilham, 'Private Sector Calls to Boycott Israeli Delegation in Doha,' *The Star*, 30 October 1997.
-'Sanctions Suffocating Gaza's Fragile Economy,' *Washington Post*, 5 December 2000.
-Shahin, Mariam, 'Undercover Business,' *The Middle East*, February 1997.
-Shalev, Shai, 'Leon Recanati Makes IDB His,' *Globes*, 3 July 2001.
-Shapiro, Haim, 'Israel, Jordan Reach Transport Agreement: Peres, Hassan Agree to Split Gulf of Eilat,' *Jerusalem Post*, 19 October 1995.
-Shapiro, Haim, 'Growing Pains,' *Jerusalem Post*, 31 January 1996.
-Shavit-Raz, Noga, 'Delta GM: Traditional Industry has Future; High Tech won't Solve Unemployment,' *Globes*, 10 December 1997.
-Shiloah, Dinah, 'Peace Dividend across River Jordan,' *The Times,* 9 April 1999.
-Shiloah, Dina [Dinah], 'In Israel and Jordan, Talk Turns to Business,' *International Herald Tribune*, 1-2 July 2000.
-Shuman, Joshua, 'Industrialists Fear Peace Accord Could Harm Economy,' *Jerusalem Post*, 7 January 1993.
-Siegel-Itzkovich, Judy, 'Peace May Fuel Software Boom,' *Jerusalem Post*, 3 October 1993.
-Sobelman, Daniel, 'Jordanian PM Blasts Opponents of Relations with Israel,' *Ha'Aretz*, 30 August 2000.
-'Special Report Jordan: US Free Trade Zones Stir Controversy,' *Middle East Economic Digest (MEED)*, 29 May 1998.
-Steinberg, Robbie, 'Gaon to Help 'Privatize the Peace',' *Ha'Aretz*, 12 March 1998.
-Steinberg, Robbie, 'News in Brief,' *Ha'Aretz*, 5 May 1998.
-Steinberg, Robbie, 'Forged Products Flooding Israel,' *Ha'Aretz*, 21 July 1998.
-'Study Examines Israeli and Palestinian Markets to Enlighten Jordanians,' *Jordan Times*, 3 June 1996.
-Suwadeh, Mervat, 'Likud Victory Dissuades Jordanian Businessmen from Investment in West Bank, Gaza,' *Jordan Times*, 5 June 1996.
-Tabbaa, Lamia, 'Tabbaa Urges Government to Include Private Sector Businessmen in Official Delegations,' *Jordan Times*, 20 November 1996.
-Taher, Ghadeer, 'Jordan, Israel, and the Palestinians: One Partner Too Many,' *Jordan Times*, 31 May 1998.
-Taher, Ghadeer, 'Jordanian and Israeli Phone Firms to Try to Settle Dispute,' *Jordan Times*, 1 December 1998.
-Tal, Dalia, 'District Committee Approves Jordan Gateway for Deposit,' *Globes*, 13 February 2000.
-Toukan, Alia A., '80% of Jordanians Still Believe Israel is Enemy – Poll,' *Jordan Times*, 7 January 1998.

-Toukan, Alia A., 'Peace Treaty Anniversary Far from Festive,' *Jordan Times*, 26 October 1998.
-Tsuriel, Keren, 'Survey of Manufacturers: 38% of Enterprises Favour Status Quo with Palestinians,' *Globes*, 19 October 1999.
-Tsuriel, Keren, 'Manufacturers: We oppose Economic Separation from Palestinians,' *Globes*, 7 December 1999.
-Tsuriel, Keren, ''99 Software Exports up 33% to $2 Bln,' *Globes*, 25 January 2000.
-Tsuriel, Keren, and Gadi Golan, 'New Horizon to be Sold to Century of Jordan, Hong Kong Company for $1.78 mln,' *Globes*, 16 May 2000.
-Tsuriel, Keren, 'Manufacturers Association Proposes Compromise: Import only 2,000 High-tech Workers,' *Globes*, 12 July 2000.
-Tsuriel, Keren, 'The Economics of Ideology,' *Globes*, 20 July 2000.
-Tsuriel, Keren, 'Joint Jordanian-Palestinian Industrial Zone to be Set Up in Jericho,' *Globes*, 10 August 2000.
-Tsuriel, Keren, 'Business Meeting with Abdullah Cancelled; Benny Gaon: All Projects Stalemated,' *Globes*, 22 August 2000.
-Tsuriel, Keren, 'Manufacturers: Cooperation Endangered due to Jordan-US, EU Free Trade Zone Agreements,' *Globes*, 22 August 2000.
-Vivekanand, P. V., 'Cement, Steel to be Jordan's First Exports to Palestinians,' *Jordan Times*, 6 May 1995.
-Vivekanand, P. V., 'Jordan to Seek Israeli Restraints on Movement of Goods to W. Bank' [sic], *Jordan Times*, 17 June 1995.
-Vivekanand, P. V., 'Jordanians Split over Economic Impact of Possible Strain in Ties,' *Jordan Times*, 26 August 1995.
-Vivekanand, P. V., 'Transport Operators Gear up to Start Jordan-Israel Traffic,' *Jordan Times*, 30 January 1996.
-Vivekanand, P. V., 'More Jordanians now Support Normal Ties with Israel – Opinion Poll,' *Jordan Times*, 4 March 1996.
-Vivekanand, P. V., 'Ministry Says Israeli Fair is not its Concern; Event Delayed by 3 Weeks,' *Jordan Times*, 5-6 December 1996.
-Vivekanand, P. V., 'Cairo Conference Shrouded by Uncertainties of Peace Process,' *Jordan Times*, 16 November 1996.
-Vivekanand, P. V., 'Government Maintains Neutral Stand in Regards to Israelis Trade Exhibition, *Jordan Times*, 31 December 1996.
-Wertheimer, Stef, 'Peace's New Priorities, *Jerusalem Post*, 4 November 1993.
-Wertheimer, Stef, 'Singapore as Parable, *Ma'ariv*, 8 October 1999 (English translation provided by Mr. Wertheimer).
-'Work Starts on PA Industrial Parks,' *Jerusalem Post*, 15 February 1996.
-Yudelman, Michal, 'Histadrut Won't Refund "Tax" Deducted from Palestinian Workers' Pay,' *Jerusalem Post*, 16 August 1994.
-Zlotowski, Michel, 'Peres, Arafat Sign Investment Fund Accord, *Jerusalem Post*, 21 January 1998.

Reports and Websites:
-1997 Census on Population, Housing and Establishment, Palestinian Central Bureau of Statistics (PCBS), www.pcbs.org/english/phc_97/popu.htm.
-Abu El-Haj, Ribhi, *The Israeli Electronics Industry*, Paper Presented to the Economic and Social Commission for Western Asia (ESCWA) Expert Group Meeting on the Impact of the Peace Process on Selected Sectors, 23-25 June 1997, Amman, E/ESCWA/ID/1997/WG.I/21.

-Amir, Shmuel, et al, *Alternative Models of Economic Arrangements within the Framework of a Permanent Settlement between Israel and the Palestinian Authority*, Draft sponsored by the Foreign Ministry of Japan, 23 March 1999.
-Arab Palestinian Investment Company (APIC) website, www.apic-pal.com.
-Astrup, Claus, and Sebastien Dessus, *Trade Options for the Palestinian Economy: Some Orders of Magnitude*, World Bank, October 2000.
-Awartani, Hisham, and Samir Awad, *Palestinian-Israeli Joint Ventures: Constraints and Prospects*, Economics Department, Centre for Palestine Research and Studies (CPRS), www.cprs-palestine.org/economy/94/joint.html.
-Blacklist of Jordanian Companies Dealing with Israel, *Muqawama (Resistance)*, Newsletter of the Professional Associations' Anti-Normalisation Committee, 21 January 2001 (*Arabic*).
-[Bouillon, Markus], *Jordan: US Free Trade Agreement*, Oxford Analytica Daily Brief, 18 October 2001.
-[Bouillon, Markus], 'Country Assessment: Israel,' *International Standards Compliance Index*, Research Department, Oxford Analytica, June-July 2001.
-[Bouillon, Markus], 'Country Assessment: Jordan,' *International Standards Compliance Index*, Research Department, Oxford Analytica, June-July 2001.
-*Building a Prosperous Peace: Amman '95*, published by the International Press Office, The Royal Hashemite Court, Amman 1995.
-CA IB Investment Bank of the Bank of Austria Group, *Economic Update Israel*, 28 June 2000.
-Centre for Palestine Research and Studies (CPRS) website, www.cprs-palestine.org.
-Century Investment Group website and Omar Salah biography, www.qiz.com, and www.centuryinvest.com/omarsalah.asp.
-Co-ordinating Bureau of Economic Organizations (CBEO), *Economic Implications of the Establishment of Autonomy in the Territories and Ways for its Integration with the Israeli Economy*, February 1993 (Hebrew, *Lishkat ha-teum shel ha-irgunim ha-kalkali'im, Bhinat ha-shlakhot ha-kalkaliyot shel hakamat ha-otonomiya b'shtakhim v'drakhey shiluva b-kalkalat yisrael*).
-Destremau, Blandine, *The Restructuring Process of the Israeli Garment Industry*, Paper presented to the Economic and Social Commission for Western Asia (ESCWA) Expert Group Meeting on the Impact of the Peace Process on Selected Sectors, 23-25 June 1997, E/ESCWA/ID/1997/WG.I/22.
-Economic and Social Commission for Western Asia (ESCWA), *Trade Efficiency in ESCWA Member Countries: A Comprehensive Study*, New York 1999, E/ESCWA/ED/1999/6.
-Economic and Social Commission for Western Asia (ESCWA), *Appraisal of the Middle East and North Africa Economic Conferences*, New York 2000, E/ESCWA/ED/1999/15, 12 November 1999.
-Economic Cooperation Foundation (ECF) and DATA-HCIF, *The EPS Model: A Possible Set of Israeli-Palestinian Economic Understandings for Permanent Status*, June-November 1998.
-Elul Group website, www.elulgrp.com.
-*Evaluating the Paris Protocol: Economic Relations between Israel and the Palestinian Territories* (Draft), Study financed by the European Commission, July 1999.
-Federation of Israeli Chambers of Commerce (FICC) website, www.tlv-chamber.org.il.
-*The Flow of Investments into the al-Hassan Industrial Estate During 1999*, Internal Report Obtained from the Investors Services Bureau at the al-Hassan Industrial Estate, September 2000 (Arabic, *Harakat al-istithmar fi medinat al-Hassan al-sina'iya li-'am 1999*).
-Government of Israel, *Development Options for Regional Cooperation*, October 1994.
-Government of Israel, *Development Options for Cooperation: The Middle East/East Mediterranean Region 1996*, Version IV, August 1995.
-Government of Israel, *Programs for Regional Cooperation 1997*, November 1996.

BIBLIOGRAPHY 221

-Government of Israel, *Partnerships in Development 1998*, November 1997.
-The Institute for Peace Research, *2001 Survey: Attitudes of the Arabs to the State of Israel*, http://orae.fes.de:8081/fes/docs/NAHER_OSTEN/2001%SURVEY.HTM.
-*Interim Progress Report on Regional Development Projects*, April 2000 (ongoing database project), Israeli Ministry of Regional Co-operation.
-Irbid Chamber of Industry, *Quarterly Report: First Quarter 2001*.
-Israel Manufacturers Association (IMA) website, www.industry.org.il.
-Israel Manufacturers Association (IMA), Division of Foreign Trade and International Relations, *Joint Ventures in the Karni Park: Required Conditions, Findings and Conclusions, in combination with the Findings of the Israel Export Institute*, May 1997 (Hebrew, *Agaf sahar huz v'ksharim binleumi'im, hitahdut ha-ta'asiyanim b'yisrael, Mizamim meshutafim be-Park Karni: tnayim nidrashim, mimza'im v'maskanot, b'shiluv mamza'ay makhon ha-yizu'a ha-yisraeli*).
-Israel Manufacturers Association (IMA), *Final Economic Status Between Israel and the Palestinians: The Standpoint of the Manufacturers Association*, November 1999 (Hebrew, *Hitahdut ha-ta'asiyanim, Hesder ha-keva' ha-kalkali beyn yisrael l'falestina'im: 'emdat hitahdut ha-ta'asiyanim*).
-*Jordan: A Winning Business Destination*, Ministry of Planning, November 1997 (6 vols.).
-Jordan Commercial and Industrial Estates Corporation (JCIEC), *Annual Report 1998*.
-The Jordan Rift Valley Steering Committee of the Trilateral Economic Committee/The HARZA JRV Group, *Jordan Rift Valley Integrated Development Study Final Report: Master Plan, Description of Master Plan Projects*, August 1997.
-Lakind, Stacey, and Yigal Carmon, 'The PA Economy – Free Market or Kleptocracy? Part I: Economic Policy,' *MEMRI (The Middle East Media and Research Institute) Inquiry and Analysis No. 10*, 7 January 1999, www.memri.org/ia/IA1099.html.
-Letter from Prime Minister Binyamin Netanyahu to Stef Wertheimer, 4 February 1999.
-Letter from Prime Minister Ehud Barak to Stef Wertheimer, 13 September 1999.
-*National Economic Dialogue Conference: Conference Conclusions and Private Sector Recommendations*, Ramallah, 30 May 2000, published by Paltrade.
-Palestine Development and Investment Company PADICO) website, www.padico.com.
-Palestinian Academic Society for the Study of International Affairs (PASSIA) website (Gaza and West Bank map), www.passia.org/palestine_facts/MAPS/wbgs1.html.
-Palestinian Central Bureau of Statistics (PCBS), *PCBS – Foreign Trade Statistics*.
-Palestinian Central Bureau of Statistics (PCBS) and Palestinian Authority (PA), *Current Account Data Series*, 1998.
-Palestinian Industrial Estates and Free Zones Authority (PIEFZA), Document ANR20008, Dated 2000/12/11.
-Palestinian Industrial Estates and Free Zones Authority (PIEFZA), *Jenin Industrial Estate Feasibility Study*.
-Palestinian Industrial Estates and Free Zones Authority (PIEFZA), *Nablus Industrial Estate Feasibility Study*.
-Palestinian Trade Centre (Paltrade) website, www.paltrade.org.
-The Peaceworks, Inc. website, www.peaceworks.com.
-Regional Economic Development Working Group (REDWG) Monitoring Committee Secretariat, *Monthly Chronologies: First Annual Issue*, May 1998-April 1999.
-Royal Scientific Society (RSS), *Studies About the Economic Implications of Peace in the Middle East on the Hashemite Kingdom of Jordan*, Vol. 1, September 1994 (Arabic, *Al-jam'iya al-'ilmiya al-malikiya, Dirasat hawl al-athar al-iqtisadiya li'l-salam fi al-sharq al-awsat ala al-mamlaka al-urdunniya al-hashimiya*).
-Royal Scientific Society (RSS), Peace Follow-Up Unit, *Follow-Up Report on the Trade and Economic Cooperation Agreement between Jordan and Israel in the Treaty of Peace*, April 1998.
-Sea of Life (Jordael Co.) website, www.aseaoflife.com.

-Seitz, Charmaine, 'PA Commercial Holdings Made Public,' published on the Jerusalem Media Communications Centre (JMCC) website, www.jmcc.org/media/report/2000/Jun/4b.htm.
-Siemens website, www.siemens.com.
-*Twenty Fifth Annual Report, 1990* (Amman: Central Bank of Jordan, Department of Research and Studies, 1991).
-United Nations Conference on Trade and Development (UNCTAD), *Palestinian Merchandise Trade in the 1990s: Opportunities and Challenges*, UNCTAD/GDS/SEU/1, 23 January 1998.
-United Nations Conference on Trade and Development (UNCTAD), *The Palestinian Economy and Prospects for Regional Cooperation*, UNCTAD/GDS/SEU/2, 30 June 1998.
-United Nations Conference on Trade and Development (UNCTAD), *Cooperation between the Palestinian Authority, Egypt and Jordan to Enhance Subregional Trade-Related Services*, UNCTAD/GDS/SEU/3, 14 February 2000.
-United Nations Development Programme (UNDP) and Royal Scientific Society (RSS), Peace Follow-Up Unit, *Follow-Up Report on the Obstacles Exporters to Israel and the PNA Face*, July 1998 (Arabic, *Wahda mutabi'a al-salam, Al-'aqabat al-latti tuwajih al-musaddirin min al-urdunn illa isra'il wa al-salta al-wataniya al-filastiniya*).
-United Nations Development Programme (UNDP) and Royal Scientific Society (RSS), Peace Follow-Up Unit, *Follow-Up Report on the Transportation Agreement between Jordan and Israel in the Peace Process*, Report No. 10, February 1999 (Arabic, *Wahda mutabi'a al-salam, Taqrir mutabi'a 'an ittifaqiya al-naql bayn al-urdunn wa isra'il damn mu'ahida al-salam*).
-United Nations Development Programme (UNDP) and Royal Scientific Society (RSS), Peace Follow-Up Unit, *Follow-Up Report on the Qualifying Industrial Zone (QIZ)*, Report No. 14, November 1999.
-United Nations Office of the Special Coordinator in the Occupied Territories (UNSCO), *Quarterly Report on Economic and Social Conditions in the West Bank and Gaza Strip*, www.arts.mcgill.ca/mepp/unsco/.
-United States Central Intelligence Agency (CIA), *Atlas of the Middle East*, January 1993.
-United States Department of State, *Country Commercial Guide: Jordan, 2001*, www.state.gov/www/about_state/business/com_guides/2001/nea/jordan_ccg2001.pdf.
-United States Department of State, International Information Programs, *Middle East Peace Process Chronology*, usinfo.state.gov/regional/nea/summit/chron.htm.
-Wertheimer, Stef, *Cross-Border Industrial Parks – a 'Peace Bridge'*, April 1999, Proposal for the Establishment of an Industrial Park: Egypt, Gaza, and Israel, ISCAR Ltd.
-World Bank, *Developing the Occupied Territories: An Investment in Peace* (Washington, D. C.: International Bank for Reconstruction and Development [IBRD]/World Bank, 1993), 5 vols.
-World Bank, *Middle East Peace Talks, Regional Co-operation and Economic Development: A Note on Priority Regional Projects* (Washington, D. C.: IBRD/World Bank, 1993).
-World Bank, *Emergency Assistance Program for the Occupied Territories* (Washington, D. C.: IBRD/World Bank, 1994).
-World Bank, *The West Bank and Gaza. The Next Two Years and Beyond* (Washington, D. C.: IBRD/World Bank, 1994).
-World Bank, *Peace and the Jordanian Economy* (Washington, D. C.: IBRD/World Bank, 1994).
-World Bank, *Claiming the Future: Choosing Prosperity in the Middle East and North Africa* (Washington, D. C.: IBRD/World Bank, 1995).
-World Bank, *Jordan Privatization Note*, Privatization Technical Assistance Mission, 9-15 December 1995.
-World Bank, Country Data and World Development Indicators websites, www.worldbank.org/data/ and devdata.worldbank.org/.
-Young Entrepreneurs Association (YEA), *Annual Report 1999*.

Articles, Books, and Theses:

-Aarts, Paul, *Dilemmas of Regional Cooperation in the Middle East* (The Lancaster Papers: Current Research in Politics and International Affairs, No. 4, published by the Department of Politics and International Relations, Lancaster University, 1999).

-Abed, George T., ed., *The Palestinian Economy: Studies in Development under Prolonged Occupation* (London: Routledge, 1988).

- Abu Shair, Osama J. A. R., *Privatization and Development* (Houndmills: Macmillan, 1997).

-Adiv, Assaf, 'Israeli Textile in Crisis. No Alternative for Arab Women,' *Challenge*, No. 40.

-Aharoni, Yair, *Structure and Performance in the Israeli Economy* (Tel Aviv: Cherikover, 1976; Hebrew).

-Aharoni, Yair, *The Israeli Economy: Dreams and Realities* (London: Routledge, 1991).

-Aharoni, Yair, 'The Changing Political Economy of Israel,' *The Annals of the American Academy of Political and Social Science*, Vol. 555 (January 1998, special issue on Israel in Transition).

-Aliboni, Roberto; Tim Niblock, and E. G. H. [George] Joffé, eds., *Security Challenges in the Mediterranean Region* (London: Frank Cass, 1996).

-Allison, Graham, and Philip Zelikow, *Essence of Decision: Explaining the Cuban Missile Crisis* (New York: Longman, 2nd ed., 1999).

-Anderer, Gilbert, *Die Politische Ökonomie eines Allokationssystems: Jordanien und die internationale Arbeitsmigration seit 1973* (Frankfurt: Peter Lang Verlag, 1991).

-Arad, Ruth; Zeev Hirsch, and Alfred Tovias, *The Economics of Peacemaking: Focus on the Egyptian Israeli Situation* (London: Macmillan, 1983).

-Arian, Asher, *The Second Republic: Politics in Israel* (Chatham: Chatham House, 1998).

-Arnon, Arie, et al, *The Palestinian Economy: Between Imposed Integration and Voluntary Separation* (Leiden: Brill, 1997).

-Arnon, Arie, and Avia Spivak, 'Economic Aspects of the Oslo Peace Process: The Disappointing Consequences of an Incomplete Agreement,' *Israel-Palestine Journal*, Vol. 5, No. 3-4 (Autumn-Winter 1998).

-Arnon, A. [Arie], and J. Weinblatt, 'Sovereignty and Economic Development: the Case of Israel and Palestine,' *Economic Journal*, Vol. 111 (June 2001).

-Ashley, Richard K., 'Untying the Sovereign State: A Double-Reading of the Anarchy Problematique,' *Millennium*, Vol. 17, No. 2 (1988).

-Ashley, Richard K., and R. B. J. Walker, eds., *Speaking the Language of the Exile: Dissidence in International Studies*, special issue of *International Studies Quarterly*, Vol. 34, No. 3 (1990).

-Awartani, Hisham, and Efraim Kleiman, 'Economic Interaction Among Participants in the Middle East Peace Process,' *Middle East Journal*, Vol. 51, No. 2 (April 1997).

-Ayubi, Nazih N., *Over-Stating the Arab State: Politics and Society in the Middle East* (London: I. B. Tauris, 1995).

-Bahiri, Simcha, 'Gaza and Jericho First: The Economic Angle,' *Israel-Palestine Journal*, Vol. 1, No. 1 (Winter 1994).

-Bahiri, Simcha, 'Economic Separation or Integration: A Rejoinder to Dr. Samir Hazboun,' *Israel-Palestine Journal*, Vol. 3, No. 2 (Spring 1996).

-Baldwin, David A., ed., *Neorealism and Neoliberalism: The Contemporary Debate* (New York: Columbia University Press, 1993).

-Baskin, Gershon, and Zakaria al-Qaq, eds., *Israeli-Palestinian-Jordanian Trade: Present Issues, Future Possibilities*, Israel-Palestine Centre for Research and Information (IPCRI), Commercial Law Report Series, April 1998.

-Baskin, Gershon, and Zakaria al-Qaq, *A Reevaluation of the Border Industrial Estates Concept*, Israel-Palestine Centre for Research and Information (IPCRI), Commercial Law Report Series, December 1998.

-Baylis, John, and Steve Smith, eds., *The Globalization of World Politics* (Oxford: Oxford University Press, 1997).
-Beblawi, Hazem, and Giacomo Luciani, eds., *The Rentier State* (London: Croom Helm, 1987).
-Ben-Ami, Shlomo, 'Koor Ready to Cooperate,' *Israel-Palestine Journal*, Vol. 1, No. 1 (Winter 1994).
-Ben-Porath, Amir, *State and Capitalism in Israel* (Westport: Greenwood Press, 1993).
-Bichler, Shimshon, and Jonathan Nitzan, 'Military Spending and Differential Accumulation: A New Approach to the Political Economy of Armament – The Case of Israel,' *Review of Radical Political Economics*, Vol. 28, No. 1 (May 1996).
-Blin, Louis, and Philippe Fargues, eds., *L'Economie de la Paix au Proche-Orient/The Economy of Peace in the Middle East* (Luisant: Maisonneuve et Larose/CEDEJ, 1995), 2 vols.
-Booth, Ken, and Steve Smith, eds., *International Relations Theory Today* (Cambridge: Polity Press, 1995).
-Bouillon, Markus, and Olaf Köndgen, 'Jordaniens Friedensdividende 1994-1998. Eine Bestandsaufnahme', *KAS-Auslandsinformationen*, No. 9/1998.
-Bouillon, Markus, and Ralph Stobwasser, 'Israel and the Occupied Territories,' in Sara and Tom Pendergast, eds., *Worldmark Encyclopaedia of National Economies*, (Farmington Hills: Gale Group, 2002; 4 vols.).
-Brand, Laurie A., *Jordan's Inter-Arab Relations: The Political Economy of Alliance Making* (New York: Columbia University Press, 1994).
-Brand, Laurie A., *Women, the State, and Political Liberalization: Middle Eastern and North African Experiences*, (New York: Columbia University Press, 1998).
-Brand, Laurie A., 'The Effects of the Peace Process on Political Liberalization in Jordan', *Journal of Palestine Studies*, Vol. 28, No. 2 (Spring 1999).
-Brewer, Anthony, *Marxist Theories of Imperialism: A Critical Survey* (London: Routledge, 1980).
-Bruno, Michael, *Crisis, Stabilization, and Economic Reform: Therapy by Consensus* (Oxford: Clarendon Press, 1993).
-Brynen, Rex, 'Buying Peace? A Critical Assessment of International Aid to the West Bank and Gaza,' *Journal of Palestine Studies*, Vol. 25, No. 3 (Spring 1996).
-Bull, Hedley, *The Anarchical Society* (London: Macmillan, 1977).
-Burchill, Scott, et al, *Theories of International Relations* (Houndmills: Palgrave, 2nd ed., 2001).
-Burton, Henry J., *The Promise of Peace: Economic Cooperation between Egypt and Israel* (Washington D.C.: Brookings Institution Staff Paper, 1980).
-Calvert, Peter, The Foreign Policy of New States (Brighton: Wheatsheaf, 1986).
-Çarkoğlu, Ali; Mine Eder, and Kemal Kirişci, *The Political Economy of Regional Cooperation in the Middle East* (London: Routledge, 1998).
-Carr, E. H., *The Twenty Years' Crisis: An Introduction the Study of International Relations* (London: Macmillan, 1939).
-Chandhoke, Neera, *State and Civil Society: Explorations in Political Theory* (London: Sage, 1995).
-Cox, Robert W., *Production, Power, and World Order: Social Forces in the Making of History* (New York: Columbia University Press, 1987).
-Cox, Robert W., with Timothy J. Sinclair, *Approaches to World Order* (Cambridge: Cambridge University Press, 1996).
-Der Derian, James, and Michael J. Shapiro, eds., *International/Intertextual Relations: Post-Modern Readings of World Politics* (New York: Lexington, 1989).
-Dessler, David, 'What's at Stake in the Agent-Structure Debate?' *International Organization*, Vol. 43, No. 3 (Summer 1989).
-Deutsches Orient-Institut, *Nahost-Jahrbuch 1988: Politik, Wirtschaft und Gesellschaft in Nordafrika und dem Nahen und Mittleren Osten* (Opladen: Deutsches Orient-Institut, 1989).
-Diwan, Ishaac, and Michael Walton, 'Palestine between Israel and Jordan: The Economics

of an Uneasy Triangle,' *The Beirut Review*, No. 8 (Fall 1994), special issue on The Economics of Middle East Peace.

-Diwan, Ishaac, and Radwan A. Shaban, eds., *Development Under Adversity: The Palestinian Economy in Transition* (Washington, D. C.: IBRD/The World Bank and Palestine Economic Policy Research Institute [MAS], 1999).

-Dixon, W. J., 'Democracy and the Management of International Conflict,' *Journal of Conflict Resolution*, Vol. 37, No. 1 (1993).

-Doherty, Joe; Elspeth Graham, and Mo Malek, eds., *Post-Modernism and the Social Sciences* (London: Macmillan, 1992).

-Doyle, Michael W., 'Kant, Liberal Legacies, and Foreign Affairs,' *Philosophy and Public Affairs*, Vol. 12, No. 3 (1983).

-Doyle, Michael W., 'Liberalism and World Politics,' *American Political Science Review*, Vol. 80 (1986).

-Drezon-Tepler, Marcia, *Interest Groups and Political Change in Israel* (Albany: State University of New York Press, 1990).

-Economist Intelligence Unit, *Country Profile: Jordan, 1998-1999* (London: EUI, 1998).

-El-Ferra, Majed, and Malcolm MacMillen, 'External Constraints on Manufacturing Development in Israeli-Occupied Gaza,' *Middle East Journal*, Vol. 36, No. 1 (January 2000).

-Elizur, Yuval, and Eliahu Salpeter, *Who Rules Israel?* (New York: Harper and Row, 1973).

-Elmusa, Sharif S., and Mahmoud El-Jaafari, 'Power and Trade: The Israeli-Palestinian Economic Protocol,' *Journal of Palestine Studies*, Vol. 24, No. 2 (Winter 1995).

-Evans, Peter B.; Dietrich Rueschemeyer, and Theda Skocpol, eds., *Bringing the State Back In* (Cambridge: Cambridge University Press, 1985).

-Evans, Peter [B.]; Harold K. Jacobson, and Robert D. Putnam, eds., *Double-Edged Diplomacy: International Bargaining and Domestic Politics* (Berkeley: University of California Press, 1993).

-Farsoun, Samih K., and Christina E. Zacharia, *Palestine and the Palestinians* (Boulder: Westview Press, 1997).

-Fawcett, Louise, and Andrew Hurrell, eds., *Regionalism in World Politics: Regional Organization and International Order* (Oxford: Oxford University Press, 1995).

-Feige, Edgar, 'The Economic Consequences of Peace in the Middle East,' *Challenge*, New York, January-February 1979.

-Feiler, Gil, 'Creating Jobs for the Palestinians,' *Israel-Palestine Journal*, Vol. 1, No. 1 (Winter 1994).

-Finnemore, Martha, *National Interests in International Society* (Ithaca: Cornell University Press, 1996).

-Fishelson, Gideon, ed., *Economic Cooperation in the Middle East* (Boulder: Westview Press, 1989).

-Fishelson, Gideon, 'The Peace Dividend: Regional Trade & Cooperation,' *Israel-Palestine Journal*, Vol. 1, No. 1 (Winter 1994).

-Fisher, Stanley; Dani Rodrik, and Elias Tuma, eds., *The Economics of Middle East Peace: Views from the Region* (Cambridge: MIT Press, 1993).

-Fisher, Stanley, et al, eds., *Securing Peace in the Middle East: Project on Economic Transition* (Cambridge: MIT Press, 1994).

-Fisher, Stanley; Patricia Alonso-Gamo, and Ulric Erickson von Allmen, 'Economic Developments in the West Bank and Gaza since Oslo,' *Economic Journal*, Vol. 111, (June 2001).

-Flamhaft, Zima, *Israel on the Road to Peace: Accepting the Unacceptable* (Boulder: Westview Press, 1996).

-Frank, Andre Gunder, *Capitalism and Underdevelopment in Latin America: Historical Studies of Chile and Brazil* (New York: Monthly Review Press, 1967).

-Frank, Andre Gunder, *Latin America: Underdevelopment and Revolution. Essays on the Development*

of Underdevelopment and the Immediate Enemy (New York: Monthly Review Press, 1969).
-Freedman, Robert O., ed., *The Middle East and the Peace Process: The Impact of the Oslo Accords* (Gainesville: University Press of Florida, 1998).
-Frisch, Hillel, and Menachem Hofnung, 'State Formation and International Aid: The Emergence of the Palestinian Authority,' *World Development*, Vol. 25, No. 8 (1997).
-Garfinkle, Adam, *Israel and Jordan in the Shadow of War: Functional Ties and Futile Diplomacy in a Small Place* (London: Macmillan, 1992).
-Garfinkle, Adam, *Politics and Society in Modern Israel: Myths and Realities* (Armonk: M. E. Sharpe, 1997).
-Gharaibeh, Fawzi A., *The Economies of the West Bank and Gaza Strip* (Boulder: Westview Press, 1985).
-Gill, Stephen, ed., *Gramsci, Historical Materialism and International Relations* (Cambridge: Cambridge University Press, 1993).
-Gilpin, Robert, *The Political Economy of International Relations* (Princeton: Princeton University Press, 1987).
-Ginat, Joseph, and Onn Winckler, eds., *The Jordanian-Palestinian-Israeli Triangle: Smoothing the Path to Peace* (Brighton: Sussex Academic Press, 1998).
-Grieco, Joseph M., *Cooperation Among Nations: Europe, America, and Non-Tariff Barriers to Trade* (Ithaca: Cornell University Press, 1990).
-Guyatt, Nicholas, *The Absence of Peace: Understanding the Israeli-Palestinian Conflict* (London: Zed Books, 1998).
-Haas, Ernst B., *The Uniting of Europe: Political, Social, and Economical Forces, 1950-1957* (London: Stevens, 1958).
-Haas, Ernst B., *Beyond the Nation-State: Functionalism and International Organization* (Stanford: Stanford University Press, 1964).
-Haas, Marius, *Husseins Königreich: Jordaniens Stellung im Nahen Osten* (Munich: Tuduv Verlag, 1975).
-Haidar, Aziz, *On the Margins: The Arab Population in the Israeli Economy* (London: Hurst, 1995).
-Halbach, Axel J., et al, *Regional Economic Development in the Middle East: Potential Intra-Regional Trade in Goods and Services Against the Background of a Peace Settlement* (Munich: Weltforum Verlag, 1995; ifo Institut für Wirtschaftsforschung München, ifo research reports, Department for Development and Transformation Studies 84).
-Halbach, Axel J., et al, *New Potentials for Cooperation and Trade in the Middle East: An Empirical Analysis* (Munich: Weltforum Verlag, 1995; ifo Institut für Wirtschaftsforschung, ifo research reports, Department for Development and Transformation Studies 85).
-Harik, Iliya, and Denis J. Sullivan, eds., *Privatization and Liberalization in the Middle East* (Bloomington: Indiana University Press, 1992).
-Hazboun, Samir, and Simcha Bahiri, 'Palestinian Industrial Development and Israeli-Palestinian Attitudes to Cooperation,' *Israel-Palestine Journal*, Vol. 1, No. 4 (Autumn 1994).
-Henry, Clement M., and Robert Springborg, *Globalization and the Politics of Development in the Middle East* (Cambridge: Cambridge University Press, 2001).
-Hogan, Michael J., and Thomas G. Paterson, eds., *Explaining the History of American Foreign Relations* (Cambridge: Cambridge University Press, 1991).
-Hopgood, Stephen, *American Environmental Foreign Policy and the Power of the State* (Oxford: Oxford University Press, 1998).
-Hudson, Michael C., ed., *The Palestinians: New Directions* (Washington, D. C.: Centre for Contemporary Arab Studies, Georgetown University, 1990).
-Huleileh, Samir, 'Crash Program for Economic Survival,' *Israel-Palestine Journal*, Vol. 1, No. 1 (Winter 1994).
-Huleileh, Samir, and Gil Feiler, *Guidelines for Final Status Economic Negotiations between Israel*

and Palestine, Israel-Palestine Centre for Research and Information (IPCRI), Commercial Law Report Series, November 1998.
-Ikenberry, G. John; David A. Lake, and Michael Mastanduno, eds., *The State and American Foreign Economic Policy* (Ithaca: Cornell University Press, 1988).
-'Israeli Impediments to Investment in Palestine,' prepared by the Economic Office at the Orient House, *Israel-Palestine Journal*, Vol. 3, No. 3-4 (Autumn-Winter 1996).
-Jawhary, Muna, *The Palestinian-Israeli Trade Arrangements: Searching for Fair Revenue-Sharing*, Palestine Economic Policy Research Institute (MAS), December 1995.
-Joffé, George [E. G. H.], ed., *Jordan in Transition: 1990-2000* (London: Hurst, 2001).
-Kadri, Ali, and Malcolm MacMillen, 'The Political Economy of Israel's Demand for Palestinian Labour', *Third World Quarterly*, Vol. 19, No. 2 (1998).
-Kanafani, Nu'man, *Trade Relations between Palestine and Israel: Free Trade Area or Customs Union*, Palestine Economic Policy Research Institute (MAS), December 1996.
-Kanafani, Nu'man, 'Trade – a Catalyst for Peace?' *Economic Journal*, Vol. 111 (June 2001).
-Katzenstein, Peter J., ed., *Between Power and Plenty: Foreign Economic Policies of Advanced Industrial States* (Madison: University of Wisconsin Press, 1978).
-Keohane, Robert O., *After Hegemony: Cooperation and Discord in the World Political Economy* (Princeton: Princeton University Press, 1984).
-Keohane, Robert O., ed., *Neorealism and its Critics* (New York: Columbia University Press, 1986).
-Keohane, Robert O., 'International Institutions: Two Approaches,' *International Studies Quarterly*, Vol. 32, No. 4 (1988).
-Keohane, Robert O., *International Institutions and State Power: Essays in International Relations Theory* (Boulder: Westview, 1989).
-Khader, Bichara, and Adnan Badran, eds., *The Economic Development of Jordan* (London: Croom Helm, 1987).
-Kindleberger, Charles P., *The World in Depression, 1929-1939* (Berkeley: University of California Press, 1973).
-Kleiman, Ephraim, 'The Waning of Israeli *Etatisme*', *Israel Studies*, Vol. 2, No. 2 (Fall 1997).
-Knorr, Klaus, and Sidney Verba, eds., *The International System: Theoretical Essays* (Westport: Greenwood Press, 1961).
-Krasner, Stephen D., *Defending the National Interest: Raw Materials Investments and US Foreign Policy* (Princeton: Princeton University Press, 1978).
-Krasner, Stephen D., 'Review Article: Approaches to the State, Alternative Conceptions and Historical Dynamics,' *Comparative Politics*, Vol. 16, No. 2 (January 1984).
-Lawrence, R. Z., *Towards Free Trade in the Middle East: The Triad and Beyond* (Cambridge: Institute for Social and Economic Policy in the Middle East, Harvard University, 1995).
-Lederman, Jim, 'The Economics of Middle East Peace,' *Orbis*, Vol. 39, No. 4 (Fall 1995).
-Lederman, Jim, 'The Investments that Cement Arab-Israeli Peace,' *Middle East Quarterly*, Vol. 3, No. 1 (March 1996).
-Linklater, Andrew, 'The Question of the Next Stage in International Relations Theory: A Critical-Theoretical Point of View,' *Millennium*, Vol. 21, No. 1 (1992).
-Linklater, Andrew, *Beyond Realism and Marxism: Critical Theory and International Relations* (Houndmills: Macmillan, 1990).
-Lukacs, Yehuda, *Israel, Jordan, and the Peace Process* (Syracuse: Syracuse University Press, 1997).
-Maman, Daniel, *Institutional Linkages between the Economic Elites and the Political and Bureaucratic Elites in Israel: 1974-1988*, Doctoral Dissertation, Hebrew University of Jerusalem, July 1993 (Hebrew, *Mazavei Mifgash beyn Elitot Kalkaliyot le-Elitot Politiyot v'Menhaliyot be-Yisrael*).

-Maman, Daniel, 'The Power lies in the Structure: Economic Policy Forum Networks in Israel,' *British Journal of Sociology*, Vol. 48, No. 2 (June 1997).
-Maman, Daniel, 'The Social Organization of the Israeli Economy: A Comparative Analysis,' *Israel Affairs*, Vol. 5, Nos. 2-3, (Winter-Spring 1999, special issue on Israel: The Dynamics of Change and Continuity).
-Mansour, Antoine, *Subcontracting Arrangements between Israeli and Palestinian Firms*, Lecture delivered at the Palestine Economic Policy Research Institute (MAS), 3 July 1997, www.palecon.org/masdir/notes/mas13.html.
-Mazur, Michael P., *Economic Growth and Development in Jordan* (London: Croom Helm, 1979).
-Merhav, Meir, ed., *Economic Cooperation and Middle East Peace* (London: Weidenfeld & Nicholson, 1989).
-Milward, Alan S., *The European Rescue of the Nation-State* (London: Routledge, 1992).
-Mitrany, David, *The Functional Theory of Politics* (New York: St. Martin's Press, 1975).
-Moore, Pete W., *Doing Business with the State: Business Associations and the Rentier State in Jordan and Kuwait*, Manuscript, March 1999.
-Moravcsik, Andrew, 'Taking Preferences Seriously: A Liberal Theory of International Politics,' *International Organization*, Vol. 51, No. 4 (Autumn 1997).
-Morgenthau, Hans, *Politics Among Nations: The Struggle for Power and Peace* (New York: Knopf, 1949).
-Murphy, Emma, 'Structural Inhibitions to Economic Liberalisation in Israel,' *Middle East Journal*, Vol. 48, No. 1, (Winter 1994).
-Nasr, Mohamed, 'Industrial Survey – 1994: Main Results, Report No. 1,' *First Reading in PCBS Statistical Report Series*, Palestine Economic Policy Research Institute (MAS), April 1997.
-Nasr, Mohamed, and Bassam Badran, *The Impact of the Peace Process on the Textile and Garment Industry in Palestine*, Lectures Delivered at the Palestine Economic Policy Research Institute (MAS), 28 August 1997, www.palecon.org/masdir/notes/mas14.html.
-Nasr, Mohamed, *Opportunities and Potentials for Palestinian Industrialization*, Palestine Economic Policy Research Institute (MAS), September 1997.
-Neufeld, Mark, *The Restructuring of International Relations Theory* (Cambridge: Cambridge University Press, 1995).
-Nevo, Joseph, and Ilan Pappé, eds., *Jordan in the Middle East: The Making of a Pivotal State 1948-1988* (Ilford: Frank Cass, 1994).
-Niblock, Tim, and Emma Murphy, eds., *Economic and Political Liberalization in the Middle East* (London: British Academy, 1993).
-Niblock, Tim, and Rodney Wilson, eds., *The Political Economy of the Middle East*, Vol. 4: Economic and Political Liberalization (Cheltenham: Edward Elgar, 1999).
-Nonneman, Gerd, ed., *Political and Economic Liberalization: Dynamics and Linkages in Comparative Perspective* (Boulder: Lynne Rienner, 1996).
-Owen, Roger, *State, Power, and Politics in the Making of the Modern Middle East* (London: Routledge, 1992).
-Oye, Kenneth A., ed., *Cooperation Under Anarchy* (Princeton: Princeton University Press, 1986).
-Parker, Christopher, *Resignation or Revolt? Socio-Political Development and the Challenges of Peace in Palestine* (London: I. B. Tauris, 1999).
-Peleg, Ilan, ed., *The Middle East Peace Process: Interdisciplinary Perspectives* (Albany: State University of New York Press, 1998).
-Peres, Shimon, *The New Middle East* (Shaftesbury: Element, 1993).
-Peters, Joel, *Pathways to Peace: The Multilateral Arab-Israeli Peace Talks* (London: The Royal Institute for International Affairs, 1996).
-Piro, Timothy J., *Managers and Minerals in a Monarchy: The Political Economy of Mining in Jordan, 1970-1989*, Ph.D. dissertation, George Washington University, 1992.

-Piro, Timothy J., *The Political Economy of Market Reform in Jordan* (Lanham: Rowman & Littlefield, 1998).
-Plessner, Yakir, *The Political Economy of Israel: From Ideology to Stagnation* (Albany: State University of New York Press, 1994).
-Plotkin, Lori, 'The Doha Conference: A Post-Mortem,' *Peacewatch*, No. 149 (Washington, D. C.: The Washington Institute for Near East Policy, Special Reports on the Arab-Israeli Peace Process, 21 November 1997).
-*Politics and the State in Jordan, 1946-1996*, Collection of Papers Given at the International Symposium at the Institut Du Monde Arabe, Paris, 24-25 June 1997.
-Putnam, Robert D., 'Diplomacy and Domestic Politics: The Logic of Two Level Games,' *International Organization*, Vol. 42, No. 3 (Summer 1988).
-Rabe, Hajo, *The Political Economy of Palestine: The Transformation of Economic Elites after Oslo*, paper given at a PASSIA meeting, 30 April 1998; www.passia.org/index_pfacts.htm.
-Radi, Lamia, *L'Elite Palestinienne: Strategies de Survie et Modes d'Influence, 1967-1997*. Doctoral dissertation, Institut d'Etudes Politiques de Paris, Cycle Superieur d'Etudes Politique, 1997.
-Razin, Eran, 'Location of Entrepreneurship Assistance Centres in Israel,' *Tijschrift voor Economische en Sociale Geografie*, Vol. 89, No. 4 (1998).
-Retzky, Allan, 'Peace in the Middle East: What Does it Really Mean for Israeli Business?' *Columbia Journal of World Business*, Vol. 30, No. 3 (Fall 1995).
-Richards, Alan, and John Waterbury, *A Political Economy of the Middle East* (Boulder: Westview, 2nd ed., 1996).
-Rivlin, Paul, *The Israeli Economy* (Boulder: Westview Press, 1992).
-Robinson, Glenn E., 'Defensive Democratization in Jordan', *International Journal of Middle East Studies*, Vol. 30, No. 3 (August 1998).
-Rogan, Eugene L., and Tareq Tell, eds., *Village, Steppe and State: The Social Origins of Modern Jordan* (London: British Academy Press, 1994).
-Roy, Sara [M.], 'Separation or Integration: Closure and the Economic Future of the Gaza Strip Revisited,' *Middle East Journal*, Vol. 48, No. 1 (Winter 1994).
-Roy, Sara M., *The Gaza Strip: The Political Economy of De-Development* (Washington, D. C.: Institute for Palestine Studies, 1995).
-Roy, Sara [M.], 'De-Development Revisited: Palestinian Economy and Society since Oslo,' *Journal of Palestine Studies*, Vol. 28, No. 3 (Spring 1999).
-Roy, Sara [M.], and Karen Pfeiffer, eds., *Research in Middle East Economics. The Economics of Middle East Peace: A Reassessment, Vol. 3* (Stamford: Jai Press, 1999).
-Russett, Bruce M., *Grasping the Democratic Peace: Principles for a Post-Cold War World* (Princeton: Princeton University Press, 1993).
-Ryan, Curtis R., 'Peace, Bread and Riots: Jordan and the IMF,' *Middle East Policy*, Vol. 6, No. 2 (Autumn 1996).
-Ryan, Curtis R., 'Jordan and the Rise and Fall of the Arab Co-operation Council,' *Middle East Journal*, Vol. 52, No. 3 (Summer 1998).
-Saba, Joseph, 'Palestinian Economy: Remarks on Competition,' *Palestinian Economics System: Planned or Market-Oriented?* Seminar Report Series, Economics Department, Centre for Palestine Research and Studies (CPRS), www.cprs-palestine.org/economy/98/economy.html.
-Sadan, Ezra, 'The Best Way for Both Sides,' *Israel-Palestine Journal*, Vol. 1, No. 1 (Winter 1994).
-Said, Edward, *Peace and its Discontents: Gaza-Jericho, 1993-1995* (London: Vintage, 1995).
-Salfiti, Farida, *Israel's 'Peace Dividend:' The Jordanian Case,* Centre for Palestine Research and Studies (CPRS), Department of Strategic Analysis, March 1997.
-Samara, Adel, 'Globalization, the Palestinian Economy, and the "Peace Process",' *Journal of Palestine Studies*, Vol. 29, No. 2 (Winter 2000).

-Sanbar, Moshe, ed., *Economic and Social Policy in Israel: The First Generation* (Lanham: University Press of America and The Jerusalem Centre for Public Affairs/Centre for Jewish Community Studies, 1990).
-Sarsar, Saliba, 'Economic Implications of an Arab-Israeli Settlement,' *Scandinavian Journal of Development Alternatives and Area Studies*, Vol. 16, No. 3-4 (September-December 1997).
-Shaban, Radwan A., *Towards a Vision of Palestinian Economic Development*, Palestine Economic Policy Research Institute (MAS), September 1996.
-Shafik, Nemat, ed., *Economic Challenges Facing Middle Eastern and North African Countries* (Houndmills: Macmillan in association with the Economic Research Forum for the Arab Countries, Iran and Turkey, 1998).
-Shafir, Gershon, 'Business in Politics: Globalization and the Search for Peace in South Africa and Israel/Palestine,' *Israel Affairs*, Vol. 5, Nos. 2-3 (Winter-Spring 1999, special issue on Israel: The Dynamics of Change and Continuity).
-Shafir, Gershon, and Yoav Peled, eds., *The New Israel: Peacemaking and Liberalization* (Boulder: Westview, 2000).
-Shalev, Michael, *Labour and the Political Economy in Israel* (Oxford: Oxford University Press, 1992).
-Shalev, Michael, 'Have Globalization and Liberalization "Normalized" Israel's Political Economy?' *Israel Affairs*, Vol. 5, Nos. 2-3 (Winter-Spring 1999, special issue on Israel: The Dynamics of Change and Continuity).
-Sharkansky, Ira, *The Political Economy of Israel* (New Brunswick: Transaction, 1987).
-Sheffer, Gabriel, 'Structural Change and Leadership Transformation,' *Israel Affairs*, Vol. 5, Nos. 2-3 (Winter-Spring 1999, special issue on Israel: The Dynamics of Change and Continuity).
-Shtayyeh, Mohammad, *Israel in the Region: Conflict, Hegemony or Cooperation*, Palestinian Economic Council for Development and Reconstruction (PECDAR), 1998.
-Smooha, Sammy, 'The Implications of the Transition to Peace for Israeli Society', *The Annals of the American Academy of Political and Social Science*, Vol. 555 (January 1998, special issue on Israel in Transition).
-Solingen, Etel, 'Quandaries of the Peace Process,' *Journal of Democracy*, Vol. 7, No. 3 (1996).
-Spiegel, Steven L., ed., *The Arab-Israeli Search for Peace* (Boulder: Lynne Rienner, 1992).
-Walker, R. B. J., *Inside/Outside: International Relations as Political Theory* (Cambridge: Cambridge University Press, 1993).
-Wallerstein, Immanuel, 'The Rise and the Future Demise of the World Capitalist System,' *Comparative Studies in Society and History*, Vol. 16, No. 4 (September 1974).
-Wallerstein, Immanuel, *The Modern World-System: Capitalist Agriculture and the Origins of the European World Economy in the Sixteenth Century* (New York: Academic Press, 1974).
-Waltz, Kenneth N., *Theory of International Politics* (New York: McGraw-Hill, 1979).
-Waltz, Kenneth N., 'Realist Thought and Neo-Realist Theory,' *Journal of International Affairs*, Vol. 44, No. 1 (1990).
-Wendt, Alexander, 'The Agent-Structure Problem in International Relations,' *International Organization*, Vol. 41, No. 3 (Summer 1987).
-Wendt, Alexander, 'Anarchy is What States Make of It: The Social Construction of Power Politics,' *International Organization*, Vol. 46, No. 2 (Spring 1992).
-Wendt, Alexander, *Social Theory of International Politics* (Cambridge: Cambridge University Press, 1999).
-Wilber, Charles K., and Kenneth P. Jameson, eds., *The Political Economy of Development and Underdevelopment* (New York: McGraw-Hill, 5th ed., 1992).
-Wilson, Rodney, ed., *Politics and the Economy in Jordan* (London: Routledge, 1990).
-Wright, J. W., ed., *The Political Economy of Middle East Peace: The Impact of Competing Trade Agendas* (London: Routledge, 1998).

-Wright, J. W., and Laura Drake, eds., *Economic and Political Impediments to Middle East Peace* (Houndmills: Macmillan, 2000).
-Yetiv, Steve A., 'Peace, Interdependence, and the Middle East,' *Political Science Quarterly*, Vol. 112, No. 1 (1997).
-Yishai, Yael, *Land of Paradoxes: Interest Politics in Israel* (Albany: State University of New York Press, 1991).
-Yishai, Yael, 'Interest Politics in a Comparative Perspective: The (Ir)Regularity of the Israeli Case,' *Israel Affairs*, Vol. 5, Nos. 2-3, (Winter-Spring 1999, special issue on Israel: The Dynamics of Change and Continuity).
-Zilberfarb, Ben-Zion, 'The Israeli Economy in the 1990s: Immigration, the Peace Process, and the Medium-Term Prospects for Growth', *Israel Affairs*, Vol. 3, No. 1 (Autumn 1996).

Index

Abbas, Yasser 95
Abdel Hadi, Ibrahim 70
Abdullah, Samir 68, 71, 120
Abraham, Daniel 53, 108, 109
Abu Hassan family 40
Abu Hassan, Khaldoun 61, 100, 113
Abu Hassan, Mamduh 60, 66, 67, 112
Abu Issa, Issam 121
Abu Mazen (Mahmoud Abbas) 95, 108, 119
Abu Nada, Hashen Hussein Hashem 95
Abu Shair, Osama 40
Abu Zayyad, Fuad 115
Abul Ragheb, Ali 114, 115, 116
Admon, Mayor 110
Africa Israel Investments 82
agency law 70, 93, 94, 124, 142, 143, 145
agent-structure problem 13
Agish 86
agriculture 8, 23, 28, 36, 41, 57, 64, 70, 90, 110
Aharoni, Yair 30
Alami, Muhammad 70
Al-Aqsa Intifada *see* Intifada, second
al-Assad, Hafez 109
Al-Ayyam 120
Albemarle 76
al-Dalil Estate 80, 81
Algeria 73
al-Hamouri, Muhammad Noureddin 66
al-Hassan Industrial Estate 63, 64, 77, 78, 79, 80, 81, 82, 113, 115, 136, 137
al-Hikma Pharmaceuticals 101, 115
al-Kronz, Sa'adi 92
Allison, Graham 15, 16, 17
al-Qassem, Laith 117
Al-Ra'i 86
Al-Ram 69, 125
al-Rifa'i, Zayid 39
al-Shamma', Emad 62, 63, 81, 115, 116
al-Tarifi, Jamal 94
al-Wazir, Jihad 72

Amidar 109
Amman Chamber of Commerce (ACC) 39, 40, 60, 112, 113, 117
Amman Chamber of Industry (ACI) 39, 40, 60, 61, 100, 112, 113, 117
Anani, Jawad 3, 208
anarchy 11, 12, 13
anti-normalization 65, 66, 113, 116, 117, 118, 136, 137, 139, 140, 153
Antverg, Joseph 95
AOL 77
Apex Mutavim 82
Aqaba 63, 76, 86, 115
Arab Bank 38, 48, 77, 89, 120
Arab boycott 3, 41, 45, 51, 52, 53, 56, 57, 60, 69, 80, 100, 129, 131, 154, 161, 167
Arab Businessmen Association (ABA) 39
Arab Industrial Co. (AIC) 71, 101, 124
Arab markets 53, 58, 100
Arab Palestinian Investment Company (APIC) 46, 50, 89, 94, 95, 120, 123, 155
Arab Potash Company (APC) 36, 37, 76, 87
Arab Technology Systems (ATS) 71, 91, 125
Arab world 4, 45, 52, 54, 68, 70, 71, 73, 107, 112, 152
Arafat, Yasser 48, 49, 57, 87, 94, 95, 107, 108, 109, 119, 120, 121, 122, 144, 145, 147, 160
Aramex 87, 114
Arava Development Corporation 90
Arens, Moshe 105, 106
Arison Investments 29, 130
army (Jordanian) 77
army (Israeli) 105, 106, 107, 109
Asfour family 40
Ashdod 92
Asheri, Avraham 58, 108
Ashley, Richard 13

assassination (Rabin) 109
assassination (Mishal, attempted) 135
Association of Palestinian Chemical Industries 124
AT&T 120
Atar, Abraham 53
auditing office 122
Austria Bank 52
authoritarianism 164
Awadullah, Bassem 117
Awartani, Hisham 121
Ayeni, Bunmi 89
Azar, Wasef 61
Azorim Investment 29

B. S. T. 53
backlash (against peace) 128, 146, 154, 157, 160, 162, 168, 170
back-to-back transportation 66, 84, 98, 101, 102
Bagir 79
balance of power 11, 151
Balqa Applied University 115
Bamieh, Saeb 68, 73, 124
Bank Ha'Poalim 26, 29, 57, 59, 106, 130
Bank Leumi 29, 57, 108
Bank of Israel 108
Bar, Gabby 53, 110, 111
Barak, Ehud 94, 106, 108, 109, 110, 111, 132, 134, 135, 154, 158
Barham, Ibrahim 91, 125
Bashir, Salaheddin 115
Battikhi, Anwar 115
Bdeir family 39, 40, 113, 117
Beilin, Yossi 108, 109, 129
Ben-Ami, Shlomo 106
Ben-Gurion Airport 86
Ben-Gurion, David 28
Ben-Haim, Oded 108
Benvenisti, Rafi 108, 110
Bethlehem 97, 123, 172
Bezeq 76
Bichler, Shimshon 31
"Big 7" 33, 36, 40, 112, 113
big business 29, 30, 31, 39, 46, 51, 52, 53, 57, 58, 59, 70, 73, 87, 111, 112, 127, 128, 130, 131, 170
bilateral relations (Jordan-Israel) 60, 135
bilateral track 2, 124

Bilbeisi family 40, 66
Birzeit Palestine Pharmaceuticals Co. 69, 125
blacklist 65, 118
Blizovsky, Yoram 129
blue-collar jobs 140, 162, 168
border markets 58, 93
Boscan International 63, 64, 80, 81, 82, 116, 137
bourgeoisie 19, 20, 40, 46, 48, 153, 156
Brand, Laurie 7, 8, 18, 33, 38, 39, 140
Brewer, Anthony 20
Britain 32, 62
bromine 76
budget deficit 27
bureaucracy 38, 39, 40, 112, 119
business associations 48, 56, 61, 112, 114, 116, 117, 127, 136, 138, 146, 157, 158, 160

Caesarea Wardinon 54
caesarism 154
Camel Grinding Wheel Works (Gamal) 86
Camp David 3, 106, 109, 132, 146, 160
Caniel 78
Capital Management Corporation 91
capitalism 14, 15, 21, 30, 58, 138, 139, 140, 153, 168
Cargal 150
Çarkoğlu, Ali 5, 6, 17, 133, 146, 151, 161, 163
Carr, E. H. 11
Cartels Authority (Israel) 95
casino (Jericho) 88, 109
Catarivas, Dan 110
cement 9, 12, 29, 46, 64, 87, 94, 97, 98, 101, 102, 109, 121, 122, 135, 153
Central Bank of Jordan 33, 60, 112
centralization 96, 120, 125, 127, 144
Centre for Jewish-Arab Economic Development 91, 150
Centre for Middle East Peace and Economic Cooperation 109
Centre for Palestinian Research and Studies (CPRS) 121
Century Investment Group 62, 63, 64, 76, 77, 78, 79, 80, 86, 115, 117, 118, 136

Israeli Arabs 30, 54, 71, 106, 130, 134, 153, 164
Israeli business 30, 31, 48, 51, 58, 59, 76, 106, 111, 128, 129, 130, 131, 132, 133, 136, 149, 150, 154, 157, 168
Israeli businesspeople *see* Israeli entrepreneurs
Israeli economy 3, 28, 30, 31, 43, 46, 51, 67, 70, 71, 72, 73, 85, 108, 129, 130, 132, 134, 154, 157
Israeli entrepreneurs 53, 54, 55, 57, 61, 87, 102, 103, 128, 131, 132, 135, 149, 150, 151, 152, 154, 155, 157, 167
Israeli exports 27, 43, 85, 130
Israeli goods *see* Israeli products
Israeli importers 56, 59, 93, 94, 102
Israeli imports 55, 68, 85, 88, 92
Israeli manufacturers 48, 58, 70, 82
Israeli market 41, 43, 67, 69, 71, 72, 78, 86, 92, 93, 96, 97, 98
Israeli political economy 30, 31, 128, 130, 131, 133
Israeli products 41, 55, 59, 69, 92, 93
Israeli Shippers Association 107
Israel-Jordan Chamber of Commerce 52, 55, 85, 107
Israel-Jordan peace treaty 1, 54, 60, 61, 62, 65, 67, 83, 86, 107, 138, 149, 154
Israel-Palestine Centre for Research and Information (IPCRI) 125
ITI 120
Itzik, Dalia 109

Jaber, Abdel Malik 73, 120, 208
Japan 23, 52, 53, 130
Jenin 66, 88, 89, 96, 119
Jenin Industrial Estate 89, 90
Jerada, Muhammad 94
Jericho 88, 89, 97, 109, 123
Jerusalem 37, 52, 62, 69, 70, 97, 110, 120, 122, 123, 146
Jerusalem Business Conference 52
Jerusalem Cigarette Company (JCC) 70
Jerusalem Development and Investment Company (JEDICO) 97
Jerusalem Media communications Centre 122, 123
Jerusalem Pharmaceuticals 101, 125
Jerusalem Times 125

JETT bus company 62
jewellery 77, 84
Joint Economic Committee 92, 124
joint ventures 5, 8, 31, 52, 53, 55, 62, 64, 68, 71, 72, 73, 74, 76, 77, 80, 81, 82, 86, 89, 90, 91, 93, 106, 110, 115, 117, 128, 131, 136, 151
Jordache 80
Jordan Cement Factories Corporation (JCFC) 36, 37, 39, 87, 94, 97, 98, 113, 116, 136
Jordan Ceramic Industries Company (JCIC) 37, 60, 66, 67, 112
Jordan Electric Power Company 113
Jordan Engineering Industries Company (JEIC) 36
Jordan Engineers Association (JEA) 65
Jordan Export Development and Commercial Centres Corporation (JEDCO) 54, 66, 100
Jordan Fertilizer Industries Company (JFIC) 36
Jordan Gateway Zone 80, 82, 106, 112
Jordan Glass Industries Company (JGIC) 36
Jordan Investment Corporation (JIC) 36, 37, 38
Jordan National Bank 77
Jordan Petroleum Refinery Corporation (JPRC) 36, 37, 60, 113
Jordan Phosphate Mines Company (JPMC) 36, 37, 60, 113
Jordan Telecommunications Company (JTC) 36, 76, 113
Jordan Times 65, 208
Jordan Trade Association (JTA) 66, 99, 115, 117
Jordan Valley 87, 98
Jordan Vision 2020 114, 117, 138
Jordanian agent 65, 86, 87
Jordanian business 61, 97, 135
Jordanian Businessmen Association (JBA) 39, 40, 60, 65, 66, 112, 113, 115
Jordanian businesspeople *see* Jordanian entrepreneurs
Jordanian economy 33, 36, 41, 66, 137
Jordanian entrepreneurs 60, 61, 65, 66, 67, 76, 82, 87, 97, 100, 149, 167, 168, 171

Jordanian exports 85, 99, 102, 132
Jordanian Food Manufacturers Association 150
Jordanian goods *see* Jordanian products
Jordanian imports 55, 61, 97, 99, 102
Jordanian labour 80, 82
Jordanian manufacturers 81, 98, 100, 101
Jordanian market 53, 73, 101
Jordanian political economy 112, 137, 138, 162
Jordanian products 66, 83, 85, 86, 99, 100, 101
Jordanian Special Forces 108
Jordanian workers 76
Jordanian-American Business Association (JABA) 114, 116, 117, 138
Jordanians of Palestinian origin 32, 38, 66, 97
Jubran, Nakhleh 71, 101, 124, 125

Kabariti, Abdul Karim 112, 115
Kadamani, Yahya 62
Kadri, Ali 51
Kakish, Kamal 66, 99
Karni border crossing 89, 92
Kassem, Hassan 71, 91, 125
Katz, Yoram 106
Katzenstein, Peter 16
Kawar family 40, 87, 114, 115, 116, 117
Keohane, Robert 11, 12, 13, 14
Kerak 80, 87
Khaddourie park 57, 72, 88, 89, 91
Khader, Hussam 95, 122, 144
Khatib, Abul Elah 116
Khoury, Ramzi 95
Khoury, Sa'id 40
Kibbutz 86, 96
Kimche, David 109
King Abdullah 33, 41, 56, 73, 87, 113, 114, 115, 116, 117, 118, 127, 132, 137, 138, 139, 140, 151, 154, 158, 159, 167
King Hussein 38, 54, 55, 56, 61, 75, 81, 102, 103, 108, 113, 115, 118, 135, 136, 137, 139, 140, 141, 154, 158, 161
King's Palestinians *see* Palestinian G7

Kirişci, Kemal 5, 6, 17, 133, 146, 151, 161, 163
Kitan 54, 55
Knesset 58, 105, 108, 109, 134
know-how 54, 58, 74, 75, 82, 103, 131, 151, 152, 167
Koko, Ovadia 95
Kolber, Jonathan 28, 53, 108
Kolitz, David 106, 107
Koor 26, 28, 29, 52, 53, 57, 77, 78, 94, 106, 107, 108, 111, 130
Korea 54
Krasner, Stephen 16, 17
Kupat Holim 69
Kuwait 33, 115

labour costs 54, 55, 57, 81, 131
Labour party (Israel) 1, 24, 26, 28, 31, 34, 42, 106, 108, 129, 130, 134, 157
labour-intensive industries 54, 131, 134
Laks, Gadi 55
Lauder, Ron 109
Lautman, Dov 52, 54, 55, 56, 57, 59, 77, 107, 108, 111, 130, 132, 152, 155
Lebanon 48, 157
legitimacy 160, 171
Lenin 14
level-of-analysis debate 6, 9, 15, 20
liberal zone of peace *see* democratic peace theory
liberalization 1, 5, 7, 17, 23, 29, 33, 39, 41, 85, 96, 105, 112, 128, 129, 131, 134, 138, 139, 140, 141, 148, 150, 154, 161, 162, 163, 164, 165, 168, 169
licensing 45, 55, 70
light industry 23, 57
Likud 3, 106, 107, 109, 134, 135
Lime and Stone Production 96
Linklater, Andrew 20
Lipkin-Shahak, Amnon 106
Lisbon 122
lobbying 7, 77, 80, 81, 117, 124, 132
Lodzia 54, 81
Lower House (Jordan) 39, 118, 140
lower segments of society 134, 144, 152, 169, 171
loyalty 38, 40, 44, 121, 126, 143, 154
Lubetzky, Daniel 90

Ma'ariv 87
Maayah, Tareq 67, 72, 73, 91
MacMillen, Malcolm 51
Macpell 54
Maiman, Yossi 106
Majali, Abdul Salam 112
Malam Group 57, 77, 79, 91
Maman, Daniel 31
manual labour 75, 76, 152, 167
manufacturing 8, 26, 32, 36, 38, 44, 51, 54, 55, 56, 59, 73, 75, 77, 80, 81, 83, 85, 90, 96, 117, 131, 133, 136, 138, 143, 150, 151, 152, 154, 157, 167
Maor, Galia 108
Maoz, Hanan 91
marginalization 134, 144, 164, 168
market economy 26, 33, 49, 59, 72, 126, 138, 140, 162
marketing 54, 58, 69, 97, 98, 131, 151, 152, 167
Marxism 14, 15
Marxist 11, 14, 19
Mashav 76
Masri family 38, 40, 91, 119, 120, 155
Masrouji, Muhammad 125
means of production 19, 72, 156
MENA conferences 2, 3, 53, 60, 61, 70, 75, 76, 80, 88, 106, 108, 110, 113, 119, 136, 143
    Amman 1995 2, 37, 53, 54, 60, 62, 66, 70, 88, 110, 113, 136, 143
    Cairo 1996 2, 37, 54, 60, 70, 136
    Casablanca 1994 2, 53
    Doha 1997 2, 3, 54, 61, 70, 76, 80, 136
merchants 31, 39, 46, 58, 59, 68, 70
Meretz party 129, 130, 157
Merhav 106, 208
Merrill Lynch 106
Metalco Heating Systems 99
metals 29
Middle East Bank for Reconstruction and Development (MEBRD) 76
Mifalei Tovala 29
Migdal Insurance 91
military industry 27, 28
Milu'im 107
mining 36, 38, 114
Ministry of Industry and Trade (Israel) 53, 55, 58, 110, 111

Ministry of Industry and Trade (Jordan) 61, 85, 116
Ministry of Planning and International Co-operation (PA) 95
Ministry of Regional Co-operation (Israel) 71, 108, 110
Ministry of the Economy and Trade (PA) 68, 73, 92, 124, 125, 126
Mitrany, David 9, 10, 12
monarchy 41, 112, 118, 138, 140, 141, 159, 161, 171
monopolies 26, 46, 49, 87, 88, 94, 96, 120, 121, 122, 126, 143, 147, 150, 160
monopolization 92, 94, 119, 144, 145
Morgenthau, Hans 11
Mossad 135
Motorola 79
Mu'asher, Maher 117
multilateral track 2, 3, 46, 75
Muqawama (Resistance) 64, 65
Murad, Haidar 61, 98, 113
Murphy, Emma 129, 161, 163
Muslim Brotherhood 4, 139

Nabahin, Jaber 126
Nablus 88, 89, 95, 119, 121, 144
Nablus Chamber of Commerce 119
Nablus Industrial Estate (NIE) 90
Nahum, Moshe 55, 111
NASDAQ 114
Nasruddin, Talal 69, 125
Nassar Investment Company 46, 124, 126
National Bottling Co. 57, 126
National Economic Dialogue 72, 126, 146
nationalist aspirations 14, 119, 141, 145
nation-building 145
natural gas 76
Nazareth 53
Near East Energy Company (NEEC) 76
negotiations 1, 3, 15, 59, 72, 76, 82, 83, 87, 92, 98, 100, 106, 107, 111, 115, 116, 119, 124, 125, 126, 128, 129, 131, 132, 142, 144, 146, 147, 148, 155, 157, 158, 159, 160
Neo-Functionalism *see* Functionalism

Neo-Liberal Institutionalism 11, 12, 13, 15, 18
Neo-Marxism 14, 18
Neo-Neo debate 12
Neo-Patrimonialism *see* Patrimonialism
Neo-Realism *see* Realism
Nesher 87, 94, 97, 98
Nestlé 130
Netanyahu, Binyamin 3, 56, 66, 67, 105, 107, 109, 110, 111, 118, 128, 132, 134, 154, 157, 158, 168
Netherlands 77, 78
neutrality 137
new elite 49, 114, 115, 116, 117, 127, 137, 138, 139, 140, 144, 149, 151, 154, 158, 159, 160, 167, 168, 170
New Histadrut *see* Histadrut
NGOs 145, 159
Niblock, Tim 161, 163, 164
Nilit 54
Nitzan, Jonathan 31
Nonneman, Gerd 161, 163
non-tariff barriers 41, 69, 75, 85
normalization 4, 6, 60, 61, 65, 68, 70, 77, 112, 113, 114, 117, 118, 127, 136, 137, 139, 140, 141, 149, 150, 154, 158, 159, 170
Nortel 130
Northern International and Industrial Company (NIIC) 89, 90
Noufal, Abdel Hafiz 92, 124
Nuqul family 38, 114

occupation 41, 44, 45, 46, 48, 69, 94, 95, 102, 125, 126, 143, 147, 160, 165, 167, 169
Ofakim 77, 79
oil 32, 33, 48, 76, 87, 102
old elites *see* traditional elites
opinion polls 146
Oracle 71, 91
organizational behaviour model 15
Orient House 69
Osem 54, 93, 130
Oslo Accords 1, 41, 56, 62, 68, 69, 70, 108, 119, 135, 150
Oudeh, Fuad Muhammad 126
outsourcing 73, 97, 131, 136, 150, 151, 152, 167

overseas markets 73, 74, 83, 105, 130, 149, 167
Overseas Private Investment Corporation (OPIC) 115

PADICO 45, 50, 57, 58, 73, 88, 94, 97, 110, 118, 119, 120, 123, 143, 155
palace (Jordanian) 38, 39, 113, 116, 132, 135, 136, 137, 138, 139, 141, 165
Palestine Cement Co. *see* Palestine Commercial Services Co. (PCSC)
Palestine Commercial Services Company (PCSC) 46, 87, 94, 95, 97, 98, 109, 120, 121, 122, 123
Palestine Liberation Organization (PLO) 46, 48, 49, 88, 118, 119, 121, 124, 141, 159
Palestine Securities Exchange (PSE) 46, 120, 147
Palestinian agents 70, 93, 100
Palestinian Authority (PA) 41, 43, 44, 45, 46, 48, 49, 50, 52, 56, 57, 58, 59, 60, 61, 67, 68, 69, 70, 71, 72, 73, 75, 76, 85, 87, 88, 91, 92, 93, 94, 95, 96, 97, 98, 99, 100, 101, 102, 103, 105, 106, 107, 109, 110, 118, 119, 120, 121, 122, 123, 124, 125, 126, 127, 128, 131, 132, 141, 142, 143, 144, 145, 146, 147, 148, 150, 151, 153, 154, 155, 159, 160, 164, 165, 167, 168, 170, 171
Palestinian business 44, 45, 46, 67, 70, 71, 72, 73, 88, 93, 119, 120, 147, 149, 152, 155
Palestinian Businessmen Association (PBA) 66, 70, 124, 125
Palestinian businesspeople *see* Palestinian entrepreneurs
Palestinian Chambers of Commerce, Industry, and Agriculture 124
Palestinian Chambers of Trade and Industry 100
Palestinian Diaspora 48, 118, 151, 155
Palestinian Economic Council for Reconstruction and Development (PECDAR) 49, 119, 124, 208
Palestinian economy 3, 41, 44, 45, 46, 48, 49, 50, 59, 70, 72, 92, 100, 101, 120, 142, 147

Palestinian Electricity Company 90
Palestinian entrepreneurs 21, 40, 45, 48, 52, 56, 66, 67, 68, 69, 70, 75, 87, 94, 100, 106, 125, 141, 143, 144, 146, 149, 151, 152, 153, 167, 169
Palestinian Expatriate Businessmen's Conference 119
Palestinian exports 45, 71, 72, 73, 92, 93, 101
Palestinian Federation of Industries 69, 124, 125, 126
Palestinian Food Producers Association 67, 101, 124
Palestinian G7 38, 40, 46, 48, 50, 97, 114, 118, 119, 120, 148
Palestinian goods *see* Palestinian products
Palestinian importers 56, 67
Palestinian Industrial Estates Development Co. (PIEDCO) 46, 57, 58, 73, 88, 89, 120
Palestinian Industrial Estates and Free Zones Authority (PIEFZA) 89, 90, 120
Palestinian International Bank 121
Palestinian Investment Promotion Authority (PIPA) 125
Palestinian IT Association (PITA) 91, 125
Palestinian labour 43, 44, 48, 49, 57, 58, 74, 87, 131, 134
Palestinian Legislative Council (PLC) 95, 122, 144
Palestinian market 51, 53, 57, 66, 67, 69, 71, 98, 99, 100, 101, 102, 143, 149, 155, 157
Palestinian National Council (PNC) 119
Palestinian political economy 49, 120, 144, 146
Palestinian products 41, 43, 58, 69, 70, 71, 73, 101
Palestinian Trade Promotion Corporation (PTPC) 98
Palestinian workers 88
Palrig 79
Paltel 46, 110, 120, 123
Paltrade 68, 71, 72, 73, 120, 124, 125, 126, 146
paradigm 161

Paris Protocol 43, 68, 69, 70, 71, 92, 93, 102, 106, 132, 142, 143, 145
Parker, Christopher 145, 146
party politics 164
patrimonial capitalism 137, 138, 139, 140, 141, 145, 162
Patrimonialism 41, 138, 139, 140, 145, 146, 148, 159, 168
Paz 77, 78, 95
Paz Chen 77, 78
PDI Peace Development 53
peace dividend 4, 52, 53, 61, 75, 80, 93, 99, 104, 131, 135, 141, 161, 168
Peace Now 157
peace of the elites 141, 164, 168
Peace Technology Fund 57, 90, 110, 120, 123
Pedasco 95
Peilim Portfolio Management 59
Peres Centre for Peace 57, 71, 90, 91, 106, 107, 108, 109, 110, 120
Peres, Shimon 1, 2, 4, 52, 106, 107, 108, 109, 110, 111, 112, 128, 130, 132, 133, 134, 157, 158, 163, 168, 208
permanent status *see* final status
Peters, Joel 2, 208
Petra Drilling 60, 113
Petra Engineering 64, 86
petroleum 36, 46, 94, 95, 106, 109, 131
pharmaceuticals 69, 71
PLO *see* Palestine Liberation Organization (PLO)
Pluralism 16, 17, 18
Pohoryles, Samuel 110
Polgat 54
policy-making 6, 16, 48, 49, 124, 125, 134, 154, 155, 156, 157, 158, 160, 164
political and economic elites 5, 16, 23, 30, 31, 33, 39, 41, 49, 50, 92, 96, 104, 105, 112, 116, 118, 120, 124, 127, 128, 138, 140, 141, 156, 159, 160, 164, 167, 169, 170, 171
political opposition 136, 164
political stability 2, 4, 5, 129, 133, 141, 145, 148
Post-Structuralism 13
potential 1, 2, 4, 19, 21, 43, 54, 56, 59, 62, 63, 67, 69, 73, 74, 90, 91, 96, 101, 107, 132, 135, 136, 142, 167
Poultry Farmers' Association (Israel) 56

poverty 43, 44, 118, 140, 141, 147, 159, 164, 167, 168, 170
pragmatism 62, 63, 139
preference formation 16, 22
Preventive Security Forces 95
Prince Hassan 55
Private Sector Co-ordinating Body 125, 126
Private Sector Executive Committee (PSEC) 60
privatization 27, 33, 36, 39, 40, 41, 51, 98, 112, 113, 133, 138, 162, 164
problem-solving theory 170
production costs 45, 55, 59, 131
professional associations 6, 30, 31, 65, 136
Propper, Dan 54, 57, 108, 111
protectionism 27, 48, 54, 96, 126
protests 55, 82, 122, 139, 140, 162
public opinion 60, 65, 66, 134, 137, 160
public rejection 51, 135, 137
public sector enterprises 40
Pundak, Ron 110
Putnam, Robert 15, 16, 17

Qalqiliya 90
Qastal QIZ 80
Qatar 76, 108, 121, 123, 136
Qualifying Industrial Zones (QIZ) 55, 61, 62, 63, 64, 73, 75, 76, 77, 78, 79, 80, 81, 82, 85, 86, 89, 90, 96, 111, 115, 116, 117, 132, 136, 137, 138, 141, 149, 151, 154, 155
Qurei, Ahmad (Abu Ala) 119, 124

Rabe, Hajo 49
Rabin, Yitzhak 1, 52, 53, 81, 106, 107, 108, 109, 111, 130, 157, 158
Rablawi, Sami 95
Rafah 58, 88, 89
Rafah-Keren Shalom industrial park 88, 89
Rajoub, Jibril 95
Ram, Uri 134
Rama International 72, 73, 97
Ramallah 54, 65, 66, 67, 72, 91

Rashid, Muhammad (Khaled Salam) 87, 94, 95, 121, 122
rational choice 12
raw materials 14, 26, 44, 63, 64, 69, 70, 83, 86, 142, 152
Rawabdeh, Abdul Raouf 114, 118, 140
REACH initiative 114, 116, 138
Realism 9, 10, 11, 12, 13, 14, 15, 16, 18, 21
Recanati family 29, 130
reform 1, 23, 27, 33, 39, 41, 54, 112, 113, 114, 115, 116, 117, 127, 137, 138, 140, 141, 158, 159, 161, 162, 163, 164, 165, 168, 171
refugee camps 46
regime security 141
regional business council 60
regional economic co-operation 3, 4, 6, 9, 51, 112, 127, 150, 151, 166, 167
regional economic development 2, 107, 129, 130, 143
Regional Economic Development Working Group (REDWG) 75
regional integration 2, 3, 10, 70
regional markets 74, 92, 94, 129, 150, 151, 167
remittances 32, 33, 41, 43
rentier economy 32
rentier state 39, 41, 44
rentier system 138, 142
repression 140, 141, 148, 154, 158, 159, 164
resentment 122, 135, 153, 157, 159, 160, 162, 167, 170
revolution 14, 122, 171
Richards, Alan 161, 164
riots 33, 122, 134, 139, 140, 153, 162, 168
Rochman, Dov 111
Rotem Amfert 29
Rothschild, Danny 109
Roy, Sara 3, 43, 44
Royal Jordanian 77, 113
Ruggie, John Gerard 13
rules of origin 82, 89
Rum & Golf Co. 86, 87

Sabagh, Hassib 40, 48
Sabra and Shatila 121

Index

Saddam Hussein 61
Safad Electrical and Electronics Ltd. 91
safe passage 69
Safi Salt 87
Safra Group 82
Saifi, Riyad 113
Salah, Omar 62, 64, 77, 78, 79, 80, 81, 116, 117, 118, 136, 137, 155, 159
Salameh, Hassan 94, 121
sales tax (Jordan) 113, 140
Salfiti family 38
Salt Industries 29
Samco 91
Samman, Moayyad 100
Sara Lee 130
Sari International 62, 63, 81
Sassower, Gadi 100, 107
Saudi Arabia 3, 50, 73, 77, 136
Savir, Uri 108
Sawt al-Salam 64, 65
Schneller, Otniel 106
Schools Online at Middle East (SOLAM) 91
Sea of Life 82
secret account *see* Fund B
security checks 66, 69, 70, 101, 152
security services 50, 109, 121
Segev, Amit 53, 96
Segev, Yitzhak 109
Senate (Jordan) 39, 60
separation 19, 43, 58, 67, 68, 71
settlements 96
sewing workshops 55
Sha'lan, Fawaz 117
Shaath, Nabil 95
Shahal, Moshe 106
Shaheen, Deeb 86, 87
Shalev, Michael 29
Shamir, Shimon 62
Shamir, Yitzhak 51, 129
Shamrock Group 28, 78, 130
shareholders 64, 89, 94, 120
Sharikat al-Bahr 46, 95, 120
Sharon, Ariel 109, 110, 134, 135, 146, 154, 158
Sharon, Omri 109
Shas 105
Shefer and Levy fuel transport company 95
Shikun v'Pituah 29

Shitrit, Meir 109
Shohat, Avraham 108, 110
Shor, Amiram 57, 77
Shouman family 38, 40, 48, 119, 120
Shtayyeh, Muhammad 119, 208
Shurdom, Ihsan 77
Shustak, Yossi 92
Siemens 67, 72, 73, 82, 91
Siemens Data Communications (SDC) 82, 91
Singapore 54
Single European Act 10
Sinokrot Global Group 67
Sinokrot, Mazen 67, 70, 101, 124, 125, 126, 142
small and medium-sized enterprises (SME) 23, 28, 30, 32, 33, 38, 39, 41, 45, 46, 49, 50, 127, 143, 144, 147, 155, 166
small economy 30, 41, 48, 57, 58
Smooha, Sammy 133
social contract 19, 40, 135, 139, 141, 153, 164, 168, 169
social democracy 153
social forces 7, 9, 15, 16, 17, 19, 20, 21, 22, 156, 164, 170, 171
social foundations of international relations 13, 15
social relations of production 19, 20, 21, 156
Social Security Corporation (SSC) 36, 53, 77
social unrest 146
socialization 13
socio-economic conditions 155, 160, 164, 170
Sofer, Avi 111
software 57, 77, 79, 82, 131
Solel Boneh 26, 29
Solingen, Etel 161, 163
Soltam 28
Sonol 95
Sous, Tareq 67, 71, 172
South Asia 63
South East Asia 52, 53
Special Economic Zone (SEZ) 63, 115
Specialized Industrial Compounds 62
spill-over *see* Functionalism
stalemate 4, 54, 60, 70, 90, 130, 135
state interests 12, 13, 16, 19

State Revenue Administration (Israel) 106
state-society complex 9, 18, 21, 22
state-society relations 16, 18, 19, 22, 145, 156, 166, 169, 170
stone and marble 46, 71, 96
Strauss Dairies 57, 130
strongman 154, 158, 159
structural adjustment 33, 162
subcontracting 8, 43, 44, 45, 55, 68, 72, 74, 79, 81, 82, 86, 94, 96, 143, 144, 150, 152, 168
subsidies 26, 27, 33
suicide bombings 43, 44, 69, 171
survival 11, 18, 96, 114, 138, 159, 161, 163
systemic structuralism 11, 14, 15

Tabba'a family 39, 40, 60, 113
Tabba'a, Hamdi 39, 60, 65, 112, 113
taboo 168, 170
Tadiran 52, 53, 78, 82
Taher, Thabet 60
Tajammu'at QIZ 80, 81, 115
Talhouni family 40, 62
Tambour 93
Tamir, Doron 111
Tannus, Badia 53
Tarawneh family 87
tariffs *see* customs
Tawil, Samer 116
tax fraud 94, 121
Tayyeh, Abdallah 81, 116, 137
Team 95
technology 27, 28, 55, 74, 75, 80, 91, 103, 131, 151, 152, 167
technology transfer 55, 80
Tel Aviv 62, 71, 77, 86, 87, 90, 91, 95, 110, 121, 122
telecommunications 10, 29, 46, 120
Telrad 28, 52, 57, 130
Temple Mount *see* Haram al-Sharif
terrorist attacks *see* suicide bombings
Teva Pharmaceuticals 57, 107, 108, 129
textiles 29, 43, 44, 52, 53, 54, 56, 63, 67, 69, 70, 71, 75, 76, 77, 79, 80, 81, 82, 85, 86, 89, 96, 97, 126, 131, 133, 151, 172
The Peaceworks, Inc. 90

third world *see* developing countries
Tira, Oded 56, 59, 106, 108, 111
Tnuva 93
tobacco *see* cigarettes
Tokyo 122, 147
Tossetti Shoe Factory 96
Touq, Muhyieddin 115
Touqan family 40, 61, 115
tourism 8, 46, 76, 90, 114
trade 2, 5, 8, 10, 25, 27, 32, 33, 35, 43, 44, 45, 46, 49, 52, 55, 58, 59, 61, 62, 64, 66, 68, 70, 72, 73, 75, 83, 85, 86, 87, 92, 93, 96, 97, 98, 99, 100, 101, 102, 103, 106, 108, 117, 122, 124, 125, 126, 128, 130, 131, 132, 139, 141, 142, 143, 144, 145, 147, 148, 149, 150, 151, 152, 155, 158, 160, 169
trade agreement 54, 72, 81, 85, 97
trade deficit 32
trade fair 65, 71, 136
trade union 28, 48
traders *see* merchants
traditional elites 112, 113, 114, 118, 137, 138, 140, 141, 158
traditional industries 55, 133
training 36, 91, 138
Transclal 86, 87, 94
transit trade 61, 99
Transjordanians 38, 40
transparency 12, 105, 126, 147, 163, 165
transportation 29, 55, 66, 69, 75, 83, 84, 85, 86, 87, 95, 98, 100, 101, 102, 103, 107, 132, 143, 148
transportation agreement 62, 83, 100, 102, 106
transportation costs 70
tribes 41, 87
TRIDE fund 82
trucks 45, 70, 83, 84, 92, 95, 101, 102, 142
Tulkarem 57, 88, 91, 96
Tunisians 49, 118, 120
Turkey 54
two-level games 15

UN embargo (against Iraq) 33, 60, 81, 87
unemployment 27, 33, 43, 44, 118, 134, 140, 141, 142, 147, 159, 164, 167, 168

Unilever 130
Union of Local Authorities (Israel) 90
Union of Palestinian Textile Industries 125
United Nations Conference on Trade and Development (UNCTAD) 92, 93, 103
United Nations Relief and Works Agency (UNRWA) 41, 115
United States 2, 15, 32, 33, 45, 48, 54, 55, 61, 62, 67, 77, 78, 79, 80, 82, 85, 89, 99, 111, 115, 116, 118, 130, 137, 138, 139, 140, 141, 149, 158
United Steel Mills 94
University of Science and Technology 82
US market 55, 80, 82, 111, 132

Vardi, Yossi 53, 77, 108, 110
VAT 56, 103
venture capital 52, 77, 82
Veteran Warriors Association (Palestinian) 121
Vishay 77
Visuality Systems 82, 91

wages 26, 43, 55, 82, 90, 133, 139, 161
Walker, Rob [R. B. J.] 13
Wall Street Journal 87
Wallerstein, Immanuel 14
Waltz, Kenneth 11, 12, 13
war of movement (Gramsci) 171
war of position (Gramsci) 171
warm peace 1, 136, 137, 139, 154, 158, 159, 162
Waterbury, John 161, 164
Welfare Association (Palestinian) 46, 48
Wendt, Alexander 13
Wertheimer, Stef 58, 108
Western liberal democratic state 17
Widerman, Sam 82, 91
Wolff, Gideon 86
working class 19, 133, 162
working conditions 82
World Bank 2, 25, 35, 38, 42, 208
World Economic Forum 2, 62
world order 20, 21
World Trade Organization (WTO) 33, 62, 115, 116, 137, 139, 141, 149, 158
world-systems theory 14, 15
Wright, J. W. 5, 6, 133, 146

Yativ, Steve 131
Yiftah Co. 95
Yona, Mordehai 87
Young Entrepreneurs Association (YEA) 114, 116, 117, 138
Yungreis, Michael 107

Zara Investments 62
Zarqa 80, 115
Zikit 54
Zim 63, 107
Zionist labour movement 156
Zou'bi, Fawaz 114